DAVIS AND LEE AT WAR

STEVEN E. WOODWORTH

UNIVERSITY PRESS OF KANSAS

©1995 by the University Press of Kansas
All rights reserved

Published by the University Press of Kansas (Lawrence, Kansas 66049), which was
organized by the Kansas Board of Regents and is operated and funded by Emporia State
University, Fort Hays State University, Kansas State University, Pittsburg State University,
the University of Kansas, and Wichita State University

Library of Congress Cataloging-in-Publication Data

Woodworth, Steven E.
    Davis and Lee at war / Steven E. Woodworth.
      p. cm. – (Modern war studies)
    Includes bibliographical references and index.
    ISBN 0-7006-0718-8 (cloth)
      1. Davis, Jefferson, 1808–1889–Military leadership. 2. Lee, Robert E. (Robert
Edward), 1807–1870. 3. Confederate States of America. Army–History. 4. United
States–History–Civil War, 1861–1865–Campaigns. I. Title. II. Series.
E467.1.D26W8 1995
973.7'3–dc20
                                                  95-22706

British Library Cataloguing in Publication Data is available.

Printed in the United States of America

10 9 8 7 6 5 4 3 2 1

The paper used in this publication meets the minimum requirements of the American
National Standard for Permanence of Paper for Printed Library Materials Z39.48–1984.

For Leah

CONTENTS

ILLUSTRATIONS

Photographs

Maps

PREFACE

Born in Kentucky, Jefferson Davis grew up in Mississippi, and in the latter state he lived well over three-fourths of his eighty-one years. There, on the river just below Vicksburg was his prewar plantation, Brierfield, and there on the gulf coast near Biloxi was his postwar home, Beauvoir. With Mississippi he seceded and joined the Confederacy, and as a Mississippian he was elected its president. Throughout the conflict his home state's defense and the welfare of its troops were never far from his thoughts. Yet today this Mississippian's mortal remains lie buried, not in the soil of his own state, but in Hollywood Cemetery in Richmond, Virginia. The four years of service that identified Jefferson Davis so intensely with Virginia that its capital seemed the only natural place for his permanent interment form the subject of this book.

In 1861 the fledgling Confederacy's national capital was located at Richmond primarily because Virginia, the Confederacy's most populated, prestigious, and industrially powerful state, was strategically located near the United States capital and was anticipated to be the theater of the war's most decisive fighting. The capital was moved to Richmond because public opinion in the South held that the region's foremost military hero, President Jefferson Davis, should be in Virginia to direct operations and perhaps even take personal command in the field. Over the next four years Davis did his best to fill that role, directing the war in Virginia through generals of his choosing and occasionally flirting with the possibility of personal command. Historically, his role in these events has been largely eclipsed by his choice of Robert E. Lee to command the Confederate army in Virginia. With the president's continued support and cooperation, Lee became so successful that he obscured Davis's role in the Virginia war to the point that in the modern popular mind, Abraham Lincoln is juxtaposed not to Davis but to Lee. The conflict in Virginia is viewed, and often treated by scholarly historians, as Lee's rather than Davis's.[1] In this book I endeavor to adjust that misperception.

My earlier work, *Jefferson Davis and His Generals: The Failure of Confederate Command in the West*, reveals that the Confederate president suffered severely from indecisiveness and overreliance on old friends in his ultimately unsuccessful efforts to direct the war in the vast theater of operations west of the Appalachians.[2] But how did Davis perform in the far different—and much narrower—field of operations in Virginia? Did his personal proximity to the fighting and the high priority of this front because it encompassed both capitals allow him to cope with demands more adequately? Did he display the same weaknesses here as he did in the West? Might he have accomplished even more in Virginia than he did, and if so, what and how?

Lee himself has become the topic of some controversy among scholarly historians for his conduct of operations in Virginia. His detractors assert that his grand strategy was overwhelmingly offensive and therefore inappropriately expensive;[3] his defenders counter that he in fact acted on the strategic defensive.[4] I endeavor to show that although Lee did pursue a largely offensive grand strategy, his policy was in fact one of two possible ways in which the South could conceivably have obtained its independence. The other, the thoroughly defensive, survival-oriented grand strategy so much praised by many modern scholars, was the strategy of Jefferson Davis, and the tension between Davis's ideas and Lee's offensive quest for early victory is the central feature of the climactic stages of Davis's war for Virginia and the Confederacy.

The war had been over less than a year when Jefferson Davis wrote to his wife Varina, "The power to compare and sift testimony is as necessary to a historian as to an attorney, and I hope the faculty will be put in exercise proportionate to the field our time has offered."[5] With the hope that my own faculties may be found at least as nearly proportionate to so large a field as Davis's were to the field on which he contended, such comparing and sifting is one of the purposes of this book.

ACKNOWLEDGMENTS

I am delighted to be able to express my gratitude for the kindness of those who have helped in the completion of this work. Once again, Lynda L. Crist and Mary S. Dix of the Papers of Jefferson Davis project have been uniformly helpful and encouraging. Ira G. Gruber helped me develop the concept for the book, and Mark Grimsley, William J. Miller, Brooks D. Simpson, Michael B. Ballard, and Steven H. Newton read a rough draft and gave me a number of very valuable suggestions for improvement (they are not responsible, of course, for any errors in this work). Theodore P. Savas and David Woodbury graciously provided the high-quality original maps. Finally, very special acknowledgment is owing to my very special and supportive wife, Leah. It is neither an empty conventionality nor an exaggeration to say that without her patience, support, and warm encouragement, this book would not be.

1

THE MANTLE OF WASHINGTON

"I am President Davis!" shouted the pale, stern-faced man as he reined in his horse. "Follow me back to the field!" His clear voice rang out over the babbling of stragglers, the moans of the wounded, and the commands of surgeons. From the distance came the rumbling of a battle still hanging in the balance. Powder-blackened, sweat-streaked faces turned toward him, some with the glassy eyes of men who had seen enough of fighting for one day, others with a spark of excitement as they recognized the man whom the newborn Confederacy hailed as its most popular leader and foremost military hero, President Jefferson Davis. Many of the wounded cheered, and some of the uninjured who had thought they could stand no more of combat took new courage, shouldered their rifles, and turned back toward the battlefield.[1]

It had been the same all the way from Manassas Junction, where the president and his aide—who was also his nephew—Joseph R. Davis, had found a pair of horses and couple of Gen. P. G. T. Beauregard's staff officers to take them to the front. The senior staff officer, Col. Thomas Jordan, had remonstrated against the chief executive's going into such danger. The president, however, was not to be deterred. Had he been fainthearted, he would not have been there. Detained by administrative duties in Richmond through Saturday, July 20, 1861—Congress was convening and had to be addressed—Davis had chafed to be present at the battle expected at Manassas, a vital rail junction thirty miles south of Washington. Sunday morning he had left his paperwork and, accompanied by his aide, boarded the train for the scene of action.

As they neared the junction, dust clouds and the sound of firing told them the battle was joined. The president was dismayed, not only because he had desired to be present, but also because it was by no means certain that the reinforcements he had ordered to Manassas would be there by this time. Without them, Beauregard could hardly hope to beat off a determined Federal attack. The insistent hammering of the guns, now distinctly audible in the distance, made plain that this attack was nothing if not determined.[2]

A throng of dispirited Confederate soldiers met them at the junction. "They crowded around the train," Davis later wrote, "with fearful stories of a defeat of our army." That was enough for the railroad conductor. It was another half mile to Beauregard's headquarters, and the conductor had no intention of encountering a rapidly disintegrating army with a closely pursuing foe. He would go no further. Davis, hoping to persuade him that things were not so bad after all, singled out of the crowd a soldier who looked more collected than his fellows and asked for a report of the battle. The soldier replied that the southern army was reeling in confused and headlong flight before the victorious Federals. That was no help. The president turned again to the frightened conductor. Davis and his aide had no horses and could get none short of Beauregard's headquarters. They must get to the field and the train was the only way. At last the conductor agreed to uncouple the engine from the rest of the train and run it forward with the president and his nephew in the cab.[3]

Thus Davis had reached Beauregard's headquarters and, ignoring the objections of the staff officers, had ridden toward the sound of the guns, calling loudly to the many stragglers he passed to turn and follow him back into the fight. He would lead them. All was not yet lost. Some rallied; others, with obvious sincerity, begged the president to go no farther as certain capture or death awaited him in the debacle they had left behind. "Fields are not won," the president remarked grimly to one of the officers riding with him, "where men desert their colors as ours are doing." Drawing rein near a small stream quite close to the battlefield, Davis found an unusually large crowd. There, in the shade of some nearby trees, Confederate surgeons had set up a field hospital. At least two able-bodied men seemed to have accompanied every wounded soldier from the field, and these solicitous friends had stayed partially out of concern for their stricken comrades and partially in hopes of staying out of the fight. Davis shouted his usual exhortation, "I am President Davis. Follow me back to the field!" In the shade by the stream Dr. Hunter McGuire was bandaging an officer's wounded hand. "There comes the president," McGuire blurted out as Davis rode down the hill "at breakneck speed." The wounded officer jumped to his feet, swung his hat, and shouted, "Three cheers for the President!" No doubt

Davis acknowledged the cheers before riding on toward the front. He did not yet know the man who had led them, but soon he and virtually every southerner would know of this man. They would call him Stonewall, for his exploits in the battle that even now was ending.[4]

As Davis rode on he encountered an ambulance bringing another wounded brigadier to the rear. This was Barnard Bee, who had that day won his own place in history not so much by anything he had done as by the few words by which he had given "Stonewall" Jackson his famous nickname. Bee was dying. A little farther Davis encountered someone who informed him his political associate Col. Francis Bartow was already dead. From the battle itself, Davis could hear a more hopeful message, for judging by the gradual receding of its steady roar, the Federals, rather than the Confederates, were retreating. At last, the president spotted Gen. Joseph E. Johnston, who had brought crucial reinforcements to Manassas from the Shenandoah Valley. As Beauregard's senior, Johnston was now the ranking officer on the field. Davis approached Johnston eagerly and, forgetting any word of greeting, blurted out while they were shaking hands, "How has the battle gone?" Johnston assured him they had been victorious.

Davis had to see for himself. Mounting up again, he rode on in the direction of the enemy's withdrawal, joined now by several more members of Beauregard's staff, including former South Carolina senator James Chesnut. A cavalry captain recognized Davis and introduced himself. The president, he insisted, should not venture so near the enemy without an escort, and the captain attached his troop to the growing cavalcade. A few tense moments occurred when they sighted a column of unknown troops just ahead. Chesnut got down off his horse to scrutinize them with his field glasses. After peering at them for some moments he announced that they were definitely hostile, and the captain and his troopers galloped to the charge. The formation turned out to be Confederate, though by the time things had gotten straightened out, the president, with an almost childlike eagerness to explore further, had pressed on to another part of the field.[5]

Everywhere he saw signs of the enemy's hasty retreat. Rifles, cartridge boxes, knapsacks, haversacks, blankets, and overcoats lay where their northern owners had dropped them in their flight. Victory had taken the place of near certain defeat, and Davis's spirits soared. Those around him could not help noticing his excitement. To one officer it seemed that the president lifted his hat to just about everyone. The troops were excited too. Tired men who had fought all day, often with nothing at all to eat in the last twenty-four hours, would be on the verge of stacking arms to sink into the sleep of

Jefferson Davis. (Courtesy of National Archives)

exhaustion when the "cry was heard along the ranks that President Davis was on the field of battle." Rifles were seized up and snapped to "present arms" as the men stood in ranks while the president rode along their lines receiving their salute with another lift of his hat. Again and again Davis stopped to deliver short, exultant speeches, and the men cheered wildly.[6]

This was the role Jefferson Davis desired for himself in war—the leader on the battlefield at the head of his troops—and if he had failed to reach the field until after the fighting had stopped, it was not because he wished it so. He had been in combat before and was confident he could handle its demands. He had, from the beginning, made no secret of the fact that he would have preferred to be the South's chief general than its highest civilian official.[7] His second wife, Varina Howell Davis, was a shrewd judge of character—especially when it came to her husband. She realized that he was eager for the battlefield but ill-suited for political leadership, despite his successful fifteen-year career in Mississippi politics.[8]

The South's political leaders might have differed with her on the last point, but they clearly shared her high estimate of his military ability. Indeed, it was as much for this reason as any other that the delegates of the southern states, meeting in Montgomery, Alabama, in February 1861, had chosen Davis. The Confederate presidency was patterned after that of the United States, which in turn had been created in the image of America's great soldier-statesman, George Washington. When the delegates at the Philadelphia Convention of 1787 had stipulated that their president be commander in chief, the picture they had in mind was that of Washington, leading the Continental Army to victory in the war for independence. Since then many nonmilitary men had held the office, and no man of military training or experience had held it during a major war. But with war looming as the likely result of their own actions, the creators of the Confederate States of America wanted a leader who reproduced Washington's combination of statesmanship and military ability. Few of the delegates or their constituents doubted that they had found him in Jefferson Davis.

Born in Kentucky in 1808, Davis had been raised in Mississippi. Though the son of a middling farmer, he had come to enjoy affluence through the success of his older brother, Joseph, a lawyer and planter who had become almost a second father to Jefferson. Graduating from West Point in 1828 with a record at best mediocre, Jefferson Davis soldiered seven years before resigning, marrying a daughter of Zachary Taylor, and taking up a plantation his brother made available to him just south of Vicksburg, Mississippi. Despite the tragic loss of his bride to malaria just weeks after their wedding, he stuck to the plantation. In the 1840s he remarried, began a career in Mississippi politics, and fought in the Mexican War. The conflict made a deep impression on him. Elected colonel of a Mississippi regiment, Davis served under his father-in-law, Zachary Taylor. He gained distinction at the battle of Monterey and near-fame at Buena Vista, where his regiment, along with some Indiana troops, stopped a Mexican cavalry charge at a crucial moment of the battle. Despite a painful wound in the foot, Davis remained in the saddle directing his troops until the crisis passed. So great was his public acclaim that President James Polk offered him promotion to brigadier general. Davis declined, preferring to reenter politics. In the 1850s he served as secretary of war in the cabinet of President Franklin Pierce and later as a member of the Senate's Military Affairs Committee. When the representatives of the cotton states formed their Confederacy in February 1861, no other southerner matched Davis's combination of political, administrative, and military experience.[9]

His personality was—and is—harder to read than his resume. His postmaster general and good friend John H. Reagan concluded that Davis had "two characters—one for social and domestic life and the other for official life." The private Davis was "one of the most pleasant and genial men" Reagan had ever known. In his official capacity, however, Davis was "wholly given up to duty"—a nice way of saying he was mule stubborn.[10] A proud man, Davis was intensely concerned that others perceive him as strong, wise, and virtuous. He strove to be just that, and often was; when he was not, he strove to look that way. He rarely admitted a mistake.[11] As secretary of war he had gone to absurd lengths in unseemly exchanges of letters with subordinates, trying to prove them wrong and make them admit it.[12] Disagreement provoked him. In later years Varina commented with surprising candor on her husband's character. "He was abnormally sensitive to disapprobation," she wrote. "Even a child's disapproval discomposed him. He felt how much he was misunderstood, and the sense of mortification and injustice gave him a repellent manner."[13] Certainly, Davis was reserved in public. Most southerners at the outset of the war—even those high in the Confederate government—knew little of his personality.

The South expressed unbounded confidence in its new president, and many in the North were impressed as well. The *Richmond Dispatch* hailed him as "a tower of strength, with the iron will, the nerve, the energy and decision of Andrew Jackson and more than Jackson's knowledge and general education," while the *Cleveland Plain Dealer* called him a "genuine son of Mars," and the *Bangor Democrat* opined that his was "one of the very, very few gigantic minds which adorn the pages of history." The South hoped and expected that Davis would take the field in person. The *Richmond Examiner* confidently proclaimed that "with him, the victory would be certain, and chance become certainty." While the capital was in Montgomery, newspapers there had reported enthusiastically that Davis was having his old

Mexican War sword sharpened by a local gunsmith.[14] As late as June 1861, the president's close friend Leonidas Polk wrote that he believed Davis would "take the field in person."[15] The common soldiers shared the universal faith in Davis. "When Jeff goes to the encampments," Varina wrote, "they go on like wild Indians, scream, catch hold of him, call out 'I am from Tennessee, I'm from Kentucky, I'm from Mississippi, God bless your soul.' "[16] Virginian Albert Taylor Bledsoe summed up the South's confidence in the man it had chosen as commander in chief when he called Davis the *"one* great man to whom all hearts turn."[17]

This intense faith in Davis's martial abilities and the expectation that he would personally lead the army to victory were factors behind the shift of the Confederacy's capital from backward but centrally located Montgomery to prestigious—and threatened—Richmond. The prestige was important too, of course, for Virginia, which had seceded only after the Confederate attack on Fort Sumter in mid-April, was the state of Washington, Jefferson, Madison, and others of honored memory. Still, the exposed position of Virginia on the frontier of the Confederacy adjacent to the Federal capital made it likely that state would be the scene of the war's first—and as most then confidently expected, only—major battle. A clamor thus arose to get Davis there, the most practical means being to relocate the capital. On April 27, Virginia's secession convention voted to invite "the President of the Confederate States and the constituted authorities of the Confederacy . . . whereon in their opinion the public interest or convenience may require it, to make the city of Richmond or some other place in this State, the seat of government of the Confederacy."[18]

Prominent persons urged Davis to go. Louisiana politician John Slidell wrote to exhort him to place himself at the head of the army and seize Washington.[19] Bledsoe chimed in again. "Your presence is desired in Richmond," he wrote, "nay, it is longed for, by every man, woman, and child in the State. . . . You would be worth more than 50,000 men to us. . . . Virginia is to be the principal seat of the war. . . . All eyes, and hearts turn to you." *"We greatly need a deliverer,"* he concluded, *"and we look to you."*[20] Virginia politician Roger A. Pryor telegraphed Confederate Secretary of War Leroy P. Walker to warn of the impending threat of Federal invasion of Virginia and complain of confusion within the Richmond leadership. "Extremely important President Davis be there."[21] Whether the Virginia leadership was indeed as confused as Pryor claimed, considerable confusion did exist between Virginia governor John Letcher and Confederate authorities in Montgomery. That in itself was a persuasive argument for on-the-spot

Confederate leadership in Richmond.[22] Letcher himself also requested Davis's presence because of the threatening military situation.[23] On May 16 it was the aged Virginia disunionist Edmund Ruffin who wrote to exhort Davis, "For the salvation of our cause come immediately and assume military command."[24]

Davis was willing enough and probably rejoiced at the decision of the provisional Confederate Congress on May 21, 1861, to adjourn the following Tuesday, the twenty-eighth, and reconvene at Richmond on July 20. In the interim, the president was authorized "to have the Executive Departments with their archives removed . . . to the new seat of government."[25] On Sunday evening, May 26, Davis and his party pulled out of Montgomery on a train bound for Richmond. Accompanying him was a small entourage: Secretary of State Robert Toombs, volunteer aide Louis Wigfall–a Texas politician–and his wife, nephew Joseph R. Davis, and an old army crony of the president's, now commissary general, Lucius B. Northrop.[26]

The first problem to be encountered in the transfer was the president's own health, a problem with which he would struggle throughout the war. On the very day of the departure for Richmond, a clerk in the Confederate War Department noted in his diary, "The President is sick today–having a chill, I believe."[27] Indeed, Varina reported that her husband was sick and in bed aboard the train for a good part of the trip. She also accurately identified the cause of his sickness, "anxiety and unremitting labor."[28] Davis was a worrier who fretted incessantly about details that should have been handled by cabinet secretaries, aides, or even departmental clerks. His anxiety to appear competent and successful–along with the gnawing fear that he might not be quite good enough–drove him to work and worry until his health failed.[29]

During the previous three decades he had been sick a good deal; now he was worse than ever. Throughout the war Davis suffered from an appalling catalog of physical illnesses. Besides numerous and severe fevers, chills, and the like, he suffered excruciating attacks of facial neuralgia. This seems to have been a condition caused by a form of the herpes virus, the same that causes "fever blisters" and shingles, and was probably a lingering result of a case of the latter. Such a virus is most serious when it affects the facial area, precisely where it attacked Davis. It can, and in his case did, cause permanent corneal damage. He was described as suffering frequent and painful corneal ulcers, and by the time he became Confederate president a dull whitish film appeared to cover his left eye, which was blind. Several times during the 1850s and during the war itself, the inflammation of his remaining eye seemed so severe that his family and friends feared he would lose its sight as well. Aside from its effect on his eyes, the neuralgia could send intense pains shooting through the nerves of the face. Its attacks could be triggered by respiratory infections, fevers, tensions, and stress, and these the president had almost continually.[30] Invariably, he drove himself through the pain to continue doing his duty.

Some efforts had been made to keep the president's departure for Richmond secret, and the poor state of his health made public fanfare undesirable, but it was no use. Virtually every time the train stopped, if only for wood or water, crowds gathered and began clamoring for a speech from the president. "Where is President Davis?" shouted the crowds, "Jeff Davis!" "The old hero!" Davis's friends tried to explain that the president was not well, and sometimes it worked. On at least one occasion a number of well-wishers actually filed past the window of the president's car, silently viewing the sleeping president. One was heard to murmur, "If he can only pull through the war!" More often, however, Davis seems to have been awakened by the row and to have addressed the crowd despite his ailments. A newspaperman thought the president's voice "flute-like," and the people seem to have thought his oratory inspired, for they responded with vociferous cheers. The other politicians, Wigfall and Toombs, were then prevailed upon to speak, in a scene repeated again and again throughout the two-and-a-half-day trip.[31]

In Goldsboro, North Carolina, there was a special twist. As Davis sat taking his supper in the dining room of the hotel, he found himself suddenly surrounded by young ladies, some of whom fanned him while others decked him with garlands of flowers. From outside, where the local volunteer companies had been drawn up in formation in his honor, came the boom of cannons and the blaring tones of a military band tooting away for all it was worth at a selection of the most rousing martial airs. "It was," a reporter for the *Richmond Enquirer* observed, "a most interesting occasion." He did not record whether the president suffered from indigestion, although it seems likely.[32]

The reporter did, however, record his impressions of the public mood along the way. "The whole soul of the South," he wrote, "is in this war; and the confidence manifested in our President, in the many scenes which transpired on this trip, shows that the mantle of Washington falls gracefully upon his shoulders. Never were a people more enraptured with their Chief Magistrate than ours are with President Davis." Everyone, it seemed, young and old, was eager to see him and to shake his hand. "This trip," the newsman continued, "has infused a martial feeling in our people that knows no bounds."[33] The expectation and confidence of the South in its new president's military leadership could not have been more obvious.

As the president's train at last neared its destination early on the morning of Wednesday, May 29, 1861, it was met at Petersburg by a delegation of Virginia dignitaries, including the governor of Virginia and the mayor of Richmond. These men then accompanied him the remaining miles to the new Confederate capital. At the station there were more cannon firing another salute and the by now customary enthusiastic crowds. The Virginia dignitaries escorted Davis to an open carriage, in which he was driven triumphally through Richmond to the Spotswood Hotel, his quarters until a more permanent residence could be arranged. The crowds did not go away, of course, and the president obliged them by appearing at a window of the hotel to address them briefly before retiring to partake of what one wag called "a capital breakfast." Then he was shown to room 83, the Spotswood's finest parlor, which the proprietor had decorated with Confederate flags and a coat of arms. There he spent most of the remainder of the day meeting important people—and those who thought they were—and generally transacting the business of politics. Such matters laid aside, the president made his way out to the fairgrounds, where large numbers of the newly mustered volunteer troops were encamped, and large numbers of civilians were generally present to gawk at them and their efforts at drill. Once again Davis made a brief speech to an enthusiastic crowd.[34]

The next few days brought more ovations, serenades, and speeches, but in the midst of such distractions Davis continued to devote a substantial share of his attention to what he knew to be his most pressing task and what the public believed him best able to do, directing the military forces of the Confederacy. The Richmond papers might note with interest that when Mrs. Davis arrived in the city several days after her husband, she brought, along with the family and its various other effects, the president's gray horse and his military saddle with a compass mounted on the pommel—proof positive, as far as the editors were concerned, "that the President will lead the army."[35] The most important aspects of that leadership, however, had little to do with horses or saddles, and the president had been actively engaged in them for some weeks now.

The task of setting up the Confederacy's military arrangements had begun in Montgomery before the guns of Fort Sumter had triggered Virginia's secession. Among the first decisions Davis had had to make were those concerning personnel, the individuals who would be his chief lieutenants in making decisions and shaping policies. Curiously, Davis selected Leroy Pope

Walker of Alabama as his secretary of war, a man whose military experience was limited to a few years as a militia officer. The main reason for his selection seems to have been the fact that Walker had been a leading advocate of secession and Alabama needed some representation on the cabinet.[36] Davis himself, however, had been accounted a better than average secretary of war in the previous decade, and in keeping with popular expectation and his own inclination, he intended to give close personal attention to the affairs of the War Department. Even if he had not felt his own ability adequate to compensate for any lack in the secretary, such a purely political decision in that official's selection would have constituted no break with precedent. James Madison, during the War of 1812, and James K. Polk, during the Mexican War, had each selected purely civilian secretaries of war who brought nothing to the nation's war effort besides sundry experience in politics and civilian administrative duties.[37] The secretary of war was to be an administrative assistant in the Davis administration, never more than an adviser—and sometimes not even that—in strategic decisions that the president was determined to make himself.

For his other top collaborator at the seat of government, Davis created the new position of adjutant and inspector general and filled it by appointing Samuel Cooper, who had held the position of adjutant general in the U.S. Army for the past nine years. When the Confederate Congress, later that spring, authorized the rank of full general, Davis appointed Cooper as the senior full general of the army. The rank and the office sounded important, and sometimes Davis talked as if he meant them to be. In fact, the adjutant and inspector general was a glorified paper shuffler, replacing the old U.S. Army's general in chief position. During the 1850s that office had been held by the aged but brilliant Winfield Scott, with whom Davis had carried on a long and bitter bureaucratic feud as secretary of war. Since he found Scott a nuissance, Davis asserted that a general in chief was an unconstitutional duplication of the president's authority as commander in chief.[38]

Cooper, who had been Davis's ally in the bureau wars of the previous decade, would fill the administrative place of the discontinued office in the new Confederate government, and Davis would fill the rest. It was a natural arrangement between these two men—Davis, who was eager to direct Confederate strategy, and Cooper, who was an aged and plodding desk soldier, most at home in the dustiest recesses of a routine peacetime bureaucracy. In effect, he became the president's chief military clerk for the entire war. Little else could be done with him. Too decrepit to take the field and holding a staff rank that would not even allow him legally to command troops except at a much lower grade, he was, besides being the president's old friend, a brother-in-law of prominent Virginia politician James M. Mason.[39] Davis would have had difficulty getting rid of him and was probably not inclined to anyway. So Cooper stayed on and kept on shuffling papers, while direction of Confederate strategy and operations remained solidly in the hands of Jefferson Davis, who was happy to have it so.

With Virginia's secession late in April it had become obvious that the Old Dominion would be the scene of some of the war's most crucial fighting. The geographic stage on which these events were to be played out could be envisioned roughly as a box. The northern side of the box was the Potomac River. From this direction, Union forces could draw supplies, and so this side of the box may be thought of as a Union base of operations. The same can be said of the eastern side of the box, Chesapeake Bay. Here Union naval supremacy allowed the North to insert and supply armies from this direction. The southern side, the Virginia–North Carolina line, was of course a Confederate base, but the western side was the most interesting feature and the Confederates' biggest geographical advantage. This was the Shenandoah Valley, a strip of rich farmland nestled at the foot of the Allegheny Plateau on the west and screened from piedmont and tidewater Virginia on the east by the towering Blue Ridge. Its agricultural bounty made it a Confederate supply source in its own right, while its macadamized Valley Pike, one of the best roads in Virginia, made it an effective conduit for other supplies moving north to support Confederate armies. Thus the western side of the box was a Confederate base of operations. Nor was that all. The Shenandoah Valley was also a sheltered route by which a Confederate army, screened from its opponent by cavalry detachments holding the Blue Ridge passes, could approach the North's vitals. Beyond the Potomac, the Valley's northern extension led to within striking distance of Baltimore, Philadelphia, Harrisburg, and Washington itself. Since the Valley slanted northeast to southwest, it offered no comparable advantage for Federal use.

The geographical feature most promising for the North was Virginia's river system. East of the Blue Ridge, the state's rivers all flowed due east to the Chesapeake, offering tempting opportunities for the exploitation of Union seapower and the ability to move supplies by water. The James River was navigable all the way to Richmond, the South's vital point in Virginia both emotionally and industrially. Other rivers, from the Rappahannock on the north of Richmond to the Appomattox on the south, posed threats as well. Yet the final geographic advantage possessed by the Confederacy—and

The Virginia Theater
1861-1865

40 miles

Theodore P. Savas

one that all but negated this last northern opportunity—was the fact that any Union army moving on Richmond by way of the rivers would be badly out of position to defend its own sensitive area—Washington—while any Union army that essayed to advance on Richmond while covering Washington would move down from the north and so find the rivers obstacles rather than highways.

Within this theater of operations, Davis now proposed to direct the Confederacy's defenses. He found the situation there during late April and early May frustrating. Virginia was still in the process of formalizing its entry into the Confederacy, and in the meantime it claimed to be a nominally independent state whose military forces were merely allied to those of the Confederacy. In fact, it was manifestly obvious to everyone, especially Davis and the top authorities in Virginia, that the state would very shortly become a part of the Confederacy and its army would be absorbed into the Confederate forces. The resulting situation was confusing. Fortunately it did not last long, and the Federals were in no position to take advantage of it. Still, Davis's correspondence on the subject betrayed a certain tense foreboding that he might be held responsible for the direction of military operations of which he was virtually ignorant.

On April 26 he had Walker telegraph Virginia's Governor Letcher seeking information about the size, organization, and deployment of the state's army. When no answer came by May 1, Davis had Walker renew the request, adding the almost querulous warning, "Until this information is received, it is impossible for the President to determine in what manner he can best execute the convention between your Commonwealth and this Government, by which that force was made subject to his control."[40] Letcher replied the same day.[41] Still Davis remained uncertain of his authority in Virginia and on May 6 inquired of Letcher again through the secretary of war, "Do you desire this Government to assume any control over military operations in Virginia? If so, to what extent?"[42] About the same time, apparently dissatisfied with the limitations of such formal channels as dispatches to the governor of Virginia through the secretary of war, Davis opted for a more immediate link to the Virginia forces by writing directly to the major general commanding Virginia's state army, Robert E. Lee.

Lee was an 1829 West Point graduate and distinguished veteran of the Mexican War, where he had served on the staff of Winfield Scott. He was widely recognized as one of the most accomplished officers of the Old Army, and Davis himself seemed to share the conventional high estimation of Lee's ability. When in the mid-1850s as secretary of war he had presided over the creation of two new, crack cavalry regiments, the pride of the army, he had assigned Lee to be lieutenant colonel of one of them.

The secession crisis had produced very mixed feelings in Lee. Although he was, in his attitudes toward slavery, his contempt for abolitionists and Republicans, and his preference for southern Democratic candidate John C. Breckinridge for president in the election of 1860, very much a typical southerner, he also recognized, as did many other reluctant Confederates, that the Constitution held no right of secession for the states.[43] In a letter to his son written in January 1861 he admitted,

Secession is nothing but revolution. The framers of our Constitution never exhausted so much labor, wisdom and forbearance in its formation, and surrounded it with so many guards and securities, if it was

Robert E. Lee. (Courtesy of National Archives)

intended to be broken by every member of the Confederacy at will. It was intended for "perpetual union," so expressed in the preamble, and for the establishment of a government, not a compact, which can only be dissolved by revolution, or the consent of all the people in convention assembled. It is idle to talk of secession. Anarchy would have been established, and not a government, by Washington, Hamilton, Jefferson, Madison, and the other patriots of the Revolution.[44]

Lee knew where his duty lay, but like many other southerners felt drawn in another direction. "A Union that can only be maintained by swords and bayonets," he wrote in the same letter, "has no charm for me."[45]

But Virginia did charm him. He loved the state and recoiled at the thought of siding against it and with the antislavery northerners he so much disliked. On the horns of this dilemma, he vacillated somewhat during the months leading up to Fort Sumter, sometimes talking as if he would fight for Virginia, whichever side it took, and sometimes as if he would resign from military life entirely, return to his home state, "and go to planting corn."[46] Then Virginia seceded, and Lee struggled with his conscience about what to do next. His conscience lost, and he resigned from the U.S. Army. Then, urged by representatives of Governor Letcher, who held out promises that he would command Virginia's troops, Lee offered his services to his state and found himself major general commanding the army of a would-be independent state of Virginia before his resignation from the U.S. Army had had time to be processed and accepted.[47] The impropriety of this disturbed Lee, but he had made his decision to go with his native state, and the rest had followed naturally and with a speed that surprised and embarrassed him.[48]

Lee quickly got down to the business of setting Virginia on a war footing and did a good job of it. He had troops raised, trained, equipped, and stationed at such key points as Norfolk, Manassas Junction—guarding the direct overland rail route from Washington to Richmond—and Harpers Ferry, at the lower (northern) end of the strategic Shenandoah Valley, just across the Potomac River from Maryland. In organizing an army from scratch, he briefly had the aid of his old comrade Joseph E. Johnston.

Johnston was a West Point classmate of Lee, and his career had paralleled that of his fellow Virginian. At each step of promotion Johnston had been just even with, or sometimes a bit behind, Lee. That was a matter of utmost concern to Johnston, for whether it was direct competition with Lee, or whether it was merely a desire to command others, Joseph Johnston craved promotion with an almost bizarre intensity. Every officer could be expected to aspire to higher rank—Lee certainly did—but with Johnston the passion for advancement drove him to patterns of behavior that sometimes seemed oddly out of step with his normally dignified demeanor.[49] At West Point Johnston had risen to the rank of cadet lieutenant only to be reduced to the ranks for his final year, possibly because the commandant and faculty

Joseph E. Johnston. (Courtesy of National Archives, 111-B-1782)

thought he was taking himself and his minor promotion altogether too seriously. So pompous was his behavior that his fellow cadets nicknamed him "the Colonel."[50] For a time, it appeared that was as close as he would get to such a rank, for after eight years in the army he was still a lowly first lieutenant. In frustration he resigned in 1837, explaining to his brother, Beverly, that he did this "principally because, from the rules of our service, of promotion by regiments, any of my juniors who had the luck to be assigned to regiments in which promotion was less slow than in that to which I belonged had got before me on the army list."[51] That was characteristic of the man. He could not stand having others get before him, and if they did, he was sure it had been a matter of mere luck.

Civilian life suited Johnston less well than he had anticipated, and when a few years later a corps of topographical engineers was added to the army, Johnston successfully sought a commission in it, hoping this new branch of the service might be the fast track to promotion. He accepted the commission, however, only after obtaining a guarantee that he would be accorded the same rank and seniority as if he had not temporarily left the army.[52] As a quick route to advanced rank, the topographical engineers proved to be a disappointment, but in 1846 came the dream of every junior officer panting for promotion: war. In the Mexican War Johnston got himself a commission as a lieutenant colonel in a temporary, wartime-only regiment. Delighted with this two-grade jump in rank, he was soon enraged to find that with the end of hostilities the regiment was disbanded, and his rank, as had been specified from the outset, returned to its previous level. For the next eight years he carried on a running battle with the War Department, including Secretary of War Jefferson Davis, in the attempt to gain recognition for his claim that he was still a lieutenant colonel.[53] Promotion continued slower than Johnston wished in the topographical engineers, though he carefully ingratiated himself with any and all in the army hierarchy who might be able to help him along. In disgust he wrote his brother in 1851, "In the Topl. corps there is no promotion, a thing I desire more than any man in the army."[54]

Actually Johnston had been advancing about as well as anyone in the Old Army and better than most. That did not satisfy him. During the 1850s, whenever new regiments were formed, he applied for commission in them with higher rank. When Secretary of War Jefferson Davis had the new First and Second Cavalry Regiments formed, Johnston finally got his wish. At the same time that his friend and rival Robert E. Lee was made lieutenant colonel of the Second Cavalry, Johnston gained similar rank in the First. Then, near the end of the decade, he achieved an even more exciting success. With his relative John B. Floyd serving as secretary of war in the administration of James Buchanan, Johnston began pulling bureaucratic strings, first to gain official recognition for his bogus claim to be entitled to the rank of full colonel and then to have himself appointed to fill a recent vacancy in the office of quartermaster general. The post came with the staff rank of brigadier general. Johnston, thanks to his inside connections and his lack of compunction about using them, got the job and the rank. At last he had gotten ahead of Lee. Of course, it was only staff rank and did not entitle him to command troops at that level—had he at that time actually taken command of troops in the field, he would have functioned at his previous "line" rank of lieutenant colonel—but for Joseph Johnston, rank was rank, and he was happy to have all he could get of whatever sort and by whatever means obtained.[55]

Virginia's secession had triggered Johnston's resignation. Reaching Richmond a few days after Lee had assumed command of all the Virginia forces, he called on Lee immediately, and at Lee's recommendation received the same rank that Lee already had in the Virginia service, major general. Lee assigned Johnston to command the Virginia forces "in and about Richmond," with the task of training and organizing the volunteers then flocking into the capital.[56] The Virginia convention, however, still in session and turning its attention now to the organization of the state's military, had other ideas, at least about the rank Johnston should hold. It decided that high military titles should not be allowed to proliferate too freely. One major general was enough for Virginia, and Lee was the one. Johnston was offered a brigadier general's commission instead. Though this would still have left him second in rank only to Lee within the Virginia forces, Johnston was bitter.[57] Declining the proffered commission, he reported himself sick.[58]

That was the situation when, in the first week of May, Davis, frustrated with the cumbersome system of gaining information on the Virginia forces by dispatches to the governor sent through the Confederate secretary of war, wrote directly to Lee, relating his desire for information and also offering commissions as Confederate brigadiers—the highest rank in the Confederate Army—for both Lee and Johnston. Davis further requested that one or both of the generals come to Montgomery to discuss the Virginia front. Lee was busy these days. He answered promptly if laconically that Johnston was sick, he himself could not get away from the pressing demands of organizing the Virginia forces long enough to come to Montgomery, and Davis could get all the information he needed from Senator Robert M. T. Hunter, then on his way to Montgomery on other business. He concluded, "My commission in Virginia [is] satisfactory to me."[59]

The dispatch must have rankled the president. Davis liked to hold long, some would say interminable, discussions with those to whom he turned for advice. On other occasions he did not respond well to anyone's suggestion that one could be too busy or otherwise more importantly occupied than to rush to such conferences with the president, and he tended to resent those who turned down commissions he offered.[60] On top of all that, Lee had suggested that he could get the information he needed about Virginia from Hunter, a politician with no military training. Did Lee take the president for a mere civilian politician himself? Having sent such a dispatch to Jefferson Davis, Lee did well not to receive a sharp rebuke in reply, and though he probably never knew it, he could thank the fact that Davis, harassed and sick as he was, was not nearly as harassed and sick—and irritable—as he would become before the war was over.

Although Lee did not know it, he came near to having another problem with the president. Lee was following a cautious policy in Virginia, admonishing his more aggressive outpost commanders that they must do nothing to bring on a Federal offensive before the state was prepared to receive it.[61] An informant sent to Virginia by Walker thought such restraint smelled of treachery.[62] Davis set little store by the report, for on May 10 he designated Lee, still in his capacity as a Virginia officer, to command all Confederate troops operating within the state.[63]

About that time Davis wired Johnston directly. Since Lee had taken Johnston's word that he was too sick for duty, he had not informed Johnston of the president's previous offer of a brigadier's commission.[64] Receiving the offer from Davis, along with an invitation to come to Montgomery for consultation, Johnston made a remarkable recovery. Telegraphing his acceptance, he departed soon after, and by May 15 was in Montgomery.[65] Davis held a high estimate of Johnston. Along with Lee he had been one of the most highly regarded officers of the old service. Although Johnston may or may not have resented the fact that while heading the War Department and later as a member of the Senate Military Affairs Committee Davis had not always agreed with his extravagant claims to higher rank, the president himself showed no awareness of any previous strains in his relations with the general.[66] And now, of the two renowned Virginia officers, Johnston seemed the more cooperative. Davis assigned Johnston to take command, under Confederate auspices, of the Virginia forces at Harpers Ferry.[67]

Johnston's mission pointed up the strange and confusing situation developing in Virginia. Lee first learned of Johnston's assignment when the latter, no doubt pleased with having gotten ahead of Lee again, this time in the regular Confederate service, wrote him from Abingdon, Virginia, on his way to his new post, enclosing a copy of his orders and airily informing him that "the President intends to assemble an army near Harpers Ferry."[68] Lee must have wondered what else the president intended to do in Virginia of which the nominal commander of Confederate forces in the state knew nothing. On the other hand, Lee was not the only one who was in for surprises. Davis had told Johnston to stop off at Lynchburg on his way north and take whatever of the troops there he might need as reinforcements for the small force already at Harpers Ferry, but when Johnston reached Lynchburg, he found no troops.[69] Clearly an abysmal lack of communication existed between the Confederate authorities in Montgomery and the leadership of the Virginia forces.

Whatever Lee may have thought of Davis's failure to inform him of Johnston's assignment to the Harpers Ferry command, he probably felt a measure of relief that someone he could trust would be taking over that vital position. Up to that point, the commander at Harpers Ferry had been Col. Thomas J. Jackson. An 1846 graduate of the U.S. Military Academy, Jackson had served with distinction in the Mexican War, resigned from the army to take up a teaching position at the Virginia Military Institute (V.M.I) in 1851, and taught there until the outbreak of the war.[70] Quickly given a colonel's commission in the new volunteer forces, Jackson had been assigned command at Harpers Ferry by order of Governor Letcher himself, who placed great confidence in Jackson's personal knowledge of northwestern Virginia.[71] Whether Lee was familiar with Jackson's reputation as an eccentric at V.M.I. or not, he soon may have come to think that the former professor was a bit unpredictable. His dispatches tended to speak of "throwing" bodies of troops about this way and that as if they were javelins. It made him sound excitable, if not downright overwrought.[72] He also showed a surprising and—as far as Lee was concerned—misplaced streak of aggressiveness. Jackson had recognized at once that Harpers Ferry, situated as it was in the bottom of a bowl formed by the high ground on either side of the Shenandoah and across the Potomac, would be possessed by whoever possessed the heights. Accordingly, he made plans to seize them, including those north of the Potomac in Maryland. That was not good politics for the Confederacy, which was making much of its purely defensive intentions and simultaneously trying to woo a hesitant Maryland out of the Union. Besides that, it was a violation of Lee's basic policy of doing nothing that might arouse northern forces into aggressive action before Virginia preparations were complete. He tactfully cautioned Jackson against such a course, but the former professor insisted that it was necessary and went ahead.[73] Lee had serious misgivings.[74] Thus in all likelihood it was not without some relief that Lee viewed Davis's assignment of Johnston to the key post at the mouth of the Shenandoah.

Johnston reached Harpers Ferry on May 24 and sent Jackson a note asking him to have copied and distributed to the troops a general order of Johnston's

assuming command of the post.[75] This was Jackson's first news that anything of the sort was in the wind. As an officer of the state of Virginia, he
took his orders from Lee, who of course had not alerted him since he was
himself ignorant of Davis's doings. Punctiliously, Jackson informed Johnston, "Until I receive further instructions from Governor Letcher or General
Lee, I . . . decline publishing the order." He was cordial enough about it,
offering Johnston and his staff all the information and assistance he could,
but he simply refused to hand over command without some indication that
the move was authorized.[76] Proper information was available shortly, and
Jackson cheerfully complied. Johnston took the matter in stride and held no
grudge against his conscientious new subordinate. But the incident was
another illustration of the fact that the defenders of Virginia were not
working efficiently together, and the efforts of the Confederate government
in Montgomery to direct operations from a distance were only making
matters worse. In general, the process of shifting military control of Virginia
from state to Confederate authority had not been a smooth one, and the
confusion of the Harpers Ferry incident was acted out in less significant areas
a number of times.[77]

It was this state of confusion that had helped convince Davis his presence
in Virginia was necessary, and so when the Confederate Congress gave its
approval, he lost no time—sick though he was—in heading for the threatened
state. Even as he traveled north, spending a good portion of the trip flat on
his back and much of the rest making speeches and waving to crowds, he was
also planning and arranging operations in a military theater that would now
be specially his own. At one of his stops on May 28 he wired ahead to Lee,
"What news today[?] Communicate with me at Goldsboro tonight."[78] Lee
had left Richmond that day on an inspection trip to Manassas, but Virginia
adjutant general Robert S. Garnett sent a reply with such inconsequential
information as had come in that day, which the president presumably found
time to read after the fanfares, cannon salutes, and drapings with flower
garlands were over for the night.[79] Of much more consequence was another
telegram Davis sent during one of the breaks on the journey northward. This
one was to Confederate Brig. Gen. P. G. T. Beauregard, then stationed
at Charleston, where he had presided over the reduction of Fort Sumter
six weeks before; it summoned him to Richmond to be briefed for service
in Virginia.[80]

A Louisiana Creole, Pierre Gustave Toutant Beauregard had finished
second in the West Point class of 1838. In Mexico he had won two brevets
and been twice wounded. Though junior to Lee and Johnston, he was one of

Pierre G. T. Beauregard. (Courtesy of National Archives, 111-B-1233)

the rising stars of the Old Army. When his state seceded he resigned his captain's commission and offered his services to the Confederacy.[81] Davis made him brigadier general and gave him command of the forces menacing Fort Sumter, where he directed the war's opening scenes. Short, dapper, flamboyant Beauregard won instant fame rivaling Davis's.[82] He received the president's summons May 28, left Charleston the next day, and arrived in Richmond on the thirtieth.[83] The city turned out en masse to welcome its second celebrity and war hero in as many days. As with Davis the previous morning, an elegant carriage was waiting at the depot to transport Beauregard in style to his own accommodations at the Spotswood. Beauregard protested that the coach-and-four was too extravagant, ostentatiously insisting on more modest accomodations. An ordinary carriage was found, and the general finally went on his way to another hotel.[84]

That same day, Lee had returned from his visit to the outpost at Manassas. Anxious to talk with Lee, Davis summoned him to a conference at his quarters the next day. The president would later assert that at this time he had had "unqualified confidence" in Lee.[85] That was an exaggeration, yet despite Lee's failure to visit Montgomery and his lack of interest in a Confederate commission, Davis had made him a brigadier general in the Confederate army and wisely continued, to some degree, his overall control of forces in Virginia.[86] That, however, was a policy with almost more exception than application, as the president and Lee exercised a sort of coleadership in Virginia, Davis directing the areas that most interested him and Lee taking the remainder.[87] As Lee and the president conferred on May 31, Lee described to him the strategic significance and the condition of the force at Manassas, where he had left 5,000 men guarding the key rail junction and Richmond's most direct link with the productive and strategically important Shenandoah Valley.[88]

At some point Beauregard was shown in and joined the discussion. It was one of Davis's typical decision-making conferences, and he was never hasty about such things. Hours went by in what Beauregard described as "a full interchange of views." Davis at first thought the Louisianan should be sent to Norfolk, but so thoroughly did Lee impress upon him the importance of Manassas and the nature of the threat it was under that the president changed his mind and directed Beauregard to leave as soon as possible for that point instead.[89] In fact, the president became so fascinated with the defense of Manassas that he more or less took the direction of affairs on that front out of Lee's hands, leaving the Virginian to handle the seemingly more mundane areas such as Norfolk and the rest of coastal Virginia.[90]

Beauregard would have liked to have stayed "a day or two" in Richmond "in order to prepare himself better for the field," as he put it, and, one suspects, to enjoy the almost universal adulation of the populace, but both Lee and Davis believed strongly that no time was to be lost, and so, with whatever regrets, Beauregard took the train for Manassas the next day, June 1, 1861, and arrived there that afternoon.[91] If he was less than happy to be there—at least quite so soon—he was no more pleased with the orders that were to govern his operations. Davis had had Lee draw up the orders, and both of them agreed that the best policy for the present in Virginia was avoiding anything that might provoke a Federal response for which they were as yet unprepared. Beauregard later complained that the defensive policy was all wrong, that it gave up the initiative and allowed him no discretion.[92] For the moment, however, he was little inclined to advance. He had been less than two days at his new post when he wrote the president that the situation was all but hopeless. The entrenchments, he conceded, were tolerably well planned, but the location was next to impossible for defense, at least with a force anywhere near the size of his own. The enemy had all the advantages, and if he advanced, Beauregard asserted, the Confederates would have no choice but to fall back toward Richmond, hoping for a lucky opening, or to meet the enemy at one of the fords of Bull Run, a stream just north of Manassas, and "sell our lives as dearly as practicable."[93] Davis may not have been quite sure what to make of this sudden cry of desperation from his general, for he apparently sent no direct answer to it.

At the end of the first week of June, Davis confronted serious problems with Johnston at Harpers Ferry. Lee had been handling this situation, but Johnston was proving almost impossible to deal with, and the difficulty and importance of the matter led him to present it to the president. Davis had made clear to Johnston when they had spoken in Montgomery that he considered the position a vital one, key to the Shenandoah Valley, and wanted it held. On May 25, Johnston's first full day in command at the post, he had made a "careful examination of the position and its environs" with the assistance of his chief engineer officer, Maj. William Henry Chase Whiting.[94] Whiting was an unusual character. He had not only graduated first in the West Point class of 1845 but also set a record of academic achievement that was to stand for another half century. Unquestionably brilliant, Whiting also had a darker side to his personality, a strange instability. Later in the war, rumors would make the rounds that he was a heavy drinker. He was given to occasional outbreaks of shockingly impulsive behavior. Several months later, when the president offered him command of a Mississippi brigade, Whiting responded with an insulting letter. Most important, he was an incurable pessimist.[95] Longstreet later wrote that although Whiting was "of brilliant, highly cultivated mind, the dark side of the picture was always more imposing with him."[96]

Whiting was the last man Johnston needed to have near him at such a time. If Johnston cared for anything as much as rank, it was reputation. He wanted others to think him perfect and had an inordinate fear lest he should appear to fail. One associate noted that in prewar days he had had a reputation as a fine marksman, but this observer, more astute than others, had noted that for all his reputed skill, Johnston rarely brought back any game when he went hunting. The reason was that he had not fired. The shot was never quite right, the situation always less than perfect, and Johnston would not endanger his reputation for marksmanship by risking a shot unless it was a sure thing.[97] Now, assigned to command a crucial forward outpost of the badly outnumbered Confederacy, Johnston needed boldness, audacity, and the ability to make the best of bad circumstances. He had little enough of those traits in his own character, and Whiting would provide just the wrong influence.

As the general and his chief engineer rode around the Harpers Ferry position, they fed each other's fears "that it could not be held against equal numbers by such a force as then occupied it."[98] This reflected on both the position, which Johnston and Whiting considered untenable, and the troops that held it. Johnston had little respect for the undisciplined volunteer troops that made up his command; they were another part of the imperfect situation that threatened to mar his reputation. Once when he spoke disparagingly of their probable fighting qualities, a volunteer officer spoke up for his outfit, "If these men of the Second Virginia will not fight, you have no troops that will." "I would not," Johnston glumly replied, "give one company of regulars for the whole regiment!"[99]

In this frame of mind he began complaining to Richmond before he had been in command for forty-eight hours. "Our force is too small. . . . This position can be turned easily," and he begged for Lee's "views and instructions."[100] Johnston wanted to pull back from Harpers Ferry, but he wanted someone else to take the responsibility for ordering it. And so he went on from day to day bombarding Lee with complaints of the hopelessness of his situation and begging for "precise instructions."[101] Lee assured him that other commands were covering the flank approaches that he was regarding with such horrified apprehension, that the abandonment of Harpers Ferry "would be depressing to the cause of the South," and that Lee thought the place could be held, at least for the time being. If Johnston actually found himself threatened by an overwhelming force, he was authorized on his own discretion to make a fighting retreat.[102] That was not good enough for Johnston. He wanted out and on someone else's orders. "Would it not be better," he insisted, "for these troops to join one of our armies, which is too weak for its object, than be lost here?" By June 6 he was complaining that he had received "no instructions," despite Lee's patient attempts to instruct him and Davis's previous thorough briefing in Montgomery.[103] Reassurances elicited from Johnston only increasingly elaborate rationalizations of his contention that Harpers Ferry was a hopeless position and ever more insistent pleas that his force be withdrawn. In frustration Lee finally had to "lay it before the President."[104]

Davis's response paralleled Lee's and hit at the heart of the issue. The president did not "think it probable that there will be an immediate attack" by the Federal troops that Johnston professed to fear most, those advancing through what is now West Virginia.[105] Whatever might be the difficulties involved in holding Harpers Ferry, and they were real and major, the Confederates had to bear in mind the probable disorganization, unpreparedness, and confusion of the enemy. Even a weak defense might turn back an even more feeble—and perhaps irresolute—attack, and a good bluff might forestall attack in the first place, possibly long enough to allow Davis to find significant reinforcements. Besides, Harpers Ferry was important not only strategically and as a source of supplies but as a link with potentially rebellious Maryland.[106] Every day that it could be held was a small victory for the South.

Still, Johnston persisted in complaining. Finally, on June 13, the president had had enough. Retaining a remarkable degree of respect and even affection for the contrary general, Davis used Cooper to send what was obviously his own rebuke, apparently in hopes that this oblique means of communication would spare Johnston's feelings and preserve good relations between general and president.[107] The letter he dictated to Cooper, however, revealed a president who was courteous, respectful, and irritated. He "inferred" that Johnston considered the authority granted him inadequate, that he held it necessary to retreat before the enemy was present, without even an effort to put up a fight. He reminded the general that "in all the directions which have been given to you" great confidence was placed in Johnston's "sound judgment and soldierly qualifications" and that he had been expected to use his discretion. It was impossible, Davis had Cooper say, for enemy movements to be foreseen and detailed directions given from the capital. The commander on location had to make decisions. Davis still doubted the position was as threatened as Johnston seemed to think, but "as you seem to desire . . . that the responsibility of your retirement should be assumed here, and as no reluctance is felt to bear any burden which the public interest requires," Johnston was hereby authorized to retreat whenever he felt it necessary. Davis hoped that in that case the people of the valley would rally to him in such numbers that he would be able to turn successfully on his pursuers. Stressing the reasons for holding Harpers Ferry, the men in Richmond concluded on a conciliatory note:

> It is but justice to add that the greatest confidence is placed upon your capacity to inspire others with the soldierly qualities you have so often exhibited, and that the most unlimited confidence is reposed in you both as a commander and a patriot. For these reasons it has been with reluctance that any attempt was made to give you specific instructions, and you will accept assurances of the readiness with which the freest exercise of discretion on your part will be sustained.[108]

It was a remarkably patient and generous letter. Davis would do his best to work with Johnston, but Johnston would have to shoulder the responsibility of generalship.

By this time, however, Johnston's nerves had him jumping at shadows. On June 13, the same day Cooper wrote Davis's letter, Federals operating out of Pennsylvania raided Romney, fifty-five miles west of Harpers Ferry. Johnston mistook this minor incident for a harbinger of the arrival of Federals then advancing through West Virginia, whose appearance he feared would turn his position.[109] Wasting no time, he had the Potomac railroad bridge blown up at 4:00 A.M. the next morning and had two regiments on the road to Winchester with the rest preparing to follow.[110] By June 15, Johnston's forces were clear of Harpers Ferry, leaving the railroad and other facilities there in ruins. Johnston's men gleefully derailed massive locomotives into the river and torched twenty-ton gondolas of coal. The fires burned for weeks.[111] Johnston, in his state of near panic, had vastly exceeded the extent of destruction Davis had expected him to leave in his wake.[112] As much of the property thus destroyed belonged to the Baltimore and Ohio Railroad, Johnston's action had a negative political effect in Maryland.

During the withdrawal toward Winchester, Johnston received Cooper's letter of two days before. Although he welcomed "the President's authority to abandon Harper's Ferry," he took vigorous exception to the suggestion that he was guilty of "desiring that the responsibility of my official acts should be borne by any other person than myself," an imputation he found intolerable. "I know myself to be a careless writer," he admitted, but insisted that "nothing in my correspondence with my military superiors" gave basis to such an idea.[113] Two days later Johnston wrote that he had taken up a position about twelve miles north of Winchester but had hopes of doing little more than delaying the enemy advance. "The want of ammunition," he related, "has rendered me very timid."[114] The president, continuing to use Cooper as a front man in his exchange with Johnston, directed a conciliatory reply. "The fullest reliance was placed" in Johnston's "zeal and discretion." All that was desired was to resist enemy invasion as much as possible, and for that purpose it was necessary that Johnston keep his superiors in Richmond better informed of his situation, plans, and needs. In return, the high command would do its best to support him.[115]

A few days later Davis saw an opportunity to improve still further the temporarily strained relations with Johnston. Taking the occasion of a successful raid by a subordinate of Johnston's, Davis wrote to congratulate Johnston and to discuss the present strategic situation, mentioning his constant efforts to reinforce Beauregard at Manassas and the possibility of Johnston's combining with Beauregard against an attempt to turn the Manassas position on the left, between the two Confederate forces. "I wish you would write whenever your convenience will permit and give me fully both information and suggestion," Davis concluded. "I am sure you cannot feel hesitation in writing to me freely and trust your engagements will permit you to do so frequently. With earnest wishes for your welfare & happiness I am very truly your friend, Jefferson Davis."[116]

In reply, Johnston wrote a letter at least equally warm and friendly, full of information about the condition of his force and his plans for the future. He was eager to cooperate in Davis's suggested descent on the flank of any force threatening Beauregard from the west and sounded more confident of victory than in his previous communications. He apologized for any inconvenience that may have been caused to the president by two personal representatives he had sent to Richmond in the preceding weeks. Col. Francis Thomas, his chief ordnance officer, had gone to seek ammunition, about which Johnston confessed to being "almost in a panic." While there, Thomas "undertook to explain [to Davis, Johnston's] views, necessities and wishes." Now, with some embarrassment, Johnston excused himself for sending him, and for dispatching a member of Congress—who happened to be visiting him—to explain his course of action to the president and try to get the president to approve it. This irregular method of reporting was also embarrassing to Johnston now that he was sure of the president's approval, but by way of excuse he explained that he had been too busy deploying his troops to take time to write. Concluding his letter, Johnston wrote, "We require now, I think, but one thing to make speedy success certain–that you should appear in the position Genl. Washington occupied during the revolution. Be assured that it would be worth many thousands of good troops to us. Civil Affairs can be postponed–or left to the Vice President." And he signed himself, "Most respectfully & truly Your friend & ob[edien]t se[rvan]t."[117]

Davis would have liked nothing better than to take the field but probably would not have shared Johnston's cavalier willingness to let civil affairs take care of themselves. Still, the letter was friendly, confidential, and highly flattering. This first eruption of difficulty with Johnston seemed to have been completely healed, leaving their relationship stronger than ever and rich in prospects of future cooperation.[118] Yet it had cost Davis something. Two days after Johnston's abandonment of Harpers Ferry, news of the retreat reached Richmond as a rumor, and War Department clerk John B. Jones heard "murmurs against the government" for the first time in the Confederacy, noting in his diary that "so far, perhaps, no Executive had ever such cordial and unanimous support of the people as President Davis." Ultimately the president's fund of public goodwill at this early point in the war proved adequate to cover the discontentment of the people with an action they did not understand but blamed on Davis nevertheless. Within another two days Jones was noting that "the city is content at the evacuation."[119]

While the difficulty with Johnston over Harpers Ferry was being worked out during the month between May 25 and June 26, 1861, Davis also had to give his attention to other fronts and other generals. On June 8 the Virginia forces were officially absorbed into the ever-increasing number of Confederate troops already entering the state.[120] This left Lee in a curious position. Though he still ranked as a brigadier in the Confederate army, it was not clear whether he had a command. To a friend he confided his own uncertainty, and the friend expressed the opinion that the friction involved in the transfer of authority from Virginia to the Confederacy had brought Lee into bad odor with President Davis.[121] Lee remained wisely quiet on that subject but wrote his wife that he "should like to retire to private life" but would stay in the service if Virginia needed him.[122] Virginia did need him and so did the president. Within a few days, without any formal announcement being made, Lee clearly was continuing to direct affairs in coastal Virginia, while Davis dealt with Manassas and now Harpers Ferry. Both men would take a part in overseeing Confederate efforts in West Virginia. This arrangement was apparently so satisfactory to Davis that he came to rely on Lee more and more, constantly enlarging the Virginian's sphere of responsibility.[123] Lee was courteous and respectful–the type of subordinate Davis liked to work with–and he was also efficient and reliable, traits any president could appreciate in an officer. By June 12, War Department rumor correctly had it that Lee would be the third man named to the newly authorized rank of full general, just behind the president's old West Point associate and Mexican War friend Albert Sidney Johnston, and that he would be stationed in Richmond to aid in the central direction of the war effort.[124]

This was good, because the president needed all the help he could get. In handling the Manassas line and its high-strung commander, Beauregard, Davis had taken on a trying task. During the week or so following the frantic dispatch in which he had suggested that he and his command would have to "sell our lives as dearly as possible," Beauregard began discussing with members of his staff a grandiose and unrealistic scheme for taking the offensive in Maryland. He found a ready audience among his unusual staff. Mary Chesnut, whose husband was a member of that group, called it "truly a wonderful collection of ex-governors–generals–U.S. senators."[125] James Chesnut, himself a former U.S. senator, had for some weeks had a "mania" about carrying the war into Maryland and may have encouraged Beauregard's farfetched conceptions.[126]

At any rate, on June 12 Beauregard wrote a brief letter to Davis outlining his plan and gave it to Lt. Col. Samuel Jones of his staff to take to the president along with more extensive oral explanations. Jones arrived in Richmond the next day and presented Beauregard's plan to Davis. The Creole's letter began by stating that his views "ought to be acted on at once." Next, it assumed that the enemy was about to attack and overwhelm Johnston. Rather than wait for this, Davis should withdraw Johnston's force, leave small detachments to cover the passes of the Blue Ridge, and send Beauregard's and Johnston's combined armies to take Arlington and Alexandria, thus threatening Washington and checkmating the enemy. If this did not work, Beauregard assumed, the Federals would conveniently advance on Richmond "on three or four different lines of operation." In that case, the various Confederate forces should gradually fall back toward Richmond and then take advantage of the opportunity provided to use interior lines and combine for a crushing victory over each Federal column in succession. "I beg, and entreat," he concluded, "that a concerted plan of operations should at once be adopted by the Government for its different columns, otherwise, we will be assailed in detail by superior forces, and either be cut off or destroyed entirely."[127]

It was a remarkable letter for a brigadier general to send to his commander in chief. Beauregard had thrown together a plan with inadequate information about the enemy's, and even his own, forces. He had ignored serious problems with which he had every reason to be aware–his army's shortage of wagons and complete lack of the siege artillery that would be needed to take the Federal entrenchments opposite Washington. And he had assumed that the enemy would behave cooperatively, either by failing to advance into the void created by Johnston's withdrawal–thus taking Beauregard in flank and rear just as he was attacking Washington–or by being so obliging as to advance toward Richmond neatly divided up into nickle and dime packages for Beauregard to gobble up at will.[128] On top of that, the Creole had written as if he would command his and Johnston's combined forces. Yet by this time Davis had informed both generals that those who held the rank of brigadier general in the regular Confederate army would be raised to the new rank of full general, while brigadiers in the provisional Confederate army would not. Johnston's commission was regular; Beauregard's, provisional. Thus Beauregard was actually offering to take command of his superior officer.[129] Finally, by demanding "a concerted plan of operations," he implied that Davis had none and was taking the country to destruction.

June 13 was a busy day for Davis, and one has to wonder at his patience. After carrying on extensive conversations with Jones, Davis composed a reply to Beauregard that same day. Addressing Beauregard–as he would Johnston nine days later–"My Dear General," Davis wrote a remarkably mild and conciliatory letter. One by one, he gently but clearly pointed out the problems with Beauregard's plan. Agreeing that it would be nice to take Arlington and Alexandria and so threaten Washington, he assured the general that he would soon have reinforcements equal to the numbers in Johnston's forces, and if such numbers would allow Beauregard to carry out that part of his plan without opening himself to a Federal counterblow through the Shenandoah Valley, well and good. "To your request that a concerted plan of operations should be adopted," the president continued, "I can only reply that the present position & unknown purposes of the enemy require that our plan should have many alternatives." As for Beauregard's converging retreat on Richmond, Davis pointed out that Johnston's line of retreat was the railroad passing through Beauregard's position. The two forces would have to converge a long time before either approached Richmond. Davis expressed his regret that the duties of high command had kept him as yet from visiting Beauregard's headquarters and concluded, "The capacity which you have recently exhibited successfully to fight with undisciplined citizens, justifies the expectation that you will know how to use such force as we are able to furnish."[130]

If Beauregard was impressed by the president's kindness, he hid it well. Three days later he wrote Davis another letter, addressing him stiffly as "Sir" and setting forth additional unusual requests. He wanted the troops in his command organized into brigades and the brigades commanded by Gustavus Woodson Smith and Mansfield Lovell. These two men, natives of Kentucky and the District of Columbia, respectively, were members of the West Point class of 1842 but were currently serving as street commissioner and assistant street commissioner in New York City. The president must have shook his head in wonder at this suggestion that he appoint as generals and assign to important commands men who had not yet declared themselves to be on the side of the Confederacy. After this remarkable request, Beauregard went on to ask rather brusquely, "Can I be informed why it is that none of my communications to the War Department through the Adjutant-General's Department are answered?" The bureaucracy was moving rather slowly on some of the general's other eccentric demands, and he was becoming impatient. He was particularly concerned about a request he had made that all of his troops be furnished with three-inch-wide cloth sashes, "red on one side and yellow on the other, to be worn with either color on the outside, and from over the right shoulder buttoned under the left arm, or from left to right, as the officer in command shall direct," to distinguish them from the enemy in place of proper uniforms.[131] Davis referred the matter to the quartermaster general, who informed Beauregard that both he and the president considered three-inch red and yellow sashes a bit too conspicuous for the battlefield and suggested "a small rosette of the same stuff" instead.[132]

Despite Davis's prompt reaction in cutting through War Department red tape to deal with Beauregard's request, as well as his patient and respectful response to the general's ill-conceived offensive scheme, relations between the two began to deteriorate. Beauregard believed so strongly in his own genius that he considered those who disagreed with him in any way to be mere knaves or fools. It was a reflection of Beauregard's own feelings that about this time officers of his staff—in his headquarters—began referring to the president as a "stupid fool."[133] James Chesnut apparently confided to his wife that Beauregard did not have a very high opinion of Davis.[134] The president, for his part, inadvertently added fuel to the fire by a careless comment he made in jest. At a dinner with other Confederate political leaders, including the Chesnuts, he poked fun at the grandiose pretensions of some of Beauregard's staff officers. "Whoever is too fine," he joked, "that is, so fine that we do not know what to do with him—we send him to Beauregard's staff."[135] Chesnut promptly repeated the matter to the other staff officers, who were just the sort to take it—and themselves—very seriously.[136]

Beauregard remained tremendously popular, especially in Richmond.[137] Had the general public known that he was proposing offensive plans and being, in a manner, restrained by Davis, it would have liked him even better and the president less. "A vast majority of our people," wrote a Richmond diarist, "are for 'carrying the war into Africa' without a moment's delay."[138] For all the vaunted talk of wanting only to be left alone, southerners were eager to attack and invade the North. Davis sometimes spoke that way himself. In a letter to his brother written about this time, he regretted the South's previous inability to take the aggressive and blamed it on the divided loyalties of Virginia. If that state had been as solid as the cotton states, he lamented, "perhaps we might now have been contending for the bank of the Susquehanna instead of retiring from the Potomac." Confederate troop strength was increasing, however, and the president hoped "before long to be able to change from the defensive to an offensive attitude. It will be thus only," he continued, "that we can hope to check the progress of the war by teaching the enemy its evils." Not only did he hope to see Confederate forces soon on the offensive, but he planned to be at their head himself. He had been busy, he told his brother, "organizing & preparing" in Richmond, but "when it is possible to leave here I wish to be on the lines," and he hoped his brother by that time would be in Richmond to take care of Varina and the children. This was all the more important to him as he apparently expected to come under enemy fire. "God knows," he wrote, "what the tide of war may bear me."[139]

Although Davis may have desired offensive action in order to hasten the end of the war, he did not consider it necessary to ultimate Confederate victory. Therefore he did not think it worth the taking of great risks, much less the pursuing of the fanciful schemes Beauregard persisted in hatching. Less than a month after the polite rejection of his mid-June plan, the Creole came up with a second and even more farfetched proposal. Curiously, Beauregard had in the interim returned to his previous pessimism, writing a politician friend in Richmond to ask, "Is it right and proper to sacrifice so many valuable lives (and perhaps our cause) without the least prospect of success? . . . Is this the way to direct and control the operations of an army in the field?" He was sure the evil could be remedied, though, "if properly represented to the President."[140] That, of course, was the reason for writing to a political friend in the first place. Hedging his bets, the general also wired the president directly, calling for 10,000 reinforcements.[141] On July 11 Beauregard wrote Davis, again complaining that he was outnumbered and discussing possible routes of retreat.[142]

So much the greater, then, must the president's shock have been when, without warning or perceivable reason, Beauregard swung back into his offensive mode.[143] On July 13, he wrote Johnston, "What a pity we cannot carry into effect the following plan of operations" and proceeded to sketch a design similar to his previous one. Johnston should join him, leaving detachments to delay the Federals he had been facing. Together they would destroy, in succession, Irvin McDowell's Union army outside Washington, Robert Patterson's Federals just north of Harpers Ferry, and George McClellan's northern force advancing through West Virginia against the ineffectual opposition of a tiny Confederate army under Robert S. Garnett. Then they would all move into Maryland and operate in the rear of Washington. Beauregard figured this program should take from fifteen to twenty-five days. The problem, as he saw it, was not being in command himself to order it done. "Oh, that we had but one good head," he wrote Johnston, "to conduct all our operations!"[144]

That same day, Beauregard dispatched a staff officer, Col. John S. Preston, to see Davis and "urge the absolute and immediate necessity of adopting [Beauregard's] plan of operations." With a few hours more thought, however, Beauregard decided he had an even better plan and a more promising means of obtaining its adoption. Having an aide take down some notes on his ideas, he entrusted them to Chesnut. Since Chesnut was a politician and a former Senate colleague of Davis's, he presumably would have a better chance of selling Beauregard's plan to the president.[145] Chesnut set out for Richmond on Sunday, July 14, and arrived at 3:30 that afternoon. Preston had not yet spoken with Davis, so Chesnut proceeded immediately to the president's quarters. Davis was sick in bed, racked with neuralgia, but when Varina told him who had come and on what errand, Davis invited Chesnut in immediately and received him "with great kindness and cordiality." They talked briefly, and then Davis asked Chesnut to return that evening when Lee and Cooper could join their discussion.

At the appointed hour the four men gathered in the parlor of the Spotswood. Chesnut presented Beauregard's revised plan, which differed from the version given to Johnston and Preston in that the timetable was even faster and less realistic. The new plan called for a slightly different endgame, with Johnston and Garnett crossing into Maryland to take Washington from behind, while Beauregard attacked it from the Virginia side. Davis and the two generals gave "respectful and earnest consideration" to Chesnut's presentation and generously allowed that the scheme was "brilliant and comprehensive." Davis and Lee, however, did see certain problems with its "adoption at this time." For one thing, Johnston did not have nearly as many troops as Beauregard seemed to think and far too few for the role the Creole had envisioned him playing. More important, the Federals were in a position that would allow them easily to fall back into powerful fortifications or to draw large reinforcements. Either way, Beauregard's plan did not promise decisive results, even in the unlikely case that the rest of the scheme should develop as its designer hoped. Lee suggested that Beauregard might do well to fall back to the south bank of the Rappahannock if necessary. Davis delayed final decision on the offensive plan until the morning of the fifteenth but still opposed it at that time.[146]

Chesnut returned to Beauregard's headquarters impressed with the points Lee had raised, particularly as to the wisdom of falling back behind the Rappahannock. He was afraid, however, to approach Beauregard on the issue, and so made his report without reference to it and tried to get Beauregard's adjutant general, Col. Thomas Jordan, to take up the point with the general. Jordan was not about to do that, and neither was anyone else.[147] The issue was moot by then, for McDowell, under political pressure to advance, gave Beauregard little more time for arrangements. On the evening of July 16, the same day Chesnut reported to him on his mission to Richmond, the general received information that Union forces were about to move on Manassas. He passed the news on to Richmond the next day.[148]

This was the solid information Davis had been waiting for to put into execution a plan he had long had in mind. Davis also knew the importance of concentrating troops for battle and, what was more, he knew when and how it should be done. Assuring Beauregard that help was on the way, he had Cooper telegraph both Johnston and Brig. Gen. Theophilus H. Holmes, stationed with a small force near Fredericksburg, to go immediately to Beauregard's assistance.[149] The Creole was tending toward panic again, announcing that his outposts were being attacked and begging Davis to send Holmes, Johnston, or any other force that could be found "at the earliest possible instant, and by every possible means." He fired back a petulant telegram to Cooper: "I believe this proposed movement of General Johnston is too late. Enemy will attack me in force tomorrow morning."[150] Holmes gave no resistance. He had offered to reinforce Manassas back in June, but Lee and Davis believed the time was not yet right and told him to wait. Now he was ready to go.[151]

Johnston was not. Throughout late June and early July, relations between Davis and Johnston had remained very good, though the general showed a prickly disposition in his dealings with Lee, who wisely kept such dealings to a minimum.[152] Johnston had written open, informative, and complimentary letters to the president, just as Davis liked his generals to do, and though he had suggested it might be well if Beauregard would "with great expedition furnish 5,000 or 6,000 men for a few days"—almost simultaneously with Beauregard's request for 10,000 reinforcements—he generally showed more confidence and readiness to meet the enemy than he was to do at almost any other time during the war. Indeed, in an unusual reversal of roles, he sometimes seemed during these weeks bolder and more pugnacious than the president. Davis, in his letters, was warm and complimentary, lamenting his inability to reinforce Johnston as he would have liked to. The two passed easily over potential topics of misunderstanding. Davis assured Johnston that he was anxious to "leave here to share the fortunes of the Army in the field" as soon as he believed he could do so without a negative effect on the central management of the war.[153] All of this might have suggested a trusting relationship that would lead Johnston to obey without question Davis's direction for a concentration at Manassas, but it was otherwise.

In the first place, the message Cooper sent Johnston was vague. "General Beauregard is attacked," the telegram read. "To strike the enemy a decisive blow, a junction of all your effective force will be needed. If practicable, make the movement, sending your sick and baggage to Culpeper Court-House, either by railroad or by Warrenton. In all the arrangements exercise your discretion."[154] Davis would later argue that only such arrangements as what to do with the sick had been left to Johnston's discretion and that the order to go to Manassas was peremptory.[155] The simplest reading of the dispatch indicates otherwise. Johnston was to "make the movement" only "if practicable." As Davis himself would later point out, it made no sense for him to leave such a decision up to the general, who had no way of judging the relative importance of his own and another's sector, but that is just what the president did.[156] Jefferson Davis was beginning to show small measures of one of his worst shortcomings: a tendency to waffle under pressure.

In fairness to the president, it must be said that Johnston habitually performed far worse under pressure and in such situations could be almost impossible to deal with. If Davis had sent him a truly peremptory order, Johnston would have been offended—sulky and uncooperative—because his discretion had not been trusted, but receiving a discretionary order, the general immediately began to wilt under the responsibility. He quickly wrote back to the president with objections, and Davis, making his second mistake, "replied at great length, endeavoring to convince him" the move was "practicable" after all, rather than simply ordering it done.[157] At the same time, Johnston telegraphed Beauregard, "Is the enemy upon you in force?"[158] Beauregard was apparently able to convince Johnston that this really was the main Federal offensive, and, satisfied at last, Johnston wired Richmond on Thursday, July 18, that he would at least give it a try.[159]

That day also saw the first action along Bull Run, the creek where Beauregard had placed his defensive line just north of Manassas. A Federal detachment approached one of the fords, exchanged fire briefly with the defenders, and finding the post strongly manned fell back. Beauregard made much of the affair, triumphantly telegraphing the president that "the enemy advanced in great force" but was repulsed.[160] Davis responded with news of additional reinforcements he was pushing along as rapidly as possible. "God be praised," he wrote, "for your successful beginning. I have tried to join you, but remain to serve you here as most useful for the time."[161]

The increasing tension of that week seemed to take its toll on Davis, as those around him noticed. "Mr. Davis is in wretched health," Mary Chesnut wrote in her diary on Tuesday. "He has trouble enough. Care, anxiety, responsibility—and then, his unlucky nervous irritation doubles the trouble."[162] Yet that evening he rode out to one of the many military encampments around Richmond to make a speech and present a silk flag to the South Carolinians of the Hampton Legion, who were soon on their way to the front.[163] The fatigue of prolonged tension and stress-induced neuralgia probably contributed to Davis's growing hesitance and uncertainty toward the end of the week. By Friday, still unsure whether Johnston was on his way and with a report that the enemy had learned of the projected concentration, Davis actually argued himself out of the movement he had so recently argued Johnston into. With Johnston out of telegraph communication, Davis had Cooper wire Beauregard, "If the enemy in front of you have abandoned an immediate attack and General Johnston has not moved, you had better withdraw [the] call upon him, so that he may be left to his full discretion."[164] The president was attempting to wash his hands of operational control in Virginia, giving one general discretion to enlarge the discretion of another general and cancel out completely all the president's previous efforts at concentration. Fortunately, Beauregard, in the path of the oncoming Federal army, was not about to forego any part of the reinforcements bound for him. "As this was not an order," he later wrote in reference to Cooper's dispatch, "I . . . continued every effort for the prompt arrival of the Shenandoah forces."[165]

Saturday, July 20, brought a new anxiety, when Johnston telegraphed Davis to inquire what his rank was in relation to Beauregard. He may have been motivated by Beauregard's concocting of schemes for taking command of Johnston's forces, and his action probably had something to do with his own desire to command others. To Davis the inquiry was deeply disturbing; Johnston had been informed of his and Beauregard's relative ranks. Why was he now treating the matter as an open question? The more the president thought about the situation, the less he liked it. He worried "lest there should be some unfortunate complication, or misunderstanding, between these officers, when their forces should be united."[166] He telegraphed Johnston that he was a full general and would know best how to make use of Brig. Gen. Beauregard and his knowledge of the situation at Manassas. "The zeal of both," he concluded, "assures me of harmonious action."[167] But Davis felt less assurance than he expressed, and became even more determined to reach the battlefield before the crucial moment.[168]

While the president hurried to dispatch his administrative duties and chafed at the necessity of remaining in Richmond to address Congress, his two generals, unbeknownst to him, twice flirted with disaster. The first mistake was Johnston's. Little given to detailed planning, he set out at first to march his army to Manassas. Only when it became apparent that this would get his troops to the field far too late to be of any service did he begin to look into the possibility of rail transport. Time would have been short even for that if Beauregard, anxious to speed the arrival of reinforcements, had not previously forwarded a large number of railroad cars.[169] Beauregard himself, however, was the author of the next brush with disaster. Suffering more delusions of Napoleonic grandeur, he wired Johnston to divide his forces, sending half directly to Manassas and having the other half march across the Bull Run Mountains north of the railroad to strike McDowell from the rear, while Beauregard would, he hoped, be attacking in front. With veteran soldiers, a trained staff, and ample supply and transport, the plan would have been daring almost to the point of madness. As things were, it was well nigh suicidal, and Johnston wisely declined to undertake it.[170] By noon Saturday, most of his troops were at Manassas. Beauregard was glad to have the reinforcements but less enthusiastic about the arrival of a superior officer.[171] Anxiously he pressed Johnston to accept his plan for the coming battle, and Johnston, ever hesitant to take responsibility, agreed. The next morning, however, he was somewhat taken aback to find that Beauregard had issued his attack orders to the army in such a manner as almost to suggest the Louisianan was still in command.[172] Events—and

General McDowell—left no time to pursue the matter, and fortunately for the South, no time to attempt Beauregard's vague, muddled, and thoroughly impractical plan to attack the northern army across Bull Run.[173]

McDowell attacked first and came close to defeating the Confederate army. Reluctantly abandoning his cherished plans, Beauregard went to the front and led the defense with admirable courage and tactical skill. Johnston, at Beauregard's urging, remained in the rear to throw in reserves where needed. By the narrowest of margins the northern attack was turned back. Many of the untrained Union regiments became disorganized as they began the retreat and subsequently fell back in increasing disorder. To this situation Davis came late on the afternoon of Sunday, July 21, suspecting the battle lost—as it nearly was—and calling on stragglers to rally and follow him back into the fight. He shared the elation of the troops and their generals as he discovered that near defeat had been turned into victory, and he rode over the battlefield savoring his first great success as commander in chief.

Davis had reason to look with considerable satisfaction on his first few months of command in Virginia. He had selected as his top generals in Virginia men who were widely held to be the best officers in the prewar U.S. Army. He had handled them well, usually giving clear direction but refusing to relieve them of the local control—and responsibility—that was necessary, as in the case when Johnston had sought absolution from responsibility for abandoning Harpers Ferry. His patience with both Johnston and Beauregard, especially considering his own painful physical problems, was truly impressive; and his use of Lee's abilities, though it did not show any early awareness of just how great those abilities were, was judicious within the bounds of Davis's limited knowledge at the outset of the war. The president had wisely demurred from Beauregard's farfetched strategic schemes and had shown both sound strategic sense and a good grasp of the realities of logistics. If he was overanxious to take command personally in the field, to wear "the mantle of Washington" in the fullest sense, his awareness of the responsibilities of his office in directing the war effort, and even in dealing with Congress, had restrained him and held him to his duty. He had displayed shortcomings only during the last tense week before the battle at Manassas, in leaving the crucial concentration of forces there to Johnston's discretion and in actually encouraging Beauregard to call off the move entirely. As it was, these mistakes did not bear the ill consequences they portended. They did, however, display the president's potential weakness under pressure. The months to come brought much more pressure on Davis and even more difficulty in dealing with his generals.

2

OUR ARMY DOES NOT ADVANCE

Tension between Davis and his Virginia generals took root even before the morrow of the great victory at Manassas. Completing his tour of the battle-field in the gathering darkness of that momentous July evening, the president turned his horse toward the village of Manassas Junction and set out on the seven-mile ride to Beauregard's headquarters at Moss Mansion, accompanied by his nephew as well as Johnston and others who had joined him for the last stages of his survey. Davis was quite anxious to hear the details of the battle, and all the way to Moss Mansion and after their arrival quizzed the generals eagerly. With growing satisfaction he listened to their accounts and finally exclaimed, "I think the news of our victory ought to be communicated, at once, to the War Department at Richmond." It was, indeed, high time for such notification. Back in the capital, the cabinet and assorted other dignitaries had waited in painful suspense at the war office for some word of the battle's issue, until Attorney General Judah P. Benjamin, a man of more than ordinary resourcefulness, thought to take a walk over to the Spotswood and pay a call on Mrs. Davis, who had, as Benjamin suspected, received a brief telegram the president sent, apparently immediately upon his arrival at Moss Mansion, announcing "a glorious but dear-bought victory."[1]

But someone needed to inform the government about the day's events, and as to who should do so, Davis showed no doubt. The senior officer present was responsible for such reports, and the president consistently felt that as a commander in chief he commanded wherever he was present. As he began to work out the wording of what he could not doubt would become a famous victory message, Beauregard came in. Learning what Davis was doing, the Louisianian boiled inwardly. He had won the battle through no merit of his own planning—though perhaps with some credit to his

41

Bull Run and the Manassas battlefield. (Courtesy of National Archives, 165-SB-7, Civil War 88)

battlefield gallantry–but he coveted every bit of its fame and feared that the president would create the impression that Davis, rather than Beauregard, had led the forces to triumph. To the Creole, this was proof positive that the president was "an ambitious man" in the ugliest sense of the word.[2] It is true that Davis was enjoying the role of field commander and that when the dispatch he wrote reached Richmond many people understood it to mean that the president had taken part in the battle, yet Beauregard could have taught Davis a good deal about ambition.[3]

"Night has closed," Davis began his telegram to Cooper, "upon a hard-fought field. Our forces have won a glorious victory. The enemy was routed and fled precipitately." He then went on to write of the booty won and the vigorous pursuit he assumed was taking place.[4] While he wrote, Beauregard's chief of staff, Colonel Jordan, came in with another staff officer, Capt. Robert C. Hill. Hill claimed to have ridden forward all the way to Centreville and found no armed enemies but much debris to indicate a complete stampede of the northern forces.[5] While Hill made his report, Davis finished up his dispatch and, to Beauregard's silent frustration, signed it himself. Then, turning his attention to the generals again, Davis inquired as to what units were involved in the pursuit. This must have caused some embarrassment for Johnston and Beauregard, for what little pursuit had been made had ceased several hours before.

Earlier that evening Beauregard and Johnston, seeing the Federal forces falling back in disorder, had each ordered Confederate units in pursuit. Neither was aware of the other's action and neither went in person to see that his orders were carried out promptly and efficiently. Consequently, the movements thus begun were uncoordinated and hesitant. Johnston's effort stumbled to a halt almost before it got started. Brig. Gen. Milledge Bonham had been ordered to take his own and Brig. Gen. James Longstreet's brigades, neither of which had been engaged, and go after the retreating Federals. He had hardly set out, however, before the brilliant but morose Whiting, of Johnston's staff, apparently got nervous and called the whole thing off.[6] Bonham had a bit of experience leading volunteers against the Seminoles and in Mexico, but he was no West Point man and may well have been intimidated by Whiting's reputation. Longstreet was not. Receiving Bonham's order to halt, Longstreet threw his hat down and stamped in impotent rage but under the circumstances had no choice but to comply.[7] Beauregard's pursuit was equally abortive. It had just begun when he received a report that Union troops were swarming across Bull Run on his right flank. Alarmed, he recalled the pursuing forces and rushed them to meet the supposed threat. In fact, the troops crossing the run were Confederate brigades that Beauregard's muddled orders had sent back and forth, march and countermarch, across the creek all day long. Though a good half hour of daylight remained, Beauregard chose not to renew the pursuit.[8]

Thus Davis was informed that at the moment—it was then near 11:00 P.M.— no one was pursuing at all. The president was dismayed. As he saw it, Jordan's report of the enemy's panic flight emphasized the beckoning opportunity. He also feared that if the defeated Federals were given leisure to reorganize, they might soon be back to renew the assault and the day's labor would be lost.[9] With what Jordan remembered as "great animation," Davis urged these considerations on the generals and suggested that the pursuit be taken up again immediately. Beauregard and Johnston were unresponsive. Pressing the matter, Davis asked "what troops were in the best position for pursuit, and had been least fatigued during the day." The obvious answer, of course, was Bonham's command. The president then "suggested," to use his own word, that Bonham be ordered to advance at once, regardless of the hour. The suggestion was met by silence. Clearly the commander in chief wanted either Johnston or Beauregard to give the order, and just as clearly neither was eager. The awkward silence was broken when Jordan spoke up and asked Davis if he would like to dictate such an order himself. The president was willing, and so Jordan sat down at the table across from Davis and began to take his dictation.[10]

Having taken active command of an army in the field, even in the middle of the night after a battle, Davis was about to learn something of the stresses inherent to the job. As he paused in his dictation to consider his next sentence, Jordan observed quietly that the officer who supposedly had been all the way to Centreville—and on whose report of Federal confusion the present action was being taken—had been known in the Old Army as "Crazy" Hill. Davis looked up, then laughed heartily, joined by the others in the room. Yet if the captain's information were false, they would have little enough reason for mirth. No one present knew Hill personally, so Davis sent for a staff officer who did. Yes, that had been the man they called "crazy." Davis had heard the nickname but knew nothing of Hill's record (which in fact showed him to be quite sane). The reputation alone was enough to sway Davis in his present state of uncertainty. Suppose the northern army was not as shattered as he had thought. Suppose it should succeed in throwing back or even soundly thrashing the pursuing force. Much responsibility now rested squarely on the president's shoulders, and he too was tired and had been under great stress. No longer willing to bear the full weight of the decision, Davis began to rehash the matter with his generals. They were already convinced that nothing more could be done, and the result was that Davis told Beauregard to issue an order for a modified pursuit in the morning, consoling himself with the reflection that by now it was so late that delay until morning was really not so much of a delay after all.[11]

Next morning Beauregard issued his order, though unbeknownst to the president it was not exactly what he had had in mind. The movement wound up being nothing more than a cautious reconnaissance, the chief accomplishment of which was to scavenge the battlefield for abandoned weapons and equipment.[12] By then a heavy rain was falling, turning the Virginia roads to muddy quagmires and putting an end to the possibility of serious pursuit.[13] But neither the weather nor the tense conference of the night before seemed to dampen the spirits of the Confederate high command at Manassas. Davis and Johnston arrived at the breakfast table before Beauregard, and during their conversation, Johnston suggested that the Creole ought to be promoted to full general in recognition of his services the day before. Davis was pleased to be able to inform Johnston that he already had the promotion written out.[14] When Beauregard came in, Davis handed him the paper. "Appreciating your services in the battle of Manassas," it read, "and on several other occasions during the existing war, as affording the highest evidence of your skill as a commander, your gallantry as a soldier, and your zeal as a patriot, you are promoted to be a general in the army of the Confederate States of America, and, with the consent of the Congress, will be duly commissioned accordingly."[15] As for Johnston, he was already a full general and that being the highest grade in the Confederate army could not be promoted. Davis did, however, show his satisfaction with him. Several of Johnston's subordinates, whom he had previously recommended warmly to the president, received promotions, some leaping several grades. Johnston's favorite staff officer, Whiting, jumped from major to brigadier general.[16] Both Davis and Johnston, as well as the men thus promoted, probably saw this as an indication of the good favor Johnston enjoyed with the president. That Davis inclined to rate Johnston as his best available general was indicated by a proposition the president made that day.

Confederate forces in what was soon to become West Virginia were in disarray. Outnumbered, outgeneraled, plagued by bickering among their own jealous commanders, and given no help by the population of sturdy mountaineers who wanted no part of the slaveholders' rebellion, the southern troops had suffered a series of defeats. Even the dispatch to the mountains of Lee's righthand man in Richmond, respected Virginia general Robert S. Garnett, had not sufficed to change the outlook, and Garnett had recently been killed in yet another Confederate debacle. With the Manassas front now secure and every passing hour bringing more evidence of the discomfiture of the Federals and the unlikelihood that they would be advancing this way again soon, western Virginia was the hot spot of the Confederate frontier, the area most likely to see battle within the next few weeks and most in need of the best possible commander. Davis apparently thought that man was Johnston, for he offered him the West Virginia command the day after Manassas. The new assignment would have been challenging to say the least, though a more naturally pugnacious officer might have jumped at the chance for it. Johnston, however, sensed that glory was more easily to be won in eastern Virginia, and in any case he was never one to take risks when he could rest on his laurels and guard his reputation instead. He replied to the president's offer by stating his belief that an even larger Federal army would be advancing on Manassas "before the end of fall," and therefore he preferred to stay where he was rather than be transferred to "much less important" service.[17]

The rest of that rainy Monday was spent by Davis in taking care of various administrative and organizational matters as well as a particular personal concern.[18] That he still considered himself very much in command in the field was manifested when early that morning, Adjutant and Inspector General Cooper, back in Richmond and unsure of the situation at the front, addressed a telegram to "Commanding Officer at Manassas." "Telegraph in few words," Cooper wired, "what is the actual state of things this morning, in order that a communication may be made to Congress when it meets at 12 o'clock today, especially as to the certainty of the victory."[19] Davis, not thinking twice about who was the "Commanding Officer" there, replied himself: "Victory complete. Advanced forces report that enemy fled in confusion through Centreville last night."[20]

That afternoon, taking along a guide who was supposed to know the locations of the various units of the army, the president set out to visit the wounded, especially a young relative of his, said to be in failing condition. Davis had managed to procure a carriage, and that was some comfort in the inclement weather, but he found himself crisscrossing the battlefield, covering many miles and visiting many field hospitals with their saddening and sometimes harrowing sights but still unable to find his young kinsman. With nightfall coming on he was about to give up the search when he happened to encounter an officer from the young man's unit, who directed him to the correct field hospital. By then, it was too late.[21]

Returning from this melancholy errand, the president held another conference with Johnston and Beauregard. His chief concern was to inquire of the generals just what they thought it might be practicable to undertake in the wake of the previous day's victory. All that day cavalry patrols had been bringing in additional evidence of the completeness of the Federal defeat. Now Davis wondered what advantage could be taken of the situation. The generals, however, were of one mind in the opinion that no further action was possible. Crossing the Potomac, patrolled as it was bound to be by U.S. warships, was out of the question. As for an advance to the south bank opposite Washington, Beauregard was especially negative, and Johnston was not inclined to differ. The Creole had been cultivating a spy or two in Washington and had by one such informant received his first information of the Federal advance several days ago. He now described at length the extensive and strongly garrisoned fortifications protecting the capital and turning to his fellow general as if seeking agreement said, "They have spared no expense."[22] He need not have worried about Johnston's approval. The Virginian, prone in any case to distrust volunteer troops, was appalled at the level of disorganization in the Confederate ranks and also painfully aware of his forces' lack of siege equipment.[23] The generals were right, and the president had to admit it. In truth, the Confederacy was in no position to capture or even seriously threaten Washington. Convinced that no more could be accomplished until the army was substantially strengthened, Davis determined to return to Richmond the next morning and bend his energies to achieving just that.[24]

About nine or ten o'clock Tuesday morning he boarded the train for Richmond. It was a jubilant city to which he returned, and he fell in quickly with the popular mood. Addressing the ecstatic citizenry gathered in front of the Spotswood, Davis described the battle in florid terms, praising the courage and skill of the victors, especially Johnston and Beauregard, and predicting that the Confederate flag would soon fly over Alexandria, opposite Washington.[25] The people were especially glad to hear this last. As one Richmond diarist noted, "The President had pledged himself, on one occasion, to carry the war into the enemy's country, if they would not let us go in peace. Now, in that belief, the people were well pleased with their President."[26] The next day the crowds were back, clamoring for another speech, which the president was apparently not loath to give them. "He is an old war-horse," Mary Chesnut wrote in her diary, "and scents the battlefields from afar. His enthusiasm was contagious." Apparently he was himself at least partially overcome by his own enthusiasm, for Chesnut also wrote, "The president took all the credit to himself for the victory–said the wounded roused and shouted for Jeff Davis and the men rallied at the sight of him and rushed on and routed the enemy." His reason for making such statements, she believed, was that he was "greedy for military fame." After the president's speech, the crowd called for more from the other politicians present including Beauregard's volunteer aide James Chesnut. Predictably, he "gave the glory of the victory to Beauregard." Afterward he told his wife that "if the president had not said so much for himself, he would have praised him" too.[27]

The Chesnuts at this point in the war were definitely Beauregard partisans and so may have put the worst construction on Davis's words, but even his staunchest supporters had gotten the idea, from his Manassas dispatches and other indications he had given, "that he was not only present" at the height of the battle "but had directed the principal operations in the field."[28] The day after the battle, Varina herself had been under the impression, and had told others, that "Jeff Davis led the center, Joe Johnston the right wing, Beauregard the left wing of the army."[29] Apparently the president's pride and enthusiasm had betrayed him into so misrepresenting the situation that without telling outright untruths he had given people the impression that his role had been more what he wished it to have been than what it really was.

That could be highly offensive to those who knew the actual facts, especially–for they were bound to hear of it quickly–men such as Beauregard and Johnston, whose greed for military fame far exceeded the president's own. Whether the wounded pride this may have occasioned was directly to blame or not, the president was soon to encounter severe difficulties in his relationships with his two chief Virginia generals.

The first problems involved the task of supplying the victorious Confederate army. If Napoleon was right in stating that an army marches on its stomach and World War II German general Erwin Rommel in asserting that "the battle is fought and won by the quartermasters before the shooting begins," then the southern army at Manassas was fit neither to move nor to fight, for in the opinion of its commanders it had been let down by the Confederate commissary and quartermaster departments. Johnston and Beauregard believed that Commissary General Lucius B. Northrop was at fault for failing to provide adequate supplies of food for the army and that Quartermaster General Abraham C. Myers had performed poorly in his task of providing, among other things, the wagons necessary to carry those foodstuffs any distance from a railroad. For some reason the Manassas commanders had not discussed the matter with Davis while he was at the front, but he had hardly left for Richmond when, probably as the difficulty of supplying the increased force at Manassas became more pressing, Beauregard had his commissary write the president to complain that Northrop was not filling requisitions and that if this kept up "most serious consequences are inevitable."[30]

Such a complaint was particularly hard for the president to take, not only because criticism of the way the war effort was being administered at the seat of government was at least indirectly criticism of him, but also because Northrop was an old friend from his regular army days back in the 1830s. They had served together under a martinet superior officer out in the Indian Territory and had encouraged each other in various acts of insubordination until one such had gotten Davis court-martialed.[31] Through it all, Northrop had stood by him, and so, as Confederate president, Davis, being the sort of man he was, responded with a blind loyalty that would brook no criticism of his commissary general. For the present, Beauregard's complaint went unanswered, probably indicating that Davis had referred to Northrop for information with which to reply and that Northrop, being the sort of administrator he was, had been a long time reporting back to him. While the president awaited Northrop's rely, Johnston dropped another vexing problem in his lap. One week after the victory at Manassas, the Virginian began to complain about the quartermaster general. "This army," he wrote, "is without adequate means of transportation" and therefore could not maneuver. Urgent measures, he felt, were needed to obtain the requisite numbers of supply wagons.[32] Davis would have taken this criticism less personally than he did that against Northrop, but coming on the heels of the other it must have been a frustrating reminder of the difficulties involved in supporting the South's combat troops.

All this would have been bad enough, but on July 29 Beauregard decided to test a new method of getting desired results out of Richmond. On that day he wired Davis, "Beg to suggest not to send any more troops here until provisions can be had. Some regiments are nearly starving."[33] That was an exaggeration, but if he had stopped there, little damage would have been done. Instead, he proceeded to write to William P. Miles and James Chesnut, both members of the Confederate Congress and both former volunteer aides of his, bemoaning in overblown language the lack of supplies and suggesting that but for this deficiency his troops would be following up their success as the South expected. "The want of food and transportation has made use lose all the fruits of our victory," he wrote. "We ought at this moment to be in or about Washington, but we are perfectly anchored here, and God only knows when we will be able to advance." Since he could not under the present conditions move anywhere at all, "Cannot something be done towards furnishing us more expeditiously and regularly with food and transportation?" Then, hitting again on the topic that was already becoming the focus of discontent among the Confederate populace, he added, "From all accounts, Washington could have been taken up to the 24th instant, by twenty thousand men! Only think of the brilliant results we have lost by the two causes referred to!"[34]

The congressmen did think of it and, as Beauregard had obviously intended, decided the matter was a fit subject for congressional investigation. Chesnut read it on the floor of that body, and the members promptly passed a formal resolution, inquiring of the president "whether or not he received any authentic information going to show a want of sufficient and regular supply of food" to the troops at Manassas.[35] The president's patience under the circumstances was remarkable. Once again he inquired of Northrop on the matter. The commissary general was adamant that Beauregard had no one but himself to blame for his supply woes. "The facts are," he wrote after the war, "that . . . General Beauregard, neglected his communications." If the general had not miserably muddled the railroad system in northern Virginia, Northrop maintained, all would have been well. This was partly true in that

Beauregard's use of the railroads had not been especially skillful, but the fact was that Northrop was far more to blame, having imposed a bureaucratic system that offered farmers below-market prices for produce and had all Virginia supplies hauled to Richmond first, then turned around and shipped back out to the armies in the field. The resulting confusion and duplication of effort was chiefly responsible for the supply crunch, such as it was.[36] The president predictably accepted Northrop's explanation as the whole truth and replied to Congress that the commissariat was "quite as good as was reasonable to expect."[37] For Davis, proving that supply failures were someone else's fault was more important than a remedy for the situation. It was one of his more serious failures as commander in chief.

To Beauregard, the president's reply was remarkably mild, though the faintest shadow of a chill seemed to have passed across it. The "My Dear Sir" of the president's salutation was perhaps just a bit more stiff and formal than the "My Dear General" he had used before. Davis went on to inform Beauregard of the congressional inquiry and then observed blandly, "Some excitement has been created by your letter." The heads of the commissary and quartermaster bureaus both felt wronged, Davis explained, and he himself had done his best. He asserted that "any failure which has occurred from imperfect knowledge might have been best avoided by timely requisitions and estimates." Then, striving to take a friendlier tone, the president stated soothingly, "I think you are unjust to yourself in putting our failure to pursue the enemy to Washington to the account of short supplies of subsistence and transportation." He reminded Beauregard that in the situation they faced after the battle and with the information they then had, little more could have been accomplished. "Enough was done for glory," Davis concluded, "and the measure of duty was full." The best course now was to try to show the people, the politicians, and the clamoring press that expectations of a Confederate capture of Washington were never reasonable in the first place rather than fanning the flames of popular expectation by trying to fix blame for a failure to do the impossible.[38]

Beauregard would have done well to have met the president's gracious response in a like spirit, but he was in no frame of mind for that. The victory at Manassas was popularly attributed to him, and basking in the first reflection of its glory he was for a few weeks the most popular man in the Confederacy.[39] The fame went straight to his head, and he began to act as if the South were his to command. Far from being ready to ease tensions with the president, he began a backstage political campaign to have Northrop turned out of office, writing to Miles to suggest that the president's crony be dumped in favor of Beauregard's own staff commissary, Col. R. B. Lee.[40] Miles informed the general that "the President has not the remotest idea of removing Colonel Northrop," but encouraged Beauregard's hubris with the assurance, "You may rely upon it, Congress and the country sympathize with you."[41] Thus fortified, the Creole sat down on August 10, nearly a week after the date of the president's letter, to write a reply. He excused his tardiness with a vague reference to his "endless occupations," one of which, of course, was plotting the downfall of the president's old friend. Trying to separate his criticism of Northrop from any suggestion of finding fault with Davis, Beauregard expressed regret that his letter to Miles had been read in Congress and assured the president, "I am fully aware that you have done more than could be expected of you for this army." Then, perhaps hinting negatively toward Davis's known tendency to interfere too much in the management of affairs under him, he acknowledged "that it is utterly impossible you should be able to direct each one of the bureaus of the War Department." But a problem existed somewhere, he maintained, and ought to be remedied. He insisted that an opportunity to capture Washington had indeed been thrown away through poor supply work, but that such an opportunity had existed not on July 21 or 22, when Davis had been at Manassas and quizzed his generals on such possibilities, but rather on the twenty-third and twenty-fourth. Finally, in the most insulting part of his letter, he contemptuously slapped aside the president's kind words for his efforts at Manassas. "We have, no doubt," he wrote, "by our success here, achieved 'glory' for our country, but I am fighting for something more real and tangible, i.e., to save our homes and firesides from our Northern invaders, and to maintain our freedom and independence as a nation." These, of course, were the very things for which Davis liked to claim he was fighting, and that must have given a special bite to the superior and self-righteous tone of Beauregard's posturing and a certain hollowness to his signing himself, "Sincerely your friend."[42]

For the moment, Beauregard's meanness failed to create a major breach with the president. Davis resisted the temptation to respond to the Creole's snide letter, and in the month or so that followed directed his correspondence to Johnston rather than Beauregard. That was more proper in any case. Besides, the president was seriously ill for much of the month of August 1861. Stricken with an attack of ague on the sixteenth, he was believed for several days to be in mortal danger. He then seemed to recover but, according to Mary Chesnut, remained "so weak that even talking in the room with him makes him flushed and feverish." September had come before he could receive visitors or even write his own letters, and some in Richmond had begun to suspect him—falsely—of faking the whole thing.[43] Still, despite the president's silence, resentment smoldered between the two and could not be wholly concealed. Just the day after Beauregard wrote his letter, War Department clerk John B. Jones noted in his diary, "There is a whisper that something like a rupture has occurred between the President and Gen. Beauregard," a result, he had heard, of Davis preventing Beauregard from taking Washington after Manassas.[44] At Beauregard's headquarters no one cared to disguise the matter. The general's chief of staff plied influential southerners with assertions that Davis, driven by jealousy, was out to engineer Beauregard's failure even if it meant the collapse of the Confederacy. Davis partisans—if not the president himself—returned the compliment. "It is no laughing matter," Navy Secretary Stephen R. Mallory told Mary Chesnut, "to have our fate in the hands of such self-sufficient, vain, army idiots."[45]

Beauregard's foremost enemy within the cabinet was his fellow Louisianan, Attorney General Judah P. Benjamin. Though immediately after Beauregard's success at Fort Sumter Benjamin had written him to offer "the tribute of a poor civilian who knows nothing of war," he had since become "inimical" to him. He was also in the process of getting on very good terms with Davis. A smooth and charming man, Benjamin had an ingratiating manner.[46] By late summer of 1861 the president had undertaken to ease his original secretary of war, the incompetent Leroy Pope Walker, out of office and put Benjamin in his place. Though efficient and hardworking, the Louisiana lawyer indeed knew nothing of war and so would be merely a conduit for the president's policies. He would carry them out, however, in such a way as seemed to him most likely to increase his own influence with the chief executive and to decrease that of others.[47] His dislike for Beauregard boded ill for the future of that general's relations with Davis.

By contrast with the increasingly strained relations with Beauregard, the president continued to get along well with Johnston during the seven weeks after the victory at Manassas. Davis's letters were friendly and complimentary, one concluding, "With affectionate remembrance to Mrs. Johnston."[48] The general, in turn, communicated frequently, keeping the president informed of Federal movements and likely intentions, possible Confederate operations, and the needs, training, and organization of the army.[49] Davis saw to it that his requests were promptly met. Each continued to sign himself, "your friend." This was just the relationship Davis wanted with his generals, and Johnston seemed content as well.[50]

In September, Johnston hinted that Davis should take personal command of the army in the field. "This frontier," he wrote, "should have but one commander–district lines should be abolished" and the army organized so as to "relieve the supreme commander of everything like drudgery–& leave him to bestow his mind upon the grand operations alone. Let me beg you to think of this–& to send the troops . . . & the commander-in-chief."[51] Davis missed the allusion to himself, and taking Johnston's suggestion as merely organizational, replied that unity of command was already provided "by the rule applying to troops who happen to join and do duty together"; Johnston was overall commander as he outranked Beauregard and their forces had been joined. The rest of the president's letter contained more kind words.[52]

Davis revealed much about his strategic ideas in this correspondence. The southern populace–or at least its press and politicians–were clamoring for offensive action.[53] Such operations might be desirable, Davis admitted, but not if they involved significant risk. "I have felt and feel that time brings many advantages to the enemy, and wish we could strike him in his present condition; but it has seemed to me involved in too much probability of failure to render the movement proper with our present means." Greater than the risks incurred by inaction, as far as Davis was concerned, was the danger of sudden disaster in a miscarried offensive. For him, that danger outweighed the potential advantage of possessing the initiative and choosing the time and place of action. "It is true," he admitted, "that a successful advance across the Potomac would relieve other places; but, if not successful, ruin would befall us."[54] It was a basically defensive grand strategy with which Joseph E. Johnston could not have been more in agreement.

Thus Davis and Johnston freely discussed the strategic situation in Virginia and seemed on their way to developing an excellent working understanding of each other. Never before had Davis's relations with one of his top generals been this good. Never would they be this good again. Even as they exchanged friendly letters during the six weeks after Manassas, the trouble that would soon boil over between them was already simmering. Its origins lay in a law passed by the Confederate Congress that spring and in Joseph E. Johnston's never-ending lust for high rank. On March 6 Congress had enacted a law guaranteeing officers of the United States Army who might resign to cast their lot with the Confederacy the same relative rank in the new service as they had held in the Old Army. Included in section twenty-nine of the bill was a provision stipulating that for purposes of command, an officer would rank according to the highest grade he had previously held within the same arm of the service in which he was presently functioning. This wise administrative reform was probably included at the instigation of Davis himself, who as secretary of war had long deplored the confusion resulting in the Old Army from a lack of such a provision. Johnston was not yet in Confederate service then and could hardly have been in the minds of the president or congressmen. The law they passed, however, would cast a long shadow over his Confederate career.[55]

When later that spring Congress authorized the rank of full general, Davis had immediately settled on four men for that grade. Carefully following the provisions of the act of March 6, he ranked them according to their previous seniority in the U.S. Army within the branch of the army in which they were to serve. Highest in rank was Samuel Cooper, a staff colonel in the old service. Slated to serve in the staff position of adjutant and inspector general in the Confederacy, Cooper was ranked accordingly. Next in seniority was Davis's old West Point friend Albert Sidney Johnston, who had been a line colonel. After him came Robert E. Lee, also a former colonel, but junior to Sidney Johnston. Fourth on the president's list was Joseph E. Johnston, and there lay the difficulty. Johnston's successful vault into the position of quartermaster general had brought with it the rank of brigadier, but only in a staff capacity. As a Confederate general, Johnston would be serving not in the staff but in the line, as a commander of troops in the field. As such, he was entitled by the act of Congress to be ranked only according to his highest previous rank in the line, and that was as lieutenant colonel. Davis, with his customary precision in matters of legal detail, accordingly ranked him fourth rather than first, as he would have been ranked had his staff promotion been admissible for such purposes.

Johnston would never admit the validity of such an interpretation–or of anything else that stood between him and a promotion. For the moment, however, he had remained ignorant of it and, interpreting the act in the superficial way most favorable to himself, had simply assumed that he was the highest ranking general in the Confederacy. That he was able to do so was the fault of the president. Though Davis seems to have informed Cooper, Lee, and Joseph Johnston, unofficially, that they were to be full generals, he did not formally send their nominations, in the order of their relative seniority, to Congress. The reason, apparently, was that Davis's old friend Sidney Johnston was not yet at hand. Stationed in California at the outbreak of the war, he had taken several months to make his way overland to the Confederacy. If Davis had published his list of generals before knowing for certain that Sidney Johnston was coming, he could hardly have included his friend's name. In that case, the former U.S. Army Pacific Coast commander, who by his seniority would otherwise have ranked second among Confederate generals, would have had to be promoted at a later date and thus could have ranked no better than fourth. Davis believed, with some reason, that Sidney Johnston was the best officer in the prewar U.S. Army and would have wanted him to hold the highest position possible.[56] Besides that, the president's loyalty to old friends was to become proverbial. Thus, apparently in order to assure Sidney Johnston a place as one of the Confederacy's original full generals, Davis delayed publishing his list of such officers until, late in August, he learned that his friend was on his way and would soon be in Richmond.[57]

Just when that list, or word of it, reached Joseph Johnston's eyes is not clear. But the first rumblings of impending trouble had come even as president and general were establishing their fine working relationship after Manassas. Three days after the battle, on July 24, Dabney Maury arrived at Johnston's headquarters with an order written by Lee under the heading, "Headquarters of the Forces." The order assigned Maury to serve as Johnston's adjutant general. "This is an outrage!" Johnston exploded. "I rank General Lee, and he has no right to order officers into my army."[58] Immediately firing off a letter to Cooper, Johnston wrote that he had already assigned another officer to those duties. He "could admit the power of no officer of the Army to annul my order on the subject; nor can I admit the claim of any officer to the command of 'the forces,' being myself the ranking General of the Confederate Army." He thought well of Maury, but this was a matter of rank.[59] The letter was referred to Davis, who apparently failed to understand the general's misconception and simply scrawled the word "Insubordinate" across the bottom of it.[60] This message, in turn, seems never to have reached Johnston.

Five days later Johnston wrote Cooper again, complaining that he was still receiving "daily orders purporting to come from the 'Headquarters of the Forces,' some of them in relation to the internal affairs of this army. Such orders," he concluded, "I cannot regard, because they are illegal." Once again the letter landed on the president's desk. Again Davis penned his endorsement, "Insubordinate."[61] The problem did not go away, and twice during the following month Johnston wrote Cooper to continue his complaints about rank.[62]

Still all remained well between Johnston and the president until September 10. By then, Johnston had learned of his ranking behind Cooper, Sidney Johnston, and Lee and had composed a lengthy and scathing letter to Davis, denouncing the president, Congress, his three superiors in rank—anyone who stood between him and the coveted position. So strident was the letter's tone that even Johnston hesitated to send it.[63] In the meantime he mailed the president a dispatch in which his anger appeared in a more controlled form. "Sir," he addressed him coldly, "it was said that during the past summer I have been censured by the two persons in Richmond highest in military rank, for not having assumed command of this army, and that they complain of the inconvenience to the service which had been produced thereby." This, of course, was a reference to Cooper and Lee, whom Johnston had already come to regard as his enemies at the capital. Johnston went on to defend the considerable independence he was allowing Beauregard and then stated,

> I have taken the liberty, more than once, to suggest to you to assume the military function of the Presidency, and to command on this northern frontier. I thought my meaning was very plainly expressed. I find I was mistaken, and that you regard one of the last expressions of this idea as not applicable to yourself. I may have written carelessly because, being by our laws *next in military place to yourself*, it did not occur to me that anyone else could be supposed to be thought of.[64]

The word "friend" was, for the first time in several months, absent from Johnston's closing. The emphasis Johnston placed on his imagined position as top Confederate general constituted little less than a challenge to Davis to say otherwise.

The president's reply was mild and soothing. "My Dear General," he began, "I can only suppose that you have been deceived by some one of that class in whose absence 'the strife ceaseth.' " Such false talebearers must have been responsible, Davis believed, for Johnston's impression that he was being criticized by Cooper and Lee. "I do not believe," he wrote, "any disposition has existed on the part of the gentlemen to whom you refer to criticize, still less to detract, from you." As for the babblings of the rumormongers, "to educated soldiers this could only seem the muttering of the uninstructed." Assuring Johnston that he considered him commanding general of the army in the field in northern Virginia, he tried to smooth over the general's almost belligerent reference to his rank. "The laws of the Confederacy in relation to generals," he wrote, "have provisions which are new and unsettled by decisions. Their position is special, and the attention of Congress was called to what might be regarded as a conflict of laws. Their action was confined to fixing the dates for the generals of the C.S. Army." On the whole it was a remarkably kind and patient reply to a well nigh insubordinate letter. Davis had done all that anyone could have done to be what he signed himself at the letter's close, "Your friend."[65]

It was to be the last time he would call himself Johnston's friend. Perhaps if his gentle response could have reached the general before he took further action, things might have been different, but Johnston allowed no time for that. On the twelfth, having waited hardly long enough for his previous letter to have reached the president, Johnston threw off restraint and mailed his outraged diatribe over the issue of rank. The nominations for full general had been illegal, it asserted, and so had their confirmation by Congress. "I now and here declare my claim," Johnston raged, "that, notwithstanding these nominations made by the President, and their confirmation by Congress, I still rightfully hold the rank of first general in the armies of the Southern Confederacy." The president's action had been "a studied indignity" and "a blow aimed at me only." "It seems to tarnish my fair fame as a soldier and as a man, earned by more than thirty years of laborious and perilous service." This sort of thing went on through several pages, and then came a lengthy legal argument. As a parting shot, he made a sneering reference to the fact that while he had served in the war's main battle up to that point, neither Cooper, nor Sidney Johnston, nor Lee had "yet struck a blow for the Confederacy."[66] As bad as all this was, it could have been a good deal worse. Johnston had composed an additional lengthy passage, sarcastically suggesting that his imagined demotion was his reward for the victory at Manassas, but had changed his mind about including it in his letter to the president.

All this came as a considerable shock to Davis, as his own letter of the thirteenth indicated he still considered Johnston a friend and was treating him with remarkable patience and gentleness. Such mildness was all the more notable in Davis, since he had been ill for weeks, a situation that tended to bring out the harshest side of the president's character. The same circumstance no doubt made Johnston's angry outburst even harder to endure calmly, for Davis was sick again—or still—and knew that Johnston knew it, for he had mentioned it repeatedly in their correspondence.[68] The general's lack of consideration would have aggravated the irritability that poor health produced in Davis. Under the circumstances, his reply was surprisingly restrained. "Sir," he wrote, "I have just received and read your letter of the 12th inst. Its language is, as you say, unusual; its arguments and statements utterly one-sided; and its insinuations as unfounded as they are unbecoming."[69] All this was true, if not very helpful, but nothing Davis could have said, short of giving Johnston the rank he coveted, would likely have been adequate to restore the general to goodwill and cheerful cooperation. As it was, Davis had resisted the temptation to follow Johnston's example in producing a lengthy screed of attempted self-justification. His curt answer at least gave Johnston no opening through which to continue the controversy. Davis had maintained his presidential dignity and shown a restraint that kept the incident's damage to a minimum, even ordering the assistant secretary of war not to place Johnston's intemperate letter in the official files.[70] Relations between president and general could continue on an official if not on a friendly basis, and once Johnston had learned of his rank, that was the best that could have been hoped for.[71]

While Johnston worried about rank, Lee had other concerns. Davis had sent him to retrieve Confederate fortunes in West Virginia. After Garnett's disaster in July, the situation there had continued grim. The fault lay partly with certain of Davis's political appointees. The political general was a special plague of Civil War armies. Chosen not for his likely ability to win battles but for the popular influence he possessed—and might use against the administration if his vanity and desire for military fame were not gratified with an appointment—the political general was a necessity to a government seeking popular support in a civil conflict. In the army itself, he was, with a few refreshing exceptions, enormously expensive in lives wasted and strategic advantages lost, but that was the price that had to be paid to convince the nation to fight. Both sides were forced to take on such prominent political figures in military roles for which they were, in most cases, totally unfitted. Lincoln, because of the more abstract nature of his side's war aims, had to make more such concessions than Davis, but the Confederate president could not escape giving a fair proportion of his appointments to politicians.[72] During the war's first year, nearly three in every ten generals he appointed were of this sort.[73]

The two political generals damaging the Confederacy's fortunes in western Virginia were John B. Floyd and Henry A. Wise. Of equal age and almost equal date of rank (Floyd was a few days senior), each politician had served as governor of Virginia during the 1850s. Floyd had served as secretary of war in the Buchanan administration and had left it under strong suspicion of graft, to say nothing of outright treason. Both men were rabid proslavery secessionists. Now, as generals, these two who had so much in common found it utterly impossible to get along, and fighting the Federals became secondary to fighting each other. One observer commented, "Floyd and Wise . . . are as inimical to each other as men can be, and from their course and actions I am fully satisfied that each of them would be highly gratified to see the other annihilated." He concluded with a comment that could have been a commentary on the whole Confederate high command in the East that summer and fall. "It would be just as easy to combine oil and water as to expect a union of action between these gentlemen."[74] A third general complicated the situation in western Virginia. Not exactly a political general–at least not a political appointment of Davis's–William W. Loring had been a politically appointed officer in the Mexican War, in which he had lost an arm, and thereafter had remained in the army. Having gone with the Confederacy, he was now, in a sense, one of its professional officers, but he brought with him all the incompetence and egotism of the worst of political generals. Each of these men commanded separate forces in the West Virginia mountains and refused to cooperate with each other or, after his arrival, Lee.

Lee's situation was delicate in any case. The war was new, and the high commands of both sides were still struggling to find workable arrangements. This was true for Davis despite his prewar experience, for nothing in America prior to the Civil War had come close to equaling it in scale and complexity. Not yet having mastered the crafting of clear and effective command systems, Davis had sent Lee over the mountains with uncertain authority and an ill-defined mission. Departing a few days after Manassas, Lee had taken no written orders and apparently was not expected to take personal command of the forces. His high rank and nominal position as commander of all Confederate forces in Virginia gave him a certain amount of authority, and this Davis hoped would, in what manner was never quite clear, secure cooperation among the various Confederate generals and direct them to victory.[75] In a letter to Johnston a few days after Lee's departure Davis wrote, "Genl. Lee has gone to Western Va.: and I hope may be able to strike a decisive blow at the enemy in that quarter, or failing in that, will be able to organize and post our troops so as to check the enemy, after which he will return to this place."[76] The Richmond *Examiner* the day before had correctly assessed Lee's mission as "a tour to the West, looking after the commands of Generals Loring and Wise. . . . His visit is understood to be one of inspection, and consultation on the plan of campaign."[77]

Davis's expectations had been vague but optimistic. After the war he wrote that he had hoped that Lee, "by his military skill and deserved influence over men," would be able to retrieve the Confederacy's fortunes in West Virginia.[78] Yet the directions given and the authority granted were not adequate to realize such hopes, and even with the best of command arrangements it might have been impossible to salvage a situation in which the enemy had so many advantages and the Confederates had Loring, Wise, and

Floyd. The three refused to cooperate, and even after Davis had Wise transferred to other duties, Lee was able to accomplish little.[79] The Confederacy lost western Virginia, and the public, which had expected great things from Lee and understood little of the difficulties he faced, was inclined to consider him a grossly overrated humbug.[80]

While Lee struggled vainly in West Virginia, Davis focused on the overland route from Washington to Richmond and the Confederate army that guarded it. September brought more of the same old haggling over supply and the lack thereof and whose fault that might be.[81] Davis was more interested in the strategic situation in northern Virginia. As the euphoria of Manassas had faded, the hope had remained in many southern minds that the Confederacy might still reap greater benefits from that battle, even though the time for harvest seemed to be past. Foremost among those who entertained such hopes was Beauregard himself. Serving now as a de facto corps commander in Johnston's army, Beauregard had spent the weeks after the battle squabbling with Richmond over the logistical problems that had prevented an advance and pressing Johnston to move forward anyway. As the supply situation had improved, Johnston had consented to press forward a little closer to Washington. Beauregard made the most of this concession and in mid-August pushed beyond Fairfax Court House and all the way to Mason's and Munson's Hills, about three miles from the Federal lines across from Washington and within sight of the unfinished capitol dome.[82]

Years later, Johnston would claim he had taken up these positions to be ready for offensive action as soon as reinforcements arrived.[83] In truth, Johnston "did not mean to have such posts . . . established" and said as much at the time in a letter to Beauregard. He saw no advantage in "placing ourselves so near enemy's works," feared that the arrangement would bring on skirmishing, and confessed that—now that the positions had been occupied—"nothing but reluctance to withdraw—to go backward—prevents me from abandoning them."[84] That reluctance, however, coupled with Beauregard's persistent urgings, was enough to hold him in place while the Creole pressed on him the dream of taking the offensive.

In this Beauregard was joined by Maj. Gen. Gustavus W. Smith. A native Kentuckian, Smith had ranked eighth in the fifty-six man West Point class of 1842. Assigned to the elite corps of engineers, he had served with distinction in the Mexican War, winning a brevet. Like many of his comrades, he had found the life of a peacetime regular army officer unrewarding and had resigned, eventually taking the position of street commissioner for New York City. When the war came, Smith hesitated. Neither the first secessions nor the news of Sumter caused him to stir from his job in New York. It was not until the chimera of Kentucky neutrality had disappeared in early September that Smith had moved to end the speculation—until then rife both above and below the Mason-Dixon Line—as to which way he would jump. He went south, arriving in Richmond on the eleventh.[85] He had already written to Davis from Nashville on the third, offering his services and asserting that "the guns at Sumter would have brought me South at once" if he had not been suffering from a serious and prolonged illness. Now, however, he was "perfectly recovered" and eager for service, and in concluding his letter did not neglect to include a flattering assurance of his "regard, friendship and admiration" for Davis.[86] For some reason, Smith enjoyed a formidable reputation out of all proportion to his military accomplishments. Hailed in the press, lauded by politicians, and recommended for an important commission by Johnston and Beauregard in a joint letter to Davis, Smith seemed a valuable accession to the cause.[87] Davis appointed him a major general and assigned him as the first officer of that rank in Johnston's army.[88]

Johnston and Beauregard received Smith enthusiastically, and the former lost no time in assigning the army's new third-ranking officer to command the segment of the army that originally had been his own, designating it the "Second Corps," while the forces that originally had been Beauregard's remained under that officer and were designated the First Corps.[89] This was a highly practical arrangement as yet without official sanction in Confederate law.[90] Smith soon fell in with Beauregard's ideas about the desirability of taking the offensive. If Smith's postwar reminiscences can be believed, he came to the army with the conviction that Davis had no "well-defined, comprehensive war policy" and "seemed to be floundering in a discursive plan for trying to protect all the assailable points in the country, hoping that something favorable would turn up from abroad." What Smith wanted, he later wrote, was an immediate offensive, and he was delighted to find that Beauregard was of the same mind.[91]

Johnston was won over, and the three then had no difficulty agreeing that to accomplish their desired offensive they would need more troops. The question was how to get the president to send them. Smith, who had just received such a high commission from Davis's hand and had not encountered the difficulties with the president that Beauregard and especially Johnston had in recent weeks, was optimistic about the possibilities of persuading the commander in chief. The day after arriving in camp he wrote Davis, stressing the army's "critical condition" and asserting, "It is essential to the welfare of the Confederate States that we should not meet with a reverse on this line."[92] Smith went further, urging Johnston "to request President Davis to visit the headquarters of the army with a view to discuss" the possibilities for reinforcement and offensive action before the onset of winter.[93] It is a measure of Smith's remarkable reputation that fall that Johnston acted immediately on the advice of an officer who had been with the army scarcely twenty-four hours and that same day, September 26, sent the desired message to Richmond. He did not, however, write to Davis. Their ugly falling out was not yet two weeks old, and he likely had no stomach for approaching the president with a request. Instead, he wrote to newly installed Secretary of War Judah P. Benjamin. Absent from Johnston's letter was any hint that the movement forward to the line in front of Fairfax Court House had been anything but his own idea. Instead, he asserted that he had advanced both in order to find more healthful campsites for the troops and "to be ready to turn the enemy's position and advance into Maryland whenever the strength of this army would justify it." So far, however, that desirable circumstance had not been realized, and since the present position inside a wide sweeping curve of the Potomac was liable to being turned on either side, it was now "necessary to decide definitely whether we are to advance or fall back to a more defensible line." Johnston said he suspected that the Confederate government was in no position to reinforce the army for taking the offensive, but "if I am mistaken in this," he wrote, "and you can furnish those means, I think it is important that either his excellency the President of the Confederate States, yourself, or some one representing you, should here upon the ground confer with me in regard to this all-important question." Dispatching a staff officer to carry the letter to Richmond, Johnston sat back to await the result.[94]

To his surprise a letter came back from Benjamin promising a visit by the president. The secretary would not promise that the army could be put in a condition to take the offensive since the Richmond authorities had not been receiving adequate reports on the army's present numbers and situation. This, Benjamin admonished, would have to change. Nevertheless, he and the president had considered Johnston's letter and decided a visit to the front was justified. Davis never needed a second invitation to visit the front lines and would go himself. The secretary informed Johnston that he could expect the president "within a day or two."[95]

In fact, by the time Johnston received Benjamin's message, the president was already on his way. The day after the secretary sent his dispatch, at 6:00 A.M., Davis boarded a special train for the front. During a brief stop at Manassas Junction, he was prevailed upon to make a few impromptu remarks to some of the Mississippi troops stationed there, and a newspaper correspondent jotted down the gist of them. Once again the president's martial ambitions rose to the surface as he spoke of the "work before them . . . in which he had come to bear with them his part." He went on to express his desire to lead them personally "to glorious victory or a patriotic soldier's grave."[96] Davis had obviously not given up his hope of being present at the head of the army at the supreme moment. Continuing his journey, he arrived at Fairfax Station that evening, where Johnston, Beauregard, and Smith met him amid the fanfare of cheering crowds and bands belting out "Hail to the Chief" and "Dixie." Mounting the horse provided for him, Davis joined the generals and their staff officers for the ride to the army's headquarters at Fairfax Court House. Both soldiers and civilians lined the road and hurrahed lustily as the president passed by. Sitting with his accustomed military erectness on the handsome white horse, Davis lifted his hat in response again and again during the four-mile journey.[97] On their arrival they found that there had been some sort of a misunderstanding as to the selection of a house for the president's lodging during his visit. Just what it was is not clear, but it was finally resolved by Beauregard's inviting Davis to stay with him at his headquarters, a "comfortable brick house in the outskirts of the village." Davis asked Johnston and Smith to meet him there the next day for the important discussions that were the reason for his visit.[98]

At the appointed hour the generals arrived, and the conference began. For the first hour of the discussion Davis took the lead and dwelt on matters of army organization.[99] He objected to the existence of corps, since they were unauthorized by the letter of the laws that the Confederate Congress had passed establishing the army.[100] According to Beauregard, he also objected to the existence of divisional organization and resisted the generals' urgings to appoint officers of appropriate rank to command them. If so, he quickly relented.[101] Smith had said little. Now he broke in "with some abruptness," as he described it, and brought the discussion to the main issue. "Mr. President," he asked, "is it not possible to put this army in condition to assume the active offensive?" He then launched into a forceful statement of his belief in the need for such an offensive. The others soon joined in the discussion. They pointed out advantages in an early movement by Confederate forces—the disorganization of the Federals as they assembled their army and the skill and high morale of the Confederate troops. They also discussed the disadvantages of delaying action until spring—an idle winter's demoralizing effect on Confederate troops, the impossibility of substantially increasing their numbers, the certainty of a vast increase in Federal numbers, and, worst of all, the prospect of the expiration of the one-year enlistments of most of the Confederate troops. On these matters, Smith thought, "there seemed to be little difference of opinion."[102]

What then was to be done? As usual, Beauregard had devised a plan and previously presented it to his fellow generals. Smith had embraced it with enthusiasm, Johnston with reluctance, and they had agreed to present it to Davis.[103] Beauregard's strategy applied not only to the devising of the plan but also to obtaining its acceptance by the commander in chief. Now that the time had come to present the scheme, the Creole wisely left Smith to expound it, no doubt hoping that the new general's better relations with the president would boost its chances of approval.[104] The idea was for a small diversionary force to remain near the army's present position while the main body, suitably strengthened by the additional troops the generals hoped to get from Davis, would move directly north and cross the Potomac at a nearby ford that Beauregard was having reconnoitered. Once in Maryland the army would be maneuvered so as to threaten Washington from the rear. Beauregard hoped they might even seize the Federal capital before the new Union commander George B. McClellan could shift enough troops across the Potomac to stop them. Even if the northern general could get there in time, Beauregard believed the Confederates could easily defeat a Federal army that would be demoralized, disorganized, and coming up piecemeal in its dash from camps south of the Potomac. At any rate, McClellan would have to fight at a disadvantage. The capture of Washington should, Beauregard thought, provide generous stocks of supplies, and the victorious Confederate army could then take up the defensive again, now on the northern frontier of Maryland rather than Virginia.[105]

Smith continued to plead his case insistently. "Mr. President," he said, "is it not possible to increase the effective strength of this army and put us in condition to cross the Potomac and carry the way into the enemy's country? Can you not," he persisted, "by stripping other points to the last they will bear, and, even risking defeat at all other places, put us in condition to move forward? Success here at this time saves everything; defeat here loses all." He went on to give specific examples of how he thought Confederate losses elsewhere might be made good by means of a victory north of the Potomac. "In short," as he later summed up his argument, "that success here was success everywhere, defeat here defeat everywhere; and that this was the point upon which all the available forces of the Confederate States should be concentrated.[106]

This was a gambler's counsel indeed. Still, it had a certain logic. Perhaps it might be better to let victory or defeat ride on a single roll of the dice than to play the sure thing when that was a certainty of slow defeat.[107] It all depended on one's view of the Confederacy and its strength. Confederate materiel and manpower shortages were givens. The question then was whether southern will to victory, coupled with the natural advantages of the defender, would be enough to overcome these handicaps in a long war. If not, then the army must lunge forward in hopes of a quick victory, even if the chances were almost equally great for quick defeat, since those would be about the best odds the South could hope for. On the other hand, if southern stubbornness and a long, inconclusive, and costly war could fatally sap northern morale, then patient caution was the wiser course. Beauregard, and apparently Smith, tended to the former view; Davis, to the latter. He would support offensive action to hasten victory, but not if it meant gambling away the Confederacy's certainty of independence through patient endurance. This strategy may have been purely instinctive with Davis, for he never articulated it; yet it obviously guided his actions.

Davis's first question, once Smith had finished speaking, focused on the size of the risks involved. Proceeding as was customary in formal councils of war, Davis asked the lowest ranking general to give his opinion first. Turning to Smith, he asked what was the lowest number of troops he thought necessary to undertake such a campaign. The general demurred, suggesting that this was a matter for Johnston to decide. Davis insisted, however, and Smith finally stated that 50,000 was the smallest force with which he "would consider it advisable to undertake the contemplated campaign," and then only provided that the additional 10,000 men needed to bring the army up to that strength were not new recruits but seasoned soldiers. Davis wanted to know what Smith meant by "seasoned soldiers," and the general explained that he meant men such as the 40,000 presently in the army's ranks.[108] Expressing no opinion, Davis turned next to Beauregard and asked how many troops he thought the plan would require. The Creole replied that he thought 60,000 would be more realistic and made the same stipulation as to their quality. Johnston, when asked in his turn, agreed with Beauregard.[109]

Davis was shocked. According to his postwar account he had not previously realized that the chief purpose of the meeting was discussing what reinforcements he could supply, though how he could have been under such a misconception after reading, as he presumably had, Johnston's letter to Benjamin is unclear. He also seems to have been confused about the number of troops then present and how many additional would be needed to bring the army up to the necessary strength. Davis had apparently hoped that reinforcements already sent since Manassas would have given the army the requisite numbers. Indeed, he was counting on it. With him on his journey from Richmond he had brought a military engineer's sketches of the falls of the Potomac "to show the feasibility of crossing the river at that point."[110] The generals had not been the only ones contemplating a campaign into Maryland, and Davis, true to form, may well have hoped to be at the head of such a victorious advance. Now with his generals informing him that ten to twenty thousand more men would be necessary to make such an advance, he was bitterly disappointed. He turned resentful and defensive as well, since their clear implication was that the additional troops could be sent if he could but summon the nerve to take the necessary risks elsewhere.

His attitude was exposed by the next question he put to the generals, once again beginning with Smith. Whence did the general think such troops should be drawn?[111] It was an absurd question for a commander in chief to ask of a general whose responsibility and knowledge did not extend beyond a small theater of operations in northern Virginia, but it was intended to suggest, unfairly, that if the generals—who knew little of other fronts—could not specify a source of reinforcements, then they could not expect him to do so either. Once again, Smith tried to beg off, but Davis insisted. The general tried to excuse himself on the grounds that he had been in the Confederate States less then a month, but the president persisted. Finally, Smith stated that he would take them from the large and inactive force at Pensacola "or any place, or places, from which they could best be spared, rather than throw away the chance offered by the contemplated campaign."[112] Johnston steadfastly refused an answer to the same question. Bitterly, Davis spoke of his disappointment, of the shortage of arms in the Confederacy, and of the fact "that the whole country was demanding protection at his hands and praying for arms and troops for defense." He then stated in no uncertain terms that "no re-enforcements could be furnished" to the army except perhaps for 2,500 or so raw recruits.[113]

Despondently, the generals then turned to discussing whether it might not be better to "run the risk of almost certain destruction fighting upon the other side of the Potomac" with the troops then in the ranks. This, too, was dropped, and the conversation lapsed. Davis then spoke up and suggested that they make a few small-scale raids during the winter. Perhaps a force could slip across the Potomac and overpower an isolated Union division or two. Perhaps by erecting batteries on the south bank they could seal off a segment of the lower Potomac against Federal gunboats and thus use it to cross a detachment into pro-Confederate eastern Maryland.[114] Here was Davis's sort of offensive warfare, with limited risks. For him the risk of a door-die offensive that weakened the rest of the Confederacy far outweighed that posed by the prospect of slow and indecisive attrition. The generals, however, were in no mood for half measures. Besides, they considered some of the president's proposed raids to be downright foolhardy and were probably right. Politely they raised a few objections to the ideas but assured him that "if any opportunity should occur offering reasonable chance of success, the attempt would be made."[115] Here was a clash of two fundamentally different grand strategies: Davis's policy of outlasting the North, and Beauregard's quest for quick victory. The Creole, despite his considerable mental gifts, was not the practical planner to make his visions appear as achievable realities, and so, for now, Davis firmly imposed his own approach.

The meeting broke up near midnight. The next day Davis had hoped to continue reviewing the troops, but a dripping, all-day rain deterred him. So strong was his desire to see and be seen by the soldiers that he decided to extend his visit. Thursday, October 3, rewarded him with clearing skies and a drying landscape. By noon the event could get under way. Accompanied by the generals and their staffs, Davis rode along the front of the brigades drawn up for review. To a watching newspaper correspondent, it was an impressive spectacle, with "drums beating, flags dipping, bands playing, horses prancing," as regiment after regiment snapped to "present arms."[116] Davis was in his element. He was brought back to reality by a message from Richmond notifying him that his wife, then seven months pregnant, had been involved in a serious carriage accident. Setting out for the capital that evening, Davis was again met by enthusiastic crowds at the train station. Pressed to make a speech, he kept his remarks brief. "Generals Beauregard and Johnston are here, the orators of the day," he proclaimed. "They speak from the mouths of cannon, of muskets and of rifles; and when they speak, the country listens. I will keep silent."[117] Back in Richmond, he found Varina battered but basically sound, and a doctor reassured the anxious parents that the child in her womb had suffered no harm.[118]

Short though the president's visit to the army had been, and unproductive in his discussions with the generals, it had a positive effect on the army's morale. Some soldiers wondered if Davis's presence meant offensive operations.[119] Others simply observed that the visit had "roused enthusiasm once more to fever heat."[120] For that matter, it probably had done no harm to Davis's state of mind either. He always reveled in being among his troops, and their vociferous welcome was a soothing balm after the increasingly vitriolic attacks in some elements of the Confederate press. Some papers were accusing Davis of being solely responsible for the failure to pursue after

Manassas as well as for the present inaction of the army.[121] The inaction after the great victory had perplexed the Confederate people as well. Even one staunch Davis supporter had confided sadly in his diary, "Our army *does not advance.*"[122] But whatever doubts the public might have, at least the soldiers still seemed to respect him, and Davis valued their opinions a good deal more than those of the press. The president could also take some satisfaction in the fact that while his relations with Johnston were at best correct, he enjoyed very good relations with the other two top generals on that front. He had been on warm terms with Smith throughout their wartime association, and the disappointment at Fairfax Court House did not alter that. Although relations with Beauregard had been badly strained toward the end of the summer, they now seemed to be entirely mended.

Throughout the late summer and early fall of 1861, Davis had striven hard, despite his chronically poor health, both to strengthen the army in northern Virginia and to maintain friendly relations with its generals. His success had been mixed. With Beauregard and Smith his patience and kindness thus far had been successful, while on Johnston they had been wasted. The president had been right to rank the generals as he had, but having done this, he probably could not by any means have retained the friendship and cordial cooperation of the rank-hungry Johnston. If Davis made any mistake in his dealing with Johnston, it was probably that he did not shelve the general immediately after the abusive and insubordinate letter protesting rank. Characteristically, the president overestimated both his and his general's ability to work smoothly together in a professional capacity despite bitter personal animosity. In strengthening the army he was handicapped partially by his reliance on the mediocre Northrop but far more by the simple industrial and material weakness of the Confederacy.

The disagreement with the generals at Fairfax Court House had keyed less on the South's total material strength than on a highly subjective assessment of what sort of war was most to its advantage. The position Davis took reveals much about his basic outlook on the conflict and the Confederacy's chances of success in it. To him, time was on the side of the South. Offensive action might be congenial to the southern temperament, and possessing the initiative was undoubtedly an advantage, but none of that was worth the risk of defeat on this front or elsewhere. If to the generals a policy of passive defense seemed a long but sure road to final defeat, to Davis the best policy was the one that offered the lowest chances of crushing defeat in the next few months. Beyond that, he trusted something would turn up. Thus more by attitude than by conscious adoption of a policy, the president tended toward a defensive strategy of dogged national survival. The army did not advance, and there followed an anxious winter that saw bitter clashes not between armed masses but among the handful of individuals whose cooperation was vital to the smooth function of the Confederate high command in Virginia.

3

A MUTINOUS AND
DISORGANIZING SPIRIT

Peace and good harmony with generals were things Davis valued highly, but by this point in the war, he was making at least one marked exception to that rule. Joseph E. Johnston was beyond the pale as far as the president was concerned. Although he still maintained an implicit—perhaps irrational—faith in the general's military skill, Davis was not inclined to waste any more kindness on the haughty Virginian. The president corresponded frequently with Beauregard and Smith during the month of October but let Benjamin handle what communication was needed with Johnston, mostly matters of army organization.[1]

The organizational issue closest to Davis's heart was his plan to have same-state regiments brigaded together. This he believed would be good for morale and was at least implied in the acts of Congress providing for the raising of the army. It appealed to his states' rights beliefs as well as to his own state pride. He was especially galled to notice during his recent visit to the army that "Mississippi troops were scattered, as if the State was unknown."[2] Davis envisioned a system of organization, both in size and composition of units, similar to that in the Mexican War army of Zachary Taylor, in which he had served. He revealed something of his feeling for the crusty old general who had been his father-in-law when he stated that "many" in that "little army . . . would no sooner have questioned his decisions or have shrunk from him in the hour of danger than if he had been their Father."[3] Army reorganization thus seemed to be little less than a filial duty for the president.

Johnston and his subordinates had no use for the idea. They liked the brigades the way they were, had little appreciation for political considerations, and—especially in Johnston's case—disliked anything that smacked of meddling by a superior authority. Johnston pleaded the risk of attempting to reorganize the army in the face of a northern offensive that he claimed to expect in a few days. At the conference Davis had agreed that Johnston could wait until things seemed a bit safer, but back in Richmond as days passed with neither the desired reorganization nor an enemy attack, he had Benjamin start pressing the general for compliance. Davis even went so far as to issue an order containing a detailed table of organization for the entire army, spelling out divisions, brigades, and the state affiliations of the regiments that should compose them. Again, however, he acceded to Johnston's request that the reorganization be carried out "only when it might be done safely." Johnston continued to drag his feet. He had from the first no intention of obeying the president's orders if he could possibly help it, and his excuses had been lame at best. The offensive he had claimed to fear had been the farthest thing from McClellan's mind. Worse, while danger of attack supposedly prevented the organizational changes the president wanted, it did not, apparently, prevent Johnston and the other generals from carrying out certain changes that they desired. Davis still wanted regiments brigaded by states but not badly enough to sack a general who all but refused an order to do so. The result of the general's intransigence and the president's persistence was a chilly but correct exchange of correspondence between Johnston and Benjamin, with no discernible result except a widening of the breach between Davis and his army commander.[4]

The problems with Johnston seemed to motivate Davis to greater efforts toward good relations with the other officers, and for most of the month of October, he succeeded. Smith still had not given up on an offensive and continued to importune the president by letter in almost the same terms he had used in person at Fairfax Court House.[5] In response, Davis assured him that the impossibility of a major offensive was "painful" to him too and suggested that the smaller-scale raids he had urged might prevent the drop in morale Smith feared as a result of an idle winter in camp. He was equally patient when Smith took up Johnston's refrains about the undesirability of the kind of brigading by states that was so important to Davis, as well as other organizational matters. In each case Davis gently explained the reasoning behind his decisions, much as he was doing almost simultaneously in letters to Beauregard, who had voiced some of the same concerns. Both Beauregard and Smith he addressed as "My Dear General," and to each he signed himself "Very Truly Your Friend." For Johnston, who had chosen to make himself a personal enemy, simple orders, relayed through the secretary of war or the adjutant and inspector general, would suffice. To Smith and Beauregard, Davis spoke as to friends, revealing much of his thinking and even a little of his feeling. Beauregard was the recipient of Davis's reminiscence about his service in Taylor's army.[6]

It was a strange situation. The president felt a mixture of personal dislike and professional respect for his chief general, while he had both warm personal and high professional regard for his two subordinate generals. He believed he could use Johnston notwithstanding their personal animosity. "My recollections of my military life," he later wrote in reference to another situation, "do not enable me to regard as necessary that there should be kind personal relations between officers to secure their effective cooperation in all which is official."[7] Yet the arrangement prevailing in northern Virginia in October 1861 could not have worked well. The president's willingness to subvert the chain of command by corresponding directly with Beauregard and Smith gave ample notice of that. In any event, the situation turned out to be short-lived.

Smith and Johnston became very close. The senior general was, as one of Smith's aides observed, "absolutely devoted to General Smith," and the warm feelings were reciprocated. The two dined together routinely at a common mess, and their personal staffs were virtually merged into one.[8] The closer Smith drew to his commanding general, the higher the probability of his falling out with the president. When he did, near the end of October, the ostensible occasion of the quarrel was trivial almost to the point of absurdity. Smith had a favorite young lieutenant named Horace Randal, and Randal had a couple of grievances. For one thing, another young officer whom he had outranked in the Old Army had now gotten ahead of him in the Confederate service. For another, he was stationed in delightful, sunny, and–for a young officer seeking glory–almost terminally boring Pensacola. He wanted a promotion and transfer to a fighting front and saw prospects for both in assignment to Smith's staff. Resigning his commission in the army at Pensacola, he came to Smith's headquarters. The general took up his cause and pleaded the case with the president in two early October letters. Davis was sympathetic but maintained that Randal's duty was to remain at his post in Pensacola.[9]

Smith was not satisfied, and he then did something very foolish. He decided to force the president's hand. On October 25, he wrote Davis informing him that he had already assigned Randal to a position on his staff "and the fact has been announced." He asked that Davis grant Randal the highest possible rank for a senior aide-de-camp. The implication, of course, was that the president would not embarrass a senior general by failing to ratify a decision he had already announced to his troops. That was Smith's mistake. Davis was very sensitive to being robbed of his prerogative, and it was always a dangerous thing to push him into a corner on the assumption that he dared not take certain actions. He wrote back to Smith a kindly letter only slightly less friendly than the others he had written that month. Carefully he explained that the position Smith wanted for Randal was not authorized by law. In any case, to appoint Randal now would "encourage the idea that an officer, who from personal considerations and without the sanction of his commanding Genl. should retire from the service at Pensacola, might expect the premium of a higher appointment upon application being made at Richmond." As for the appointment's having already been announced, the president admonished Smith that a general's recommendation could not "be enhanced by the announcement in orders of the fact that you had made it" and confessed that he was "at a loss to perceive why the fact of your having made a nomination was announced in orders to the troops."[10]

Smith was not mollified, and Johnston's influence probably had something to do with his attitude. Receiving the president's kind but firm letter on November 2, he scrawled a note across the margin, expressing his bitterness. He had decided, he said, not to answer this letter because all his requests and recommendations were being rejected. Other generals had larger staffs, and it was just unfair. "It is clearly useless," he concluded, "for me to expect any aid or consideration at the hands of the Executive."[11] Henceforth Smith, like his friend Johnston, considered Davis an enemy and acted accordingly. When several days later another young aspirant for a commission sought Smith's recommendation to the president, the general replied to the effect that "recent circumstances forbade [him] to make a special call upon" Davis. The young man then appealed directly to the president and in doing so revealed Smith's attitude.

Davis immediately wrote the offended general, offering to appoint Randal a first lieutenant in the provisional—rather than the regular—army, if that was what he and Smith really wanted. He assured Smith he had meant no unkindness to him or to Randal. "Neither the circumstances nor the state of my feelings," he wrote, "incline me to alienation from any one who confronts our common enemy."[12] That failed to satisfy Smith, who wanted to know why Randal could not be given a commission in one of the few authorized regiments of the regular Confederate army and then detailed to his staff. Patiently, the president explained that those vacancies were filled, but when Congress authorized a new regiment some two and a half weeks later, Davis promptly granted Randal the rank he and Smith had sought so long and acrimoniously. Perhaps embarrassed by the general's persistently frosty tone, Davis had this last piece of good news relayed to Smith by an aide.[13] Smith apparently never expressed his gratitude.

By this time Davis had even more serious problems with Beauregard. The Creole's flamboyant ways occasionally brought him into friction with the legal-minded and unimaginative president and the lawyerly secretary of war who represented him so accurately. Late in the summer, Beauregard had gotten the idea of raising a company to man a newfangled rocket battery that he hoped might be good for scaring ill-trained northern troops, but this scheme fell afoul of Confederate law since it did not provide for the newly recruited company to elect its own commander. Beauregard was duly informed through Benjamin that his plan was illegal.[14] Then there was the matter of Beauregard's official position. Ever since his army and Johnston's had joined on the eve of Manassas, the two generals had considered their separate forces as two distinct corps within an army. It was a wise, practical, but unfortunately illegal arrangement. Confederate law as yet provided for brigades and divisions only—no corps. Naturally, Davis hewed to the letter of the law and probably saw no difficulty in such a course. After all, Taylor's (much smaller) Mexican War army had not had corps. Strangely though, he does not seem to have caught on to what the generals were doing until his Fairfax Court House visit. A few days later, he notified Beauregard that since corps did not exist, he could not command one.[15] A personal factor made this bad news even harder for the general to take. In his effort to maintain good relations with the Creole, Davis seemed to be using Benjamin to handle his less pleasant correspondence, and something in the secretary of war's manner rankled Beauregard.

The general fired back a letter to Benjamin requesting that if he did not command a corps, he be relieved of his "present false position."[16] After stewing on his grievance a few more days, he wired Davis directly, "Please state definitely what I am to command if I do not command a Corps in consequence of latter being unauthorized."[17] At the same time he wrote the president a letter, more fully airing his irritation. He protested the "unusual & offensive style" of the secretary's letters, accused him of ignorance in military matters, and asked Davis to judge between himself and "the functionary at his desk, who deems it a fit time . . . to write lectures on law—while the enemy is mustering in our front."[18]

The bit about Benjamin's military ignorance was, of course, a trifle awkward, since the secretary's every military decision was—unknown to

Beauregard–dictated by the president. Davis seemed to overlook this, however, and continued his friendly policy toward the general. He and Benjamin had each already written in response to Beauregard's request to be relieved. The president's was a long, confiding letter, most of it given to discussing his ideas about army organization. Toward the end he mentioned the general's request but protested that Beauregard was indispensable in his present position. He praised the Creole's ability and "moral power" over his troops and concluded, "My appreciation of you as a soldier and my regard for you as a man cannot permit me willingly to wound your sensibility or to diminish your sphere of usefulness."[19] Benjamin also wrote the same day, and though he tried to be conciliatory he ended up sounding supercilious to the offended general.

> I beg to say in all kindness, that it is not your position which is false, but your idea of the organization of the Army as established by the act of Congress, and I feel confident you cannot have studied the legislation of Congress in relation to the army. You are second in command of the whole army . . . , and not first in command of half the army. The position is a very simple one, and if you will take the pains to read the sixth section of the "act to provide for the public defense" . . .

And so the secretary went on at some length in a vein that could hardly have been more inflammatory to Beauregard.[20]

To make matters worse, Benjamin's irritating letter seems to have arrived a day before Davis's soothing one, though both were dated the same day.[21] The general responded with an angry letter to Davis, complaining of the "unwarrantable tone" used on him by "the present incumbent of the War office." He would leave it to the public to judge "whether or not I have 'studied' aright the legislation of Congress . . . ; whether as the honorable secretary *courteously* advises, I have taken the 'pains' to read the laws of Congress . . . or whether in my ignorance of that legislation, I require enlightenment after the manner of the communication enclosed." "With this," he concluded, "I shall leave it to your Excellency, an educated soldier, keenly alive to all the sensibilities which our profession & associations engender, to shield me (for the present) from these ill timed unaccountable annoyances."[22] Receiving Davis's letter the following day he wrote again, this time in a much better frame of mind. In a friendly tone he thanked Davis for his kind words and respectfully explained his ideas about army organization but promised to carry out "cheerfully" whatever the president might order.[23]

And so the remainder of October passed with Davis diligently attempting to smooth the feathers Benjamin had ruffled. He assured Beauregard that the secretary had meant no harm and indeed had high respect for the general. He praised the Creole's "genius and gallantry" and spoke of his exploits "amid the smoke and blaze of battle." In a final appeal to Beauregard to put the quarrel behind him, Davis wrote a paragraph that in its kindly—well nigh fatherly—tone almost rivaled some of Lincoln's letters to his more difficult generals:

> Now, my dear sir, let me entreat you to dismiss this small matter from your mind. In the hostile masses before you, you have a subject more worthy of your contemplation. Your country needs all of your mind and of your heart. You have given cause to expect all which man can do, and your fame and her interests require that your energies should have a single object. My prayers always attend you, and, with confidence, I turn to you in the hour of peril.[24]

Beauregard seemed to calm down. It had not been easy, but Davis had apparently succeeded in preserving good relations with at least one difficult general.

Four days later someone showed Davis a copy of the Richmond *Dispatch*, which contained a synopsis of Beauregard's report on the Battle of Manassas. Beauregard's Manassas report was long overdue, and this was the first Davis had heard of its existence. He was shocked and outraged at what he read in the newspaper. The synopsis depicted Beauregard as having submitted a plan that would have led to the capture of Washington and Baltimore and the Confederate occupation of Maryland had not the president unaccountably vetoed it. It also seemed to lay a disquieting amount of emphasis on Davis's hesitance about ordering Johnston over from the Shenandoah. Furious, the president sent to the War Department for the report, and the next day it landed on his desk. It seems the offending document had arrived in Richmond two weeks before, on October 15, but no one had thought to tell the president about it. Strangely, it was dated August 25, a fact that Beauregard later explained on the basis that he had decided to expand the report after it was first written, taking considerable time doing so, and had forgotten to change the date.[25] In reality, the report was not quite the indictment of Davis that the newspaper account made it sound.[26] Though Beauregard had not been able to resist showing off his grandiose plan in a detailed and thoroughly superfluous retelling, he had at least admitted that it "was not accepted at the time, from considerations which appeared so weighty as to more than counterbalance its proposed advantages."[27]

Such refinements were lost, however, on the enraged president. Glancing over the report, he satisfied himself, as he expressed it in a letter to Beauregard that day, that "the newspaper statements were sustained by the text of your report." A disagreement over strategic policy "could have no appropriate place in the report of a battle," and its appearance there and—worse still—in a sensationalized newspaper report looked very much like "an attempt to exalt yourself at my expense." Besides, when had Beauregard ever submitted anything like a formal written plan of campaign?[28] Of course, the general's reference was to the plan Chesnut had submitted orally back on July 14, but as far as Davis was concerned, only written proposals counted. In any case, Beauregard's pre-Manassas plan had been such a flight of fancy that little of it had stuck in the president's mind except the request for massive reinforcements.[29] The claim that an actual plan of campaign had been proposed and rejected was, to Davis's mind, a gross distortion. Not content merely to protest to Beauregard, Davis on the same day tacked a lengthy note to the offending report, refuting those allegations he believed were unwarranted. The order to Johnston was no more discretionary than it should have been, the vague plan submitted by Beauregard's aide was totally impractical, and, most important, for whatever opportunities may have been missed "responsibility cannot be transferred to the Government at Richmond, which certainly would have united in any feasible plan to accomplish such desirable results."[30]

The publication of the synopsis of Beauregard's report set off a flurry of recriminations, and before Davis's letter reached the general, Beauregard himself was thoroughly caught up in the controversy. Like Davis, most readers of the synopsis interpreted it as an attack on the administration, and several individuals—Beauregard thought they were "office holders in the War & State Departments"—wrote letters to the Richmond papers defending Davis and attacking the general.[31] On November 3, Beauregard responded to these himself in a letter to the editors of the Richmond *Whig*. Melodramatically heading his letter "Centreville, within hearing of the enemy's guns," Beauregard denied having anything to do with the leaking of his report. He protested that he was not seeking public accolades and cared nothing for popularity, but it all had a hollow ring to it.[32] Even some of Beauregard's adoring public were a little put off by the letter's grandiose heading and insincere modesty.[33]

On top of everything else, the Confederacy held its first and only presidential election under its regular constitution on November 6. Davis had thus far

Judah P. Benjamin. (Courtesy of National Archives, 111-B-1867, Civil War 143)

been serving only as provisional president, and though he was the only candidate for the regular six-year term that fall, some of Beauregard's political friends had been making ill-concealed efforts to engineer the general's election in Davis's place.[34] Nothing came of the efforts, but they naturally did nothing to improve Beauregard's standing in the president's eyes or in the eyes of his secretary of war.

How Beauregard's report had gotten into the paper in a form especially insulting to the president and why the actual report was not brought to Davis's attention for more than two weeks after its belated arrival at the War Department has never been satisfactorily explained. The person who seemed to take the most pleasure in the affair was Secretary of War Benjamin. The day before Beauregard wrote his ill-advised letter for publication, Benjamin discussed the controversy with War Department clerk John B. Jones. The secretary gave his account of the rights and wrongs of the matter, and Jones confided in his diary that he was very persuasive. What really rankled the secretary was that after he had rebuked Beauregard, "the general had appealed to the President." Now, the secretary gloated, Beauregard "had ascertained who was *strongest* with the President."[35]

Actually, Beauregard had not yet ascertained that, but he was about to. The president's stiff letter did not reach him until November 6. On the fifth, Beauregard responded to a previous letter of the president's, trying to reconcile him to Benjamin. He accepted Davis's assurance that Benjamin had meant no offense. Still, Beauregard insisted that the secretary must use a nicer tone when addressing him and not presume to question his motives. He complained that Benjamin saw every issue as a legal problem and warned lest army and general both "be put into the straight-jackets of the law."[36] That was not a very good thing to say to Jefferson Davis at the best of times, for he had a great respect for the law and never reacted well when his attempts at conciliation were met with this sort of haughty, grudging acceptance. Now, coming on top of Beauregard's recent publicity play in the Richmond papers, this letter was particularly inflammatory and brought another stinging rebuke. Beauregard's complaint about the secretary's tone met with no sympathy. "I do not feel competent to instruct Mr. Benjamin in the matter of style," Davis wrote. "There are few who the public would probably believe fit for that task." His grievance about Benjamin's legal orientation received even less consideration. The secretary of war was not, Davis pointedly observed, the only one "to look at every exercise of official power in its legal aspect, and you surely did not intend to inform me," the president continued, "that your army and yourself are outside of the limits of the law. It is my duty to see that the laws are faithfully executed, and I cannot recognize the pretension of any one that their restraint is too narrow for him."[37]

When Beauregard's explanation of the affair regarding his Manassas report finally arrived, it was no more satisfactory to the president. The general seemed not to realize how offensive his course had been or how angry Davis was. Glibly contradicting his commander in chief he maintained that the discussion of strategy did indeed belong in the report and even offered a few misapplied history lessons as attempted proof. He assured the president that he had not been trying to make himself look good at Davis's expense and suggested that such thoughts had been planted in Davis's mind by "that parasite class ever surrounding . . . the elevated." Although he expressed his honor at having Davis's friendship and the hope that "by no act of mine, I will ever forfeit [your] respect & esteem," he offered the highly ambiguous comfort of saying that being president "requires more ambition" than he had and that he had "always pitied, more than . . . envied those in high positions."[38] Political ambition is something Davis had told Beauregard he did not have, and the Confederate president certainly wanted no one's pity, least of all the haughty Creole's. Beauregard's final touch in his letter of reply to the president's accusations was to enclose a copy of his letter to the Richmond *Whig*, though how he thought that document would soothe the president's offended pride is hard to imagine.[39]

By this time Davis had thoroughly gotten over the illusion that he was on friendly terms with any of his top eastern generals. If the generals wanted to indulge in fixing blame and assigning guilt, Davis could play that game as well as any and with considerably more relish. Unbecoming in generals, this practice was particularly unfortunate in a commander in chief, but Davis had acted presidential long enough and was now ready to indulge his propensities with a vengeance. Within days of reading Beauregard's report, he had written to Chesnut, Cooper, and Lee, asking for their recollections of the disputed pre-Manassas meeting, and to Johnston, seeking testimony from him as to whether the administration had held the army back from anything it was possible to do. In lame excuse for such efforts at self-justification, he asserted that the recent attacks on him had "acquired importance from the fact that they have served to create distrust, to excite disappointment, and must embarrass the Administration in its further efforts to . . . provide for the public defense."[40] The various officers replied over the next few days, more or less confirming Davis's view.[41] Chesnut added to his reply a pious hope for "harmony & heart co-operation of those who are chief & chosen instruments in the direction of our affairs," for which Davis thanked him and insisted "that our cause is to me so far above any personal considerations that I can find no difficulty in fully co-operating with any one who can and will promote its success."[42] The statement was equivocal and not entirely candid, but Davis wanted it to be true. He did strive to work with generals he loathed insofar as he believed his duty required it, but of "heart co-operation" there could be no question.

By early November 1861 relations between Davis and the three top-ranking generals in Virginia had deteriorated to the point of cold formality and scarcely veiled hostility. Having gotten a late start at the battle of self-justification, Davis that month resorted to the awkward expedient of asking his enemies to supply his ammunition. He had neglected to keep copies of much of his correspondence with the generals over the past months and so dispatched a friend, Charles D. Fontaine, to army headquarters with letters to each of the three generals requesting that Fontaine "may be permitted to take such copies from the originals in your possession." The generals had little choice but to comply.[43] Privately, Beauregard continued to "snarl at the president" while at the same time he carried on his own campaign of securing testimony and piling up evidence to justify his contentions against Davis.[44] Smith maintained his petty and unreasonable demands for Randal—who had now become quite a favorite of Johnston as well—and would be satisfied with nothing the president did.

Having lost hope of staying on good terms with Smith and Beauregard, Davis actually moved toward an attempted reconciliation with Johnston, for whom he had always retained his respect as a general if not his liking as a person. Early in November Johnston was fuming about the latest move of the Richmond authorities, the transfer of one of his brigades to the Shenandoah Valley. Although that sector also came under Johnston's recently conferred authority as commander of all Confederate forces in northern Virginia, he did not appreciate meddling by superiors. Since Davis had, as had become his custom, used Benjamin to convey this order, Johnston's renewed animosity was toward the secretary of war. To a friend he wrote sarcastically that "the Secretary of War will probably establish his headquarters within this department soon."[45] He also wrote, in more restrained tones, to Benjamin himself, complaining of the move. Davis, in a marked change of approach toward the proud Virginia general, now responded personally to Johnston's letter, and although salutation and closing were formal rather than friendly, the overall tone was mild and conciliatory. The president explained the need for the action and assured Johnston of continued reinforcements as the Confederacy's resources allowed. "I will show this reply to the Secretary of War," Davis concluded, "and hope there will be no misunderstanding between you in future. The success of the army requires harmonious co-operation."[46]

In a further attempt to secure "harmonious"—if not "heart"—cooperation, Davis later that month dispatched his friend, Mississippi politician Lucius Q. C. Lamar, to army headquarters, which by now had been moved back to

Manassas, as the army had withdrawn from its advanced positions after all hope of a fall offensive had been abandoned. Lamar was going to the army's new headquarters nominally as a volunteer aide to Johnston but in reality as an emissary of the president to clear up "some wrong impressions" and the "ill feeling between the Potomac generals and the President." Little is known of the details of Lamar's mission. He stayed all winter but was confined to his room by sickness during much of that time.[47] His accomplishments in the matter that was the chief purpose of his errand were probably slight, for relations between the president and Johnston were soon deteriorating again.

By early December Davis was back on the subject of army organization. Johnston still had not brigaded troops according to states, and Davis was particularly anxious—and increasingly insistent—that he do so with at least the Mississippi troops immediately.[48] Johnston continued to protest. Both men used Cooper and Benjamin as much as possible rather than do anything as distasteful as writing directly to one another. Davis's case lost none of its force by coming through the pen of Benjamin. "Fully two months have elapsed since the President's verbal expression of his desires," wrote the secretary of war. "Six weeks or more have elapsed since orders were formally issued from this Department . . . , and the President now finds the Mississippi regiments scattered as far apart as it is possible to scatter them."[49] The general continued to object that he was about to be attacked and could not safely comply.[50] Hoping to gain from the president a sympathetic hearing for his ideas, Johnston prevailed upon Davis's brother-in-law, newly promoted Brig. Gen. Richard Taylor, to go to Richmond and present his case. Taylor was by profession not a soldier but a Louisiana planter. Son of a president and himself a man of unusual refinement, Taylor possessed great charm and the ability to get along with very diverse types of people. He also possessed the respect and affection of Jefferson Davis, but in this case the influence of a friend failed to sway the president. He did "listen patiently" to Taylor's appeal but would not give an inch. Nor could Taylor, upon his return to the army, budge Johnston from his intransigence.[51]

At this point the situation was complicated by the entry of an additional participant. Johnston's friend, the not entirely emotionally stable W. H. C. Whiting, was commanding one of the army's brigades. Since Whiting was from Mississippi, Davis had designated him to command one of the two new, all-Mississippi brigades he envisioned. Whiting liked the brigade he had and was eager to take Johnston's side in the current quarrel. On December 19 he wrote and forwarded through channels a feisty letter to the president, stating that he did not want a Mississippi brigade and telling Davis how to organize the army. Davis responded by having the secretary of war write Johnston. "The President," Benjamin gravely informed the general, "has read with grave displeasure the very insubordinate letter of General Whiting, in which he indulges in presumptuous censure of the orders of his commander-in-chief, and tenders unasked advice to his superiors in command." If Whiting did not want a Mississippi brigade, that was fine. Of course, that would also mean that he now had no brigade and so, automatically, his commission as brigadier general in the provisional Confederate army would lapse. He would revert to his regular Confederate army rank of major of engineers and as such should report at once to General Jackson, who had recently been sent to command in the Shenandoah Valley and might be able to find some use for him. "In conclusion," the secretary wrote, "the President requests me to say that he trusts you will hereafter decline to forward communications of your subordinates having so obvious a tendency to excite a mutinous and disorganizing spirit in the Army."[52]

Johnston interceded for Whiting, apologizing for forwarding the letter and pleading that Whiting was needed in his present post.[53] The president remained adamant that the order must stand, yet despite Johnston's twice repeated call for a replacement for Whiting, none was sent, and the theoretically demoted general continued to exercise his command. All the while, Johnston unaccountably seems to have said nothing about the matter to Whiting himself.[54] Eventually thinking better of his rash communication, Whiting sent in a request that it be returned to him for "modification." Some time thereafter he heard a rumor that Davis "had expressed much displeasure" about the letter. Thoroughly chastened, Whiting wrote Davis a letter of humble apology "for any thing objectionable in the phraseology of that letter, a phraseology due rather to my temperament than my reasons." He admitted that he had been wrong in some of his assertions and assured the president that he had nothing against Mississippi or its soldiers.[55] Davis was not placated in the least, replying stiffly that Whiting's demotion "was demanded by a just regard to good order and discipline, and was due to the men who had been assigned to your command and against a connection with whom you had entered a protest." He was less inclined to forgive Whiting because the offending letter was "the third occasion when it had become proper to notice the discourteous & insubordinate tone of your correspondence on official subjects." It would, the president affirmed, be returned to Whiting for a rewrite.[56] And there, somewhat curiously, the entire matter seemed to end. Whiting apparently never submitted his revised letter, and Davis never saw to it that his order for the general's removal was carried through. This was perhaps understandable, for he soon had other things to occupy his attention.

While the bickering went on between Benjamin (on behalf of the president) and Johnston regarding the reorganization of the army, Beauregard continued to make a nuisance of himself. In January he became the focus of a political squabble within the Confederate government when some of his supporters in Congress as well as in the Virginia House of Delegates sought to have his report published, including the portion that was offensive to Davis. Queried as to his wishes in the matter, Beauregard telegraphed the speaker of the House of Delegates, "Let Congress do for the best. We must think of the country before we think of ourselves." He would have done better to have stopped there but could not resist adding a theatrical touch: "I believe Burnside's expedition is intended for Wilmington, to cut off railroad to Charleston. Let government look to it."[57] This was a gratuitous bit of grandstanding. Neither Congress nor the House of Delegates were in the position to make strategic decisions on the basis of what intelligence Beauregard might share with them. Besides, the Federal amphibious expedition under the command of Maj. Gen. Ambrose Burnside was headed not for Wilmington but for Roanoke Island.[58]

A Beauregard supporter in Congress read the general's telegram to that body and, as he informed Beauregard, "The effect of its patriotic sentiment on Congress would have been most grateful to your feelings had you witnessed it."[59] The general would have been less gratified to know the effect of his pseudopatriotic posturing on the commander in chief. Davis had political problems enough without the turbulent Creole being sufficiently close to the capital to strike poses for the benefit of Congress and otherwise stirring up strife. For that reason Davis decided to transfer Beauregard to the West, where his talents might be useful and his tongue and pen less harmful. The victor of Manassas was still too popular to be sacked outright or even transferred against his will, so Davis cleverly got one of the general's friends to talk him into accepting the move. The deal was done, and Beauregard made preparations to leave. Defiant to the last, he issued a farewell order to his troops, calling them "Soldiers of the First Corps, Army of the Potomac." He spoke of his transfer as a "temporary separation" from the Virginia army, but in fact the Louisiana general would disappear from the Virginia scene for well over two years.[60]

Amid the hostility of most of his eastern generals, Davis could still count at least one high-ranking officer who was not alienated from him. Robert E. Lee had returned in November from his failed mission to West Virginia. He was not a popular man in the Confederate press just then. Newspapers referred to him as "Granny Lee," "the Great Entrencher," and "the King of Spades" and bemoaned his "dilly-dally, dirt digging, scientific warfare." One journalist wrote that what was really remarkable about the West Virginia campaign was that "it was conducted by a general who had never fought a battle, who had a pious horror of guerillas, and whose extreme tenderness of blood induced him to depend exclusively upon the resources of strategy to essay the achievement of victory without the cost of life."[61] Davis retained his faith in Lee, and though he had missed the courtly Virginian's quiet competence in Richmond, he had another mission in mind that seemed perfectly suited for a general with an engineering background and a proclivity for "scientific warfare," one who could be trusted in top command of a department far removed from Richmond, where the president seemed to consider himself a sort of de facto theater commander. Northern amphibious expeditions had been scoring limited successes and arousing unlimited fears along the Confederate Atlantic coast. Within days of Lee's arrival in Richmond, Davis had given him orders for South Carolina. Lee was reluctant to place blame, well deserved though it might be, on his subordinates in West Virginia, but he did make sure that at least one of his problems there would not be repeated by asking Davis to spell out the nature of his authority in South Carolina. The president assured him of full powers and was impressed by Lee's modesty and magnanimity. To the governor of South Carolina Davis wrote to vouch for Lee's patriotism and ability, newspaper croakers notwithstanding.[62] Davis was no doubt relieved to have a troublesome area of the country in the hands of a man he could trust, but assigning Lee there did remove from Virginia the highest ranking general—indeed, one of a shrinking few—still on good terms with Davis.

By early February that number had suffered one more significant subtraction. Stonewall Jackson, now a major general, had been sent the previous October to command Confederate forces in the Shenandoah Valley, under the overall umbrella of Johnston's command of the whole Virginia front.[63] Jackson had held his position less than a month when he came up with a plan to take the initiative and put the enemy in his sector off balance. The first step was to take the little Allegheny mountain village of Romney, then garrisoned by a small Union force. To do this he required more force, and with Johnston's approval he asked for the division of Brig. Gen. W. W. Loring, now idle after helping to make Lee's West Virginia expedition a failure.[64] Davis left it to Loring's discretion, and when the latter responded enthusiastically, ordered the operation to proceed with the utmost dispatch.[65]

Thomas J. ("Stonewall") Jackson. (Courtesy of National Archives, 111-B-1867, Civil War 143)

By this time Jackson had conceived an even more ambitious plan and sent an aide to Richmond to present it and appeal for the necessary additional troops. Davis listened courteously to the proposal but apparently did not accept it, and the movement went forward as originally planned.[66]

Obviously, a winter campaign in the West Virginia mountains would involve some hardship, and this was made worse by one of the more severe winter storms in memory. Loring had written before the operation that with good management "there need be no suffering from the climate," but it soon became apparent that good management was precisely what was lacking in Loring's own command.[67] The general's incompetence, contrariness, and inability to control his nearly demoralized troops not only handicapped Jackson's attempt to take the Federal garrison at a disadvantage but also led to much more intense suffering in Loring's units than was experienced by the other forces in the expedition.[68] The shivering Confederates reached Romney but found that the Federals had withdrawn. Leaving Loring's force to garrison the town, Jackson pulled his own brigade back to more centrally located Winchester, in the Shenandoah Valley, whence it could readily reinforce several possible trouble spots.

Reflecting with growing envy on the superior quarters they imagined the Stonewall Brigade to be enjoying in Winchester, Loring's officers reached a frame of mind little short of mutinous. In fact, their lot was no worse than that of any Confederate troops serving in Virginia that winter.[69] Loring, however, not only allowed them to become demoralized but actually led the croaking himself. Within hearing of several officers he called Jackson's orders an "outrage," and he signed and forwarded with his approval a petition of eleven of his officers calling on the authorities in Richmond to override Jackson and withdraw the division from Romney.[70] Not content with the petition, some of his officers wrote their congressmen and one, Brig. Gen. William B. Taliaferro, with Loring's approval, traveled to Richmond to air his gripes directly to the president.[71]

The earlier mutterings among the politicians had already made Davis restless enough to have Benjamin telegraph Johnston to "examine for yourself into the true state of the case, take such measures as you think prudent under the circumstances, and report to the Department."[72] Davis intended this as an order for Johnston to go in person to that area of his department.[73] The general, however, thought of it merely as a command to have the matter investigated and accordingly sent his inspector general to check it out.[74] This misunderstanding proved to be of no real significance since Davis did not allow sufficient time for Johnston or a subordinate to reach the Shenandoah

Valley. On the morning of January 30, he entertained Taliaferro, received from his hand a duplicate copy of the mutinous petition (Loring had thought, incorrectly, that Jackson would not forward it), and listened sympathetically while he whined about conditions in Romney. Taking out a map, the president asked Taliaferro to indicate where Jackson's various forces were posted. Davis "did not hesitate," Taliaferro later wrote, "to say at once that Jackson had made a mistake."[75] The president had already decided on quick action and believed Jackson was playing favorites by keeping his old brigade in supposedly comfortable Winchester while Loring's troops suffered the lot of soldiers in Romney.[76] The same morning he talked with Taliaferro, he had Benjamin telegraph Jackson: "Our news indicates that a movement is being made to cut off General Loring's command. Order him back to Winchester immediately."[77]

Jackson complied at once, then wired in reply, "With such interference in my command I cannot expect to be of much service in the field" and therefore asked to be assigned to go back to teaching at the Virginia Military Institute or allowed to resign.[78] Nor was this a ploy to gain attention. The same day Jackson wrote to his old friend, Virginia governor John Letcher, asking that he use his influence to see that his telegram to the War Department be acted upon.[79] As the determined general later explained to Letcher, the policy of the Richmond authorities in interfering with his operations was so ruinous that "no officer can serve his country better than by making his strongest possible protest against it, which in my opinion, is done by tendering his resignation, rather than be a willful instrument in prosecuting the war upon a ruinous principle."[80]

Davis apparently would have gladly accepted Jackson's resignation, for he had recently remarked in a cabinet meeting that the general was "utterly incompetent."[81] That things did not come to that point was due primarily to Joseph E. Johnston's greatest contribution to the Confederate war effort. His first act, on receiving Jackson's letter for forwarding to the secretary of war, was to write a friendly letter to Jackson begging him to reconsider. He pointed out that the order had bypassed him entirely, thus insulting him as badly as it had Jackson. "Let us dispassionately reason with the Government on this subject of command, and if we fail to influence its practice, then ask to be relieved from positions the authority of which is exercised by the War Department, while the responsibilities are left to us." He then held Jackson's letter to see if the general would relent.[82]

Meanwhile he wrote his own letter of protest to the president. He reminded Davis that he had previously complained of "such exercise of military command by the Secretary of War." If Richmond was going to be giving orders directly to officers in the Shenandoah Valley, Johnston suggested it would be best if that region were removed entirely from his command. "A collision of the authority of the honorable Secretary of War with mine might occur at a critical moment," he explained. "In such an event disaster would be inevitable." He concluded by urging Davis to pay another visit to the front. "Your presence here now or soon would secure to us thousands of excellent troops, who otherwise will disperse [due to failure to re-enlist] just as the active operations of the enemy may be expected to begin. . . . The highest benefit," wrote Johnston with apparently unconscious irony, "would be your assuming the command."[83] To strengthen his protest, Johnston forwarded to Benjamin an appeal Jackson had made directly to his commanding general. Explaining the folly of the order from Richmond, Jackson had asked of Johnston "that the order be countermanded, and that General L[oring] be required to return with his command to the vicinity of Romney." While still holding Jackson's letter of resignation, Johnston sent in this protest with the endorsement, "Respectfully referred to the Secretary of War, whose order I cannot countermand."[84]

As the Shenandoah commander remained adamant on the issue of his resignation, Johnston, on February 7, finally had to give in and send along Jackson's letter to the secretary, writing at the bottom, "I don't know how the loss of this officer can be supplied."[85] His delay, however, had been adequate to give Jackson's friends such as Governor Letcher and Congressman Alexander Boteler time to bring the general around.[86] The day before Johnston forwarded his letter, Jackson had finally relented and written to inform Letcher that he could, if he wanted, withdraw the general's resignation. Letcher, who knew how to get things done within the world of Richmond politics, lost no time in doing so, and the services of Stonewall Jackson were saved for the Confederacy.[87]

The repercussions of this ugly affair were no prettier than the events that set them off. By this time Benjamin had already written to Johnston, informing him that the order to Jackson had been sent "at the President's instance" and arguing that the decision had been strategically sound. Yet at the same time, he made the perplexing statement that "these are mere suggestions, the decision being left to yourself."[88] In his reply, Johnston apparently chose to preserve the fiction that the order had been Benjamin's, since this gave him more latitude in denouncing it and, indirectly, its true author. He regretted "very much that you did not refer this matter to me before ordering General Loring to Winchester instead of now." As for such matters being left to his discretion, it probably would not be a good idea for him to issue any contrary orders, Johnston observed blandly, since this would tend to make "the impression that our views do not coincide, and that each of us is pursuing his own plan." His parting shot was a sarcastic suggestion that "having broken up the dispositions of the military commander, you give whatever other orders may be necessary."[89] Davis knew where that shot had been aimed, and he answered it in like spirit. "It is not surprising," he wrote the general, "that the Secretary of War should, in a case requiring prompt action, have departed from [the] usual method, in view of the fact that he had failed more than once in having his instructions carried out when forwarded to you in the proper manner." The incident had occurred, Davis insisted, because Johnston had not given his "personal attention to the case."[90] This was the lamest of excuses, for if Johnston had set out for the Valley by the fastest means of transportation immediately upon receipt of Benjamin's first telegram, he could not have arrived much before the order for the recall of Loring's troops from Romney.

Jackson generally kept to himself any reflections he might have had on the president's exercise of the role of commander in chief. On the other hand, he was not at all reticent about what he thought of Loring. "General Loring should be cashiered," Jackson told a friend.[91] Toward that end, he brought official charges against the contumacious general for "neglect of duty and conduct subversive of good order and military discipline." Forwarding the charges to Johnston, Jackson began making preparations for the court-martial.[92] That, however, was as far as the matter went. Johnston agreed with Jackson on the need for a trial, but when the case reached Richmond it ran into trouble. Benjamin asked Loring to give his side of the story, and on reading it he suggested to Davis that "it does not seem to me that any advantage to the service can result from continuing the investigation of these charges." Davis agreed, dismissing the charges with a babble of legalistic double-talk, the conclusion of which was "the charges will not be prosecuted."[93] Astute enough to realize that Jackson and Loring were unlikely to work well together, Davis had already had Loring transferred out of the Shenandoah Valley district.[94] How little he thought of Jackson's opinion and how little blame in the affair he attached to Loring was revealed just four days after he first received Jackson's charges. On February 17, Davis asked Congress for its formal approval of Loring's promotion to major general.[95] It went through, and Loring went off to take up a new post in the war's western theater, where his chief subsequent impact on the course of the conflict was in making somewhat easier Ulysses S. Grant's capture of

Vicksburg seventeen months later. He did so by refusing to obey an order from his commanding general.

For Davis the handling of the Jackson-Loring dispute was the discreditable ending of a long season of failure in his attempts to work effectively with his generals. In the seven months since the victory at Manassas, nearly every high-ranking field commander in Virginia had turned against him. Johnston, Beauregard, and Smith had fallen out with the president for reasons of their own. Whiting, still a brigadier general apparently despite the president's wishes, had also become bitterly inimical to his commander in chief. Jackson had found his operational plans frustrated and his authority undermined by Davis's actions. Even James Longstreet and Earl Van Dorn, the army's other two major generals, had soured on the president, the former in apparent sympathy with Johnston and the latter in disappointment over the size of the command he had been given.[96] Of these, Van Dorn was the least alienated, but he was soon transferred to the West. Lee, of course, had very high rank and still maintained good relations with Davis, but he was largely discredited with the public and a fair segment of the army and by this time was off supervising coastal fortifications in the Carolinas.

Not all of these difficulties reflected as badly on Davis as did the affair with Jackson. In the case of Smith, the president had gone to extreme lengths to try to placate the general. Smith, however, had grown altogether too close to Johnston, and his inclination to take the Virginian's side in the growing quarrel with Davis was probably what led him to make one impossible demand of the president after another. With Beauregard, Davis had certainly had ample provocation in the Creole's blatant glory hunting, but once his patience was exhausted he had put the worst possible interpretation on the general's every word and action. Davis had genuinely tried to be conciliating, but in the end his own wounded feelings had dictated his attitude toward Beauregard. Moving the Louisianan away from Richmond was probably the best thing Davis could have done under the circumstances and with the information then available to him, though command of New Orleans might have been a more profitable assignment for Beauregard than the assignment he received to Kentucky and Tennessee. Whiting's insubordination was clear-cut, and the president could hardly have acted differently in this case except that by showing more resolution and persistence in his determination to reduce Whiting from brigadier general to major, he could have made his captious fellow Mississippian a salutary example to other officers inclined to the same "mutinous and disorganizing spirit."

Only in the case of Jackson had Davis erred seriously—indeed, spectacularly. It was one thing to give decisive direction to field commanders as to the goals they were to accomplish and the methods and means to do so. It was another thing entirely to try to direct day-to-day movements of brigades and divisions from behind a desk in Richmond. Unfortunately, the war was to show Davis as too ready to attempt the latter and not ready enough to undertake the former. Worse still was Davis's appalling disregard of the chain of command. The president had received and encouraged criticism by junior officers of their superiors, even going so far as to discuss with Taliaferro the supposed blunders of Taliaferro's commanding officer. He had then ordered Johnston, Jackson's immediate superior, to investigate the situation but had acted before Johnston had any reasonable chance to comply with the order and without giving Johnston any notice whatsoever. If his excuse were true—and it may well have been—that an order to Johnston might not be carried out, that in itself was an indictment of Davis for leaving an all-but-mutinous general in such an important command. Finally, the president's action in dismissing the court-martial charges and then giving to Loring a promotion that must have appeared—and probably was—an expression of the commander in chief's approval of the course Loring had taken could only undermine discipline within the army. All in all, the incident reflected as negatively on Davis as any in which he was involved during the war. The fall and winter had been an exasperating time for the president in his efforts to direct the generals in Virginia, and not only his patience but also his good judgment seemed to have been severely taxed.

Whether through fault of his own or not—and in most cases it was not—Davis now had to contend with the hostility of all the high-ranking generals then exercising field command in Virginia. As the spring campaign grew closer and the South learned with apprehension of the enormous preparations being made north of the Potomac, Davis was faced with the problem of having to meet this threat by either trying to make use of officers who disliked and distrusted him or of bringing into Virginia other generals with whom he could work more harmoniously. Neither option boded well for his chances of success, and the fact that he faced such a choice was a stark reminder of the failure of his best efforts over the previous seven months.

4

SO MANY FAILURES

Even as the last acts of the Romney incident were being played out, Davis confronted a problem of far greater import. The Confederacy appeared to be collapsing. Out in Tennessee, Fort Henry fell on February 6, opening the heartland of the confederacy to northern penetration as far south as Mississippi and Alabama. Two days later, in coastal North Carolina, the small Confederate garrison at Roanoke Island was overwhelmed by a combined Federal army and navy operation. This debacle left Norfolk, with its vital navy yard—where even then a strange ironclad monster called the *Virginia* was nearing completion—vulnerable to Federal attack. It also opened a potential back-door route to Richmond, and it raised the specter of Federal amphibious forces descending without warning on any part of the enormous southern coastline. As if all this were not enough, February 16 brought the fall of Fort Donelson in Tennessee, sending into northern captivity 12,000 soldiers the South could ill afford to lose and opening the Cumberland River to northern gunboats. That meant the fall of Nashville, the South's second most important manufacturing city after Richmond, and the loss of the rich agricultural region of Middle Tennessee.

If the haste of the Confederate president's reaction smacked almost of panic, there could be no denying that the situation appeared desperate. Davis took immediate steps to shore up the Confederacy's sagging defenses in the West, but he was acutely aware of a far greater threat.[1] The South might be slowly losing the war on the other side of the mountains, but it could lose very quickly in the Virginia tidewater. Coming at the culmination of such a train of disasters, the fall of Richmond, involving the loss of its vital industrial capacity and a tremendous blow to already sagging southern morale, would likely have ended the conflict.[2] Davis was most anxious, therefore, to guarantee the safety of his capital against any possible northern foray from the coast. As the only major body of troops available for that purpose was Johnston's army encamped at Centreville, just north of Manassas, the president's next step was obvious.

On February 13 Davis wrote requesting Johnston to come to Richmond to confer on a matter the details of which he was loath to commit to paper.[3] The letter does not survive, but it must have contained not only indications of the urgency of the president's summons but also at least a hint of the subject to be discussed.[4] When Johnston received the letter on the sixteenth, he immediately wired Davis that Smith, his second in command since Beauregard's departure, was sick. Johnston was therefore "afraid to leave the army" and asked permission to delay the visit to Richmond until Smith had recovered.[5] Apparently perceiving the reason for Davis's request that he come to Richmond, Johnston, the same day, sent the president a letter. "We cannot retreat from this point," he wrote, "without heavy loss." Confederate movements were hindered by roads made muddy by winter rains, while Johnston feared northern forces would avail themselves of water transport for a possible flanking move. To Johnston, this dire outlook was made even worse by a bit of scuttlebutt he had picked up that day. Rumor had it that G. W. Smith was to be transferred to East Tennessee. Pleading the inadequacy of his staff and the lack of competent generals throughout the army, Johnston filled most of his letter with urgings that he be allowed to keep Smith.[6] In fact he need not have worried. It was not Gustavus W. Smith but Edmund K. Smith who was slated for Tennessee.

Davis received the letter early on the morning of Wednesday, February 19, and hurried to allay the general's fears. "I have not intended to withdraw General Smith from your command," he assured Johnston, explaining that he was making other transfers. Adding a note on a subject much on his mind, he wrote, "I am very anxious to see you. Events have cast on our arms and our hopes the gloomiest shadows, and at such a time we must show redoubled energy and resolution."[7] That was his only reference to the issue of pulling the army back. Discussion of such a sensitive subject would have to wait until Johnston could get away from camp for a few days. Giving the letter to an aide to be mailed, Davis then hurried off to the morning's cabinet meeting, scheduled for 8:00 in the Customs House.[8] The following Saturday was to be Davis's formal inauguration as the Confederacy's first regular president. He had prepared a draft of his formal inaugural address, and a meeting like this was the way he liked to put the final polish on such papers.

Whether the work on the address provided a convenient cover for a meeting whose purpose he did not wish known by the public or whether he simply could not forbear bringing up to the cabinet a matter that was pressing so heavily upon him, Davis raised the issue of the military situation about two hours into the discussion. He related the grizzly details of the previous week's military disasters (the fate of Fort Donelson was still unknown in Richmond at this time) and explained that "the time had come for diminishing the extent of our lines—that we had not men in the field to hold them and must fall back."[9] That all came as quite a shock to this assembly of political bigwigs. After all, Davis was the military expert among them, and if he was alarmed, the situation must be grave indeed. But the president went on. Unless Johnston's army was pulled back closer to Richmond, the city would fall. Burnside's presence on the North Carolina coast changed the entire military equation in Virginia. Now Richmond must be protected against threats from both north and south. Davis expected Burnside to move in short order against Suffolk, Virginia. That would isolate vital Norfolk and guarantee its fall. Even the politicians could see that the city in which they presently sat would be the obvious next target.[10]

Davis could not have timed what happened next any better if he had tried, and he could not have tried since he believed Johnston was still up at Centreville, tending his army in place of the ailing Smith. Yet at that moment in the cabinet's deliberations, an aide announced that General Johnston had arrived and was waiting in an outer office. Davis excused himself and stepped out to talk with him. He assured Johnston of what he had that morning written in the letter to him about Smith and briefed him on the desperate situation in the West and the steps being taken to remedy it. Finally, he informed him that he had arrived in time to take part in the discussion on the question of pulling his own army back closer to Richmond.[11] Davis then returned to the cabinet meeting with Johnston in tow. For the remainder of the day, the issue was hashed and rehashed. It was not decisive leadership, but it was the way Davis liked to deal—or to avoid dealing—with difficult matters. In the course of the deliberations Davis mentioned the fact that several different generals now shared the responsibility of guarding Richmond, including the commanders of the relatively small forces confronting Burnside. To address this potential problem, Davis revealed that he was considering bringing Lee up from his post on the southern seaboard to coordinate things around Richmond. For the moment, Lee felt the situation at Savannah looked too threatening to allow him to get away, but the president was clearly still interested.[12]

At some point in the conference, apparently as the hour began to grow late, Johnston excused himself and headed for the hotel, while the politicians went on talking.[13] In the hotel lobby he met Col. William Dorsey Pender of the Sixth North Carolina. Pender had been home on leave and was passing through Richmond on his way back to the front. Approaching Johnston, Pender asked his commanding general if there was any truth to the rumor he had been hearing ever since he arrived, that the cabinet was currently meeting to discuss the possibility of pulling the army back from the Centreville line.[14] This did not bode well for the president's attempts at secrecy, nor did it boost Johnston's scant faith in politicians.

The meeting was resumed the next morning, with still more discussion of the question of what to do with Johnston's army. The general freely conceded that withdrawal from northern Virginia was desirable.[15] He admitted to the president and cabinet that his position could be turned "whenever the enemy shall choose to advance," and that that was likely to be a good while before Johnston himself was prepared to move.[16] Still, he contended that on Virginia's dirt roads and in the present winter weather the difficulties of a withdrawal were "almost insurmountable."[17] In the end, Johnston had his way, for no order was issued for the withdrawal of the army. Davis directed Johnston to have the country behind his present position surveyed in search of a good defensive position, probably the Rappahannock River.[18] He also wanted the general to send to the rear his excess baggage, heavy ordnance, and large stockpiles of supplies, so that the army would be free to move rapidly in the event of a threat to Richmond, without the loss of items of which the Confederacy had no surplus.[19] All of that was sensible enough, indeed was probably a much wiser course than the more precipitate retreat Davis had envisioned before Johnston had so forcefully impressed on him the difficulties involved.[20] Somehow, though, it became the cause of a great deal of confusion and a further souring of the relationship between the president and the commander of the Confederacy's chief army.

Their relations were none too good as it was. After the conference finally broke up Thursday, Johnston, who was already becoming an unwitting favorite of politicians hostile to the president, attended a social gathering. By this time it was another of Richmond's poorly kept secrets that Johnston was carrying on a running feud with the secretary of war over the administration of the army. Benjamin had developed the irritating habit of bypassing the army commander in such matters and was authorizing infantry companies to convert to cavalry or artillery, or allowing aspiring officers to recruit new companies of such arms from among the army's present infantry, or simply granting furloughs to Johnston's soldiers at a rate the general feared would all but empty his camps.[21] He was also following Davis's practice of receiving and even encouraging direct communication—outside the chain of command—from Johnston's subordinates. Johnston had remonstrated that "the rules of military correspondence require that letters addressed to you by members of this army should pass through my office" and had urged that such a proper policy be followed, observing sarcastically that it would "create the belief in the army that I am its commander."[22] Benjamin paid no heed, and hostility between them grew. Thus when asked at the Richmond dinner party by a member of Congress "whether he thought it even possible that the Confederate cause could succeed with Mr. Benjamin as war minister," Johnston hesitated a moment and then "emphatically" replied that it was not.[23]

Naturally, word of this got back to Davis and must have been a further irritant, especially when on March 4 Johnston's views were cited in a congressional debate as proof of the secretary's incompetence.[24] The president was very sensitive about his appointees and interpreted any criticism of them as a personal attack on himself. Since Benjamin and, to a certain extent, Davis were presently under severe criticism for the recent military reverses, the president would have been all the more touchy about such a statement from one of his chief generals.[25]

In view of such frictions the most remarkable thing in Davis's relationship with Johnston that winter may well be the degree of respect the president retained for the high-spirited general. Davis had had a high estimate of Johnston's military skill before the war and was not quick to change his opinions. Beyond that, Johnston was in many ways a general after the president's own heart. Absent the influence of the flamboyant Beauregard, Johnston held an outlook very similar to Davis's—the South could outlast the North if only it avoided sudden catastrophe. As no great victories were necessary for Confederate independence, no great risks were to be taken in their pursuit. This similarity of outlook Davis probably sensed, and it would have drawn him to the proud Virginian despite their difficulties. That their similarity in outlook was in some ways superficial and that they differed drastically in mental toughness and dedication to the Confederate cause, Davis showed no inkling.

On Friday morning, February 21, Johnston returned to his army and Davis to his preparations for the inaugural the next day.[26] Saturday was dreary, beneath a cold, steady, winter rain. "Such a day!" War Department clerk John B. Jones wrote in his diary. "The heavens weep incessantly. Capitol Square is black with umbrellas; and a shelter has been erected for the

President to stand under."[27] Davis, pale, unwell, and suffering from neural-gia, stood under his pavilion and delivered his speech.[28] "He read it well," the favorably disposed Jones recorded, "and seemed self-poised in the midst of disasters, which he acknowledged had befallen us. And he admitted that there had been errors in our war policy. We had attempted operations on too extensive a scale, thus diffusing our powers which should have been concentrated." Davis maintained his calm demeanor at a "lugubrious" inau-gural reception at the President's Mansion that evening, despite the fact that he knew—as the public did not until the following day—that both Fort Donelson and Nashville were gone. Outside, the cold rain continued its steady dripping.[29]

It was raining in Centreville too, and Johnston's mood was as dismal as the weather. His outlook had not been improved any by an incident on the train on the way up from Richmond. An old acquaintance of his from Fauquier County had mentioned to him the same rumor Pender had asked about in the hotel. Nor could Johnston comfort himself with the reflection that perhaps, after all, only a few people had heard the news. His Fauquier acquaintance was "too deaf to hear conversation not intended for his ear."[30] If he knew of the proposed movement, all Richmond—and all the northern spies it contained—must know it as well. Still, Johnston had retained enough optimism to remark to an officer of the commissary department, on his way to see to the removal of the large stockpiles of cured meat that the depart-ment had by now succeeded in building up close in the rear of the army, that "he thought there would be no difficulty" in procuring adequate transporta-tion to get all the supplies away.[31] Yet, reflecting on the situation at his camp in the mire of northern Virginia, Johnston succumbed to his natural ten-dency to despair. While Davis went through the wearisome formalities of office back in Richmond, Johnston wrote gloomily in a letter to him, "The condition of the country is even worse now than I described it to be, and rain is falling fast." Johnston feared that some of his field artillery could not be moved under present conditions, much less his heavier guns and bulky stores, and he observed ominously, "The enemy may not allow us much time for changes of position."[32]

In the days that followed Johnston continued in the same vein. On the twenty-third he moaned of the condition of the roads, the futility of Confederate efforts in northern Virginia, and the likelihood of an early Federal advance.[33] Two days later it was more of the same, with the further disturbing comment that much "property must be sacrificed in the contem-plated movement."[34] On the last day of the month he added complaints about the management of the railroad to the rest of his repetitive litany and again warned of "great sacrifice of property."[35] His letter of March 3 was the same thing again.[36] In all of these letters appeared a repeated set of phrases that must have puzzled Davis: "The orders you have given me"; "our preparations to execute your plans"; "Your orders for moving"; if the enemy advanced, it would "compel the movement you have ordered without further delay"; and most disturbingly, "A large quantity of [public property] must be sacrificed or your instructions not observed."[37] Clearly, Johnston had a different concept of the final decision of the conference in Richmond than did Davis and the other participants, for no order for immediate withdrawal had been issued.[38]

Still anxious to restore a working relationship—if not a friendship—with Johnston, Davis responded patiently to the general's querulous letters. Writing Johnston on February 28, Davis expressed his hope that new recruitment efforts in Virginia would enable him to reinforce Johnston heavily. If, however, as he suspected, that hope proved illusory, it would be necessary to retreat—all the more reason, in view of the perceived enemy threat, to "disencumber yourself of everything which would interfere with your rapid movement when necessary" and to make the prescribed "examination of the country in your rear" so as to "select a line of greater natural advantages than that now occupied by your forces." The sooner Johnston could inform Richmond of his intended future defensive line, the more effectively could supplies be stockpiled to anticipate his wants. Meanwhile, Davis emphasized how desperately the Confederacy needed the weapons, supplies, and equipment then in use in northern Virginia and urged that they not be hastily abandoned. He was particularly concerned about the heavy artillery, adding, "Whatever can be, should be, done to avoid the loss of those guns." Davis concluded:

As has been my custom I have sought to present general purposes and views. I rely upon your special knowledge and ability to effect whatever is practicable in this our hour of need. Recent disasters have depressed the weak, and are depriving us of the aid of the wavering. Traitors show the tendencies heretofore concealed, and the selfish grow clamorous for local, and personal, interest. At such an hour, the wisdom of the trained, and the steadiness of the brave, possess a double value. The military paradox that impossibilities must be rendered possible had never better occasion for its application. . . . Let me hear from you often and fully.[39]

Such words may well have surprised Johnston, for this was the most flattering thing the president had written to him in five and a half months.

Eight days later the president wrote again in like tone. The same rains that made Confederate movement difficult would, Davis reminded Johnston, undoubtedly delay an enemy advance. Plenty of time should be available to get the siege train and supply dumps moved to safer locations. Naturally, the troops should be sheltered as much as possible. Davis still hoped to be able to reinforce Johnston adequately to hold his ground but admitted that was unlikely. "You will be assured," the president emphasized, "that in my instructions to you, I did not intend to diminish the discretionary power which is essential to successful operations in the field; and I fully rely upon your zeal and capacity to do all which is practicable." Finally, he again urged Johnston, "Please keep me fully and frequently advised of your condition and give me early information if there be anything in which I can aid your operations."[40]

Aside from the fact that Davis was trying very hard to conciliate his leading Virginia general, one other thing was clear from this correspondence: Johnston had no reasonable excuse for believing that a peremptory order of the president's required him to retreat from his present position immediately or with undue haste. In view of this fact, Johnston's mantra that he was about to retreat by order of the president at whatever material cost is puzzling to say the least. The best explanation would seem to be that the general was beginning to give way under the self-imposed strain of imagining all the different ways his Federal opponent could defeat him. Johnston seems to have felt even more alone in his responsibility since the departure of Beauregard, and this probably accounts in part for his almost frantic concern that G. W. Smith not be transferred as well. Feeling distrusted and distrustful of his superior at the War Department and shaken by Davis's revelation of Confederate disasters and suggestion that it might be necessary to pull his army back toward Richmond, Johnston was simply losing his nerve. Although dwelling on the difficulties of retreat in his letters to Davis—in order to decrease the pressure to carry out such a movement successfully—he in fact became more and more obsessed with putting a good deal more distance between himself and the enemy at the earliest possible moment. As in the case of his withdrawal from Harpers Ferry, Johnston was anxious that Davis should bear the responsibility for the movement and so tortured the president's oral instructions into a positive order to retreat. Davis, who assumed that Johnston would retreat if necessary once baggage and supplies had been secured, seems not to have picked up on the general's distorted references to his orders.

Curiously, even while Davis was responding to Johnston's nervous letters in late February and early March with some of his most conciliatory statements in months, he was allowing the ongoing difficulties between Johnston and Benjamin to fester—with ill effect on his relations to the general. Johnston, growing tired of appealing to Benjamin to cease his disruptive practices, wrote directly to Davis, describing the secretary's actions and seeking the president's "protection of the discipline and organization of this army."[41] Davis consulted Benjamin on the matter. Whatever may have driven the Louisiana politician in his dealing with Johnston, one thing was certain: Judah P. Benjamin was not the man to have for an enemy in a bureaucratic dogfight. So completely did he succeed in bringing Davis around to his way of seeing the situation that the president was moved to write Johnston, "The Sec. of War informs me that he has not granted leaves of absence or furloughs to soldiers of your command for a month past" and then only a few. He followed this up with a lesson in Confederate military law regarding the organization and enlistment of troops. He was quite willing, he assured Johnston, to protect the general's proper authority, but he was sure that "the Sect. of War . . . cannot desire to interfere with the discipline, and organization of your troops." He also observed that Benjamin had complained that Johnston was not obeying his proper orders, and Davis was inclined to believe him. "You can command my attention at all times to any matter connected with your duties," the president concluded, "and I hope that full co-intelligence will secure full satisfaction."[42]

This letter failed to secure Johnston's satisfaction at any rate, particularly since the same mailbag that brought it contained "a large package" of just the sort of orders the secretary of war had convinced Davis he had not sent for a month.[43] Worse, it was followed the next day by another rebuke from the president over Johnston's failure to carry out a minor organizational directive. "The order did not admit of discussion and I hope will be obeyed with due promptitude," Davis wrote in a terse telegram. "Military operations cannot be conducted otherwise."[44] These rebukes, combined with Johnston's not entirely unreasonable conviction that Davis was allowing an oily politician like Benjamin as well as the rest of the hidebound desk jockeys in the War Department bureaucracy to undermine his authority and disorganize his army, destroyed any remaining chance of reconciliation between general and president. Although later that month, in a rare and grudging concession to the opinion of Congress, Davis moved Benjamin from the War Department to the post of secretary of state, the damage had already been done to his relations with Johnston.[45]

While conducting these two simultaneous exchanges of correspondence with Johnston–one soothing the general's fears of the strategic situation in front of him and the other exacerbating the general's frustrations with the bureaucratic situation behind him–Davis had also moved to realize the plan for coordinating the scattered defenders of the capital that he had shared with the cabinet on February 19. He brought Lee to Richmond. The circumstances of the move were dictated by the political situation. Davis had planned to give Lee the position of "Commanding General of the Armies of the Confederate States," after the pattern used in the U.S. Army. Accordingly he had his political allies in Congress introduce a bill authorizing such an office.[46]

Strangely enough, the bill gained the enthusiastic support of Davis's increasingly numerous enemies as well, since they reasoned that the general thus appointed would, to some degree at least, supplant Davis in the active role of commander in chief. To facilitate such a consummation so gratifying to their way of thinking, these politicians saw to it that the wording of the bill that finally reached the president's desk was subtly different from what Davis had sought. The proposed act authorized the commanding general to take command of any of the Confederacy's field armies whenever he had a mind to–without reference to the president. This Davis would not have. On March 14, four days after receiving the bill, Davis returned it to Congress with his veto message. "The officer so appointed," Davis remonstrated, "is authorized to take the field at his own discretion and command any army or armies he may choose, not only without the direction but even against the will of the President, who could not consistently with this act prevent such conduct of the general otherwise than by abolishing his office." Besides, the Confederate Constitution made the president commander in chief of the armed forces, which he would not be if he could not control the discretion of this general. In a word, the act threatened civilian control of the military and was unconstitutional.[47]

By that time Lee was already in Richmond. Davis had wired him on Sunday, March 2, "If circumstances will, in your judgment, warrant your leaving, I wish to see you here with the least delay."[48] Lee replied immediately that he hoped to be able to leave Savannah by Tuesday morning.[49] Hurriedly tying up the odds and ends of business he had on hand, Lee was able to get away ahead of schedule, on Monday evening. Well before week's end he was in the capital.[50] While Lee studied the strategic situation in Virginia to orient himself to operations there, Davis cast about for a means of turning the political flank of the perverse legislators. He found one within a week of Lee's arrival. On March 13, the day before he returned the unsatisfactory bill to Congress, Davis had the secretary of war issue a routine order through the adjutant and inspector general's office: "General Robert E. Lee is assigned to duty at the seat of government; and, under the direction of the President, is charged with the conduct of military operation in the armies of the Confederacy."[51] No new office was created, no act of Congress was needed, and no threat was posed to the constitution or Davis's authority.

By the time Lee entered into his new duties, the situation between Davis and Johnston had become further strained. The general's half-deliberate misunderstanding about what was to be done with the army at Centreville had finally produced its evil effect. For Davis, the disappointment was intensified by the newly arisen hopes that it destroyed. On March 8 the Confederacy's strange new ironclad *Virginia* sallied forth from its base at Norfolk to destroy two vessels of the Union blockading squadron at Hampton Roads. On the ninth the *Virginia* fought an inconclusive battle with the Union ironclad *Monitor*, but that did not prevent Davis from drawing the very reasonable conclusion that neither Norfolk nor the Peninsula were as seriously threatened as they had appeared up to this time. Troops would not need to be shifted to that front. Indeed, some of those now there might be available for service with Johnston. That, along with the vague promises of new recruitment in Virginia, seemed to suggest a major shift in the balance of power in the northern part of that state.[52] On Monday, March 10, Davis excitedly wired Johnston, "Further assurance given to me this day that you shall be promptly and adequately re-enforced, so as to enable you to maintain your position and resume first policy when the roads will permit."[53]

Later that same day Speaker of the House Thomas Bocock hurried over to Davis's office. The president was in another cabinet meeting, but what Bocock had to say was urgent, and he had a message sent in to the president: rumor now had it that Johnston and his army were in headlong retreat.[54] Davis could not believe it.[55] The secretary of war (who was still Benjamin at this point) must look into it at once, Davis ordered. As the day wore on without news, the president seemed almost distraught, as he irritably scribbled a note to Benjamin, "Have you *not yet* sent an officer to *learn* the *facts* and *reasons*?"[56] The days that followed brought even more disturbing reports. Ammunition dumps were being blown up, food stocks were burned or left to rot in the open, even camp equipment was being put to the torch. It sounded for all the world like a routed army desperately fleeing after a catastrophic defeat. Yet if a battle had occurred, it surely would have been reported, and what intelligence did arrive indicated no Union pursuit.

Johnston's abandoned fortifications near Centreville–with logs left in the embrasures to give the appearance of cannon. (Courtesy of National Archives, 165-SB-6, Civil War 59)

Indeed, McClellan's Federals had seemed in no hurry to occupy Johnston's abandoned camps. Davis was loath to believe it all, and still no message came from Johnston himself, whom the president had recently and repeatedly admonished to communicate frequently and fully with him.[57]

The week passed. Davis gave Lee his new orders on Thursday and vetoed Congress's impertinent general in chief bill on Friday. Finally on Saturday, March 15, the long-awaited communication from Johnston arrived.[58] It was a letter from Johnston to Davis dated Thursday, March 13, from the south bank of the Rappahannock. Curiously, a shorter dispatch from Johnston to Cooper sent the previous day had not yet arrived.[59] Both messages brought the same tidings. The army had indeed abandoned its position at Centreville on Sunday evening. The rest of the rumors seemed to be true as well. "More than half of the salt meat" at the giant commissary department meat-packing plant at Thoroughfare Gap had been left behind, as well as "much more than half" of the army's baggage. This problem, Johnston maintained, was the fault of the railroad officials, whose performance had been "wretched." He further expressed his hope to be able to fall back even farther, beyond the Rapidan River, as soon as possible. In keeping with the orders that he had convinced himself Davis had given, Johnston declared himself ready to "take such a position as you may think best in connection with those of other troops."[60]

None of the dire rumors of the previous week had prepared Davis for this last suggestion. How could Johnston possibly expect *him* to select the army's new position? The general had been ordered to make a reconnaissance of the country behind him specifically in order to select a good position on which to fall back should retreat become necessary. The only thing Davis could make of the statement was that Johnston had neglected to do so and was utterly ignorant of the country between Centreville and Richmond, an incorrect but not entirely unreasonable conclusion, based on Davis's assumptions.[61] Davis replied with a brief telegram and a longer letter. In the telegram he acknowledged Johnston's letter as his first official notification of the army's movement. As for the general's implied query about what position to take, Davis could "suggest nothing as to the position you should take, except it should be as far in advance as consistent with your safety."[62] The letter made the same points only somewhat less tersely. In addition, the president expressed his surprise, wondered if Johnston had sent him a number of letters that he had not received, and emphasized that no reason existed in Richmond for the army's abandoning its position at this time.[63]

Davis had lost some of his confidence in Johnston, and it is a measure of just how much confidence he had had in the Virginia general that after all this he still retained a considerable amount. Over the next week or two, Davis learned just how great a logistical disaster the retreat had been. Over 1.5 million pounds of foodstuffs were abandoned or destroyed, giving the inefficient Confederate commissary department a setback it could ill afford. Besides vast stocks of clothing, equipment, and ammunition, Johnston had also abandoned the heavy guns that Davis had been so concerned with saving. Much as Johnston might try to shift the blame to the railroad companies or to inefficient commissary officers, the fault was primarily his. Not only had he retreated prematurely through his own loss of nerve, but he had so interfered with the operations of the railroad companies as to create the very inefficiency of which he constantly complained to Davis. As if all this had not been enough, Johnston still did not feel safe behind the Rappahannock, and when the railroads, still hamstrung by Johnston's inept oversight, were not as fast as he desired in getting the army's supplies moved still farther south, he again lost patience and on March 18 pulled back behind the Rapidan, abandoning additional stocks of meat. The needlessness of this whole sorry proceeding was underscored by the slowness of the Union forces to follow up the retreat.[64]

While Johnston had slipped into a mental state not far removed from panic and had misconstrued the instructions the president had given in

February, Davis also had undergone at least some small change in mood, though his had been in the opposite direction. After the appearance of imminent and total collapse in the midst of the mid-February defeats, the situation in early March gave cause for guarded optimism on the part of Davis. In the West Albert Sidney Johnston, with the aid of Davis's active direction from Richmond, was gathering his forces for a show-down battle that might catch the Federals off balance and regain what the Confederacy had lost the month before. In Virginia and North Carolina, northern forces seemed little inclined to press the advantage they had had after the fall of Roanoke, and the *Virginia*'s bold performance gave further grounds for hope. Lee, too, brought a different way of thinking to the Confederate high command. He was naturally aggressive, and he went to his task with a disciplined calmness. Yet despite his undoubted influence on Davis, even in these early weeks of their new association, he was merely reflecting the president's own upbeat mood when on March 16, his third day on the job, he wrote Maj. Gen. Theophilus H. Holmes, who commanded a force covering Johnston's right flank, "It is not the plan of the government to abandon any country that can be held, and it is only the necessity of the case, I presume, that has caused the withdrawal to the Rappahannock."[65] The determination to hold as much territory as possible was typical of Davis and reflected his newly recovered optimism. Whereas in mid-February the overall strategic situation threatened to require the withdrawal of Johnston's army, a month later no such impending need was seen—no reason for Johnston's withdrawal—beyond the tactical situation in his front.[66]

The withdrawal was a fact now, however, and the question was what to do next. Specifically, for Johnston at least, the question seemed to be where Davis wanted him to place his army, for preferring to see the retreat as Davis's rather than his own necessity, Johnston continued to place it in those terms. Perplexed, Davis in mid-March decided to pay Johnston a visit.[67] Always prone to involve himself in matters of detail, Davis could rarely resist the temptation to visit the front lines.[68] Below the junction of the Rapidan and the Rappahannock, Johnston's lines still followed the south bank of the latter, and there Davis met Johnston and surveyed the position. He liked what he saw, for the south bank was high and dominated the north. Asking Johnston if the same situation held true along the river all the way downstream to Fredericksburg, he was taken aback to hear the general admit "that he did not know; that he had not been at Fredericksburg since he passed there in a stage on his way to West Point, when he was first appointed a cadet."[69]

Since that had been thirty-seven years ago, Davis decided it was time for a refresher course.

Arriving in Fredericksburg late on March 21, they saw at once that the picturesque old town, sitting on the low southern bank of the Rappahannock under the dominating bulk of Stafford Heights on the north bank, was ill-sited for defense. To protect the town, the Confederates would have to hold Stafford Heights, and to investigate that feasibility Davis took Johnston as well as Holmes, the local commander, and several of their staff officers for a ride on the heights the next morning.[70] As Davis and Johnston rode along side by side, the others dropped back out of earshot, and the two carried on a lengthy private conversation, the contents of which remain unknown.[71] One thing was certain, however, and that was that holding Stafford Heights would require far more manpower than the Confederates had. As the party passed through the little village of Falmouth, just across the river from Fredericksburg, on the way back, Davis remarked to Holmes's aide and local resident J. T. Doswell, "To use a slang phrase, your town of Fredericksburg is right in the wrong place." Doswell had to admit it was true.[72]

Davis had something else on his mind. "The purposes of the enemy," he later wrote of this time, "were then unknown to us."[73] Yet the Federals were obviously up to something. In recent days ship traffic on the Potomac had indicated another seaborne operation, possibly a large one, but what was the intended target, and could this be merely a feint to divert Confederate attention away from a possible overland movement toward the Rappahannock-Rapidan line? On the twenty-first, Lee had telegraphed him from Richmond that the Federal transports that had been at Hampton Roads that morning had put to sea again. What could that mean? Lee thought it meant another movement toward North Carolina, "where a great battle is to be fought." He assured Davis that he was already forwarding reinforcements to the area but felt they needed a good overall commander. For this duty he recommended either of Johnston's top two subordinates, G. W. Smith or James Longstreet.[74] This, along with the possibility of sending troops from the northern Virginia army, may well have been the subject of the president's private discussion with Johnston, or it may be that Davis did not even need to ask what his general would think of parting with either of his subordinates. In any case, Davis telegraphed Lee on the twenty-second to go to North Carolina himself. Promptly, but with serious misgivings, Lee set out to do so. He felt his presence was needed in the capital in order to see that troops were thrown forward as rapidly as possible.[75]

In fact, Davis was even then taking steps to see that the interruption to Lee's service in the capital would be brief. Although Johnston might balk at giving up Smith or Longstreet, he was not loath to part with Holmes, an aging mediocrity whose prewar friendship with Davis assured that the president would be the last one to recognize his limitations. Besides that, Holmes was a North Carolinian, and as such very politically acceptable to command the defense of that state. Before leaving Fredericksburg Davis gave Johnston an order to send Holmes, two brigades of infantry, and two batteries of artillery to Richmond en route to points south.[76] That done, Davis boarded the afternoon mail train and headed back to the capital.[77]

The Union buildup at Fort Monroe, at the end of the peninsula between the James and York Rivers, continued, and with it Davis's uncertainty. Richmond might be threatened from the north or the east or both, and defeat on either front would likely cost him the city and the war. After he returned to the capital, Lee showed him a note from Gen. John B. Magruder, who commanded the 4,000-man Confederate force watching the growing numbers of Federals at Fort Monroe. With about 30,000 men from Johnston's army, Magruder believed he could crush the northern forces on the Peninsula.[78] Davis was interested. Assuming (correctly, as it turned out) that the Federals there had been drawn from McClellan's forces in northern Virginia, he thought that would make a northern advance against Johnston unlikely at this time.[79] Accordingly, he had Lee write Johnston on March 25 to see what he thought of the idea and to warn him to be ready for a rapid movement if called on. "The President desires to know," Lee wrote, "with what force you could march to re-enforce the Army of the Peninsula or Norfolk." He pointed out that it would take at least 20,000 or 30,000 men to get the job done there.[80] "To insure security and dispatch," Lee sent his letter by special messenger, and Johnston had it the next day. Davis, however, now experienced his own case of nerves. Growing impatient as he worried over the genuinely threatening situation on the Peninsula, by the afternoon of March 27 he could wait no longer. He wired Johnston to send 10,000 men at once.[81]

On receiving Lee's letter, Johnston, like Davis, also found the idea attractive and wrote back the next day to say he could bring 25,000 of his total 35,000-man army as soon as called for.[82] Indeed, so eager was Johnston for the endeavor that he was dismayed at the wire asking for only 10,000 of his troops and wrote Lee urging that the Richmond authorities stick with the original plan.[83] Yet at this point, Davis's nerves again got the better of him as he grew alarmed about some of the intelligence coming from northern Virginia. Could the enemy be contemplating an attack on the

Rappahannock line? The president had Lee respond to Johnston's dispatches, reminding him that there was no better place to make a stand between the Rappahannock and Richmond and suggesting that in view of the situation in northern Virginia, Johnston had better use his own discretion in deciding how many men to send.[84] Johnston must not forget that losing Staunton and the railroad connection between Richmond and the West would be even worse than losing Norfolk and the Peninsula. "The President is not at all reluctant," Davis had Lee say, "to take the responsibility of any movement of the propriety of which he is confident."[85] The problem was, of course, that at the moment Davis was not at all confident what movement might be appropriate and so was strongly disinclined to take drastic or decisive action.

At the conclusion of his letter of March 28, Lee had added, "If doubtful of the course to be pursued, he [the president] invites you to a full conference at this place, where the latest intelligence is collected."[86] Johnston took advantage of this invitation. Taking Smith with him and leaving Longstreet to mind the store back on the Rappahannock, he went to Richmond to consult with Davis for a couple of days near the end of the month.[87] By April 3 he was back at his headquarters in the field. The discussions in the capital did not seem to have resolved much, for on April 4 he wrote the president to renew his plea that he be ordered to take his entire army, or most of it, to the Peninsula at once.[88] Of course, as he explained in a dispatch to Lee sent the same day, if it were to be left to his discretion and his front was seen as threatened, then he would stop the movement of the brigades already slated for the Peninsula, adding, "The President, however, will always have the means of judging where those troops are most needed."[89]

This was not considered at all amusing in Richmond, for that same day McClellan's forces had begun their advance up the Peninsula toward the Confederate capital, now less than sixty-five miles away.[90] Lee telegraphed Johnston relaying the news and admonishing that "the movement of the troops directed from your line must immediately be made to this place . . . by order of the President."[91] That got some of the troops moving, but apparently Johnston still did not quite get the idea. Thinking the president was relying on his discretion to decide whether to weaken the Rappahannock line to send more troops to the Peninsula, Johnston wrote Lee on the sixth, "I cannot here compare the state of affairs in my front with that in front of others, and cannot, therefore, decide understandingly whether troops are less needed here than elsewhere. . . . He who directs military operations upon information from every department can."[92]

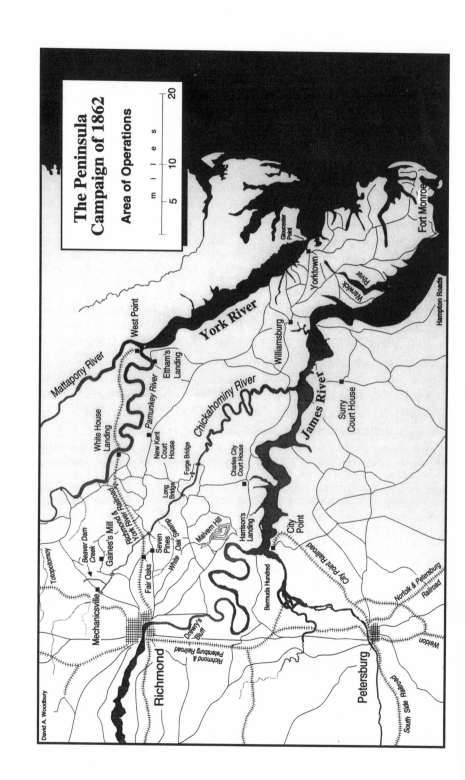

The Peninsula Campaign of 1862

Area of Operations

miles
5   10   20

David A. Woodbury

By this time, of course, Davis no longer had the least difficulty deciding where troops were most needed. The problem now lay in getting them there in time. Even as Johnston penned his last uncomprehending complaint on Sunday, April 6, the first units of his army were marching through the rain-swept streets of Richmond, and a very welcome sight they were.[93] It had been a tense weekend in the capital and even worse out at the front, along Magruder's scratch line blocking the Federal advance up the Peninsula at an insignificant watercourse called the Warwick River. The line was anchored on its left by the improved fortifications at historic Yorktown and elsewhere had the advantage of an impassable backwater or two, but undermanned as it was, it was hardly adequate to stop McClellan's mighty Army of the Potomac. What saved Richmond on April 5 and 6 was McClellan's timidity and Magruder's theatrical talent. Known in the prewar regular army for his flair in staging amateur plays to relieve the boredom at isolated frontier posts, "Prince John," as he was nicknamed, now put on his finest performance, having his relatively few infantry and artillery units march across open fields within view of enemy lines, then double back behind woods or hills to march across the same fields again looking like additional troops. Incredibly, the trick worked, and the timid McClellan settled in for a siege of the tiny force behind its makeshift fortifications.[94] April 7 was another day of steady rain, further impeding McClellan's operations. Also on that day the first of Johnston's troops began filing into the trenches at Yorktown.[95]

Now that McClellan and the main Federal army were known to be on the Peninsula, that threat could be given top priority. Davis, on April 9, ordered Johnston to Richmond with all of his troops except a small covering force to be left on the Rappahannock.[96] Johnston arrived on the twelfth, and Davis informed him that the area of his command was being expanded to include Norfolk and the Peninsula. It was a strange and ambivalent arrangement in some ways, however, because the various commanders who would be serving under Johnston were instructed "while conforming to his instructions, [to] make their reports and requisitions, as heretofore, to the proper departments in Richmond until further orders."[97] In a sense, both Johnston and the Richmond authorities would jointly command the scattered military forces operating in Virginia.

The first thing Davis wanted Johnston to do was visit the Peninsula and "examine the condition of affairs there."[98] Taking with him the brilliant but unstable Whiting, Johnston set out for Magruder's headquarters as quickly as he could and arrived there early the next morning.[99] Perhaps it was the influence of Whiting, or perhaps it was the fact that he could not possibly have gotten much sleep in the last few days; at any rate, Johnston viewed the situation along Magruder's line with a jaundiced eye. Nothing he saw pleased him.[100] Approaching Brig. Gen. Daniel Harvey Hill, the dyspeptic and sour-spirited commander of the Yorktown sector of the lines, he asked how long Hill thought he could hold out once McClellan got all of his heavy artillery up, his elaborate emplacements dug, and opened fire.

"About two days," Hill replied.

"I had supposed, about two hours," Johnston growled back.[101]

Of course, it was a given of siege warfare that if the attacker were permitted to make his "regular approaches" and employ his heavy guns, the fall of the besieged position was only a matter of time and not very much time at that. It was up to the defender to disrupt or defeat the enemy's preparations if he could. Johnston, however, was disposed to see everything in the worst possible light. By nightfall, he was convinced that nothing the Confederates could do on the Peninsula could accomplish more than delaying McClellan just long enough to emplace his artillery—plus about two hours—and this the southerners might do at the likely cost of losing their army. He determined that something else must be done. After urging for nearly three weeks that he and his army be sent to the Peninsula to deal with the Union threat there, he now found the prospect of battle intolerable. As darkness fell he began another night of travel, this time for Richmond and an attempt to talk Davis out of defending the Peninsula at all.[102]

When Davis arrived at his office on the morning of Monday, April 14, he found Johnston waiting for him.[103] Earnestly the general described Magruder's position on the Peninsula and what he thought was wrong with it. Let McClellan have the Peninsula, he urged. Instead of trying to defend it, the Confederates should, he suggested, assemble the largest army possible just outside Richmond. This would be accomplished by combining all the forces then operating for the defense of Richmond and stripping the defenses of Georgia and the Carolinas. The combined force would then meet and, as Johnston now confidently predicted, defeat McClellan in the great battle of the war just outside the Confederate capital. As he put it in later years, "Such a victory would decide not only the campaign, but the war." It was an interesting proposition from a general in whom Davis still placed a surprising degree of confidence, and the president listened to it with marked attention. He would not, however, make a decision—not yet, anyway. That, he felt, should come only after he had indulged in his favorite method of deliberation—extensive conference. Accordingly, Davis asked Johnston to return to his office about 10:00 that morning to meet with him, Lee, and recently installed Secretary of War George W. Randolph for a thorough discussion of the question. Johnston asked if he might bring with him Smith and Longstreet, and Davis readily agreed.[104]

While Davis summoned Lee and Randolph, Johnston went out to hunt up his two chief lieutenants. Longstreet he found fairly readily, but Smith was another matter. Johnston finally came across him in the Spotswood Hotel just thirty minutes before the time set for the conference. Smith, who had been working hard the last few days organizing the movement of his division, was exhausted and claimed to be ill. The precise nature of his malady has never been determined, but it had afflicted him off and on for more than a year by this time. The mysterious complaint seemed to strike hardest whenever Smith was confronted with heavy responsibility or hard decisions. For example, his "illness" had delayed for several months during the summer of 1861 his decision to go south and cast his lot with the Confederacy. Whatever it was, he had it again, and he begged to be excused from such an important conference. Johnston persisted, explaining his view of the situation and the dangers he saw in taking the army to the Peninsula. Smith gave in and hastily started writing out a memorandum summarizing his views.[105]

At the appointed time the participants came together in Davis's office. A few moments before the conference commenced, Smith pushed his memorandum into Johnston's hands. The general read it, nodded, and as the meeting got under way, handed it to Davis with the observation that he fully agreed with its statements. Davis took it and read it aloud, thus making it the basis on which the discussion was to begin. The substance of the paper was essentially the same plan Johnston had proposed a few hours before. The Peninsula was to be abandoned and the Confederates were to make ready for a showdown battle in front of Richmond with every southern soldier from Savannah to the Shenandoah.[106] Johnston then, at Davis's request, repeated to the others present the import of what he had told him earlier that morning. Davis then called on Smith, who spoke in similar terms.[107]

Randolph, in his turn, spoke against retreat. The new secretary of war had most recently been a brigadier general in the Confederate army, but he had spent eight years of his youth, from 1834 to 1841, as a midshipman in the United States Navy, resigning at age twenty-one to embark upon a legal career. Not surprisingly, Randolph was especially sensitive to naval affairs. He spoke up now to point out that abandoning the Peninsula would mean giving up Norfolk as well, with its massive Gosport Navy Yard. That would throw away "our best if not our only opportunity to construct in any short time gunboats for coastwise and harbor defense."[108] Norfolk, though seri-ously threatened, had so far been kept out of Federal hands primarily by the presence there of the formidable ironclad *Virginia*. None of those present could deny, however, that with the Peninsula gone, Norfolk would be hopelessly outflanked and bound to fall.[109] What would then become of the *Virginia* was another sobering question. Besides, Randolph continued, he was sure that if the enemy assaulted the lines around Yorktown they would be soundly defeated. Everyone readily agreed that this was true, but Johnston replied that McClellan would not assault the lines but take them by siege. In that case, he would be very difficult to stop.[110]

Yet to be heard from was Longstreet. Large of stature and imposing of appearance, Longstreet also tended to be sparing of words. His silent, dignified demeanor gave people the impression of great wisdom, which was curious since "Old Pete," as he was nicknamed, had graduated fifty-fourth out of the fifty-six men in his West Point class of 1842. Yet the bulky Georgian would never suffer from anything like an inferiority complex, and since he always acted as if he knew more than the others around him, they sometimes believed it. During the present conference he had thus far sat quietly, and Davis now called on him for his opinion. Longstreet announced that he knew McClellan and that the meticulous former officer of engineers "would not be ready to advance" for some days yet.[111] That was all well and good—and happened to be true—but Davis, at least, did not seem to think it especially helpful. With the exception of Randolph, they all knew McClellan. As a lieutenant of engineers, the present northern commander had served under Lee during the Mexican War, and his rapid advancement during the 1850s had sprung in part from the good opinion of then Secretary of War Jefferson Davis. By the end of that decade Joseph E. Johnston and Gustavus W. Smith had been two of the Ohioan's closest friends.[112] The president, therefore, may have had reason for thinking the group did not require a lecture on the personality of the opposing army commander. In any case, he interrupted Longstreet rather brusquely, speaking "of McClellan's high attainments and capacity." Offended, Longstreet decided his views were not wanted and lapsed back into his wise silence.[113]

When Lee's turn came, he spoke out strongly against Johnston's proposal and advocated the defense of every inch of the Peninsula. As midday passed and afternoon wore on toward evening, the conference developed more and more into a debate between Lee and Johnston. The pressure, or his strange illness, was getting to Smith. He became pale and talked less and less and finally not at all. Randolph had shot his bolt; besides, he hated these interminable conferences. Longstreet remained inert, and Davis continued to listen and ask questions and take no further active role in the discussion. Thus, the conference became a battle of reason and will between Lee and Johnston, two West Point roommates who had been close friends in the Old Army and had risen simultaneously, step by step, to the top of their profession. Contrary to what might have been expected in such a colloquy between two good friends of well-known reserve, this debate gradually became "very heated."[114] It was probably the only such exchange ever between these two men and very likely the most intense in which either of them, especially Lee, was involved during the course of the war. Johnston, of course, with his single-minded competitiveness about rank, especially where Lee was involved, would still have been smarting over the fact of Lee's outranking him. For Lee, the display of emotion was even more rare. He had endured deep struggles of conscience over his choice of allegiance and sometimes acted as if he felt a need to vindicate his choice by military victory. Then, too, he may have sensed in Johnston a certain weakness of character that could lead him to flinch from each approaching test of battle and go on retreating forever. Or he may simply have felt very strongly that Johnston's proposal was not the best way to protect his beloved Virginia. Whatever drove these men, they went at each other hour after hour.[115]

At 6:00 P.M. the meeting recessed, to take up again at 7:00 at the president's residence. While Smith snored on the couch in an adjoining room, Randolph and Longstreet looked on with what were probably glassy-eyed expressions, and Davis listened with rapt and nervous attention, Lee and Johnston continued to marshal argument and counterargument in a pitched battle of ideas.[116] Lee did not think it wise to strip the southern coastal defenses at this time, and since he had just come from that region a few weeks before, his word carried weight with Davis.[117] Besides, Davis had learned just two days before of the fall of Fort Pulaski, protecting the major blockade-running port of Savannah.[118] If Lee said troops were needed on the southern coast, the president was prepared to believe him. On the other hand, Johnston "maintained that if those places should be captured, the defeat of the principal Federal army [meaning McClellan's] would enable us to recover them; and that, unless that army should be defeated, we should lose those sea-ports in spite of their garrisons."[119]

Lee countered, insisting "that the Peninsula offered great advantages to a smaller force in resisting a numerically superior assailant."[120] With these advantages, Lee believed, the South could win much-needed time—time to raise and train new troops and to finish converting the existing army from its

The Confederate White House. (Courtesy of National Archives, 111-B-53, Civil War 119)

previous composition of one-year volunteers to its new system of conscripts for the war (the men were the same, but the new arrangement, as authorized by the Confederate Congress in the Conscript Act, involved tangled organizational adjustments). Johnston, however, argued that the environment on the Peninsula was conducive to all sorts of diseases. Confederate units sent there would decline through attrition without ever meeting the enemy. Since the Peninsula was so favorable for defense (never mind that Johnston had just been at considerable pains to demonstrate precisely the opposite), Magruder could hold and delay McClellan every bit as well without Johnston's troops as with them—better, then, not to commit the army to the Peninsula.[121]

Finally, Lee asserted that Johnston's plan let McClellan's host come too close to Richmond too easily. He preferred to keep his opponent at arm's length while looking for an opportunity to destroy him.[122] That was a matter almost of instinct, and Lee's fighting instincts were unquestionably different from Johnston's. The question was simply which case would appeal more strongly to Jefferson Davis. Johnston's plan offered the prospect of a smashing victory in exchange for the giddy risk of a catastrophic—and final—defeat. By contrast, Lee's program called for measured risks, careful preparation, and the holding of as much Confederate territory as possible while making the enemy fight and, one might hope, pay dearly for each mile gained.[123] While the process went on, something might always turn up, and if worse came to worst, the Confederates could then make their last stand in front of Richmond with better chances than Johnston's precipitate plan would likely have offered. For Davis, who consistently opted to hold territory and avoid risks, that was hardly any choice at all. That he had lingered so long over the decision is an indication not only of his own fatal hesitancy but also of the tremendous respect he held, even yet, for the military abilities of Johnston. That respect, however, was ultimately not enough to gain his approval for the general's plan. For the first time taking an active role in the conference, Davis announced that the Peninsula would be defended.[124]

In some ways, the president's decision was ironic. Johnston, whose radical plan Davis had rejected, was ordinarily little inclined to advocate such risks and never inclined to take them. Davis may not have sensed it—indeed, Johnston may not have realized it himself—but the general lacked the nerve to carry his present plan into execution. Joseph E. Johnston would make a career in this war of deprecating showdown battles that risked all for a chance of victory. He now advocated such a counsel of desperation probably because it was the most flattering excuse for avoiding significant contact with the enemy in the immediate future. For Johnston, once the moment of decision arrived, almost any course seemed preferable to entrusting his reputation to the fickle chances of battle. The alternative course taken, the reprieve gained, and the moment of action again approaching, he would, if at all possible, find another excuse to seek another field, another time. Ironically, Lee, whose cautious plan Davis preferred, was an aggressive risk-taker who believed the South would have to force the issue against its larger northern antagonist. That the president as yet knew none of this spared him an even greater burden of worry than the one presently ruining his health.

By the time Davis announced his decision and the conference broke up, it was 1:00 A.M. Johnston woke Smith, and together with Longstreet they left the president's residence. The commander of the Confederacy's largest army now had his orders but was determined to thwart them. "The belief that events on the Peninsula would soon compel the Confederate Government to adopt my method of opposing the Federal army," Johnston later wrote, "reconciled me somewhat to the necessity of obeying the President's order."[125] He raised no further protests and did not threaten to resign or request to be relieved, but he went to the Peninsula with every intention of retreating before any serious clash with McClellan's army. He would go through the motions of obeying the president's order to defend the Peninsula and delay McClellan while planning to retreat so rapidly as to force Davis into the course of action that debate had just failed to secure from him.

Johnston was no sooner back at the front than he began to bombard Richmond with complaints that his lines were untenable, even going so far as to request, perhaps not without a touch of sarcasm, that Lee suggest what positions his army ought to take up. Lee patiently replied that he trusted Johnston would be able "to remedy" his present position "or to assume a position better calculated for your purpose." If Johnston had views he wanted brought to Davis's attention, Lee assured him that he would be glad to do so.[126] Johnston, however, continued his complaints. "No one but McClellan," he lamented, "could have hesitated to attack."[127] When Lee, probably at Davis's insistence, wrote to see if Johnston could spare a few regiments to counter another Federal force that seemed to be threatening Richmond from just north of Fredericksburg, Johnston was horrified. If the Union force in northern Virginia, commanded by McDowell, should advance on Richmond, then Johnston saw only one alternative and that was for the president to accept the plan he had advanced at the conference in Richmond.[128] Still intent on forcing this program on his superiors, Johnston, on April 27, wrote Lee a further dismal report. McClellan, as everyone had known he would, had been "preparing . . . to attack Yorktown with heavy artillery." Once that happened, "it is certain that our guns will soon be dismounted." The York River would then be open to northern vessels, which would presumably shuttle Union troops deep into Confederate rear areas "and so compel me to fall back."[129] Lee wrote back that he would prepare for the worst, but trusted Johnston might be able to avert such an event.[130]

Johnston, however, had no intention of trying. As far as he was concerned, his note of the twenty-seventh constituted adequate notice of his impending abandonment of the Yorktown lines and retreat up the Peninsula. In any case, he was determined to be long gone before McClellan was ready to open his attack.[131] On the twenty-ninth he argued that the struggle for Yorktown was one "we cannot win" and announced that he intended to "move as soon as can be done conveniently, looking to the condition of the roads and the time necessary for the corresponding movement from Norfolk." Ominously, in view of his recent track record, he added, "The wretched condition of the roads may cause us heavy losses of materials on the march." As always, he closed with his standard refrain about concentrating at Richmond "the largest force you can collect."[132] The next day he wrote again in almost the same words. "We can never win," in the present confrontation with McClellan. Then he offered an absolutely bizarre proposal to "take the offensive, collect all the troops we have in the East and cross the Potomac with them" while a similar offensive was carried out west of the Appalachians.[133] This was a strange recommendation from a general of Johnston's unaggressive temperament, but the key was that such a course was attractive to Johnston because it was safely remote in time and place. Anything was better than facing the enemy here and now. Lee could only reply diplomatically that the president "concurs in your views as to the benefits to be obtained by taking the offensive" and was considering the "feasibility of the proposition."[134]

Neither Davis nor Lee, however, seem to have realized the urgency of Johnston's various appeals to have his force pulled off the Peninsula. It finally struck them with a considerable jolt when, on May 1, Johnston announced that he would be withdrawing the next day.[135] In consternation, Davis himself telegraphed Johnston. He had accepted, he said, the general's conclusion that he would not be able to hold the Peninsula much longer and had been making arrangements for the removal of important supplies and equipment there and in Norfolk, but "your announcement today that you will withdraw tomorrow takes us by surprise, and must involve enormous losses, including unfinished gunboats. Will the safety of your army allow more time?"[136] Spending more time in the Yorktown trenches was the last thing Johnston wanted to do, for McClellan was obviously nearly ready to begin active operations. Johnston would have moved on May 2 as planned, but finding some of his units unready on that day he delayed the march until the third.[137] On that day, the Yorktown lines were abandoned—skillfully, without McClellan's notice during the operation. Johnston also sent orders to Maj. Gen. Benjamin Huger, in Norfolk, to march his troops out of that position immediately. This "would have involved heavy losses in stores, munitions, and arms." Fortunately, Secretary of War Randolph happened to be in Norfolk at that time inspecting the preparations for withdrawal. Boldly, he ordered Huger to hold the position longer, daring a Federal attack, while the vital materials were withdrawn. Remarkably, in view of Johnston's haste, Huger was able to remain in Norfolk an additional week and then withdraw unmolested.[138] On the Peninsula, under Johnston's direct supervision, the loss of weapons, equipment, and supplies was every bit as bad as he had predicted and included all fifty-six of his heavy guns.[139]

The *Virginia,* left without a home port by the loss of Norfolk, drew too much water to retreat up the James, and her captain was left no choice but to blow up the Confederacy's most powerful warship.

It was another discouragement for an already careworn president. Two weeks before, a War Department clerk had noted that he looked "thin and haggard."[140] About the same time, his brother in Mississippi had written to express his concern about Davis's residence; Richmond looked none too secure anymore. He also suggested that Varina and the children be sent out of the apparently doomed city.[141] Then on the same day that he received the shocking news that Johnston intended to retreat from Yorktown immediately, Davis had felt called upon to deal with a difficult situation in the other portions of that general's department. If the president handled it poorly, it can at least be said for him that he had a lot on his mind just then.

When the bulk of Johnston's army had been shifted to the Peninsula, several small screening forces, each about a brigade to a division in size, had been left to cover, or at least observe, the parts of Virginia thus left exposed. Brig. Gen. Charles Field commanded a force of about 4,000 men just south of Fredericksburg, watching McDowell's 40,000 menacing Federals. Jackson had perhaps 5,000 men in the Shenandoah Valley, where he faced dual threats in the form of Union generals Banks and Fremont, who were approaching the Valley from the north and west respectively, with a combined total of about 45,000 troops. Positioned just east of the Blue Ridge, roughly between Jackson and Fields, was Maj. Gen. Richard S. Ewell, with another 8,000 troops. Jackson, senior of the Confederate commanders in the region, hoped to make some advantage of this unpromising situation. That alone would have been enough to convince more timid officers that he was insane, and the former Virginia Military Institute professor's celebrated eccentricities, grotesquely exaggerated in the press, completed the picture many had formed of a lunatic in command. Still, Jackson was not the only one who entertained thoughts that the Confederacy could gain from bold operations in northern Virginia. Back in Richmond, Lee, probably with the encouragement of Davis, began to take an active interest in such operations.[142]

Johnston had left Jackson with orders to prevent Banks from reinforcing McClellan and had generally encouraged Jackson to do whatever good he reasonably could. In keeping with these instructions, Jackson had attacked Banks at Kernstown on March 23 and gained assurance that substantial Union forces were still present in the Valley by suffering a sharp tactical defeat at their hands. In the weeks that followed, Jackson sought reinforcements and the authority to undertake a really ambitious scheme to make life unpleasant for the Federals in northern Virginia. Reinforcements, of course, were hard to come by. Around April 1, Longstreet, who was temporarily commanding on the Rappahannock while Johnston was conferring with Davis in Richmond, replied that additional troops could be had only if Longstreet, who outranked Jackson, came with them and took command. "Old Pete" wanted an independent command and explained that his presence would be necessary to give the operation "vigor and action."[143] Nothing came of that, and after Johnston moved to the Peninsula, he quickly became wrapped up in the affairs of his army there. On top of that, he was having difficulty getting information from his forces elsewhere in Virginia. The commanders of these units, including Jackson, had been ordered to communicate with Johnston through the adjutant and inspector general's office in Richmond. Somehow, whether by Lee's action, Davis's, or simple oversight, most of this information was not making it to Johnston.[144]

Davis had brought Lee to Richmond to coordinate the operations of the various forces commanding it. When Lee was in the capital the year before, Davis had established a pattern of leaving the secondary areas of action to Lee's supervision while he concerned himself with the main struggle. Thus, it is not surprising to find Lee directing the forces in northern Virginia by mid-April 1862 in hopes of achieving a strategic concentration that would disrupt Union offensive plans against Richmond. He counseled both Jackson and Ewell that since Union forces in the region were divided, they must be weak somewhere. It was up to the Confederates to find that place and concentrate their forces on it. Perhaps Ewell could link up with the Confederate force watching Fredericksburg, by now reinforced to 12,000 men and under the command of Brig. Gen. Joseph R. Anderson, for a quick strike at the Federals opposite them. If that were not feasible, then maybe Ewell and Jackson could combine against Banks. "I cannot pretend at this distance," Lee wrote Jackson near the end of the month, "to direct operations . . . , but submit these suggestions for your consideration."[145] It was just as well that Lee was exercising this supervision rather than Johnston, for even as the latter became caught up in affairs on the Peninsula, what direction he did give Jackson tended to narrow the options for aggressive action.[146] With Lee, greater stress was put on potential offensive operations, giving Jackson permission to draw Ewell's force into the Valley for his campaign there.[147]

Jackson began preparing for his offensive, but the whole thing was nearly wrecked before it got well under way. By the end of April, Ewell and his chief lieutenant, Richard Taylor, had worked themselves into a frothy rage over

Jackson's supposed madness and his disinclination to share more of his campaign plans with his subordinates than they needed to know. Taking counsel how to rid themselves of this pestilent commander, they decided Taylor should go to Richmond to convince his brother-in-law the president to send to the Valley an officer who would outrank Jackson.[148] Taylor found Davis receptive to his pleas, partly because he was very persuasive, partly because he was kin, and partly because Davis had not forgotten Romney and thought Jackson a fool. Indeed, so uncomfortable was the president with the autonomy Jackson was enjoying that he had determined on May 1 to send either Smith or Longstreet to take command of the force near Fredericksburg.[149] Either of those men in that position could be expected at least to supervise Jackson and probably prevent his undertaking any of his ambitious plans. That neither had gone was not so much Davis's doing as Johnston's, who had protested so vehemently against their departure that the president had relented. Now, just a few days later, he heard his misgivings confirmed in Taylor's appeal and promised that Longstreet would be sent to the Valley as soon as possible to supersede Jackson in command. Still cursing his commander as an "old crazy fool" but happy that he would soon be rid of him, Taylor returned to the Valley. He was to be disappointed, however. Lee, who was developing a deep trust for Jackson, seems to have prevailed on the president to let Stonewall continue without interference.[150]

Davis had narrowly avoided making a truly colossal blunder. Jackson was just the man to have in the Shenandoah Valley at this point. During the next few weeks, while Davis's attention was focused on the steadily approaching juggernaut of McClellan's army, Jackson, with Lee's encouragement, carried out one of the more brilliant campaigns of military history. With boldness and skill he defeated separate northern forces whose combined numbers far exceeded his own, confusing the Union commanders, capturing much-needed supplies and equipment, and winning for himself such fame that no living man then ranked higher in the admiration of the southern people. More important, he distracted the Federal high command just as McClellan's campaign for Richmond was reaching a crucial stage. Washington withheld McDowell's 40,000 men, whose imminent appearance on Richmond's northern horizon had been a recurring nightmare for Davis. Jackson's action and Lincoln's reaction had taken McDowell and his men entirely out of the conflict for the Confederate capital.[151] Davis played no role in the conception or execution of Jackson's whirlwind Valley campaign, but at least he had had the sense to bring Lee to Richmond and give him the necessary authority and responsibility to turn Jackson loose on the

Yankees. And he had allowed himself to be persuaded to put up a little longer with a general who had seemed crazy. Davis took this success by omission anything but gracefully. Learning of Jackson's achievements late in May, he told Varina that he had suggested something of this sort at the conference with Johnston and the others back in April. "Had the movement been made when I first proposed it," he sniffed, "the effect would have been more important."[152] Fortunately for his own reputation, Davis seems not to have grabbed at credit in the presence of anyone else. Important enough was the fact that thanks to Lee and Jackson, if not necessarily Davis, a chance still remained to save Richmond.

As events were unfolding, however, during that month of May, it appeared nothing might be able to save Richmond from the advancing masses of McClellan, and under the growing pressure and frustration, relations between Johnston and his superiors in Richmond became increasingly strained. The general, for his part, kept harping on all of his favorite complaints. He was not getting adequate information about the forces in his department elsewhere in Virginia, he needed more high-ranking officers, and he wanted all available Confederate forces brought together and placed under his command just outside Richmond. Petulantly, he suggested that if he were not permitted to draw to himself the forces then watching McDowell in northern Virginia, he did not really command that area and ought to be officially relieved.[153] Lee did his best to mollify Johnston, providing full information on operations elsewhere in the state in letters that in contrast to Johnston's were uniformly kind in tone.[154]

Meanwhile, Davis began to display an interest in trifling administrative matters that under the present extreme circumstances was little short of bizarre. On the same day Johnston pulled out of Yorktown, Davis had Lee write him to express concern that the rifles of soldiers going on sick leave were "not being turned in to the proper officers." The president, Lee warned, had dispatched an officer from the ordnance department in Richmond to go to Johnston's army and make sure every last musket was handled according to correct bureaucratic procedure.[155] Next, Davis took up—of all things—the old controversy about brigading the troops of each state together. This time he wrote to Johnston himself. "Orders were long since given to bring the practice and the law into conformity" and "I have been much harassed and the public interest has certainly suffered by the delay to place the regiments of some of the States in brigades together." In fairness, Davis was apparently taking a bit of political heat on this subject and had at least tried to insulate Johnston from the worst of it. "While some have expressed surprise at my patience when orders to you were not observed," Davis tactlessly continued, "I have at least hoped that you would recognize the desire to aid and sustain you, and that it would produce the corresponding action on your part." Since he believed the reasons Johnston had formerly offered for delaying were no longer applicable, he hoped that "you will, as you can, proceed to organize your troops as heretofore instructed," especially with respect to the troops from Mississippi. Ending the letter on a complimentary note, Davis added, "I have been much relieved by the successes which you have gained" in holding the Federals at bay during the retreat "and hope for you the brilliant result which the drooping cause of our country now so imperatively claims. . . . I hope to see you soon at your headquarters."[156] Curiously, the tone of this letter was, despite its subject matter, almost friendly. Davis apparently still wanted at least some degree of reconciliation with Johnston. Turning his attention to niggling administrative details was simply the president's way of dealing with stress.

Johnston was under stress himself and was not inclined to make allowance for his commander in chief's foibles. In a letter to his wife he described the president's dispatch as one of those "such as are written to *gentlemen* only by persons who can not be held to personal accountability"—that is, challenged to a duel. "I can not understand," he continued, "the heart or principles of a man who can find leizure [sic] in times like these to write four pages of scolding to one whom he ought, for the public interest, to try to be on good terms with."[157] It seems never to have occurred to Johnston that the same public interest might suggest that he, in turn, ought to try to be on good terms with Davis.

These days, however, Johnston was angry with his superiors, his subordinates, his circumstances, and himself. "He was," one astute judge of character concluded, "too fussy, too hard to please, too cautious."[158] As the army drew back closer and closer to Richmond, nothing seemed to go as he hoped it would. After pulling out of the Yorktown lines, the army had marched up the Peninsula toward another set of fortifications Magruder had built near the old colonial capital at Williamsburg. There, on the third day of the retreat, elements of McClellan's army caught and engaged Johnston's rear guard. The Confederate commander had no intention of remaining in the Williamsburg defenses, having already made plans to retreat, perhaps all the way to Richmond.[159] Williamsburg was for him merely an opportunity to knock the pursuing Federals back on their heels. When it was over, Johnston professed himself pleased with the battle's results, but he could not have failed to realize that it had been a dreadfully mismanaged affair.

Longstreet was bringing up the rear. How poor a job he had done at keeping his division in hand was demonstrated when the Federals caught up with him near Williamsburg and five of his six brigades became engaged before he himself chose to observe the field. Although his men had driven the enemy back several hundred yards, Longstreet now found himself with one flank in the air, almost no reserves, and facing steadily growing pressure as more Federal units moved up. What he did not know—because he did not bother to check—was that his subordinates had left some of the fortified line unmanned, creating a potentially disastrous situation. Even without such knowledge, he felt the need of reinforcements and called on D. H. Hill's division, next ahead in the column, to countermarch to his aid. News of this call for added strength reached Johnston, whom Longstreet had hitherto avoided notifying of the action, and the commanding general reached the field several hours after the battle was joined.[160]

Arriving at last, Johnston looked around and decided to let Longstreet carry on. This probably had something to do with one of Longstreet's greatest strengths as a commander, his apparently complete imperturbability on the field of battle. His great physical stature and his air of quiet, stolid self-assurance made him a great source of emotional strength to subordinates and superiors alike. Johnston thus left the battle in Longstreet's self-confident hands. That the fight did not end disastrously was largely due to the fact that none of the men in blue coats, at least none with stars on their shoulders, seem to have caught on to the matter of the empty fortifications except a single brigadier. He got his men into some of them, and when Hill and one of his brigadiers, Jubal Early, undertook to throw them out, the attack they mounted was so hasty and poorly executed that it accomplished little other than getting a great many of their troops shot. But the "fog of war" was thick that day, compounded by a literal fog. In the exchange of blunders that characterized this and many another battle, the Confederates did not commit mistakes numerous or large enough to cancel the natural and manmade advantages of their position. Johnston and Longstreet were quick to claim victory.[161]

The following day a Union force began debarking from transports well up the York River at Eltham's Landing, near Barhamsville, on Johnston's left flank. The general had been looking, rather diligently, for just this sort of thing to happen and expected a sizable body of bluecoats. Ready for them, he now seems to have hoped that the exact situation he had been itching for had finally turned up. Quickly he maneuvered his divisions toward the York until by the morning of the seventh the whole army was poised around Eltham's

Landing, waiting for the Federals to advance out from under the guns of their fleet. Then came anticlimax; the Yankees had apparently failed to read the script. They were few, unaggressive, and not inclined to walk into a trap. When the morning passed without action, Whiting was ordered to send forward a brigade of his division to "feel" the enemy. The outfit he picked consisted of three Texas regiments and one from Georgia under the command of a rangy, tawny-bearded, and very aggressive former U.S. Army officer named John B. Hood. Hood's Texans went forward skirmishing, probing for something solid out front. They went on probing for a mile and a half through the woods until they reached the riverbank and found that the Union skirmishers were back aboard their transports.[162]

By 4:00 P.M. Johnston had learned that no battle would be fought at Eltham's Landing. Enraged at this disappointment, Johnston quickly mounted up and rode off at high speed down a crowded and muddy road, with a dozen and more frantic staff officers and couriers trailing out behind, sabers clattering and hats flying off, at the best speed their horses or their horsemanship could manage. The general's mad ride was finally brought to a halt when an ambulance driver, hearing the pounding hooves coming up behind him and anxious to get out of the way of whatever it might be, steered his vehicle toward a fence at the side of the road. Unfortunately, that happened to be the side of the ambulance on which Johnston was even then attempting to pass, and the raging general now found himself boxed in between the ambulance and the fence. "I don't think I ever saw any one fly into such a fury in my life," wrote staff officer E. P. Alexander, the only one who had managed to keep Johnston in sight. He had "never before heard the general use an oath," but he did now, as Johnston, "face as red as blood," roundly cursed the startled driver and then, turning to Alexander, who had just come up, demanded, "Give me a pistol & let me kill this infernal blanketty blank." Alexander had his revolver but was not about to give it to Johnston. Pretending not to have a weapon, he "held back & looked around, while the poor ambulance driver, scared almost into a jabbering idiot, whipped at his team." The hapless man finally made good his escape, and the general's blood pressure gradually came back down out of the stratosphere. Johnston decided to spend the night at a nearby village hotel, and as Alexander observed, "The staff & couriers were arriving for an hour afterward."[163]

The incident remained unknown to most Confederates, including Davis. Johnston naturally put the best face on the Eltham's Landing affair in his report to the Richmond authorities, commending the performance of the officers engaged there. Davis had Lee express to Johnston his "pleasure" at "the handsome manner in which the enemy was dislodged."[164] Yet while the president could take satisfaction that his chosen army commander apparently knew his business and was skillfully warding off Union pursuit, Richmond remained in grave danger. On May 9, Davis decided the time had come for Varina and the children to leave the city "to relieve him from unnecessary anxiety." Varina, as was her nature, was averse to fleeing, but her husband insisted, and they decided that she and the children would remain three more days. That evening, however, as President and Mrs. Davis were hosting a reception at the Confederate White House, "a courier came to the President with despatches." Varina remembered the scene years later. As Davis "passed me on his return to the drawing-room I looked a question, and he responded, in a whisper, 'The enemy's gun-boats are ascending the river.' " The guests stayed late that evening, and the first family had little time for discussion, but after the last hand had been shaken and the last guest shown out the door, Jefferson told Varina that "he hoped the obstructions would prevent the gun-boats reaching [Richmond], but that he preferred we should go the next morning." Her protests were unavailing, and finally acquiescing, she went to tell the children.[165] The next morning, as Varina and the children boarded their train for points south, Secretary of War Randolph gave orders to his bureau chiefs to "have such of your records and papers as ought to be preserved, and are not required for constant reference, packed in boxes, for removal." He hastened to assure them that "this is only intended as a prudent step, and is not caused by any bad news from the army. There is no need, therefore, for any panic in the city, and it should be prevented by the assurance that we have every reason to think that the city can be successfully defended."[166]

For informed observers in the Confederate capital it must nevertheless have been disquieting. The signs were bad both at the White House and the War Office, and it was not so much from the army that bad news was feared. As the president's reaction to the dispatch he received during the White House reception demonstrates, the eyes of apprehensive Richmonders were on the James River. Back in February, out in Tennessee, Fort Henry had fallen to Federal gunboats. For all anyone in Richmond knew, the loss of Fort Donelson had been to the same cause, and of course Roanoke had been a similar story. Less than two weeks before, Union warships had steamed up the Mississippi and captured New Orleans. Now the like fate seemed in store for the Confederate capital, as its river lay open to Union naval forces. The southerners had begun work on obstructions in the channel and a powerful battery at Drewry's Bluff, just below the city, but this was still incomplete. Now, thanks to Johnston's hasty retreat, the James River defenses faced their supreme test. The grimness of the strategic picture was underscored when Monday, May 12, brought word of the destruction of the *Virginia* the day before.[167]

That afternoon, Davis and Lee made the ride out to Johnston's headquarters, now just twenty-five miles or so from the capital. As the Confederate forces had fallen back before him, McClellan had advanced slowly and sidled to the north so as to use the Richmond and York River Railroad as a supply line from his new base at White House Landing on the Pamunkey, a tributary of the York. He was now set to approach the Confederate capital from due east. Johnston, as his army faced McClellan's columns, had behind him the Chickahominy River. A sluggish and normally insignificant stream hardly more than a dozen yards wide, the Chickahominy angled gradually down and across the Peninsula in a generally southeasterly direction to its mouth on the James. Swollen by the recent wet spring weather to the point of inundating the tangled thickets of its extensive, spongy bottomland, the river had now become a major obstacle to military operations.

Picking their way through the swamp, Davis and Lee trotted their horses over the bridge and into the army's camps. Arriving at Johnston's headquarters, they found the general was out. When he returned, he explained that "he had been riding around his lines to see how his position could be improved." A lengthy conference followed, in typical Davis style, and the president himself later admitted that it "was so inconclusive that it lasted until late in the night." At its conclusion, Davis and Lee decided to spend the night in camp and return to Richmond the next morning.[168] Some time before they left, they must have seen and been seen by at least a portion of the troops, for Brig. Gen. Howell Cobb, a disgruntled Georgia politician who wished he were president, wrote in a letter to his wife that Davis's presence with the army had failed to call forth the usual cheering from the troops.[169] If this was indeed the case, it was highly unusual and indicated remarkably low morale. Davis himself, in a letter to Varina, made no mention of such an omission, observing only, "The Army is reported in fine spirits and condition."[170]

On the ride back to Richmond, Davis and Lee fell to discussing the previous evening's conversation. They both had to agree that nothing more definite had come out of it than that Johnston would "improve his position as far as practicable, and wait for the enemy to leave his gunboats, so that an opportunity might be offered to meet him on the land."[171] For now, that would have to suffice, though Davis was not easy about it. "If the withdrawal from the Peninsula and Norfolk had been with due preparation and a desirable deliberation," he wrote that afternoon in a letter to Varina, "I should be more sanguine of a successful defense of this city." As it was, the Drewry's Bluff fortifications were still not quite ready, and "the hasty evacuation of the defenses below and the destruction of the *Virginia* hastens the coming of the enemy's gun-boats." Considering the situation as a whole, Davis summed up his wavering faith in Johnston: "I know not what to expect when so many failures are to be remembered."[172]

Apparently, Johnston had been no more satisfied with the outcome of the conference than had the men from Richmond, though his dissatisfaction focused in the opposite direction. Davis and Lee must have no sooner disappeared into the thickets of the Chickamhominy swamp than Johnston sat down to write them a letter "in reference to the supply of provisions for [the] army in the event of Richmond falling into the hands of the enemy." He placed the finished dispatch in the hands of Maj. A. H. Cole, with instructions to discuss the matter with the authorities and find out just where they were making provisions for him to retreat on the other side of Richmond. Mounting up, the major set off on the same road the president and Lee had traveled only a few hours before. By late afternoon or early evening he was in Richmond and in conference with Davis, Lee, and Northrop. After "several hours" this discussion broke up around 9:00 P.M. Both Lee and Cole immediately wrote to Johnston in response. Lee assured him that various steps could be taken to keep his soldiers eating in the event of the loss of Richmond. "The only question is as to the best points" to begin shifting supplies, and on that issue Lee hoped Johnston might shed some light.[173]

Cole, for his part, seems to have been disgusted with the meeting. "I have not succeeded in procuring much information," he complained to Johnston. He had gained assurances, similar to those Lee mentioned in his letter, that the army could be fed, if Johnston would "indicate where your line will be south and west of Richmond in case we should be forced to give up the city." After covering a few other matters of logistical detail, he added the postscript, "They insist on your saying where you propose taking up your line in case Richmond falls. If you choose to tell them, send me a courier early in the morning, with such information as you think proper."[174] That was a curious thing for a staff officer to say to his commander regarding their nation's high command. If, as is not unlikely, Cole's attitude reflected that which prevailed at Johnston's headquarters, the general apparently believed it was his own business whether he chose to inform his commander of what he was doing, yet wanted complete information and provision by the Richmond authorities for the needs of the army he now deigned to regard as his personal retainers.

The next day the crisis atmosphere in Richmond was more acute. Obviously, Union warships would soon be testing the hastily prepared defenses of Drewry's Bluff, and if those failed to hold, the city was gone. Davis and Lee had each inspected the works personally in the preceding days, and now the president gave orders for placing a small infantry covering force around the battery.[175] Little more could be done. Johnston had apparently opted not to favor his commander in chief with his ideas as to what position to fall back on should the capital be lost. Davis, however, was determined to know where this might be, and so while elsewhere in the threatened city the Virginia legislature was meeting to resolve formally that Richmond must be defended to the last extremity, the president, cabinet, and General Lee met to decide the unthinkable: where should the army turn at bay if it were forced to flee a doomed Richmond? The strategic problem thus posed was a simple one, and Lee was ready with an immediate answer. The Staunton River, a little less than a hundred miles southwest of the capital, offered the next good place to make a stand. Lee, however, was not willing to treat the matter merely as an elementary exercise in military engineering. For Virginia he had thrown over his loyalty to the old Union and the Constitution. With Richmond gone, little would be left of the state, and Lee would know his choice to have been the wrong one. The defense of Virginia's capital was for him an intensely emotional issue. "Richmond must not be given up," he concluded, with tears running down his cheeks. "It shall not be given up!"[176]

Those must have been encouraging words for Davis, but their reality hung entirely on the handful of heavy guns and the few artillerists at Drewry's Bluff. The suspense was not to last much longer. On rainy Thursday, May 15, five Federal warships, including the powerful *Monitor* and one other ironclad, moved up the James to engage the Drewry's Bluff battery. Learning that the battle was joined at last, Davis immediately mounted up and set off to be there in person. Before he arrived, the firing had ceased. The gunners greeted him jubilantly and recounted eagerly how the battered flotilla had dropped back down the river out of range after taking a sound beating. At news of the victory, Richmond heaved a collective sigh of relief, Davis himself noting the next day that "the panic here has subsided." Confident now that the capital was safe from a sudden dash by the U.S. Navy, the president's concern could now focus increasingly on stopping the enemy's land forces. To locals who declared their willingness to see the city defended block by block and house by house, even if this meant it would be laid in ruins, he replied "that the enemy might be beaten before Richmond or on either flank, and we would try to do it, but that I could not allow the Army to be penned up in a city." Just to be sure all would remain well on the river, Davis took "a long ride through rain and mud" the next day, Friday, May 16, to check on the completion of the works along the James.[177]

Years later Postmaster General John H. Reagan recalled that about this time concern was voiced in the cabinet over the position of Johnston's army, since it faced McClellan with its back to the all but impassable Chickahominy swamps. If Johnston accepted battle on those terms, the slightest reverse could mean the annihilation of his army, which would have no chance of saving itself by timely retreat on the few and poor roads and bridges that spanned the marshes. Should not the president "call General Johnston's attention to this"? As Reagan remembered the exchange, Davis demurred, explaining "that when we entrusted a command to a general, we must expect him, with all the facts before him, to know what is best to be done; that it would not be safe to undertake to control military operations by advice from the capital." No withdrawal order was issued, and Johnston was left to his discretion. The next morning, to the relief of whatever cabinet members might have been sweating it out, word was received that Johnston was pulling back to the southwest bank of the Chickahominy.[178]

Johnston gave the order for the withdrawal on May 15, the same day Drewry's Bluff was successfully defended, and the movement continued the next day, while Davis braved rain and mud to inspect the James River defenses. Back in Richmond on Saturday, May 17, and satisfied more than ever that the gunboats could be held at bay, the president became increasingly concerned to know just what Johnston planned to do about dealing with the other pressing threat to the capital, the Union army. To gain this information and let Johnston know his own views without the fatigue of another wearisome ride in the mud, Davis sent a letter by the hand of his aide-de-camp G. W. C. Lee, son of the general and top graduate of the West Point class of 1854. Lee, the letter informed Johnston, could brief him on the "condition of the works on the James River" and provide details of the successful battle against the Union gunboats. Then Davis turned to the subject of the military situation on the Peninsula. Although the people of Richmond were determined to defend their city at any cost, Davis reiterated to Johnston his concern "that the defense must be made outside of the city." As to how this might be done, the president offered some suggestions. If McClellan continued to advance along the York River Railroad directly toward Richmond from the east-northeast, Johnston should proceed as planned.[179] He would "improve his position as far as practicable, and wait for the enemy to leave his gunboats, so that an opportunity might be offered to meet him on the land," as Johnston had communicated to Davis when he and Lee had visited the camp on the twelfth.[180]

If, on the other hand, McClellan should attempt to shift his base from the Pamunkey to the James, "the opportunity desired by you to meet him on the land will then be afforded." How this might be accomplished depended on how McClellan chose to shift his army. Odds were he would pull back down the Peninsula as he moved south, keeping on the far bank of the Chickahominy until he was in solid contact with his naval forces on the James and within range of their supporting gunfire for the crossing of the Chickahominy. That would make Johnston's task of taking on the northern army separate from the navy much more difficult. A Confederate lunge across the Chickahominy to catch McClellan in motion far from deep water was fraught with dangers and difficulties, "but if you must choose between that plan and one which gives the enemy the co-operation of his river transports and gun boats, it would seem that the balance would be on the side of the former." The grounds for such desperate counsels lay in what McClellan could do if allowed to proceed at his own deliberate pace to apply the inexorable processes of siege as he had been allowed to do at Yorktown. Should the Drewry's Bluff defenses be subjected to the same treatment, Richmond was doomed and with it the Confederacy. Of course, McClellan might just try to cross the Chickahominy right where he was, in the very teeth, as Davis imagined, of the Confederate army. For such a gift, Davis admitted, "we can hardly hope."

The president left the decision on the method for McClellan's discomfiture to Johnston's discretion. "As on all former occasions," he wrote, "my design is to suggest not to direct, recognizing the impossibility of any one to decide in advance; and reposing confidently as well on your ability as your zeal, it is my wish to leave you with the fullest powers to exercise your judgment." Hoping that Johnston might see fit to share with him some of his thoughts in such matters, Davis concluded, "Col. Lee will communicate fully with you and bear to me any information and reply which you may intrust to him."[181]

Johnston, however, had no desire to entrust anything to Lee for the president's information, nor did he choose to respond to a letter the elder Lee sent the same day that showed such a marked similarity to the president's as to suggest that the two had been in close conference about the military situation on the Peninsula.[182] Dissatisfied, Davis decided to go in person and discuss matters with Johnston. Leaving his office about noon on Sunday, May 18, he saw Postmaster General Reagan riding by and hailed him to say that after dinner he should come by and they would ride together "down to the Chickahominy to see General Johnston." Reagan shouted something in reply as he rode off, but Davis did not quite catch it. No matter; there would be plenty of time to talk with Reagan on the seventeen-mile ride to Johnston's camps, and so Davis went off to have lunch before setting out for an afternoon on horseback.[183] He was in for a surprise. What Reagan had shouted was that it would not be necessary to go all the way to the Chickahominy to see Johnston. Reagan knew because he had spent the day before and that very morning visiting the regiments from his state, Texas. Contrary to Davis's expectation that Johnston would remain close enough to the Chickahominy to "contest the crossing of that stream" should McClellan try it or even to cross himself if the Federal general was more cautious, the Confederate army had fallen back much closer to the capital.[184] The president was about to find out just how close.

The noon meal finished, Reagan and Davis met and rode toward the east side of town. As they passed through the small suburb of Rocketts, they rode over a rise and there about half a mile ahead stood row upon row of tents. What, Davis wondered aloud, could all this be? When Reagan informed him that it was Hood's brigade, a unit of Johnston's army, he simply could not believe it. "No!" he protested, "Hood's brigade is down on the Chickahominy." Reagan said he was sure since he had camped with them the night before. While the president digested this strange development and their horses walked on, the postmaster general added, "If you want to see General Johnston, he is in the brick house off to our right."

Davis was perplexed. "No," he insisted, "General Johnston is down on the Chickahominy." Reagan, however, was again in a position to speak with authority, for he "had seen [Johnston] and his staff go to that house that day." Now it finally dawned on Davis what had happened, and Reagan noted that "the look of surprise which swept over his face showed a trace of pain."[185] Johnston had taken the final step in forcing upon the government the strategy it had rejected, pulling his army back into the very outskirts of Richmond, in some places as close as three miles from the city itself. This he had done under no direct pressure from the enemy, who did not even get around to following up his withdrawal for several days afterward. When the Federals did follow, however, they found themselves within sight of the spires of Richmond and within hearing as its bells chimed the hours.[186]

How it was that Davis knew nothing of this until his shocking Sunday afternoon ride of May 18 remains a mystery. Johnston, of course, had not informed him, but in later years the general maintained that Davis must have known his position earlier since G. W. C. Lee had visited his lines the day before.[187] Although it is true that the president's aide would have met Johnston's forces southwest of the Chickahominy, the unanswered question remains how far this was from the river. The army had remained in motion throughout the seventeenth, steadily drawing back toward the capital, and it may be that Lee found Johnston considerably closer to the Chickahominy–and farther from Richmond–than Davis did the next day.[188] Lee may have assumed, as Davis undoubtedly did, that the general would halt his forces within easy striking distance of the river. It may be that Lee was simply embarrassed at the utter lack of information he had to give Davis. Assuming that Johnston must have communicated with the president by other means, he may not have thought to report to Davis something as obvious as the army's position almost within the national capital, something about which no responsible general would have failed to keep his superiors informed. In any case, the discovery of May 18 obviously came as a surprise to Davis.[189]

Recovering from his initial shock, the president decided to take Reagan's suggestion and go to see Johnston. Taking his leave of the postmaster general, he turned off to the right toward the general's headquarters, accompanied by another of his aides, Col. Joseph C. Ives. They found Johnston, and the president asked him what the army was doing just outside of Richmond. The general explained that the ground on the near bank of the Chickahominy was marshy and the supply of drinking water questionable. Johnston claimed he had simply pulled back to the first good water he could find this side of the river. Supplies were easier to come by here so close to the depots, and besides there was "the advantage of having the river in front rather than in the rear." "An advantage," Davis later observed, "certainly obvious enough, if the line was to be near to it on either of its banks."[190] Then the conversation turned ugly. Neither Davis nor Johnston recorded this part of the exchange, but Ives told Reagan what he had heard. Davis asked Johnston "if Richmond was to be given up without a battle." The general's answer was equivocal. Then Davis, apparently in considerable exasperation, said that if Johnston "was not going to give battle, he would appoint some one to the command who would."[191]

Back at his office, Davis continued to be irritated with Johnston, that same evening directing Robert E. Lee to write him a letter cautioning him about the proper behavior his troops should show toward civilians and their property. He had Lee add a summons for Johnston to report to him. "As you are now so convenient to the city the President wishes you to confer with him upon your future plans, and for that purpose desires you to see him at his office. Please say when it will be convenient for you to come in."[192] All through the next day, Davis expected to see Johnston arriving for conference, but the general neither came nor answered Lee's note. "I have been waiting all day for him to communicate his plans," Davis wrote in a hasty letter to Varina. "We are uncertain of everything except that a battle must be near at hand."[193] A battle must, of course, be fought unless Richmond was to be given up without one, and Davis was far from being the only one who was beginning to have doubts about Johnston's will to commit his army to battle. War Department clerk John B. Jones felt called upon to write "as strong a letter as I could to the President," urging that Richmond be held. "Better die here!" Jones exhorted, than abandon the chief city of Virginia and the Confederacy.[194] Rumors that the city would be left to its fate were current elsewhere too, and the legislature designated a committee to inquire of Davis the government's intentions in the matter. On Tuesday, May 20, the president set their minds at rest on that much at least by announcing that Richmond would be defended. "A thrill of joy electrifies every heart," the ecstatic Jones wrote in his diary.[195]

Davis still had to see that the army made the defense of the city he had promised its citizens. Giving up on hearing anything from Johnston on Monday, Davis resigned himself to making further frequent visits to army headquarters. To facilitate passage through the various sentry posts in Richmond and its outskirts, he had a pass for himself issued by the city's provost marshal. "The bearer," it stated laconically, "is President Davis."[196] Information from Johnston trickled in.[197] On Monday, the general had finished a report of his operations on the Peninsula up to that time and forwarded it to the adjutant and inspector general.[198] Tuesday he wrote about administrative matters but still gave no clue as to his plans for the defense of Richmond.[199] Under the circumstances, Davis was displaying considerable patience, but when Wednesday came with no clue of Johnston's intentions, that patience had reached its limit. He had Lee write a very direct and thorough request for information from Johnston. "The President desires to know the number of troops around Richmond," Lee wrote, "how they are posted, and the organization of the divisions and brigades; also the programme of operations which you propose." He concluded with the suggestion "that you communicate your views on this subject personally to the President," adding that this might be "convenient" for Johnston and "more . . . satisfactory" to Davis.[200]

The next morning Johnston sent one of his aides into the city with a letter for Lee. The dispatch itself has not survived, but judging from Lee's response, it was apparently filled with more of Johnston's complaints over the administrative arrangements in the army's immediate rear areas, matters he had thrown into some disarray by retreating so far as to entangle the administration of his field army with that of the nation's capital. Lee tactfully replied, "I can only assure you that there is no question as to the extent of your authority or command" and went on to explain the arrangements to Johnston. Of a "programme of operations" there was no hint.[201] Growing increasingly impatient, Davis decided to inspect the army and its positions himself. Riding out that afternoon with Lee, he headed for the part of the lines near Mechanicsville, north of the Chickahominy. What they found was not encouraging. The enemy seemed a bit restless that afternoon, and they could hear artillery fire in the distance, but none of the Confederate officers they met seemed to know what was afoot or even what troops were stationed next to their own. The confusion and disorganization in the southern ranks was so severe that Davis concluded that a single Federal division, had it chanced to advance at that point, could have marched right up the turnpike and into Richmond. Back in his office the next day, he wrote a sober note to Johnston, informing him of his findings. He also asked Lee to ride down to the camps again and talk things over with Johnston.[202]

With his great tact, Lee was able to get much more out of the recalcitrant general than had anyone in Richmond up to that time. McClellan had presented the Confederates with the gift Davis had thought too good to be true. He had straddled his army across the Chickahominy swamps close to Richmond and far from the presumed naval support that Johnston so much dreaded. Johnston now shared with Lee that he was contemplating an assault upon one of the sundered halves of the northern army, though which one would depend on the way the situation developed. In any case, he expected to make his attack by the following Thursday, May 29.[203] Lee also urged upon Johnston, apparently more persuasively than heretofore, the importance of his going into the city to brief Davis personally on his plans to forestall the siege McClellan was preparing to lay against the Confederate capital. Thus impressed, Johnston himself rode into the city the next day and finally met with Davis. Although their discussion did not involve the kind of detail the president would have liked, it did, when combined with his previous day's revelations to Lee, suffice to placate the president for the moment.[204] With the basic outlines of the campaign thus charted out, Davis and Johnston could turn their attention to some of their other favorite concerns, as the tension seemed to bring out their characteristic behaviors almost like nervous tics. The day after their meeting, Johnston wrote to Lee complaining that Davis had not accorded higher rank to the army's brigade and division commanders.[205] Meanwhile, Davis was writing to Johnston to urge once again—incredibly—that he brigade the Mississippi regiments together.[206] The next day the president followed up this communication with yet another dispatch on the same subject, to which he added a few lines kindly explaining that Johnston really had all the generals he could need.[207] Of course, Davis should have made additional appointments, and Johnston should have put the Mississippi troops together—both of them long ago—but this was hardly the time for such considerations. Davis, for his part, seems to have been remarkably mild about the whole thing. He was not looking for a fight with Johnston but simply doing what came naturally to him when under great pressure. With Davis and Johnston, the more things changed, the more they stayed the same.

Tension mounted as the impending showdown battle for Richmond drew closer. Lee worked hard at finding reinforcements for Johnston from elsewhere in the Confederacy; the army commander was to have his wish after all for the grand concentration in a climatic battle at the gates of Richmond. Davis fretted. Still, Johnston offered no details on his plan of attack. On Monday the president sent for Lee. What was to be done? Davis believed the Confederates must hit McClellan before he could settle in for a siege, and this could best be done north of the Chickahominy. The idea was one Davis and Lee had discussed previously and on which they were in agreement. "General Johnston should of course advise you of what he expects or proposes to do," Lee concluded. "Let me go and see him, and defer this discussion until I return." When questioned by Lee, Johnston expressed a preference for striking the Federals north of the Chickahominy, near Mechanicsville, and Lee brought the temporarily reassuring news to the president.[208] In fact, Johnston was vacillating between striking the Federals south of the river near the crossroads of Seven Pines, his first choice, or doing so at Mechanicsville, where success would be more effective in preventing the dreaded linkup between McClellan and McDowell.[209] Then on Tuesday, May 27, Johnston received a report that McDowell was moving south from Fredericksburg. This was just what he had feared, and he decided to implement the attack against Mechanicsville immediately.

The next morning Johnston requested that Lee send additional reinforcements. "Every man we have should be here," he wrote. Then, unable to resist the temptation for an "I told you so" to his former friend of Old Army days, he added, "I have more than once suggested a concentration here of all available forces."[210] Excited at the prospect of impending battle, Davis rode out to the front that afternoon, this time taking with him aide Col. William Browne. Arriving at Johnston's headquarters, they learned that the general was out riding his lines. When a courier tracked him down with word that the president was awaiting him at headquarters, Johnston sent back a request that Davis come back a few hours later, and he would have time to talk with him then. When they did talk, Johnston informed Davis of his plans to attack the next morning.[211] That evening, however, matters took a different turn. Johnston had gathered his generals at headquarters to plan the morrow's assault. The meeting was not auspicious. Smith, who was to command the attacking column, was muttering darkly about the strength of the Union position and how this was going to be a "bloody business." All the generals were considerably relieved when in the midst of the meeting news arrived that cavalry scouts now believed McDowell, who unbeknown to the Confederates had been ordered to the Shenandoah Valley several days earlier, was no longer moving south. The next day's battle would now be unnecessary, and Johnston could turn his attention again to obtaining those precise conditions for an attack in the place of his choice south of the Chickahominy.[212]

It seems not to have occurred to Johnston to notify the president of this change in plans. The next morning Davis hurried through his office work and then rode out to the Meadow Bridges, spanning the Chickahominy near Mechanicsville, "to see the action commence." He saw nothing of the sort. Riding about the Confederate lines he found troops doing everything but preparing for an attack. He could find neither Smith nor Johnston, and the subordinate generals he met seemed not to know what was going on. Where was Smith? Someone thought he had taken sick and gone into a farmhouse some yards to the rear, a not unlikely supposition given Smith's normal reaction to nervousness. The president—and the "cavalcade of sightseers" he usually attracted—scouted along the Chickahominy, startling drowsing Yankee pickets, who thought they saw a body of rebel cavalry clattering along the opposite bank. Whether Davis ever did manage to find Smith, and what the general told him if they did meet, is obscured in the confused and conflicting memories of the two men. Whatever might have passed between them, by sundown Davis had turned back toward the city sure only that no Confederate attack was imminent on that front.[213]

Johnston seems not to have known of Davis's unhappy visit to his lines. The general apparently spent a good part of the day at his headquarters attending to administrative matters, including sending Davis an explanation of his continued inability to brigade the Mississippi regiments together.[214] Somehow Davis got the idea that an assault would come off the next day, and so he took another afternoon's ride along the army's lines in the sector where combat was expected. Friday afternoon, however, proved to be as uneventful, and as rainy, as Thursday had been. Save for some inconsequential skirmishing around Fair Oaks station on the Richmond and York River Railroad, it was once again all quiet along the Chickahominy. Saturday morning, the last day of May, Davis packed up a few momentos for shipment to his family, "some valuable books and the sword I wore for many years, together with the pistols used at Monterrey and Buena Vista, and my old dressing case." In a letter he wrote to Varina that morning, he explained, "These articles will have a value to the boys in after time and to you now." In the same letter he commented on the military situation and his opinion of his generals. "Lee," he wrote, "rises with the occasion . . . and seems to be equal to its conception. I hope others will develop capacity in execution."[215] Lee, the reserved intellectual whose conceptions had been behind some of Winfield Scott's Mexican War victories, would do for the planning of operations from a desk in Richmond. Davis believed a stronger hand would be needed to lead the army to victory on the battlefield, and he still hoped, despite the many disappointments, that that hand would be Johnston's.

In mid-afternoon Davis's office work in Richmond was interrupted. Something was afoot down on the Chickahominy. Very likely his first clue was the mutter of distant artillery rising to a steady rumble that precluded any mere sparring by a battery or two on each side. This had the sound of a general engagement. Calling for his horse, the president was off at once, accompanied as usual by a couple of his aides. He was apparently one of the last in Richmond to learn that the struggle for the city was about to commence. War Department clerk Jones recorded in his diary on the thirtieth a report that Johnston would strike the Federal left south of the Chickahominy the next day. On the day of the battle he wrote, "Everybody is upon the tip-toe of expectation. It has been announced (in the streets!) that a battle would take place this day, and hundreds of men, women, and children repaired to the hills to listen, and possibly to see, the firing."[216] If fear of a security leak had prompted Johnston to forego notifying either Davis or Lee of the impending attack—for neither had received such notice—it had been a wasted frustration.[217]

As the president approached Johnston's headquarters house, he saw the general leave it hurriedly, mount up, and gallop off in the direction of the firing, which now was marked distinctly by the higher pitched rattling of massed musketry against the thundering background of the artillery. Johnston had given no indication that he saw Davis drawing near, but the two had been close enough by the time the general spurred his horse away that the staff officers who witnessed the incident "believed that Gen. Johnston saw Mr. Davis approaching, and that he sought to avoid a meeting by mounting quickly and riding rapidly to the extreme front."[218] Johnston may well have wished to avoid any awkward questions the president might have, for at that moment his plan was in disarray.[219] The situation was rapidly headed for a state of disorder every bit as distressing as the one that had brought the president's sober admonition earlier in the week.

It had all seemed so simple. Two Union corps, almost two-fifths of the Federal army, were on the south bank of the Chickahominy, tenuously linked with their comrades on the north bank by a few rickety bridges spanning the rain-swollen river. A violent storm on the night of the thirtieth had raised the river still higher and threatened to wash out the bridges altogether. That was so much the better for the plan Johnston had by then decided to put into action. He would hurl the bulk of his army against the two isolated corps on the south bank. For this purpose he would use three roads that ran roughly parallel from Richmond toward the Federal lines. On the northernmost of the three, the Nine Mile Road, the Confederate left wing would advance. The center column would advance over the Williamsburg Road, and a third column would advance on the right over the southernmost of the highways, the Charles City Road. The left wing would be the main assault, with Longstreet's division in the lead supported by Magruder's and Whiting's, and Johnston planned to take over personal direction of this drive once the action commenced. D. H. Hill's division composed the center column, and Benjamin Huger with his division on the right would support Hill and cover his flank. With reinforcements over the last few weeks having brought his total strength to 97,000—little short of McClellan's own 103,000—Johnston could hope to overwhelm a sizable portion of the Federal army.[220]

The plan had touches of brilliance, though it was perhaps a bit too complicated. If quite a number of things would work as Johnston hoped, the result would be devastating for McClellan and his army. Johnston, however, was notoriously careless of tactical detail, and he had under him a man who was best not left to his own devices. James Longstreet craved the power and recognition of independent command and was not overscrupulous in how he went about getting it. Somewhere between the two of them the plan went

James Longstreet. (Courtesy of National Archives, 111-B-2028)

fatally awry. Johnston had given Longstreet no written orders but had explained to him in person the role he expected him to play in the day's attack. Just what passed between them and what passed through Longstreet's mind during the hours preceding the attack is unknown. Longstreet may simply have grossly misconstrued his orders.[221] On the other hand, he may have decided that the idea of operating under the immediate supervision of the army commander offered insufficient opportunity to win recognition on his own. A slight alteration in the battle plan would fix that.[222]

So it was that in the early morning hours of May 31, as troops moved to their final attack positions, Whiting found his way blocked on the Nine Mile Road by Longstreet's division marching back toward Richmond. Longstreet was countermarching in order to shift his troops down to the Williamsburg Road, allowing him to come into the attack behind D. H. Hill, whom he outranked, and away from the watchful eye of Johnston. This unauthorized move also brought the Georgian's division across the path of Huger's right-wing troops as they headed for their jump-off point. At the place where the road crossed Gillies Creek, the bridge was washed out and the rain-swollen stream was to be crossed on a makeshift replacement bridge only a single plank wide. Both divisions needed to cross, and the question was whose would go first. It came down to a matter of rank, which Longstreet claimed to have more of. Each man was a major general, and the matter turned on date of rank. Huger stated his, which happened to be considerably prior to Longstreet's. Lying glibly, the Georgian confidently claimed to be the senior and ordered Huger to wait while his entire 14,000-man division walked single file over the one-plank bridge. Then, because the attack plans called for Huger to go in first, while Longstreet was in the process of putting his own division in the second wave, he had his men wait by the side of the road on the far bank of the creek while Huger's division crossed and then passed his own on its much-delayed way to the battle.[223]

The result was that the battle that was supposed to begin early in the morning did not start until 1:00 P.M. Longstreet knew who was to blame for that. A few days later he was loudly proclaiming that it was all Huger's fault. He had a way of stating these things with such assurance that people believed him, and Johnston, partly to cover up his own embarrassing failure to see to the execution of his plan, knowingly joined the deception, even persuading G. W. Smith to alter his report of the battle to correspond with Longstreet's fictional version. Huger protested and demanded a court of inquiry but to no avail. In the end, his career was ruined.[224] But all that still lay in the future, as Johnston waited impatiently at his headquarters for the sounds that would tell him that his plan for the destruction of the two Union corps had been set in motion. To the south, however, where D. H. Hill was to open the assault as soon as Huger moved into position on his right, came only silence. Nor was there any sign that Longstreet was in his place on the Nine Mile Road. Unaware of his subordinate's strange twisting of his plan, Johnston had ordered one of his aides to ride east on the Nine Mile Road until he came up with Longstreet's division, but hours had passed and he had not returned. In fact, the young officer had cantered off down the empty road all the way into Union lines, where he had been made a prisoner.[225] For several hours Johnston was in the unenviably embarrassing position of an army commander who had completely lost a 14,000-man division.

It was 10:00 before Johnston discovered what had become of the errant Longstreet. By then calling him back to his assigned sector would have taken even more time and further deranged the plan. The only option now seemed to be doing it Longstreet's way or not at all. Johnston wavered, but true to form in a man who would not so much as discharge his fowling piece unless conditions were perfect, he leaned increasingly toward the latter option, telling a staff officer "he wished the troops were back in their camps." He might have sent them there, too, had not Robert E. Lee arrived at his headquarters about that time.[226] The day before, Lee had sent Johnston a note offering to help in any way he could in the battle that everyone knew must be coming within the next week. Johnston's answer had been vague, but Lee, sensing events moving toward a climax, had ridden out anyway to see what he could do.[227] With his classmate and longtime friend and rival present, Johnston apparently found that his pride would no longer let him turn back.

Still, he seems to have hoped that perhaps his subordinate commanders might abort the attack on their own. The day wore on. Noon passed. Then from the direction of the Williamsburg Road came the unmistakable sounds of firing—musketry, Lee thought; only an artillery duel, Johnston insisted. Whether there was, as Johnston explained in his report, a strange acoustic phenomenon at work here that allowed others around the headquarters house to hear the sounds of pitched battle while Johnston heard only a sullen muttering of desultory artillery fire, or whether the general's ears were subject to his wish that the present nightmare was one from which he might yet awake is impossible to say, but such illusions, whether of ear or of mind, were soon dispelled. At 4:00 P.M. a message from Longstreet arrived. The battle had not only been joined but was nearing its decision while most of the Confederate forces planned for it remained idle.[228]

In fact, the troops on the Williamsburg Road had been hotly engaged for some three hours by this time. Bearing the brunt of the fighting was D. H. Hill's division. Hill was a difficult man, sour, critical, sometimes downright mean-spirited. He had tremendous capacity for hating and for fighting and however unpleasant he might have been to have about camp, he was just the man any commanding general would wish to have at the head of a division in combat. With vigor and skill he hammered away at the hated Yankees hour after hour.[229] Longstreet, whose seniority—genuine this time—gave him command on this part of the field, was not doing much to help. Before the war was over, the Georgian was to gain a reputation as a solid corps commander, and that renown was not entirely unearned. Longstreet had a basic nuts-and-bolts competence about him, a workmanlike grasp of the unspectacular mechanics of handling large bodies of troops in camp, on the march, or on the battlefield. In action he could generally manipulate his brigades where and when he wanted them, and that was a talent not possessed by many a Civil War general of far greater intellect and genius for the art of war. An added strength of no small significance was the sense of calmness and confidence he seemed to exude. "He was like a rock in steadiness when sometimes in battle the world seemed flying to pieces," an admirer wrote.[230] That was worth a great deal in a general. Give Longstreet a top-notch superior, one who would keep close tabs on him and who possessed both brains enough to know what Longstreet ought to do and force of personality enough to make him do it, and the Georgian could indeed be a faithful "Old Warhorse," as Lee nicknamed him. But Lee was to be the only general who would ever get solid service from the self-satisfied Longstreet. On this last day of May 1862, in the woods and fields around the Williamsburg Road, Longstreet was showing part of the reason why.

Much as he might convey the impression of profound wisdom, his actions betrayed unmistakably that he required guidance in the application of his skills. After sending in Hill, Longstreet fumbled about while Hill's four brigades did virtually all the fighting. With the other nine brigades at his disposal Longstreet accomplished next to nothing. He sent Huger's three, along with three from his own division, wandering off down Charles City Road, where they spent the rest of the day marching back and forth aimlessly in response to a series of contradictory orders from Longstreet. He posted another of his brigades to guard against an attack from his left rear—precisely the direction in which lay the remainder of the Confederate army. Only one of the two remaining brigades did he manage to put into the fight alongside Hill's struggling soldiers. In all, Longstreet used just 12,500 of the 29,500 men under his command. Yet the hard-driving Hill actually managed to make some headway, though at terrible cost in casualties. By late afternoon his troops were nearing the end of their tether, and so it was that Longstreet finally got around to informing his army commander that he had opened a pitched battle and asking that the left wing of the army advance to support his attack.[231]

This was the message Johnston received at 4:00 P.M., and that occasioned his departure from headquarters, hastened perhaps by the approach of the president to whom lengthy and embarrassing explanations would have to be given. Hurrying to the front, Johnston laid hold of the first brigades he encountered, regardless of chain of command or divisional affiliation, hastily chivvied them into line, and sent them stumbling forward through field, forest, and bog along the axis of the Nine Mile Road in the general direction of what should have been the exposed northern flank of the Federals then opposing Hill. A few hours earlier it would have been just that. Now, however, the advancing Confederate brigades—those who managed to wade the swamps and avoid getting lost in the woods—ran head-on into a big, unshaken, and seemingly unshakable Union formation. These were fresh troops, the II Corps division of John Sedgwick, which would prove to be one of the toughest fighting divisions in the Army of the Potomac under one of its most able officers. They were some of the troops Johnston had thought he would not have to deal with that day, for they had camped the night before on the north bank of the Chickahominy. In response to Hill's attack on the Williamsburg Road, their hard-nosed corps commander, Brig. Gen. Edwin V. Sumner, had ordered them across the one remaining flood-battered—in some places even partially submerged—bridge. The span had collapsed not long after, but it had held long enough to put these stubborn fighters squarely across the path of the one remaining move Johnston had thought was open to him. Now all the Confederates he could hurl at them would not be enough to push them out of the way. As the shadows stretched across the soggy landscape, one southern brigade after another in disjointed and bloody assaults lashed furiously but futilely at the Federal line.[232]

Back at headquarters, Davis had watched Johnston ride out of sight and then recognized Lee's horse standing hitched in front of the house. Going inside, the president found Lee and asked him what the musketry fire he had heard was all about. Had Davis heard it too? Lee explained he had thought so himself, but Johnston had insisted "it could be nothing more than an artillery duel." Together, Davis and Lee walked out of the house to listen more. Now they were certain. This was no skirmish but a full-scale battle. Mounting up quickly, they galloped toward the sound of the guns, followed by the president's aides. On the way they passed various bodies of Confederate troops moving up toward the fighting, and they stopped briefly at the headquarters of General Magruder, though he was apparently able to tell them little of what was going on. While they were there, Postmaster General Reagan dropped in for a moment before hurrying off again toward the sound of the firing. Davis and his party soon followed. About a mile from Johnston's headquarters they finally reached the front lines, and bullets were soon clipping twigs and tree branches around them. Before them lay a soggy oat field, on the far side of which the Federals obviously had their battle line in the thick woods that fringed the clearing. Equally obvious to any trained military man was the fact that this flanking attack—and with it the South's hopes for victory in the battle—was going nowhere until these stubborn Yankees were dislodged.[233]

Johnston had gone off to the right somewhere, but plenty of other exalted personages were in evidence along the line. Besides the president and general in chief, the secretary of war and various members of Congress dashed about bent on furthering the Confederate cause. Reagan, being apparently of a practical turn of mind, had somewhere procured a rifle and begun taking potshots at the Yankees while working his way off to the right to try to find his state's brigade. Davis, feeling that something must be done, sent a courier back to Magruder's headquarters to order him to try to get a brigade around the Union flank. Magruder, however, had gone forward himself and was nowhere to be found. When another messenger failed to locate him, Davis was on the point of going in search of him personally when one of the couriers returned with word that he had given the order to one of Magruder's brigadiers instead, and that the troops were moving up at once. But it was too late. Through the gathering dusk, Davis saw the remainder of the Confederate line go forward through the open field against the front of the Federal position. The result was another bloody repulse, and the beaten troops came streaming back through the oat field in what looked like the beginning of a first-rate stampede.[234]

Davis ordered the flanking attack called off—it would now be a waste—and spurred his horse forward to try to rally the fleeing survivors of the failed attack. Lee and the staff officers joined him in the effort. They had just succeeded, with much cajoling and pleading, in getting some sort of a battle line cobbled together again when the warlike postmaster general returned from his sector of the field. He had just left Johnston, he said, in a very forward position foolishly—as Reagan believed—exposing himself to enemy fire and deaf to the cabinet member's entreaties that he go to the rear. Now Reagan was irate that the president and the general in chief were displaying a similar lack of prudence, and he berated them hotly for taking unnecessary risks. It is probably an indication of what the heat of battle does to the processes of the mind that the postmaster general, pausing from his assumed role as sharpshooter, could feel called upon to remonstrate with high-ranking military leaders for being under fire. Davis took no heed of his objections. A few minutes later someone brought news from the right that

Johnston had been killed. "After a short interval," Reagan later recalled, "he was brought past us on a stretcher, apparently in a lifeless condition."[235]

In fact, he was conscious, though in considerable pain. He had been struck by a musket ball in the shoulder, and a moment later a chunk of shrapnel from an exploding shell had knocked him off his horse, seriously wounded. Davis hurried to the stretcher, "manifesting great concern" for the general's well-being.[236] Old differences forgotten for the moment, the president spoke in friendly terms to Johnston.[237] For now though, more pressing matters demanded attention, chief of them the question of the army's leadership now that Johnston would obviously be out of action for some months to come, if indeed he recovered at all. Just then Gustavus Smith appeared, having himself just learned of Johnston's wounding, a fact that made him by rank the new commanding officer of the army. Davis was eager to talk to him and find out his views. It would have been a difficult position for anyone, but Smith seemed to convey an impression of more than understandable inadequacy. Johnston's enthusiasm for Smith as a general seems to have been waning slightly for some time, especially since Smith had snored through the crucial meeting on the defense of the Peninsula. The army's second in command was becoming somewhat of an odd man out, and now he had only the most perfunctory understanding of the situation. He related Johnston's plan for the battle and Longstreet's alteration of it. Johnston had gone off to see to affairs farther to the right, and Smith knew nothing of what had gone on there. As for what the army's next move should be, Smith explained lamely when questioned by Davis that he really needed more information. They might be able to advance, or at least hold their ground, unless they had to retreat. The president left the interview with a distinct feeling of dissatisfaction.[238]

Davis and Lee rode the seven miles back to Richmond together. If Davis used any of the ride for reflection on the last three months, he would have had plenty to think about. His chief goal in Virginia had been the protection of Richmond and rightly so. The difficulty had come in attempting to work with Johnston toward that end. The general had refused to communicate adequately and, even more alarmingly, had displayed a tendency to lose his nerve, to retreat prematurely, and to postpone the day of battle whenever possible. Davis had retained an amazing degree of faith in Johnston, partly because of Johnston's genuine theoretical skill and partly because his cautious, low-risk approach to the war mirrored Davis's own—but without the president's intestinal fortitude. Davis had tried to improve relations with Johnston but not to the point of giving up his pet schemes about army reorganization. The president had not realized the need to give explicit instruction to Johnston. Thus he had seen his wishes twisted to meet the general's preferences in the matter of retreat from Manassas and from the Peninsula. In the end, Johnston had forced on Davis precisely the strategy he had rejected at their lengthy conference in March: a massive concentration for a desperate battle in front of Richmond. Yet even when successful at last in imposing his will on his government, Johnston had not risked battle except under heavy pressure from Davis. Had Johnston escaped the May 31 battle unscathed, there is as much reason as not to conclude that he would have abandoned Richmond without fighting a second engagement. If his record is any clue, he would have given only the shortest of notice when that time came. Yet Davis overlooked the basic character flaw in this general and continued to regard him as his most skillful commander.

Far different had been the president's relations with the man whose horse now trotted beside his own up the road to Richmond. Lee was tactful, courteous, and a pleasure to work with. He had a solid military reputation among those well acquainted with the Old Army. Davis seemed to consider him a perhaps overly cautious maker of brilliant plans—with just a trace of the intellectual's hesitancy and lack of drive—but a good officer for all that.[239] Loath to part with Lee's help in Richmond, in this crisis—with the enemy at the gates, Johnston incapacitated, and Smith incapable—Davis had no choice. Before they reached the city, he had made his decision. Turning to his companion, he announced that he was placing him in command of the army. Lee was to take over the reins first thing in the morning. With that, Davis opened a new epoch in his relations with his generals in Virginia.

5

THE STAKE IS TOO HIGH

The crash of battle split the early morning stillness of June 1, 1862. It was Sunday, but there was no Sabbath of rest for the two armies still locked in deadly embrace a few miles east of Richmond. Along the roads between the Confederate capital and the fighting front flowed long processions of human misery–the wounded, thousands of them, moving painfully along in assorted ambulances and less commodious wagons toward the inadequate facilities and dubious comforts the city could offer men in their condition. Within the city, at the plain but comfortable townhouse that served as the Confederacy's "White House," Jefferson Davis rose early. He had arrived back at the mansion after his ride to the front at about 9:30 the evening before and probably spent some hours dispatching business before retiring.[1] Pressing for his attention at this early morning hour were matters involving his top generals and the high command of the army then fighting to keep McClellan's bluecoats out of the city.

Following up his words to Lee during their ride home the evening before, he sent the general a note formally charging him with command of "the armies in Eastern Virginia and in North Carolina." Davis expressed his regret at the "unfortunate casualty" that had removed Johnston from his position and made it "necessary to interfere temporarily with" Lee's duties as general in chief under Davis "but only so far as to make you available for command in the field of a particular army."[2] The president was not eager to hear a renewed chorus of demands from the press and politicians to install a general in chief, and he apparently planned to emphasize early and often that Lee continued to fill that office.[3] In fact, over the coming months, Lee would do little more than advise Davis about affairs beyond his own army and that infrequently, but Davis's main goal was accomplished in that no general in chief was appointed to replace Lee for almost two years, and then it was by Davis's choice and a man with whom he could work.[4] For the present, Davis gave Lee written orders to "assume command . . . and give such orders as may be needful and proper."[5]

That settled, the president could turn his attention to other matters for several hours, secure in the knowledge that the intellectual and impressive Lee, rather than the unimpressive Smith, was at the helm. A few hours later, Davis once again rode toward the scene of the morning's fighting, where the sounds of battle were already subsiding into isolated spatters of picket fire. It was not an easy ride through the army's rear areas along roads choked with ambulances and supply wagons. It got no easier, and a good deal more dangerous, as he neared the front. The evening before he had urged Smith to keep the army where it was, avoiding a further withdrawal toward Richmond.[6] Now he had the impression that Lee would be seeing to it that the army held its ground. With that thought in mind, Davis rode toward last night's army headquarters. Just as he turned onto the Nine Mile Road, he saw an officer running toward him across a field. It turned out to be General Whiting, who informed the president that he was "riding into the position of the enemy." Confederate forces had pulled back after all, and the Federals, following up, were now in their place. Whiting pointed out to Davis a Union battery, "which," he added, "I am surprised has not fired on you."[7]

It was not a pleasant surprise for Davis, nor was it his last of the day. When he finally found his way to army headquarters about 1:30 and asked for Lee, he discovered that the general was not there and had not been there that morning. So shocked did Davis appear at this news that Smith was moved to asked him "if he had any special reason for supposing General Lee would be there at that time." Davis replied that he had ordered Lee to take command of the army early that morning. "Ah!" replied Smith, "in that case he will probably soon be here." Davis was invited to take a seat and await the general's arrival. Thus the president passed what could only have been an uncomfortable half-hour, making small talk with Smith. Finally, about 2:00, Lee came in.[8] He had left Richmond about an hour earlier to carry out the order given to him by the president verbally the night before and in writing early that morning.[9] That morning he was so far from taking command that he had, about 5:00 A.M., responded to a dispatch from Smith very much in the tone of a supervising general in chief operating from the capital. "Your movements are judicious and determination to strike the enemy right," he wrote to the man he was supposed to have replaced. "You are right in calling upon me for what you want. I wish I could do more."[10] It was Smith who had directed that morning's fighting, and with a vacillation and bungling that had vitiated whatever opportunities may have remained for the battle plan in which Johnston had placed such confidence little more than twenty-four hours earlier.[11] What moved Lee to delay his assumption of command remains a mystery. It may be that he wanted to allow Smith to finish the battle first, or perhaps he was embarrassed at superseding Smith at all. Maybe it was all just a little too sudden. At any rate, Lee's course was not at all what Davis expected and, at least from the president's point of view, was not a promising beginning for the new commander's tenure at the head of the army.

Smith gave Lee an extensive briefing on the morning's fighting and the situation of the army at the moment. Davis listened until about 3:00 and then left and rode out to see the army's position for himself. He rode toward the area that had seen the heaviest fighting both that day and Saturday, Longstreet's position on the Williamsburg Road. Others had the same idea, and before his tour of inspection was over he had been joined by half a dozen generals, at least three cabinet members, and assorted other luminaries. Lee himself came up before the president completed his observations and returned to the city.[12] Davis took time that evening to visit the wounded Johnston. He offered to let the general stay at the Confederate White House during his recovery, but Johnston's staff had made other arrangements.[13] Clearly, however, Johnston was to be out of action for some months to come, and the fate of the army—and the Confederacy—was to rest with Lee.

That was no reassuring thought for many a Confederate after Lee's misfortunes in West Virginia the previous fall. When he insisted that the army begin an immediate program of thorough entrenchment, his popularity dropped still further. Lee was now "the King of Spades" and compared unfavorably in the press to Jackson, whose exploits in the Shenandoah Valley, partially set up by Lee himself, were presently capturing the hearts and imaginations of the southern people. Across the lines, McClellan smugly announced that he preferred Lee to Johnston. Lee, he opined, was "too cautious and weak under grave responsibility . . . wanting in moral firmness when pressed by heavy responsibility, and . . . likely to be timid and irresolute in action."[14] No description could have fit Lee less or McClellan more, but few at this juncture would have ventured to gainsay him, even— had they been on speaking terms with the Federal commander—the officers and men of Lee's own army. A soldier in the ranks wrote home, "I know little about [Lee]. . . . But I doubt his being better than Johnston or Longstreet."[15] Longstreet himself would later write that "the assignment of General Lee to command the army of Northern Virginia was far from reconciling the troops to the loss of our beloved chief, Joseph E. Johnston." Longstreet pointed out that Lee had led an army to failure in the West Virginia campaign and although he had performed creditably as an engineer officer on the southern coast and in the Mexican War fifteen years before, those were but weak recommendations. "Officers of the line," Longstreet observed gravely, "are not apt to look to the staff in choosing leaders of soldiers, either in tactics or strategy. There were, therefore, some misgivings as to the power and skill for field service of the new commander."[16] The consensus on Lee in early June 1862 was clear. To soldiers and civilians North and South, Lee was at best a brainy and diligent staff officer of uncertain value as a leader of men or director of armies.[17]

But what was he to Davis? In later years the Confederate president would claim to have had complete faith in Lee from the very outset. No success of that general had come as a surprise to him. Lee's stunning strengths had been clear to Davis when hardly another could see them. In the wake of Lee's wartime brilliance and the memory of his courtesy, such things were easy for Davis to say and no doubt sincerely believe. In fact, however, things are rarely that simple, and Davis's assessment of Lee in June 1862 was no exception. Lee had been an engineer officer during much of his time in the Old Army, and Davis, whose low rank in his West Point graduating class precluded such service for him, seems at this time still to have harbored the same sort of prejudice against engineer officers that many Confederates were now expressing toward Lee.[18] Lee had been a handy person to have at the seat of government for directing military affairs in secondary theaters, but Davis had hitherto given no indication that he considered him of primary use in the field. In the present crisis, Lee had been the only alternative to leaving the army in the not particularly capable hands of Gustavus W. Smith. There, at least, the choice was clear.

Whatever Davis's estimate of Lee as a field commander may have been, he clearly found him likable. The president even appeared eager to maintain cordial relations with Lee and to avoid the unpleasant feelings that had, largely through no fault of his own, hindered his efforts to use Beauregard and Johnston. When, on his first full day in command, Lee sent a note to Davis asking for the appointment of several new brigadier generals, the president complied with alacrity. He granted virtually all that Lee requested that very same day, and though he made a few suggestions as to how the newly promoted officers should be employed, he was quick to add, "You will know best how to dispose of these officers." Then in a comment that was to characterize much of the relationship that would develop between these two men he added, "I give you the material to be used at your discretion." Elsewhere in the dispatch, Davis touched on what had been one of his chief irritations with Johnston, a lack of communication. "Please keep me advised," the president wrote, "as frequently as your engagements will permit of what is passing before and around you."[19]

Johnston had never kept Davis well posted on events in his front, and Davis had never been so quick and compliant in meeting that general's requests. Clearly, a new day had dawned for the force that Lee was now beginning to style as the Army of Northern Virginia. Johnston himself was one of the first to recognize this. To those who bemoaned his wounding as a disaster for the Confederacy, he explained, "The shot that struck me down is the very best that has been fired for the southern cause yet. For I possess in no degree the confidence of our government, and now they have in my place one who does possess it."[20] Johnston probably underestimated the professional esteem in which Davis still held him and overestimated the president's confidence in Lee's abilities, but he had recognized the fact that Lee had a good working relationship with Jefferson Davis that Johnston had not had for nearly a year. The difference lay not with Davis but with the generals themselves.

These early June days found Davis, as was often the case during his public life, severely hampered by illness. Sunday, the first, had been a hot day, and the president's ride to the front in that weather seems to have left him very much the worse for wear. To Lee he explained in a note the next day that he was "so unwell today that I have delayed to go out until an important contingency may require."[21] Tuesday saw temperatures in the mid-90s again, but either rising strength or growing anxiety put the president back in the saddle and on the road for the army's encampment and a personal inspection of the situation. As he rode out the Nine Mile Road he noticed a large number of horses standing hitched in front of a house on the left; among them was one he had seen Lee riding. Dismounting and entering the house, Davis found Lee in conference with his brigade and division commanders. Lee was saying little, and the subordinate officers were lamenting the evils of their situation. Whiting, characteristically, was particularly gloomy in alluding to the disparity in Union and Confederate troop strength. A few minutes prior to Davis's arrival Lee had remonstrated at such reflections. "Stop, stop," he had protested. "If you go to ciphering we are whipped beforehand." The entry of the president had not significantly changed the flow of the conversation nor deterred Whiting from a gloomy recitation of the various elements of siege craft by which McClellan was bound to beat them in the end. This was too much for Davis. He "expressed, in marked terms" his "disappointment at hearing such views." Lee explained that only a few minutes before he had "said very much the same thing." Reassured somewhat, Davis listened a few more minutes before slipping out and riding off to continue his reconnaissance.[22]

Not long after, Lee dismissed the meeting. The officers returned to their camps no wiser about his plans, but Lee had gained valuable insights into their states of mind. In an interesting postscript to the meeting, it was only a matter of days before Whiting's division was reduced by the transfer of units to less than half its previous size.[23] Meanwhile, the meeting concluded, Lee rode off after the president, catching up with him as he surveyed the front. Lee quickly turned the conversation to the present military crisis and asked what course Davis thought best to take under the circumstances. Johnston would never have dreamed of putting such a question to the president. With Lee it seemed natural. Whether the general asked in order to gratify Davis's vanity in his own military sagacity or for the purpose of obtaining valuable military advice, he got both, for Davis's pride was not unfounded. He suggested reversion to a plan that he and Lee had previously discussed for execution by Johnston's army: an attack on the portion of McClellan's force north of the Chickahominy. The original design had called for A. P. Hill's oversized division to be brought around on the exposed Federal right flank and rear. Now, however, Davis believed that in order to defeat the undoubtedly strengthened Union defenses, it would be necessary to draw Jackson's Valley army to the scene and throw it, rather than Hill's division, at the Federal flank.[24]

Lee continued successfully cultivating good relations with Davis. Feeling between them was friendly enough that when the president noticed the rough gait of the gray horse Lee had acquired in the West Virginia mountains the previous winter—a horse Lee had named "Traveler"—he offered to lend him one of his own fine horses. In a polite note, Lee declined but expressed to Davis his "full sense & appreciation of your kindness & great gratitude for your friendship."[25] Davis renewed the offer three days later, and again Lee very gently turned it down. So confident was the general now in his good relations with the president that he ventured in the same note to express disagreement with Davis's cherished scheme for brigading regiments by states. "I fear the result," he said of the plan: "Nor do I think it the best organization. I would rather command a brigade composed of regts from different states." He went on to explain why he thought so and to suggest that "officers looking to political preferment" might wish for state brigades. This was no statement to make lightly to Jefferson Davis, who on occasion had taken personal umbrage at less blunt utterances. Lee, however, smoothly glided on to conclude, "But as it is your wish . . . I will attempt what can be done."[26] A relationship carefully cultivated by both men and sound enough to allow such open and honest communication was a definite advantage to Lee and Davis.

Secure in this, Lee could turn his attention to stopping and driving back the foe that threatened Richmond. He went to work on the organization of his own army, making some improvements but unfortunately eliminating Johnston's subdivision of the force into two wings and a reserve.[27] The wing arrangement had been Johnston's way of circumventing Davis's denial of army corps. Although they had been at best makeshift formations led by their senior division commanders, they had offered some enhancement of the army's ability to maneuver and fight beyond the range of its commander's vision. If this reversion was a concession to the president, it was to prove an expensive one. Even Lee seems not to have grasped the need for corps organization until hard experience taught him that lesson.

At the same time Lee continued his emphasis on entrenchment, notwithstanding the "ridicule" of—as he put it—"troops, officers, community, & press." To Davis, Lee explained, "Why should we leave to [McClellan] the whole advantage of labour. . . . There is nothing so military as labour, & nothing so important to an army as to save the lives of its soldiers." Confident though he might be in Davis's friendly regard, Lee would never make the mistake of becoming complacent about Davis's goodwill. He cultivated it constantly. In the same dispatch, after relating some matters of internal army organization, Lee concluded, "Our position requires you should know everything & you must excuse my troubling you."[28] This was exactly what Davis had always wanted and never gotten from Johnston.

Gratified as he undoubtedly was with Lee's communicativeness, Davis was far from contenting himself with only such knowledge of the army as he could gain in dispatches. Daily he rode out to view the camps and lines for himself. Nothing, it seemed, could deter him, as his dismayed aide-de-camp and riding companion learned one day during the week after Seven Pines, when thunderclouds boiled up on the horizon. Davis rode on, and when the storm struck they were quickly soaked. The president, however, seemed to enjoy it. "The wetter we became," the aide wrote in a letter to his wife a few days later, "the higher his spirits rose." At a rain-swollen stream, Davis "ploughed" in and crossed with ease, while the less well-mounted aide had a considerable struggle getting to the other side.[29] Rain was a frequent occurrence during these days, and the roads, unpaved and now frequented by heavily loaded supply wagons, were "awful."[30] "You have seen nothing like the roads on the Chick[ahomin]y bottom," Lee wrote the president.[31] He was wrong; Davis was riding those very roads on a regular basis. "The roads to the different positions of the Army could not be worse and remain passable," he wrote in a letter to Varina.[32] Despite the fatigue and exposure, his various ailments, which were in fact closely tied to his mental and emotional state, began to abate. To Varina he described himself as being in "usual health," despite the fact that "the weather has been very inclement."[33] For Davis, it was a relief to be able to do something, anything, rather than await events in the confinement and, to him, unrewarding political activities of Richmond.

Such diversion might be healthy, but the problem remained of what to do about McClellan's army at the gates. On this question, Davis's thoughts fell more and more under the sway of Lee's persuasive mind. In a letter to his wife, the president defended Lee's policy of entrenchment, not surprising in view of the fact that Davis was also a West Point graduate. Most striking, however, was that he did so with the same ideas and in almost the same words that Lee had used in writing to him just a few days before.[34] In more consequential matters as well, the president took his lead from the general. On June 1, Alexander R. Boteler, a member both of the Confederate Congress and of Stonewall Jackson's staff, wired Richmond that Jackson's Valley force was badly threatened: "Jackson wants reinforcements immediately if possible." Boteler followed his telegram as rapidly as rails would carry him and arrived in Richmond a day or two behind it. In lengthy discussions with Davis, he explained Jackson's accomplishments, situation, and wants.[35] The president sent him back with a letter to the general, praising Jackson's accomplishments but explaining that he could send no significant reinforcements.[36] At this point, Davis was still thinking like Johnston in terms of a maximum concentration of forces near Richmond. That would soon change.

The next day Lee wrote to Davis suggesting, "After much reflection I think if it was possible to reinforce Jackson strongly, it would change the character of the War." Lee explained that he envisioned Jackson seizing the initiative and crossing the Potomac, forcing the enemy to respond and to fight on terms the Confederates would dictate. Otherwise, Lee explained, McClellan would proceed by the slow-but-sure processes of siege, and the outcome would be as certain as that foreseen by Whiting at the meeting of generals two days before. "It will require 100,000 men to resist the regular siege of Richmond, which perhaps would only prolong not save it," Lee wrote. The answer, besides Jackson's projected offensive move, was "preparing a line that I can hold with part of our forces in front, while with the rest I will endeavour to make a diversion to bring McClellan out" of his entrenchments. Hinting at what he believed to be the enemy's weakness, Lee noted that McClellan "is obliged to adhere to the [railroad] unless he can reach James river to provision his Army."[37]

This program combined aspects of Davis's own earlier suggestion with some far more daring and aggressive elements that were Lee's own. Though the grand offensive by Jackson into the North did not become a reality, the whole scheme was indicative of Lee's style of strategic thinking in the aspects that differentiated it from that of Johnston or Davis. Although the latter two would take the offensive if risks were low enough–very low indeed in Johnston's case–Lee was prepared to accept enormous risks. Johnston and Davis naturally tended to favor concentration of force first, last, and always, but Lee was willing to divide his forces in the preliminary stages of a campaign in order to disperse and confuse an enemy, the better to destroy him when Lee's forces converged for the kill. Although Johnston and, to a lesser extent, Davis, tended to feel that they gained strength relative to the enemy the farther they drew back into their own territory, Lee felt strongest when he had the enemy at long arm's length, with plenty of room to maneuver. Davis and Johnston were inclined to await the enemy's movement and react accordingly, but Lee always preferred to take the initiative himself. Most important, Davis and especially Johnston thought primarily in terms of avoiding defeat, while Lee sought victory and hoped to make it complete. At bottom, Davis and Lee seemed to differ in their conceptions of what would be needed to establish a Confederate nation. If, for Davis, the war could be won simply by not losing, for Lee, who never appeared to share his commander in chief's unquestioning confidence in the rightness or the ultimate success of the cause, it could be lost simply by not winning. A would-be nation of people whose loyalties were divided and consciences uneasy–people who felt as Lee had before committing himself beyond hope of turning back–would need resounding victories and an early peace, or its morale was bound to crumble. For the moment such differences of viewpoint and approach between the president and his new Virginia army commander were almost entirely latent, but they lay behind the new and daring strategic thinking toward which Lee drew his supportive but still uncertain commander in chief.

The sway he already held over Davis could hardly have been more dramatically emphasized than in the events of the same day, June 5. Orders from Richmond set troops in motion to reinforce Jackson, troops that otherwise would have been drawn into the army before Richmond under the old policy of massive concentration.[38] Five days later came an even greater test of the president's growing confidence in Lee. The general proposed sending two more brigades to Jackson, having him crush the Federals he now faced, then rapidly drawing him eastward to the Peninsula, where with additional reinforcements he would execute the contemplated flank attack on McClellan. That much, at least, was something Davis had long foreseen. The part about weakening the army before Richmond to reinforce Jackson first was a touch of Lee's own audacity. "McClellan will not move out of his intrenchments," Lee reminded the president, unless "forced, which this must accomplish." He promised that he could hold the Federals in their present position for another week or ten days, and Davis gave his consent.[39] With this as with other of Lee's ideas, the president was soon thinking of it as his own. "I will endeavor," he wrote Varina the next day, "by movements which are not without great hazard to countervail the enemy's policy. If we succeed in rendering his works useless to him and compel him to meet us on the field, I have much confidence in our ability to give him a complete defeat." That might open the way for invasion of the North. Meanwhile, "we are reinforcing Gen. Jackson and hope to crown his successes with a complete victory over all the enemy in the Valley."[40]

Events, however, took a different course. On the eighth, Lee had written Jackson suggesting that the "decisive moment" was approaching for the struggle for Richmond and asking whether Jackson thought he could give the Federals in the Valley the slip and bring his army to Richmond.[41] On June 13, Jackson wired his reply. The situation in the Valley was now at a standstill, and Jackson's force could come when Lee thought best. Lee sent the telegram on to Davis, noting, "I think the sooner Jackson can move this way, the better. The first object now is to defeat McClellan." Davis endorsed the document simply, "Views concurred in."[42] That set plans in motion for a Confederate offensive on the Peninsula before the end of the month. At some time during these weeks, Lee briefed Davis on the precise form this offensive would take. On the south bank of the Chickahominy, directly in front of Richmond and the bulk of McClellan's army, only a third of Lee's total strength would remain in the trenches. The rest he would concentrate on the north bank in order to gain a local numerical advantage. As soon as Jackson's force swung in on McClellan's exposed northern flank, Lee would fling the rest of his assault force at the crumbling Union line to complete the rout. Destroying the Union right would expose McClellan's railroad supply line back to his depot at White House Landing on the Pamunkey River and leave the northern general in desperate straits. Lee hoped and expected it would set the scene for what he intended should happen next: the destruction of the Union Army of the Potomac.[43]

For Davis, however, the force to be left covering Richmond was too weak. Even with the aid of its extensive entrenchments, it could not stop a determined Federal assault of the magnitude McClellan would be capable of throwing at it. Davis had a high opinion of McClellan, having favored him with a number of choice appointments when he was secretary of war and McClellan a young officer during the mid-1850s. "If," as Davis put it, "McClellan was the man I took him for . . . as soon as he found that the bulk of our army was on the north side of the Chickahominy, he would not stop to try conclusions with it there, but would immediately move upon his objective point, the city of Richmond." That could be disastrous for the Confederates. The president conceded that "if, on the other hand, [McClellan] should behave like an engineer officer, and deem it his first duty to protect his line of communication," the plan "would be a success." Lee was irritated by such implied criticism of his former branch. He "did not know," he said, that "engineer officers were more likely than others to make such mistakes." Quickly checking himself, however, Lee took a more practical approach. "If you will hold him as long as you can at the intrenchment," he assured the president, "and then fall back on the detached works around the city, I will be upon the enemy's heels before he gets there."[44]

With that, the president's consent was gained. Once again, Davis had found it impossible to refuse Lee's combination of strong arguments and—almost—unshakable courtesy. Still, it was not always a comfortable thing for Davis, with his essentially defensive outlook, to be dragged along in the wake of Lee's brilliant but fundamentally more aggressive thinking, and this made for some very mixed feelings on the president's part. He professed, and sometimes probably felt, great confidence in Lee. To William Preston Johnston, his young aide-de-camp, he said that he had "perfect confidence in Genl. Lee," and could see no reason to take personal command himself in the field since Lee was acting according to his ideas.[45] Confederate War Department clerk John B. Jones observed that the president seemed "very cheerful" as he learned more about Lee's preparations to attack McClellan.[46] To Varina, the president wrote in a June 19 letter, "Lee is working systematically and operating cordially and the army is said to feel the beneficial effect of it."[47] Not all of Davis's utterances, especially in his letters to Varina, reflected the same degree of confidence in Lee and his plans. Of one thing, however, Davis grew increasingly certain: Lee was prepared to take risks of shocking magnitude.

The opinions and attitudes of high-ranking Civil War commanders were generally reflected among the younger officers of their staffs. This was true as well in the case of the Confederacy's commander in chief, as his military aides invariably can be found to have expressed the same ideas about generals and situations that Davis himself is known to have held. Thus it is interesting to note what one of the president's staff officers was saying about Lee at this time. Col. Joseph C. Ives was an 1852 West Point graduate now attached to Davis's staff as a military aide. One mid-June day Ives was riding the lines with artillery officer Edward Porter Alexander. The topic of discussion turned to recent newspaper criticism of "Granny Lee," and Alexander expressed his uncertainty about the new army commander's nerve. "Ives, tell me this," he said. "We are here fortifying our lines, but apparently leaving the enemy all the time he needs to accumulate his superior forces, and then to move on us in the way he thinks best. Has General Lee the audacity that is going to be required for our inferior force to meet the enemy's superior force—to take the aggressive, and to run risks and stand chances?" Ives pulled up in the middle of the road. Turning in the saddle, he looked his companion straight in the eye. "Alexander," he said, "if there is one man in either army, Confederate or Federal, head and shoulders above every other in audacity, it is General Lee! His name might be Audacity. He will take more desperate chances and take them quicker than any other general in this country, North or South: and you will live to see it, too."[48]

Ives seems to have meant this as praise of Lee, and in the context of Alexander's doubts, it certainly was. But while taking "more desperate chances . . . quicker than any other general" in the country might seem a positive advantage to a thirty-two-year-old staff officer, it might not be cause for such unbridled enthusiasm in a fifty-four-year-old president on whom the mantle of responsibility for the survival of a far-flung new nation rested very heavily indeed. In a June 21 letter to his wife, the president expressed his ambivalence toward Lee's undertaking in a way that typified the naturally cautious Davis's acute discomfort at having delivered the safety of the capital and the survival of the Confederacy into the hands of a man who would willingly gamble it all for a chance to destroy the enemy army. "The stake is too high," Davis wrote, "to permit the pulse to keep its even beat," but he was "hopeful of success."[49] Though two days later he urged Varina to "be not disturbed," he clearly was disturbed himself. In that same letter, written just three days before Lee planned to launch his offensive, the president wrote of the steady improvement in the physical condition of Joseph E. Johnston. "I wish," Davis continued, "he were able to take the field. Despite the critics who know military affairs by instinct he is a good soldier . . . , and could at this time, render most valuable service."[50] At this point in the war, only one position could come into the question of Johnston's rendering service if he had been able to take the field, commander of the Confederate army defending Richmond. The president's wish that Johnston "were able to take the field" can only be understood as a wish that Johnston rather than Lee were at the helm of the army before Richmond. Thus, almost on the eve of the Seven Days' battles, Davis, despite his claims of confidence in Lee, was uncertain enough to wish the daring commander back at his desk in Richmond, where he could organize, plan, and facilitate—but not run the risk of losing the war in an afternoon.

But Johnston was not able to take the field; so for the time, Lee was the only viable choice. Davis, to his credit, gave him his support but continued to keep a close personal eye on the progress of events. The weather had changed. "The heat and dust are very oppressive," Davis explained to Varina, but the fresh air and activity apparently agreed with the president because he also confided, "I am nearly well again."[51] On the twenty-fourth, his riding took him to Lee's headquarters, but the general was absent, having gone to investigate some skirmishing along the lines south of the Chickahominy. Lee explained the situation to Davis in a dispatch later that day, admitting that the Federal probe against precisely that portion of the line that was to be weakened in preparation for the coming assault had "caused me some anxiety." Still, he was "determined to make no change in the plan" and had ordered Huger, commanding the troops in that sector, "to hold his lines at all hazards."[52] Tensions continued to rise as the next day brought an even stronger Union thrust south of the Chickahominy. Yet the resultant fighting, though noisy enough to distinguish this day, June 25, in retrospect as the first of the Seven Days, turned out to be inconsequential, and each side remained ignorant of the other's intentions.[53]

Thursday, June 26, was to be the day for the opening of Lee's great offensive. For Davis it began with a further increase in the level of tension. From Lee came word that Jackson, "in consequence of the high water & mud" from the previous day's rain, was far behind schedule and would have to make a hard march if he was to be in position for this day's assault. Nor could Lee consider delaying the assault, because he feared "from the operations of the enemy yesterday that our plan of operations has been discovered to them." Those probes south of the river must, he felt, have been intended to determine the degree of Confederate weakness there.[54] Further delay now would seal their doom, leaving southern forces badly out of position and the initiative in the hands of McClellan. Lee would have to prepare to go ahead with his attack and hope Jackson came up in time.

Always mindful of the president, Lee also took time that morning to send Davis a copy of the general order of the day as well as the signals that were to be used by the Confederates' observation hot-air balloon.[55] As a final touch, in case the president wanted to communicate with him during the day, he had a staff officer send Davis a note that "the headquarters of the Commanding General today will be on the Mechanicsville Turnpike," just across the Chickahominy from the Union-held village that gave the road its name and where Lee's attack was aimed.[56] With final preparations made and the troops, except for Jackson's, in their positions, Lee took up his post on the turnpike. Nothing remained but to await the appearance of Jackson on the enemy's right flank.

The day wore on in tense stillness. In Richmond, the waiting weighed heavy on Davis as well, and by midday he had succumbed to temptation and ridden out the Mechanicsville Turnpike to see the action. He arrived at Lee's headquarters about 2:00 P.M., though his appearance here could hardly have been what Lee had intended in notifying the president of his whereabouts. To make matters worse, Davis was not alone. As usual on such occasions, the president's comings and goings had not escaped the notice of other political figures in Richmond, several of whom, including Secretary of War Randolph and Secretary of the Navy Stephen R. Mallory, had chosen to accompany him to the field.[57] E. P. Alexander was under the impression that Davis had "ridden out from Richmond, not only to see, but anxious to participate in, the coming battle."[58] Whatever the president's intent, his presence along with that of the other assorted dignitaries must have made Lee's unpleasant situation even more so. His army sat idle, waiting vainly for Jackson to come into position, while Richmond was all but exposed to capture should the Federals grasp the situation, an event that every passing hour seemed to bring closer. All this was now to be played out under the appraising eyes of a flock of civilian politicians. No general could have relished the situation, nor did anyone in the group of high-ranking Confederates seem to be enjoying himself very much. "I have never in my life seen more gloomy faces," wrote a staff officer who observed their expressions "of weary waiting and anxiety."[59]

From Lee's position on moderately high ground south of the Chickahominy, he could see spread out before him a broad expanse of countryside, including the village of Mechanicsville. Yet he could not see, much less control, all of his army. Specifically, he could not see or know the status of Jackson's crucial flanking column or of the troops next on Jackson's right, who were supposed to go in after making contact with Jackson. The force Lee was taking into battle, even exclusive of the troops covering Richmond, was more than twice the size of any American army ever fielded before the Civil War. Europe, of course, had seen larger armies, but when such forces had been used effectively for the sort of flanking maneuver Lee now had in mind, they had been subdivided into army corps, and of these Lee had none. Nor had he any experience with them. As the afternoon progressed, it probably began to dawn on him that he had lost control of this battle.

About 4:00 P.M. the waiting finally came to an end amid the crash of musketry. Lee, Davis, and those around them observed Confederate troops advancing toward the town of Mechanicsville, driving Yankee skirmishers out of the place and swinging on toward the main Federal lines just across the marshy valley of Beaver Dam Creek. Lee correctly identified the advancing Confederates as the men of A. P. Hill's division and incorrectly assumed that Hill had, in accordance with orders, waited until Jackson had appeared on the Federal flank and begun to roll up the northern end of the enemy's line.[60] In fact, Hill's advance was a factor of his own impatience.[61] Jackson was still struggling with terrain, poor maps, poor staff work, and fatigue—his own and that of his troops—in his effort to get into position. Thinking the plan was finally working, Lee ordered Longstreet to commit his division as well. It was only after conferring with Hill on the battlefield a few minutes later that Lee realized the true state of affairs. Faced with an impossible situation, he decided that the only course now was to continue the attack. To stop was to invite a devastating response by handing the initiative back to McClellan after having given away the main idea of the Confederate plan. The Federal position behind the creek appeared impregnable, strongly held by both infantry and artillery, but the Confederates would have to make their attack and hope for the best.[62]

Grimly, Lee sat his horse where the turnpike topped a gentle knoll just outside Mechanicsville affording another open view of the fields before Beaver Dam Creek. He had crossed the Chickahominy in the rear of his troops and now watched as they launched their forlorn advances into the maelstrom of Union defensive fire. A good bit of that fire was artillery, and some of it was aimed at Confederate rear areas including Lee's vantage point.

Oblivious to the whistling and bursting shells around him, Lee remained intent on the drama unfolding in the valley before him until he noticed a party of mounted men also braving the artillery fire not far off. Davis had hurried forward with the advance of the army, followed by his gaggle of mounted politicians. They had galloped across the rickety bridges over the two channels of the Chickahominy just behind the lead brigade of Confederate infantry and even before that brigade's artillery could get over.[63] Now Davis, like Lee a few yards away, watched the progress of the desperate battle with nervous absorption.

This was too much for Lee. Riding over to Davis, he saluted stiffly. "Mr. President," he said gravely, "who is all this army and what is it doing here?" Obviously embarrassed, Davis replied, "It is not my army, General." He meant that the crowd of sightseers had come on its own in his wake. Lee was not satisfied. "It is certainly not my army, Mr. President," he said, "and this is no place for it." Meekly Davis replied, "Well, General, if I withdraw, perhaps they will follow me." With that he tipped his hat to Lee and turned his horse away from the enemy. The political cavalcade followed. Once out of sight of Lee, however, Davis doubled back and returned to the battlefield, still under enemy fire—an exploding shell killed a Confederate soldier within a few feet of him—but safely beyond Lee's gaze at least for the moment.[64]

Former U.S. senator and current Davis staff officer James Chesnut related to his wife several days later what was apparently a second encounter between president and general, probably during this day's fighting. As Chesnut described it, "General Lee rode up and, bowing politely, said, 'Mr. President, am I in command here?' " Naturally, Davis had answered in the affirmative. "Then," Lee continued, "I forbid you to stand here under the enemy's guns. Any exposure of a life like yours is wrong. And this is useless exposure. You must go back." Chesnut recalled Davis's reply as "Certainly I will set an example of obedience to orders—discipline must be maintained." Once again, however, Davis seems merely to have given the slip to Lee and remained on the field.[65]

For all his eagerness, the president had nothing very inspiring to watch. What was happening to A. P. Hill's division down in the valley of Beaver Dam Creek was not pretty. Seeing the attack in the process of failing, Davis decided to intervene. Support, he believed, would be necessary from the troops of neighboring division commander D. H. Hill. Not bothering to contact Lee or even Hill, Davis wrote out an order and committed it to a courier to be delivered directly to brigade commander Roswell S. Ripley, instructing Ripley to bring his regiments into the attack on the right of

A. P. Hill's troops. This was an intelligent move. If an infantry assault was to be made at all, then Ripley's brigade ought to have been part of it. In fact, unknown to Davis, Lee himself had issued an order for the same movement only a few minutes before.[66] Still, a commander in chief who intervened in brigade-level tactical decisions on the battlefield, bypassing two layers of the chain of command including an army commander in whom he was supposed to have absolute confidence, was badly out of his proper role.

The battle of Mechanicsville was probably beyond saving anyway. Without the planned flanking attack, the frontal assaults against such a strong position as that behind Beaver Dam Creek never had much of a chance. The brigades committed suffered heavy casualties. On the Union side, losses were a few score of men and the never very robust nerve of George B. McClellan. Having won a lopsided victory, with a slight advantage in numbers, and with only weak Confederate forces separating the main body of his army from the enemy capital—facts that never seemed to come into clear focus in McClellan's mind—the Union general decided the only course left to him was retreat. The railroad back to White House Landing on the Pamunkey would be abandoned and the Army of the Potomac would undertake the desperate expedient of attempting to fall back to a supply base on the James River. By thus snatching defeat out of the jaws of victory, McClellan breathed life back into Lee's failing offensive effort. The tide of battle was about to swing in the Confederates' favor, not because Lee was a better strategist or tactician than McClellan or because his men were better fighters than the Yankees but because he had more nerve. Since Davis had from the outset been in a position to call the whole thing off but had, however reluctantly, let it go on, some of the credit for nerve belongs to him as well.

None of this was clear on the morning after the Mechanicsville fiasco. All that was apparent was that the Federals had abandoned their impregnable position and withdrawn to the east. Lee could only assume that Jackson's movement had spooked the enemy or that he had done them more damage than appeared in the previous day's fighting. His reaction was to pursue, taking advantage of the opportunities presented by McClellan's retreat and hoping to make good his original purpose of cutting off and bagging the whole army. The next five days witnessed a series of savage battles, as the corps commanders of the Army of the Potomac, with little help or coordination from McClellan, strove to stave off Lee's intended result and the hard-fighting, long-suffering blueclad soldiers blunted one Confederate thrust after another. Yet at the end of each fight they were compelled by their general's lack of nerve to turn their backs and plod on in retreat. For Lee, it was a week of frustration. The roads on the Peninsula were poor and confusing, and bad maps only made the situation worse. His staff seemed inadequate for the complex task of helping him manipulate so large an army, and some of his unit commanders—notably Jackson—found the conditions especially crippling. All of these difficulties came on top of the basic problem that Lee was trying to maneuver an army of over 90,000 men in a series of wide-sweeping and complex movements, yet that army's largest units were divisions. Lacking corps organizations as well as large numbers of experienced staff and line officers, it simply was not the instrument for execution of Lee's bold but complicated plans.

Davis was on the field each day and may have slept there some or all of the nights.[67] Lee carefully kept him informed of the progress of the action, and Davis in turn made sure that the general was notified of his whereabouts.[68] At the battle of Gaines Mill, on June 27, Lee anticipated a powerful Federal artillery bombardment of a farmhouse in which Davis had taken up his post of observation. A courier from Lee warned the president, who left the premises only a few minutes before it was virtually shot to pieces in the cannonade.[69] Davis apparently knew when Lee was warning him of real danger and when the general simply wanted him off the field in order to be rid of the president's persistent gaze over his shoulder.

It was natural for many civilians back in Richmond to believe that Davis, with his military experience and reputation was, as War Department clerk John B. Jones put it, "on the field directing every important movement in person."[70] In fact, the president generally refrained from further exercises of command and contented himself with the role of observer. An exception came on the night of June 28. Inspecting the lines south of the Chickahominy, Davis warned the officers commanding there that the Union forces opposite them "would," he thought, "commence a retreat before morning." He "gave special instructions as to the precautions necessary in order certainly to hear when the movement commenced" and entertained high hopes of the mayhem that might be wrought among the Federals when they were caught in the act of retreating. Once again, Davis's assessment of the situation proved correct, with the enemy withdrawing during the night. The president's instructions, however, were not heeded, and the retreat went unmolested.[71] This wise but unsuccessful foray into battlefield command remained the exception. For the most part Davis, sometimes with aides and sometimes alone—the rest of the politicians had apparently grown weary— rode "the lanes and orchards near the battlefield, . . . issued no orders; but awaited results."[72]

Somehow in the midst of such activity Davis managed to carry out the more conventional duty of a commander in chief in having the War Department order troops previously guarding the back door to Richmond on the south bank of the James to move north of the river and then downstream in support of Lee. This was another alert move, since McClellan's retreat made the troops superfluous where they were and their addition helped make good some of the fearful losses Lee was taking during this week of battles.[73]

On June 29 another miscarried attempt to crush the Federal rear guard saw Magruder's division clash with Union forces at Savage's Station. Magruder failed to press home his attack vigorously and got no support from nearby Confederate units. Once again the result was failure. Among the Confederate casualties was one of Magruder's brigadiers, Richard Griffith, badly wounded. Griffith had been Davis's adjutant back in the old Mississippi Rifles during the Mexican War. Now Davis sought him out as he was being carried off the battlefield. "My dear boy," the president said as he leaned over Griffith, "I hope you are not seriously hurt." But Griffith was and died that evening in Richmond.[74]

The next day, June 30, Lee hoped to cut off Federal retreat by seizing the vital crossroads at Glendale. The battle was to commence as soon as Huger's artillery opened on the enemy from the north. By 11:00 A.M., the troops of the main Confederate column of attack, those of Longstreet and A. P. Hill, were in place, and the wait for Huger began. About 2:30 the report of a few guns was heard to the north. Thinking this the sign that Huger was going in, Longstreet ordered his own artillery to open up. While the word was being passed to the batteries, Longstreet sat his horse in what he described as "a little clearing of about three acres, curtained by dense pine forests." It soon became a very popular place. Lee rode up, followed by his staff, and joined Longstreet in waiting for the sounds that would signal the beginning of their culminating attack. Next to arrive was the president himself, accompanied by aides. Anticipating Lee's stock objection to his presence, Davis succeeded in doing what few enemy generals ever did: he took the initiative away from Lee. "Why, General," he said as soon as they came within speaking distance, "what are you doing here? You are in too dangerous a position for the commander of the army." Witnesses failed to record whether Lee showed irritation at this. He seldom did. "I'm trying," he answered, "to find out something about the movements and plans of those people," meaning the enemy. Then, not to be deterred by the president's attempted preemptive strike, he continued, "But you must excuse me, Mr. President, for asking what you are doing here, and for suggesting that this is no proper place for the commander-in-chief of all our armies." If Lee was rarely deprived of the initiative, Davis was never bettered in stubbornness. "Oh," he replied, "I am here on the same mission that you are." Having dueled to a draw, both men remained where they were.[75]

Longstreet remembered the conversation that followed as quite pleasant, as the participants were "anticipating fruitful results from the fight." At this point, Longstreet's batteries finally opened, but with unintended side effects. The more numerous, well served Union guns gave back considerably better than they were getting. Though out of sight of the Federal gunners, the collection of high Rebel brass had the misfortune to be unwittingly ranged almost immediately by the fast-firing Federal artillery, and the little clearing suddenly became a very lively place. "The second or third shell burst in the midst of us," Longstreet remembered, "killing two or three horses and wounding one or two men." Things apparently went on like this for some time. Finally, up rode A. P. Hill, who without salutation of any kind announced abruptly, "This is no place for either of you, and, as commander of this part of the field, I order you both to the rear!"

"We will obey your orders," the president replied, and together Davis and Lee rode back a ways but halted still under the enemy's fire. Hill, finding them there a few minutes later, was adamant. "Did I not tell you," he burst out again, "to go away from here? And did you not promise to obey my orders? Why, one shell from that battery over yonder may presently deprive the Confederacy of its President and the Army of Northern Virginia of its commander!" There was no arguing with the man. Davis and Lee finally pulled back out of range.[76]

Neither man considered his scouting activities finished for the day. Later that afternoon Davis encountered Lee returning from viewing the beginning of the Federal withdrawal over Malvern Hill. Once again Davis admonished Lee for taking risks with his personal safety, and again Lee protested that such methods were the only way to get reliable information.[77] Davis's own reconnaissance that afternoon was for a time hindered by the fact that he could not obtain a guide with sufficient knowledge of the tangled back lanes and roads of the Peninsula to show him how to get from one Confederate column to another.[78] He still managed to be present that evening when green troops from the division of Maj. Gen. Theophilus Holmes broke under the noisy but relatively ineffective fire of the big guns mounted on Union warships in the James River. At least Davis said the fire was ineffective, and he was that day becoming quite a connoisseur of the business end of artillery firing exercises. The troops were of a different mind in the matter, and it was with difficulty that Davis managed to get them to stop running and form line again about a half mile from their original position. No sooner had he completed this arduous task, however, than another of the monster shells burst "in the top of a wide-spreading tree, giving a shower of metal and limbs, which," as Davis wryly observed, "soon after caused them to resume their flight in a manner that plainly showed no moral power could stop them within the range of those shells."[79]

The day's fighting was a disappointment to Lee. Huger and Jackson somehow failed to get into action, and although Hill's and Longstreet's troops fought hard, they were unable to trap and destroy the Federals nor to prevent their withdrawal to Malvern Hill. On that eminence they waited on the morning of July 1, barring further pursuit. Lee was not ready to give up his quarry. All that night he worked hard to sort out his army and prepare it for one last lunge at the enemy. Trying to control his unwieldy army without the aid of an adequate staff was proving too much for him. By the morning of July 1, he had not slept in at least twenty-four tense and trying hours and confided to Longstreet that he was very tired and not feeling well at all.[80] He asked Longstreet to turn his division over to the second in command and accompany Lee that day in case the need arose for Longstreet to take over leadership of the army.[81] Longstreet's stolid self-confidence was reassuring even to his commander.

Some time later that morning, they encountered D. H. Hill, who had been making some inquiries of his own among the local citizens regarding the lay of the land ahead. His conclusion was not encouraging. "If General McClellan is there in force," he said, indicating the gentle swell of Malvern Hill that brushed the southeastern horizon, "we had better let him alone." Longstreet laughed. "Don't get scared," he chided, "now that we have got him whipped."[82] Jackson arrived about noon for conference with Lee and the other generals. He advised flanking the Federals off their dominating hilltop position while Longstreet was for plowing straight ahead. This time, Lee took Longstreet's advice. The Confederates would assault Malvern Hill.[83]

The affair was a horrible fiasco. The preparatory artillery bombardment was partial and uncoordinated and was hammered into silence by Federal counterbattery fire almost before it got started. That demonstration of the overwhelming Union firepower on Malvern Hill should have precluded the infantry ever going forward at all, but so muddled and sloppily written were the orders to the division and brigade commanders that they felt compelled to march their men out of the woods and up the open slope into the meat grinder of massed Federal artillery and musketry.[84] "It was not war," D. H. Hill later wrote, "it was murder."[85] A Union officer who surveyed the scene of the fighting from his vantage point on the hilltop the next morning was appalled at the sight of over 5,000 bodies strewn across the slope, noting that "enough of them were alive and moving to give the field a singular crawling effect."[86]

Once again, Lee had lost control of the army. Indeed, all but prostrated by his effort to do the impossible in taming such a cumbersome beast, the general apparently had a struggle keeping his own thoughts clear and well sorted. At this point, of course, Davis could do little about that. To the extent that any of the difficulty sprang from him, it was the fruit of policies he had adopted more than six months before. Conflict with Beauregard notwithstanding, Davis should have allowed the army to be organized into corps over the winter. That might have made it substantially more suitable to translate Lee's operational genius into victory on the battlefield. If Davis ever became aware of this mistake, he never admitted it. Yet what he did recognize as duty, he was careful to do. On the afternoon of Malvern Hill, he did what little he could.

Before the assault, Lee had ordered Maj. Gen. Lafayette McLaws to find suitable positions for artillery to bombard Malvern Hill in preparation for the assault. McLaws was absent on this mission for some time, and when he returned to where Lee was, he found the commanding general asleep under a tree. Remarkably, Davis himself was watching over Lee and urged McLaws not to wake him as he had been up all night. The sound of their voices, however, was enough to arouse the sleeping general, and he immediately sat up and gave his attention to McLaws's report.[87] If the attack on Malvern Hill showed less than Lee's ordinary tactical acumen, it may well be due to the fact that by the afternoon of July 1, Lee was physically at the end of his tether. Davis, for his part, had refrained from any sort of assumption of command or veto of Lee's plans, of which he must have known in advance. Lee's aggressiveness as an army commander had from the start been unnerving to the president, but having cast his lot with Lee, Davis commendably refrained from minute intervention on the field of battle. Though the result might have been unfortunate in this case, the precedent was far more promising for good results than had been Davis's behavior at the outset of the offensive, when he had bypassed Lee to give orders to a brigadier at Mechanicsville. Davis had come to the battlefield to observe but also to do what he could to help. Sometimes, as at Mechanicsville, that help might be inappropriate, however correct tactically. Yet even Davis's northern counterpart could offer no more touchingly humble example of a willingness to do whatever might bring victory a little closer than Davis's quietly watching over the sleeping Lee.

Next morning the last Federal rear-guard cavalry pulled off of Malvern Hill, following the rest of the Army of the Potomac as it completed its retreat, intact, into the fortified camp at Harrison's Landing on the James River. Lee sent Davis a note informing him of this and stating that the army would follow the enemy as best it could under the circumstances.[88] Later, the president surprised Lee by dropping in at his headquarters at the Poindexter house on Malvern Hill while Lee conferred with several of his generals. Accompanied by nephew Joseph R. Davis, then serving as one of his military aides, Davis came in out of the rainy, chilly weather just as Lee and Jackson were discussing the present tactical outlook.

Dr. Hunter McGuire, Jackson's medical director, inferred Lee's surprise from the somewhat flustered greeting he gave Davis. As McGuire recalled it, Lee "said not, 'Mr. President,' but 'President, I am delighted to see you.'" Once introductions were made and greetings exchanged among the Davises, Lee, and Lee's aide Maj. Walter Taylor, Davis turned and looked questioningly toward a tall, rough-hewn, somewhat ungainly officer standing nearby. Jefferson Davis and Stonewall Jackson had never met face to face. While Davis was occupied with Lee, McGuire leaned over and "told Gen. Jackson in a whisper who the august visitor was," though Jackson would hardly have required such information. His feelings toward Davis, however, were none too cordial, for he had not forgotten the Romney campaign and Davis's intervention in Loring's favor during that affair. "He stood," McGuire recalled, "as if a corporal on guard, his head erect, his little fingers touching the seams of his pants, and looked at Davis." Lee broke the tense silence, though he still seemed a bit flustered. "Why President," he said, "don't you know General Jackson? This is our Stonewall Jackson." Davis was not one to extend cordiality that he knew would not be reciprocated. He bowed stiffly. Jackson, ever conscious of the requirements of military discipline, saluted crisply, "the salute," recalled McGuire, "of an inferior to a superior officer."

Such awkward social necessities out of the way, Lee and Davis went to the dining room table and spread out their maps to discuss the military situation. Lee briefed the president on the previous day's fighting and on what was known of the present whereabouts of McClellan's army. As the discussion continued, the onlookers were struck with the ascendance of one mind over the other. "Every now and then," recalled McGuire, "Davis would make some suggestion; in a polite way, Gen. Lee would receive it and reject it. It was plain to everybody who was there that Lee's was the dominant brain." The clear tendency of the conversation, in which Longstreet also took at least some part, was that the best policy would be to give up the pursuit of McClellan. Jackson, who was listening in silence in a corner of the room, was a study in unhappy facial expressions, from one of simple anxiety to that of deeply troubled "mental agony." Jackson, virtually alone among Lee's generals, believed McClellan was defeated and ought to be pursued. His disappointment when Lee's decision went against this was intense, and during the days that followed his staff had occasion to notice a number of "outbursts of temper."[89]

Davis spoke with Jackson personally later that day, and though the general kept himself under strict control, he did not disguise the fact that he disagreed with the decision that had been made. "They have not all got away," he said quietly, "if we go immediately after them." But Jackson's was the only voice Davis heard express such opinions.[90] Lee believed that "under ordinary circumstances," that is, if the army had moved and fought as he had envisioned, "the Federal army should have been destroyed."[91] He realized, however, that the moment of opportunity had passed and saw nothing to be gained by further offensive action. Again, Davis wisely left such a tactical decision in the hands of Lee. As was coming to be usual, he agreed with Lee's assessment of what had happened, writing his wife a few days later, "Had all the orders been well and promptly executed, there would have been a general dispersion" of McClellan's army.[92] The president meanwhile was intensely aware of the worn down condition of the Confederate troops. "To the fatigue of hard marches and successive battles," he wrote after the war, "enough to have disqualified our troops for rapid pursuit, was added the discomfort of being thoroughly wet and chilled by rain." With the thought of relieving the soldiers' suffering, Davis sent out to the surrounding area to see if he could purchase, at any price, a supply of whiskey large enough to provide a ration to each man, but without success.[93]

With the active campaigning now at an end for the present, Davis returned to Richmond. Lee was careful to keep him posted on developments with daily dispatches. During the next few days he could report only that the enemy held an impregnable position along the James but showed no inclination to leave it.[94] Davis, for his part, was an almost equally diligent correspondent. In his first letter back in Richmond, he admitted, "My office work fell behind while I was in the field, but no public interest, I hope, was seriously affected." He agreed that leaving McClellan unmolested for the moment "must be regarded as necessary" but suggested, without any hint of pressure, a few ideas that might be considered as possibilities for dislodging McClellan. He assured Lee that "the entire confidence reposed in you would suffice to secure my sanction to your view" regarding the movements of the army. "I would not," Davis wrote, "be regarded as interfering with the free exercise of your discretion." He urged Lee not to hesitate to ask for "anything which you think would be more promptly or certainly executed by my personal attention" but admonished the general once more "against personal exposure either in battle or reconnaissance." Back in the capital, the president also devoted himself to renewed efforts to fill the vacant ranks of Lee's army, which had lost about one man in five during the bloody fighting of the Seven Days.[95]

These costly Seven Days' battles had delivered the Confederate capital and driven McClellan's threatening army out to a more acceptable distance, but they had failed to accomplish the rest of Lee's purpose of substantially destroying that army, dealing a blow to northern morale that might bring the war to an early end. As the results had been mixed, so too was public reaction to Lee's generalship. Among the newspapers, the Richmond *Dispatch* reported, "The rise which this officer has suddenly taken in the public confidence is without a precedent." At the same time, other papers claimed that the successful plan of campaign had in fact been Johnston's, while still others reported as if Jackson was as much the hero of the Peninsula as he had been of the Valley.[96] John B. Jones noted in his diary, "Lee does not follow up his blows on the whipped enemy, and some sage critics censure him for it."[97] Within the army, opinion was also divided. Lafayette McLaws wrote to his wife during the midst of the week of battles, "General Lee is rapidly regaining, if he has not already regained entirely, the confidence of the Army and the people as a skillful and even a dashing officer."[98] On the other hand, frustrated politician-turned-general Robert Toombs wrote to a political associate after the campaign, "Lee was far below the occasion. If we had had a general in command we could easily have taken McClellan's whole command and baggage."[99] But Toombs never forgave a professional soldier for having more military knowledge than he did.

Davis himself showed increased confidence in Lee. He had, at times, expressed such confidence in Lee before the battles. Sometimes he had, with some reluctance, acted on that confidence. After the Seven Days the president said no more of returning Johnston to the Virginia command. For a time, Davis showed no sign of reluctance in granting Lee a completely free hand, but that did not mean the president's fundamental outlook toward the war and its winning had changed. Davis had never opposed offensive action if it seemed to offer some chance of success within the limits of his willingness to take risks. Now, riding the crest of the Seven Days' victory and with the remarkable Lee in command, he was ready to allow those limits to be stretched—temporarily but considerably. To Varina he wrote that there might be some surprises in store for the enemy "and some things they have not dreamed which we may do." Even as he mentioned his efforts to secure new recruits throughout the Confederacy, he eagerly predicted that "if our ranks were full we could end the war in a few weeks." He was also optimistic that victories on the field of battle might translate into the favorable intervention of the European powers. "There is reason to believe," he told the first lady, "that the yankees have gained from England and France as the last extension, this month, and expect foreign intervention if we hold them at bay on the first of August." Exuberantly he concluded, "Our troubles you perceive have not ended but our chances have improved so I repeat be of good cheer."[100] Yet if Davis was, at least temporarily, ready to pursue a quick victory, some lingering differences of outlook would continue between the president and his new Army of Northern Virginia commander. Although a quick victory might be desirable to Davis, to Lee it was imperative.

Even more eager to strike a blow at the enemy was Jackson, probably out of sheer innate aggressiveness. Disappointed when Lee remained noncommittal about an offensive proposal he put to him shortly after the Seven Days, Jackson decided to go over his commander's head. For this purpose he once again chose Boteler. Perhaps still remembering the Romney incident and undoubtedly sensing Davis's basically defensive attitude, Jackson surmised incorrectly that Lee did not have an entirely free hand and that the real problem lay with the president. Explaining the matter to Boteler, Jackson said, "So great is my confidence in General Lee that I am willing to follow him blindfolded. But I fear he is unable to give me a definite answer now because of influences at Richmond, where, perhaps, the matter has been mentioned by him and may be under consideration. I therefore want you to see the President and urge the importance of prompt action." Davis heard Boteler out as he expounded the details of Jackson's plan but took no action.[101]

The question of what to do next, however, was about to be taken out of Confederate hands. Back on June 26, the day Lee's Peninsula offensive had started, Lincoln had authorized the organization of a new Federal "Army of Virginia." The new force was to be under the leadership of successful western commander John Pope and was to consist of the various Federal units, amounting to considerable strength in aggregate, that up to that point had been operating separately in northern Virginia and the Shenandoah Valley. Pope's army was to protect Washington, threaten Richmond from the north and west, and relieve pressure on McClellan. During the next two weeks Pope's force drifted southward just east of the Blue Ridge, posing an increasingly insistent problem for the Confederate high command in Virginia.[102] To make matters worse, Pope issued various orders and proclamations that succeeded in both alienating his own troops and convincing the Confederates that he would henceforth treat hostile civilians more like rebels and less like protected noncombatants than heretofore. Davis took monstrous umbrage at this and fired off to Lee a dispatch that fairly sputtered with rage. Henceforth, "General Pope and his commissioned officers" were to be treated as "robbers and murderers" and most emphatically not "to be considered as prisoners of war." He concluded by instructing Lee "to communicate to the commander-in-chief of the armies of the United States the contents of this letter."[103]

Like Davis, Lee seemed horrified to find that the Confederacy's enemies, some thousands of whom he had but recently been instrumental in killing or wounding, now proposed to wage real war against the Confederacy. The conflict was working on Lee's thinking as much as it was on the thinking of Pope and other northerners of like mind. As always, though, Lee was more restrained in his expressions than was Davis. Although he did stoop to calling Pope a "miscreant," his strongest words as to what should be done about him were simply, "He ought to be suppressed if possible."[104]

Lee was already taking steps, a fortnight before Davis's bombastic proclamation, to "suppress" John Pope and his army. He could not afford to ignore McClellan just yet, but on July 13 he decided to send Jackson north to the vicinity of Gordonsville on the vital Virginia Central Railroad, where he would be in a position to counter Pope. If Davis raised any objection or offered any caution in regard to this move, no record of it remains. Nevertheless, Lee acted cautiously in the matter of pulling troops out of Richmond, being careful not to alarm the president with fears that the city might be exposed to capture by a reinforced McClellan. Such concerns dictated that the force detached be a small one, a few brigades at most. Despite questions about Jackson's performance in the Seven Days, Lee showed no hesitation in naming his fellow Virginian to this key independent command, an assignment whose importance was far out of proportion to the relatively small number of Confederate troops involved. Apparently Jackson's Seven Days' performance had not fallen as far short of Lee's expectations as critics then and since have claimed.

To ensure mutual understanding, Davis, Lee, and the army's top generals held a conference on July 13 at the Confederate White House. Davis, Lee, and Jackson remained in conversation long after the others had departed.[105] By the eighteenth, Lee, though still apprehensive that McClellan would be reinforced and that the enemy would "leave no stone unturned to capture Richmond," nevertheless was beginning to hope that the new Federal approach might offer a renewed opportunity. Far from giving up the hope of winning a crushing victory, Lee wrote eagerly in a dispatch to Davis of his "hope of striking a blow" at the enemy.[106] These were not the words of a man who had given up on decisive battles.[107]

The next day Jackson reached Gordonsville, securing, for the moment, the Virginia Central Railroad and with it the capital's connection to the rich granary of the Shenandoah Valley. Pope was just to the north, at Culpeper, within the triangle formed by the confluence of the Rapidan and Rappahannock Rivers, on the Orange and Alexandria Railroad. As yet, however, with the small force Lee had detached to him, Jackson was in no position to "suppress" Pope. For Lee, the strategic situation was a difficult one. Besides Pope's 56,000 at Culpeper, he also had to worry about another 11,000 at Fredericksburg, where they posed a potential threat to Jackson's line of communications, the Central Railroad between Gordonsville and Richmond. Then there were another 10,000 or so Federals on transports in the Chesapeake and, of course, McClellan's army at Harrison's Landing, reinforced now, bigger than ever, and uncomfortably close to Richmond. Still, the general whose name might have been audacity demonstrated as much, along with his faith in Jackson, by ordering A. P. Hill's oversized division to Gordonsville. Lee's nerve was tested a week later when, on August 5, elements of the Army of the Potomac advanced menacingly up the James to the old Malvern Hill battlefield. Lee countered the move with the troops he still had on hand, and McClellan quickly backed down.

The situation remained threatening enough on the James to preclude, for the moment, Lee's further weakening of his own force to strengthen Jackson, but he wrote his trusted lieutenant suggesting quick action against Pope but leaving the matter to Jackson's discretion. "I must now leave the matter to your reflection and good judgment," Lee wrote. "Make up your mind what is best to be done under all the circumstances which surround us, and let me hear the result at which you arrive."[108] Jackson was always quick to take up Lee's suggestions, and in this case he had actually anticipated his commander's wish and had his troops in motion across the Rapidan and toward Pope. On August 9 he defeated a detachment from Pope's command at the battle of Cedar Mountain, just south of Culpeper, before pulling back to the south side of the Rapidan. Encouraging as this might be to Lee, it did not remove the threat to the Virginia Central, and so on the thirteenth he dispatched Longstreet, his next most trusted commander, to take an additional two divisions to Gordonsville, while a weak division was posted at Hanover Junction to cover the Virginia Central against a possible movement from Fredericksburg.

Although this left little to counter another possible move by McClellan, Lee was becoming increasingly convinced that such a move was not in the works. That would leave him free to go west himself and take charge of the suppression of Pope. Other reasons may also have pressed Lee to go to Gordonsville. Longstreet, the capable but simple mechanic of the battlefield, whose attempts to engineer victory at both Williamsburg and Seven Pines had produced dire results, outranked Jackson. Once in Gordonsville, he would command. Lee appreciated Longstreet's strengths, and if he recognized the weaknesses, he kept a tactful silence on them. Whatever his assessment of the Georgian's qualifications for independent command, Lee had made other plans before Longstreet had even reached Gordonsville. On the evening of August 14 he wrote to Davis, "Unless I hear from you to the contrary I shall leave for G[ordonsville] at 4 A.M. tomorrow." He explained that he needed to oversee the large troop buildup there and added, "When you do not hear from me, you may feel sure that I do not think it necessary to trouble you. I shall feel obliged to you for any directions you may think proper to give."[109] Davis apparently felt the need neither to restrain Lee nor for the moment to give "directions."

The next day, from Gordonsville, Lee wired the president to "put R. H. Anderson's division in motion tomorrow," to come up in support behind Lee's now substantial forces at Gordonsville. Without demure, Davis directed that the appropriate orders be issued to Anderson "immediately."[110] The following day, Lee wrote at greater length. He believed—incorrectly—that the Union force at Fredericksburg had joined Pope. He also surmised—correctly this time—that McClellan's army was about to be withdrawn from its base on the James River. "In that event," he reasoned, "the war will for a season at least be removed from Richmond & I would recommend that the troops be removed too." Besides, he continued, getting the army's camps away from the proximity of a major city would be good for health and discipline and would do the city no harm either. "If it can be ascertained that McClellan is moving," he concluded, "unless his quarters can be beaten up, I would recommend that another division follow Andersons."[111]

Beating up McClellan's "quarters," disrupting and damaging his army as it was in the vulnerable process of embarkation, was exactly what Davis had in mind. It was therefore with some disappointment that he learned on the morning of August 17 that McClellan had made good his escape unnoticed and unmolested.[112] The wires carried the news to Lee that same day. In an apologetic letter to Davis, Lee expressed his chagrin "that General McClellan's force has escaped us." He felt "greatly mortified," for McClellan "ought not to have got off so easily." Lee went on to express his dissatisfaction with D. H. Hill's performance in command of the force that was supposed to be watching McClellan. Hill, he concluded, was not up to independent command. "Left to himself he seems embarrassed and backward to act."[113] Hill would stay with the army for now—reduced to his old command of a single division—but Lee had his eye on him.[114]

Other officers had had it a good deal worse in the wake of the Seven Days. Lee was anxious to rid his army of certain generals whose incapacity he believed was in part responsible for its failure to carry out his plans. He went about it quietly but effectively and with the full cooperation of Davis. G. W. Smith was kept in an insignificant post as commander of the city of Richmond itself. Benjamin Huger's command was reduced from a division to a desk, as he became part of the War Department bureaucracy. John B. Magruder and even the president's friend Theophilus Holmes were sent west, the almost invariable direction of travel for unsuccessful Civil War generals, all the way to Texas and Arkansas respectively. With these men gone, Longstreet and Jackson were Lee's ranking lieutenants, and starting with Jackson's detachment to counter Pope, Lee began arranging his army into two wings—corps in fact—under these two men. Whether he had just recognized the utility of corps for handling a large army in far-ranging maneuver or whether he had just arrived at a means of making such organization acceptable to the president, he left no record. Davis, for his part, made no further objection. With an army now more or less purged of high-ranking incompetents, organized into effective army corps, and more experienced overall, Lee hoped that Pope would not escape as easily as had McClellan.

For this purpose, as soon as he received word of McClellan's withdrawal, he wrote Davis to renew his urging that the remaining forces around Richmond move west to join him against Pope. "The troops had better march, beginning at once," he wrote, "using the railroad as far as it goes." Briefly and clearly spelling out the arrangements to be made for this movement, almost as if to a subordinate rather than to his commander in chief, he tactfully concluded: "I beg you will excuse my troubling you with my opinions and especially these details, but your kindness has led you to receive them without objection so often that I know I am tempted to trespass. I am getting the troops in position near the fords . . . of the Rapidan . . . the process is slow and tedious. I hope to succeed by tomorrow."[115] In fact, the endeavor in which Lee hoped to succeed involved a good deal more than merely positioning his troops near the river, as though he would cover the fords to block a Union advance. That same day the troops of the Army of Northern Virginia were moving into position for an offensive that Lee hoped would trap Pope in the pocket formed by the confluence of the Rappahannock and Rapidan Rivers, but this hope proved as vain as that of annihilating McClellan's army down on the Chickahominy. Inexperienced officers and unclear orders delayed preparations for the assault until, late on August 18, Pope realized his danger and began a withdrawal north of the Rappahannock. Observing the completion of Pope's movement from a vantage point south of the Rapidan the next morning, Lee turned to Longstreet, who had accompanied him to the hilltop, and sighed in disappointment. "General," he said sadly, "we little thought that the enemy would turn his back upon us thus early in the campaign."[116]

If Lee's sole purpose had been to turn Pope out of his position and open more country from which the Confederates could draw supplies, the view across the Rapidan would have revealed pure success and no cause for sighing. Clearly, Lee's heart was still set on decisive battle.

With Pope having taken up a very strong position on the north bank of the Rappahannock, Lee had to give up, for the moment, his plans of striking a blow and instead pause to consider his next move. He dared not pause long if he still hoped for decisive victory over Pope, for massive Union reinforcements from the Army of the Potomac and from the forces around Fredericksburg drew nearer every day. On August 21 Lee wrote Davis to inform him that he had crossed the Rapidan in pursuit of Pope. Lee's information seemed to indicate a general shifting of the Federal effort in Virginia in his direction. "Can Richmond be held," he asked the president, if the Union move was matched by a corresponding westward shift of Confederate troops?[117] Three days later, before he could receive a reply from Richmond but with time running short for defeating Pope, Lee ordered Jackson to march the next morning, swinging his corps, or wing, in a wide arc west and north and into the rear of Pope's army. The operation smacked of a classic Napoleonic maneuver for the annihilation of an opponent's army. As to just what Lee hoped to accomplish by it, one thing at least is clear. Such a turning movement would force Pope out of his strong position, compelling the northern general either to fight at a disadvantage or to retreat. With Jackson's hard-marching columns driving to within three dozen miles of the Federal capital, Lee could have had few doubts as to which choice Pope would make.[118]

Next day, as Stonewall's troops began the daring maneuver, Lee was on hand at Jackson's Jeffersonton headquarters, just south of the Rapidan, to see them off. Lee had been writing Davis on an almost daily basis, but from Jeffersonton he fired off a stream of dispatches to Richmond revealing his understandable agitation at undertaking a movement involving division of his outnumbered army in the presence of the enemy. To Davis he wired early that day, "I believe a portion of McClellan's army has joined Pope[.] Expedite the advance of our troops."[119] Sometime later he telegraphed directly to G. W. Smith, who was commanding the Richmond garrison, ordering him to join Lee "with all the troops available," subject to the president's approval. A subsequent dispatch informed Davis of this.[120] Meanwhile, the president had written on the twenty-first to inform Lee that Smith would be remaining in Richmond, and that the defense of the city against any sudden Union attack required the maintenance of the force at Hanover Junction besides five brigades in and around the city itself.[121]

To Lee's requests for reinforcements, Davis responded with assurance that the troops covering the Virginia Central, Lee's line of communication, would be sent forward, though "their advance uncovers that line to attack by the enemy from Fredericksburg." Davis also agreed to release two of the five brigades he had planned to retain for the defense of the capital, as well as all of the cavalry around Richmond. The president was far from comfortable with all of this. He related reports of possible Union activity down on the Peninsula and observed that with no cavalry, "we shall be less able to get early information" of any designs the Federals might have on the city. As if all that were not bad enough, Davis lamented that should the capital indeed be threatened, the only available reinforcements for it would be the small numbers of raw recruits at Petersburg and in North Carolina. "Confidence in you," Davis concluded, "overcomes the view which would otherwise be taken of the exposed condition of Richmond, and the troops retained for the defense of the capital are surrendered to you on a renewed request."[122] The president's confidence in his Virginia commander was indeed great, but Lee once again was playing for a higher stake than Davis liked to contemplate. The three brigades retained in Richmond revealed a commander in chief willing to begin hedging his bets.

Lee received the message the next evening, August 27, near White Plains, Virginia, little more than a score of miles from Pope's main supply depot at Manassas Junction. By that time he had more good tidings for the president. Indeed, at a noon pause near Salem that day, he had penned a dispatch notifying Davis of the exciting news that Jackson had the night before seized Manassas Junction, bagging a tremendous haul of much-needed provisions as well as an assortment of locomotives, railroad cars, guns, and prisoners. When Pope turned to confront this severing of his supply line, Lee had taken Longstreet's corps and swung north in Jackson's track to unite his army squarely across the Federal communications and force a showdown fight. Thus it was that Lee came to be near Salem that noon, just west of Bull Run Mountain and poised to throw this remaining half of his army into the Union rear. Unaware of the president's compliance with his wishes expressed two days before, he continued in his noon note to press the need for more troops. Mentioning several units of McClellan's army now present with Pope, he concluded with what sounded like a command: "Expedite the reinforcements ordered."[123]

Davis received the dispatch the next day and responded immediately. He congratulated Lee on the successes gained and assured him that "the rein- forcements asked for by you have been sent forward." Also coming up from Richmond, the president informed Lee, was Brig. Gen. William N. Pendleton, chief of artillery of the Army of Northern Virginia.[124] Pendleton had been with the army's artillery reserve, lingering in the Richmond area several days after the march of Lee's other units.[125] While there, he had conversed extensively with Davis, who informed Lee in his August 28 dispatch, "Genl. Pendleton left here fully possessed of my views, and charged to communicate them to you."[126] Pendleton, a West Point contemporary of both Lee and Davis, was well qualified to serve as a go-between, though the exact content of his briefing to Lee is not recorded. Two days later, Davis explained it to Lee as being a means to "give you such information as would enable you to show me with the necessary precision how I could best promote the success of your operations and generally secure that co- intelligence between us which is desirable to both."[127] Pendleton rode hard, and by the time Davis was writing those words on August 30, was already with Lee.[128]

In the meantime, momentous events were occurring at the front. On the evening of August 28, Jackson's wing clashed with a Federal brigade near Groveton, where Jackson had taken up a strong position to await the arrival of Lee with Longstreet's wing. They joined up the next morning. Also

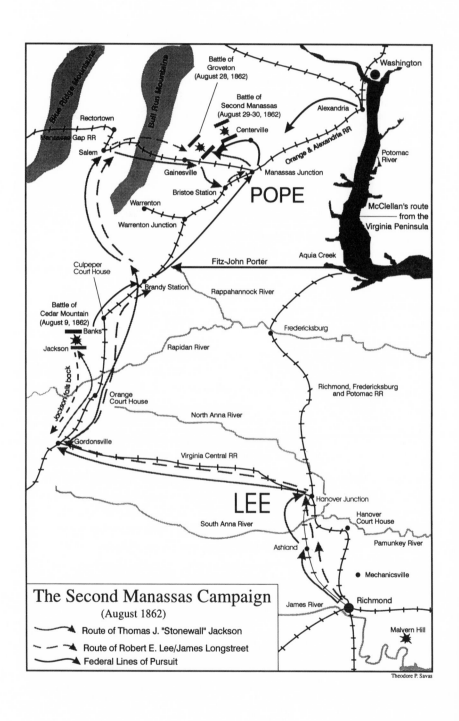

The Second Manassas Campaign
(August 1862)

Route of Thomas J. "Stonewall" Jackson

Route of Robert E. Lee/James Longstreet

Federal Lines of Pursuit

Theodore P. Savas

arriving on the field that day was the balance of Pope's army. Unaware of the presence of the second half of the Rebel army, Pope launched a daylong assault on Jackson. Despite the strong Confederate position, the determined Federals came near to breaking his line. By evening, however, it was apparent that Jackson would hold, and Lee got off another dispatch to Davis recounting the army's successes thus far.[129] Next morning, still ignorant of Longstreet's presence, Pope renewed his attacks, with half the Rebel army almost athwart the flank of his assaulting columns. Lee had been eager to attack the previous afternoon, when Jackson was hard-pressed and before more reinforcements could join Pope. Longstreet had contended it would be best to wait for additional Confederates to come up and for the tactical situation to develop more fully. In the end, his counsel prevailed, and his troops rested on their arms.

While Lee waited on the field of battle to launch the assault he hoped would ruin Pope, he wrote a longer letter to Davis. Explaining that his maneuver had "drawn the enemy from the Rappahannock frontier and caused him to concentrate his troops between Manassas & Centreville," Lee went on to state, "My desire has been to avoid a general engagement." Here was the most striking example thus far of a tendency Lee was already developing to downplay his goals in their presentation to Davis. He could not have failed to sense the president's caution, and he was always careful to cultivate the chief executive's feelings. In discussions of strategy, that meant placing his own daring schemes in the most conservative light possible. Thus his purpose in this campaign, he blandly informed the president, had been "by maneuvering to relieve the portion of the country" lately occupied or threatened by Pope's army. That was all true enough—as far as it went. Lee did hope to move the Federals out of the agriculturally rich Virginia piedmont. He knew as well as anyone how much the army would need the crops now growing there, and he made sure to add a few lines in his letter to Davis urging "proper exertion" on the part of the commissary department in getting all it could out of that area while the getting was good.

Yet he had much more in mind. He might tell Davis he had desired "to avoid a general engagement." After all, if Pope or any and all other Federal commanders chose to respond to repeated turning movements by retreating again and again all the way to Washington—or Philadelphia—or Boston—that would be fine with Lee, but that is not to say he actually expected to accomplish his goal without pitched battle. The kind of maneuvers that would throw the Federals out of Virginia, threaten Washington, and deflate northern morale were bound to goad even the most inert of northern generals into offering or forcing a battle. Since battle must then be given, Lee would seek to find in it the spectacular victories that would not only bolster southern spirits but also break–quickly and finally–the northern will to continue the struggle. Nor would this day's fighting on the plains of Manassas be enough. Even as he listened to the crash of battle along Jackson's lines and waited for the moment to unleash a decisive counterattack, Lee wrote Davis, "In order that we may obtain the advantages I hope for, we must be in larger force, and I hope every exertion will be made to create troops & to increase our strength & supplies."[130] That meant new recruiting and could have no possible bearing on the battle then in progress or even the present campaign. Clearly, "to obtain the advantages" Lee hoped for meant engaging the enemy in decisive battle.

Longstreet's lines finally rolled forward. The outflanked Federals fought stubbornly and retired in good order, without the panic that had marked the Union flight from this field the year before. Still, Second Manassas was a dramatic Confederate success, stunning the North, rejoicing the South, and impressing foreigners. Contemplating the newly won field about 10:00 that night, Lee was able to write Davis, "This army achieved today on the plains of Manassas a signal victory over combined forces of Genls McClellan and Pope."[131] Nor was he finished yet. The next day the Confederates moved to cut off Pope's retreat and clashed with Federals at Chantilly, barely twenty miles from Washington. A vicious little fight ensued, prevented from becoming a vicious big fight only by a rip-roaring thunderstorm that dampened everyone's powder, turned the roads into morasses, and generally made further combat impractical. Pope slunk back into the Washington defenses, and Lee had to content himself with an impressive but not annihilating victory.

For Davis, the suspense continued a few days more before he could receive news of Second Manassas. Even as Lee was preparing to write his exultant dispatch announcing victory, Davis composed for Lee a letter that was a remarkable mixture of elation and foreboding, caution and daring. Congratulating Lee on Jackson's successes through the twenty-ninth, Davis could not help reminding his general that he had dispatched the requested reinforcements from Richmond at a time when McClellan "was still upon our flank and a force at Fredericksburg seemed to threaten" the line of communications with Lee's army. He observed that his release of two of the city's five garrison brigades left the safety of the capital dependent on the enemy's "ignorance or want of enterprise." Still, if the enemy would refrain from threatening Richmond, Davis was willing to send a small force to demonstrate toward Fredericksburg if that would help Lee's present campaign. Finally, he expressed hope that Pendleton would be able to brief Lee adequately on Davis's outlook.[132] Once again Davis revealed himself as willing to follow Lee's strategy but harboring grave reservations, for Lee's strategy was not consistent with the president's own basic approach to the war.

The general's next letter, written three days after the battle, made this shockingly clear. "The present seems to be the most propitious time since the commencement of the war," Lee wrote, "for the Confederate Army to enter Maryland." He went on to explain that the Federal army had retreated to Washington, and although he might threaten that city, he could not afford to attack or besiege it while it was strongly held by the enemy. The Union would need time, he thought, to make good its losses and restore the organization of its Virginia army. This was the opportunity. "The army is not properly equipped for an invasion of an enemy's territory," Lee admitted. Shoes, clothes, and wagons were in poor condition and short supply. "Still," Lee argued, "we cannot afford to be idle, and though weaker than our opponents in men and military equipments, must endeavor to harass if we cannot destroy them." The danger involved in such a move, and Lee's explanation of the need for accepting it, reveal much about the Virginia general's approach to the war. "I am aware," Lee explained, "that the movement is attended with much risk, yet I do not consider success impossible."[133] For Lee, "much risk" was to be taken in an endeavor whose success was merely "not impossible" because ultimate success was indeed impossible by means attended with less risk.

That was never Davis's outlook. His confidence in Lee was now put to the test again and for an even higher stake. For the moment, his reaction was silence. Whether because of his chronic ill health or because he was simply stunned by Lee's audacity, he made no reply to Lee's September 3 letter. For the next week, Lee wrote to Davis daily, sometimes twice a day, explaining the movement and keeping the president posted on its progress. "I shall proceed to make the movement at once," he wrote on the fourth, "unless you should signify your disapprobation." Further, if all went well, he proposed "to enter Pennsylvania, unless you should deem it unadvisable upon political or other grounds." The president's silence was all the authorization Lee sought for this bold move, and he gave Davis no time to respond.

Lee worried about the problem of supplies. For ammunition, a supply line would have to be kept open to Richmond. Subsistence stores he hoped to draw, in part at least, from the country through which he was campaigning. In Virginia, his own country, and Pennsylvania, the enemy's, this would be a fairly straightforward matter. In Maryland it would not. Part of the reason for the move was to stir up secessionist feeling in that state, and heavy-handed methods would be counterproductive to say the least. For such ticklish political business, Lee wanted help and asked Davis that Maryland's former governor, now in Richmond, be sent to accompany him. Moving as rapidly as he had proposed, Lee crossed the Potomac on September 6, near Leesburg, Virginia, east of the Blue Ridge, so as to threaten Washington and Baltimore and thus keep the main Union army tied down covering those cities. He had already made plans, however, to abandon his line of communications along the Virginia Central beyond Culpeper and instead open a supply line through the Shenandoah Valley. For the moment, the Federals seemed as stunned by the move as Davis had and made no perceptible response.[134]

The Confederate president came to life after reading Lee's letter of September 4. Did Lee anticipate a sticky political situation in Maryland? Did he require the services of a politician with the army? Davis purposed to do better than send the former governor of Maryland–the Confederate president would go himself. His habits were well established in this regard. Davis had joined the army only just too late for the first battle of Manassas, had come to headquarters in the fall of 1861 when an advance seemed imminent, and had been on the field of battle at Seven Pines and throughout the Seven Days. He was a military man as well as a politician, and he had to sense the true meaning of Lee's move across the Potomac. Whatever Lee might write in his dispatches about merely harassing the enemy, this move smelled of a showdown fight, and Davis meant to be there. Accordingly, he left Richmond on the sixth or seventh and traveled as far as the Rapidan, probably in the vicinity of Orange Court House. There, on September 7, he wrote Lee, presenting him with a suggested proclamation to the people of Maryland to be issued in explanation of the army's presence in that state. He also added that he planned to continue on and join Lee north of the Potomac.[135]

Though a visit from the president was not at all a welcome proposition to Lee, the general himself had recently been ruminating on the political implications and possibilities of the move into Maryland, concluding that the time may well have come to end the war. In a letter that crossed Davis's notification of his intended visit, Lee set forth his views to the president. "The present position of affairs, in my opinion," he wrote, "places it in the power of the Government of the Confederate States to propose with propriety to that of the United States the recognition of our independence." He went on to assert that the Union was no nearer restoration than when the North had first set out with that goal over a year before. Nothing could convey this impression more forcefully than the presence of Lee's army on northern soil and within striking distance of the national capital. "Such a proposition," he explained to Davis, "coming from us at this time, could in no way be regarded as suing for peace; but, being made when it is in our power to inflict injury upon our adversary, would show conclusively to the world that our sole object is the establishment of our independence and the attainment of an honorable peace."[136] The early peace Lee seemed determined to win might be within reach, but first there was a matter to be settled with the Army of the Potomac, for the present still concentrated around Washington.[137]

As earnestly as he desired political fruits from his present military undertaking, Lee seems not to have been anxious to have Davis with him. During the Seven Days he had betrayed considerable embarrassment at Davis's presence. This was understandable, since the presence of the commander in chief created a situation in which the army—theoretically at least—had two commanders on the field, and one could never know when Davis might choose to turn theory into practice, perhaps bypassing whole layers of the chain of command to give an order directly to a subordinate officer. In all fairness, Davis had, considering his background, shown admirable restraint in such things, but Lee's uneasiness was at least equally understandable. Lee also may have begun to sense the increasingly clear difference in outlook between his own approach to the war and the president's.

In any case, Lee's reaction to Davis's letter was quick and decisive. He immediately wrote out a dispatch to the president. "While I should feel the greatest satisfaction in having an interview with you, and consulting upon all subjects of interest," he assured Davis, "I cannot but feel great uneasiness for your safety should you undertake to reach me." Not only would the journey be rough and tiresome, Lee explained, but the president would run the risk of capture by Union cavalry patrols. Again he explained his intention to abandon his supply line east of the Blue Ridge, and reiterated, "I must, therefore, advise that you do not make an attempt that I cannot but regard as hazardous." In case all of this persuasion failed, Lee also dispatched his aide, Maj. Walter H. Taylor, to ride back and meet Davis at Warrenton and renew the attempt to dissuade him.[138] The latter measure proved to be unnecessary. Taylor rode hard, leaving Lee's headquarters in Frederick, Maryland, at noon on September 9 and reaching Warrenton the next day. By that time, however, he learned that Davis, accepting Lee's arguments, had returned to Richmond.[139]

The president did not act on the basis of Lee's urging in one matter, however, and that was approaching the Union government with an offer of peace in exchange for independence. Davis offered no refusal to Lee's suggestion; indeed, he offered no reply or explanation of any sort. Instead, he seemed to be waiting for something. Under the circumstances, this awaited culmination could only have been one thing. Any militarily astute observer could see that a great battle was impending north of the Potomac. Lee's invasion made that event as certain as the falling of that autumn's leaves and a good deal more imminent. No peace overture now could stay this inevitability, nor could so acute a politician as Davis have supposed for a minute that the Lincoln government would entertain such a proposal without at least this final appeal to battle. If Lee should prove victorious in the coming clash, the proposal of peace would carry that much more weight. If he should fail, any previous Confederate peace proposal would become ludicrous. The best course, then, was to wait. From Richmond came complete silence on the subject of Lee's suggested peace initiative.

If Lee's political timing was perhaps a half beat off tempo, his sense of the flow of military events was as sharp as ever. The impending clash of arms was as clear to him as it was to Davis. He sought it. This march across the Potomac was no mere raid. In a classic turning maneuver, Lee was in the process of placing his army so that it could threaten the enemy's vital rear areas while its own communications, running southwest through the Shenandoah Valley behind the protective screen of the Blue Ridge, were secure. He was following a design he had settled on at the outset of the campaign. After crossing the Potomac east of the Blue Ridge so as to force the Union army to pull out of Virginia and concentrate on Washington, he would swing west to open communications through the Shenandoah Valley.[140] This Valley supply line was to fill not only the army's cartridge boxes, caissons, and limbers, as Lee had mentioned to Davis in his letter of September 5, but–contrary to what he had stated in that letter–the army's haversacks as well.[141] In his letter to Davis on September 9, Lee stated, "I shall move in the direction I originally intended, toward Hagerstown and Chambersburg, for the purpose of opening our line of communication through the valley, in order to procure sufficient supplies of flour."[142]

Flour, made into hardtack, comprised the bulk of the army's diet and of its supply needs. In arranging to have "sufficient supplies" brought up the well-paved Valley Pike (a flourishing route for freight wagons in prewar years), Lee would be setting up a full-service supply line, which would drastically change the rules of how he needed to operate north of the Potomac. It

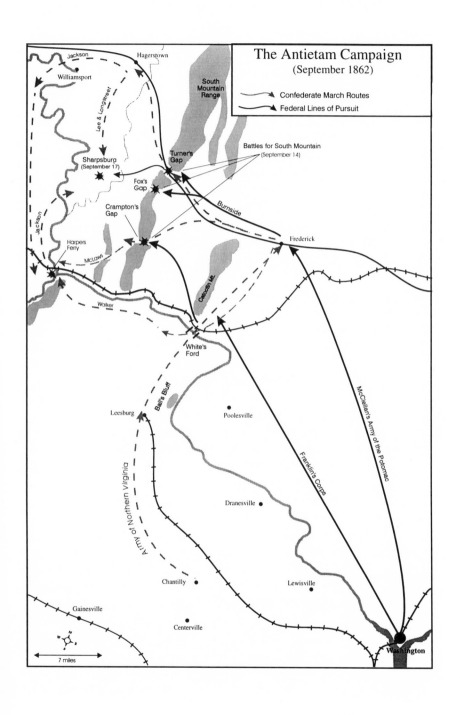

The Antietam Campaign
(September 1862)

Confederate March Routes

Federal Lines of Pursuit

Jackson

Hagerstown

Williamsport

South Mountain Range

Lee & Longstreet

Turner's Gap

Battles for South Mountain
(September 14)

Sharpsburg
(September 17)

Fox's Gap

Crampton's Gap

Burnside

Frederick

Jackson

Harpers Ferry

McLaws

Ocatoctin Mt.

Walker

White's Ford

Ball's Bluff

Leesburg

Poolesville

McClellan's Army of the Potomac

Army of Northern Virginia

Franklin's Corps

Dranesville

Chantilly

Lewisville

Gainesville

Centerville

Washington

7 miles

opened the possibility of an extended stay, for unlike the commander of a raiding army that must draw its foodstuffs from the land over which it passes, Lee would be able to keep his army concentrated and stationary, forcing McClellan to come to him on ground of his own choosing. That was just what McClellan would have to do. When an army is turned, it must either fight or retreat. Lee had turned the northern army again, and a Union retreat that gave up Washington and Baltimore was simply out of the question. If his plan worked, Lee could be confident that the Federals would attack him regardless of whatever disadvantages of position he could impose on them. Lee planned to be prepared to wait as long as necessary for that desirable event and then make the most of it, hoping for another victory on the order of Second Manassas or even greater.[143]

The problem that developed as the campaign progressed was that not all of the northern players were following the script. Lee had supposed that as soon as his army reached Frederick, Maryland, astride the National Road and controlling all the practical routes between the Shenandoah Valley and Washington or Baltimore, "the enemy's forces in the Valley of Virginia, which had retired to Harpers Ferry and Martinsburg would retreat altogether from the State." Having been turned and being too badly outnumbered to take on Lee's army in battle, these troops were to slink off quietly and let Lee get on with the campaign. "In this," Lee informed the president in a September 12 letter, "I was disappointed."[144] The Federals had stayed put and were prepared to stand a siege. As long as they were there, Lee could not carry out his plans for a sustained presence in Maryland and Pennsylvania. He could still make a raid, of course, but that was not what he wanted. The Federals on the Shenandoah would have to be removed. Confident that the plodding McClellan, now once again in command of the opposing army, would allow him plenty of time, Lee divided his army into several detachments, sending them about to gain the high ground on all sides of Harpers Ferry. They were not within supporting distance of one another should they come under attack, but for the moment Lee apprehended nothing of the sort, even though his scouts had reported on the ninth that "the enemy are pushing a strong column up the Potomac River."[145] Indeed, his army was sprawled across a remarkable amount of Maryland and Virginia real estate, from the troops threatening Harpers Ferry on the Virginia side of the river, to others at the passes of South Mountain (the northward extension of the Blue Ridge), to advance pickets at Middleburg, on the Pennsylvania line. It was nothing if not audacious. To keep the president fully informed of developments, Lee sent him a copy of the order, Special Orders no. 191, directing this dispersed movement to take Harpers Ferry while maintaining a presence in Maryland.[146]

In a further misfortune, this highly sensitive document proved to have rather too wide a circulation. Another copy of the same order, intended for division commander D. H. Hill, was lost and eventually found its way unbeknownst to Lee into the hands of George McClellan. The delighted Union general proclaimed it "a paper with which if I cannot whip Bobby Lee I will be willing to go home."[147] He had the right idea. The fact was that any competent and energetic commander would, with this information, be able to snap up the isolated and vulnerable fragments of Lee's dispersed army one after the other. Fired with expectancy at the possibilities spread before him, McClellan moved with unwonted celerity. He was not, of course, quick enough to catch and destroy Lee's army piece by piece—he was, after all, McClellan—but it was a very near-run thing.

Using the troops most readily available, Lee was able to delay McClellan at the passes of South Mountain just long enough for the scattered detachments of his army to reunite near the western Maryland town of Sharpsburg. His front faced east toward the valley of Antietam Creek and the gathering forces of McClellan's army. Behind him was the Potomac, crossable at a single ford. Another rear-guard action like the one at South Mountain would have allowed him to get his army, generally intact, back onto the relatively safe soil of Virginia. Instead, Lee opted to stand and fight. McClellan had some 87,000 men in his ranks; Lee, less than half that number.[148] With the river at his back, Lee could well face final ruin if his line was broken. In short, the decision to accept battle at Antietam was audacity run amok.

Yet it was for this that Lee had come north. He intended to force the Federals to attack him on ground of his own choosing, and he intended to beat them when they did, just as he had done at Second Manassas. Although the unfortunate scramble created by the loss of Special Orders no. 191 had narrowed the options for choice of a battlefield, the position on the hills west of Antietam Creek was a strong one. Retreat, of course, would be disastrous, but Lee did not figure on retreating. He counted on his skill and the hesitance of McClellan, his men's fortitude and what he hoped would be the demoralization of the northern rank and file, to give him victory. It was on this last count that he erred most. The northern troops were to prove themselves every bit the fighters their southern foes were despite the discouraging impact of a summer of defeat and retreat.

Throughout the day on September 17, McClellan pushed elements of his army forward in piecemeal and uncoordinated attacks, committing only

46,000 of his troops and thus neutralizing his advantage in numbers. Still the gritty Federals came within a hair's breadth of exacting from Lee the gravest penalty for his audacity. For the Confederates it was a desperate struggle. Several times during the morning the army tottered on the brink of final disaster. Fighting like wounded grizzly bears, the gray-clad troops turned back one Union thrust after another, as Lee desperately shifted troops to his badly threatened left and center. Then, just past midday, the Confederate right gave way. As Union troops swarmed to the outskirts of Sharpsburg, the end appeared to have come for the Army of Northern Virginia. Watching from a distance, Lee squinted through the battle smoke, trying to sort out the various bodies of troops wheeling across the ridge where his line had been as another formation moved up from the south. Just then a young artillery officer galloped by, carrying a telescope. Lee stopped him and, pointing to the ridge, asked, "What troops are those?"

The lieutenant offered him his telescope, but Lee had injured his hand in a fall several days before, and his fingers were swathed in bandages. "Can't use it," he explained, holding up his hand. "What troops are those?"

The lieutenant looked. "They are flying the United States flag," he announced.

Lee pointed to the other formation. "What troops are those?"

Again the young officer peered through his glass. "They are flying the Virginia and Confederate flags," he replied at last.

With a calmness that must have belied enormous relief, Lee announced, "It is A. P. Hill, from Harpers Ferry."

The last of Lee's troops had reached the battlefield, having marched seventeen miles in seven hours. Only their timely arrival blunted the last Union assault. Gradually the firing ceased. It had been the bloodiest single day in American history. Some 11,000 Confederates and 12,000 Federals had fallen. Never again, until Appomattox, would Lee's army be this close to destruction.

As nightfall brought a merciful close to the day's fighting, Lee had an opportunity to extricate his shattered army from the very tight corner in which it now found itself, drawing back across the river into Virginia. Nothing could have been farther from his mind. When his generals gathered that night after dark to make the doleful reports of the day's fighting and losses—Longstreet reported things were "as bad as can be"; Hill complained, "My division is cut to pieces"; Hood, almost in tears, moaned that he had "no division left"—Lee put to them the question of whether the Army of Northern Virginia should go over to the offensive in the morning. It was, in

Ambrose Powell Hill. (Courtesy of National Archives, 111-BA-1190)

the words of artillery officer E. P. Alexander, "sublime audacity." His subordinates were understandably hard put to appreciate it at the moment. The officers were unanimous in advising that the army get out of Maryland while the getting was good—before another sunrise. Lee sent them back to their commands to shore up their lines and collect what stragglers they could. "If McClellan wants to fight in the morning," he told them, "I will give him battle again." When daylight returned to the bloodstained ridges overlooking Antietam Creek, Lee intended to give McClellan battle whether he wanted it or not. Stonewall's topographical engineer, Jed Hotchkiss, described him as "eager to renew the battle." Even the pugnacious Jackson had grave misgivings but loyally did his best to keep them from anyone but Lee. When Lee suggested the Confederates bring up a few batteries onto some high ground in Jackson's sector and blast the way open "for falling on the Federal right," the latter suggested taking an artillery officer to view the ground and give his opinion on the feasibility of this project. To Lee's "great disappointment," the officer came back with the report that it was "not only impracticable, but extremely hazardous." Alexander summed up the result: "Fortunately for somebody, [Lee] decided to stand on the defensive."[149]

Throughout the day on Thursday, September 18, the two armies stared at each other across the valley of Antietam Creek. Lee lacked the ability to attack and McClellan the nerve. By evening it would have been clear to Lee that the present standoff was not to his advantage. With appearances at least somewhat salvaged by the extra day spent daring McClellan to do his worst, Lee began his withdrawal back into Virginia during the wee hours of the morning of September 19. Before noon the last Confederate units were across the Potomac. Although Lee had held his ground in the face of enemy attack, winning a hollow tactical victory, he had nevertheless suffered strategic defeat. With the Army of the Potomac in front of him and his back against the Potomac River to the west, Lee now found the tables turned on him with respect to lines of supply. In this situation, his enemy's supply line ran directly and safely back behind the Union army, while his own, running off to his right down the Shenandoah Valley, was vulnerable. McClellan's advance, though too slow to reap the fruits of the discovery of Special Orders no. 191, had nevertheless been fast and forceful enough—catching Lee unprepared at first with his army scattered—to cut off Lee's options, checkmate his offensive movement, and force him to withdraw defeated into Virginia.

But Lee was not finished. If one turning movement failed, he would try another. No sooner were his troops back on Virginia soil than he set them to marching up the Potomac toward Williamsport, fifteen miles north of Sharpsburg. Here he hoped to cross back into Maryland and march the ten miles to Hagerstown.[150] This would put him about twelve miles north-northeast of McClellan and on the Federal right flank. Although the move would expose both armies' communications about equally, it would renew the threat by Lee's army to the northern countryside, while a move by

McClellan toward Lee's supply line would only draw him up the Shenandoah and farther from the scene of decisive combat. The timid McClellan would, Lee reckoned, become "apprehensive about his communications."[151] The Union commander would then attack Lee in his chosen position near Hagerstown, and Lee hoped "to defeat the enemy at that point."[152]

Lee had gone so far as to have his cavalry occupy Williamsport before he gave up the idea. A temporary setback in a rear-guard action on the Virginia side of the Potomac on the nineteenth compelled Lee to countermarch part of his army in order to prevent the potentially fatal consequences should McClellan, entirely out of character, move energetically to trap the Confederates against the Virginia bank of the Potomac before Lee could recover the initiative. No real danger threatened, but with the incident over, Lee concluded that it would be unwise to press matters further. "The condition of the army prevented further offensive action," he explained in a letter to Davis several days later. "Nor is it yet strong enough to advance advantageously."[153] On the same day, September 25, G. W. C. Lee, the general's son and the president's military aide, wrote to Davis from near Martinsburg, where he had traveled on a fact-finding mission for the president. "The road from Harrisonburg to Winchester & from Winchester to Martinsburg was full of stragglers," he reported. Some of these seemed to be the walking wounded, but most had simply seen enough of fighting to last them a while and had wandered off to put some distance between themselves and the scene of likely battle. "I am told," the president's aide continued, "that the whole country is full of them, in every direction." Seeking the reason for this circumstance, he wrote, "The men of our army have been in a measure worn out by long marches and hard fighting, and are poorly clad, with many of them without shoes." Another reason might have been the soldiers' realization that in the battle on the other side of the Potomac, as G. W. C. Lee reported from what he had heard, "they got the worst of it."[154]

The elder Lee knew it too. "Desertion and straggling," he explained to Davis, had so thinned the ranks of the army that "it was unable to cope with advantage with the numerous host of the enemy" and so had been forced to withdraw from Maryland.[155] Indeed, the problem of straggling had been growing for some weeks and now seemed to threaten the very existence of the army. On September 7 Lee had written Davis, "I find that the discipline of the army . . . has not been improved by the forced marches and hard service it has lately undergone. . . . One of the greatest evils . . . is the habit of straggling from the ranks."[156] A week later he had to admit that "the vice of straggling" was so widespread that it was impossible to come up with any solid estimate of the casualties in the Second Manassas campaign.[157] After the battle at Sharpsburg and the return to Virginia, the problem actually grew worse.[158] Lee mentioned it to Davis almost daily during the week after the battle, apologizing, "My desire for the welfare of the army and the success of the war induces me to trouble you very often." The absent-without-leave were "scattered broadcast over the land," many of them engaging in "destruction of private property." Men were "feigning sickness, wounds, &c., deceiving the guards and evading the scouts." Others threw away their shoes in order to have an excuse to fall out of ranks. "Many of them," Lee wrote, "will not stop until they reach their distant homes," while others simply remained "aloof" in the vicinity of the army. "Unless something is done," the general warned, "the army will melt away." In fact, upwards of 20,000 men were absent from the army's ranks, ranks already thinned by some 47,000 casualties in the twelve weeks since the launching of the Seven Days' battles.[159]

Nor was this the sum of the army's weaknesses. When G. W. C. Lee sent his report to Davis, he had stated, "The officers with whom I have conversed say that our troops were shaky from the day they went into Maryland . . . , that if even the few (comparatively) who were present had fought with the usual spirit at both Boonsboro, and Sharpsburg, the enemy would have been badly whipped."[160] This statement is hard to credit in view of the fact that those troops had held the Sharpsburg ridge in the face of slightly superior numbers of northern troops and had suffered one-fourth their numbers as casualties in doing so. Still, the president's military aide was not the only one who held this opinion, especially after the battle. The general himself was far from confident in the present temper of his army. He explained in a letter to Davis that he considered the best move at present would be to carry out the left-handed turning maneuver he had envisioned immediately after the battle, moving on Hagerstown, Maryland, and aiming to defeat the enemy there. "I would not hesitate to make" this movement, Lee wrote, "even with our diminished numbers, did the army exhibit its former temper and condition." As it was, though, "the hazard would be great and a reverse disastrous."[161] Three months of hard marches and fearful battles had simply pushed many of the soldiers beyond the limits of human endurance. Physically or emotionally exhausted, they could do no more at present. As Alexander put it, by the end of the fighting at Sharpsburg, "the Confederate army was worn & fought to a perfect frazzle."[162]

Lee had done his best to end the war that summer. He had endeavored to destroy McClellan's army along the Chickahominy and Pope's, first in the corner of the Rappahannock and the Rapidan and then on the plains of Manassas. Foiled each time, he had nevertheless won impressive victories that had rolled back the northern armies, blunted both points of the two-pronged Union threat to Richmond, and made a potentially very significant impact on public opinion both north, south, and abroad. His daring cross-Potomac turning movement was designed to establish a fully supplied, long-term Confederate presence on the soil of Maryland and Pennsylvania, forcing a headlong Federal attack that he hoped to receive on ground of his own choosing. The resulting Union repulse would then, he hoped, set the stage for a victory more crushing and complete than that at Second Manassas. The breathtaking boldness and ingenious conception of the plan are testimony to Lee's prowess as a general. Yet this time he had overreached himself. His brave plan foundered on the Union refusal to abandon Harpers Ferry, the loss of Special Orders no. 191, the resilience of the northern troops even after a summer of defeat, and the exhaustion of the Confederate troops by that same summer's operations. Through all of the summer's campaigns, Lee's actions speak clearly of the fact that he saw quick victory as necessary for the Confederacy. That a man of Lee's intelligence knowingly chose to accept enormous risks in order to purchase the chance of an end-the-war battle is proof he believed the Confederacy's chances grew slimmer with every passing month. This was not an unreasonable view. The North had a preponderance of men, money, and materiel. Intangible but more important, many southerners—including Lee—had been unsure of the rightness of the Confederate cause in the first place. That would produce brittle morale that might break under the strain of a long war. His bid for quick victory having fallen short and his army exhausted, Lee regretfully informed the president, "I am, therefore, led to pause."[163]

Much as this pause obviously chafed Lee, it could only have come as a relief to Jefferson Davis. The president had watched with interest the development of Lee's grand offensive north of the Potomac, sending G. W. C. Lee to gather even more information than was provided by the almost daily dispatches from the elder Lee. Davis was in very poor health for much of this time, and his condition was probably aggravated by worry about the campaign in progress coupled with his inability to take the field with the army. Waiting idly in Richmond while momentous events were being decided was never easy for the high-strung president. As for the invasion of Maryland, he had hoped to see something of this sort a year earlier, but he had never been willing to take risks on this scale in order to accomplish it. That he had done so now showed the degree to which he had been swept along by Lee's daring.

His respect for Lee's intellect and appreciation of Lee's pleasant personality had grown by the end of the Seven Days into a deep confidence in Lee as a general. During the summer months, this confidence had led Davis even to set aside his own basic approach to the war. Instead of surviving and striking what small blows it could with minimal risk, the Confederacy would this summer, at Lee's behest but under Davis's direction, wager heavily on long-odds gambles for an early peace. Davis had put his money on Lee, and through each round of the summer's nerve-racking game, he had followed the general's lead, supporting his efforts even to the point of paring the Richmond garrison down to a single weak division of infantry. He had not spared reminding Lee, sometimes almost querulously, of the dizzying risks they were taking, but he took them just the same, with an effort of will that one can only admire. The stakes were too high for a man of Davis's temperament to play the game coolly, but play it he would nevertheless.

Still, his fundamental approach to the war remained unchanged. Though he might bear with Lee in grasping for the summer's opportunity, he still showed indications of believing that the Confederacy's best hope of independence lay in stubborn survival that avoided defeat and simply outlasted the northern will to preserve the Union. His desire to join Lee with the army would seem to imply some limit to his trust for the general, perhaps an urge to place boundaries on Lee's seemingly boundless appetite for taking risks. In the same manner, his sending of Pendleton to brief Lee on his "views" and "secure . . . co-intelligence between" them just two weeks after Lee left the Richmond area is hard to explain unless Davis had begun to sense that Lee's fundamental approach to winning the war was at variance with his own. With the gamble for quick victory having been taken but not gained, Davis would, during the year that followed, gradually and haltingly move toward a stronger assertion and at least a partial implementation of his own ideas for gaining Confederate independence.

6

BETWEEN THE DEFEAT OF AN ARMY AND ITS RUIN

With Lee's army safely back on Virginia soil, and McClellan's quiescent north of the Potomac, Davis and Lee could turn their attention to matters of organization. Active campaigning had filled the first four months of Lee's tenure in command, and some matters had of necessity been held in abeyance. Other problems resulted from the wear and tear of week after week of constant marching and fighting. During the reprieve granted by McClellan— while stragglers returned to the ranks and sick and wounded recovered and rejoined their regiments—the president and his chief eastern general made use of the time to improve the army's command system, discipline, and organization.

First there was the problem of poor discipline, for which Lee believed poor regimental officers were responsible.[1] He wanted ineffective officers out and sought from Secretary of War Randolph authority to carry out a thorough housecleaning.[2] Randolph brought the matter to Davis. The secretary explained that "the present condition of the Army of Northern Virginia" required a change in the system of selecting officers and that Lee had been "unable to devise any expedient by which he may avoid the alternative of violating law or of exposing his army to ruin."[3]

The problem lay in the laws by which Congress had organized the army. In keeping with popular democratic ideals, officers below the rank of general were to be elected by their troops when the regiment was organized and thereafter replaced by promotion within the same regiment. The leaders thus selected proved unlikely to know the rudiments of their military duties. Remedying the problem of poor officers had to start with some change in the law, and Davis was the man peculiarly suited by background and position to recognize this and communicate it successfully to Congress. This he did in part. In response to Lee's first mention of poor discipline within the army early in September, Davis asked Congress to set up a special court-martial commission to enforce more rigorous discipline.[4] Congress complied a couple of weeks later, but the resulting law, though necessary and welcome as far as it went, naturally missed the basic structural flaw in the Confederate system of choosing officers. It took time for Davis to see this. At first, he endorsed Lee's complaints, "Legislation is not necessary."[5] Eventually Davis came around and asked Congress for legislation permitting the president to circumvent the election and promotion system by assigning to a poorly officered regiment a qualified man from another outfit in the same brigade.[6] Congress responded with a convoluted arrangement. A special examining board could be set up in each military department to try the competency of officers. An officer found wanting could be removed but replaced only from the same regiment. Only if all the officers within a regiment proved to be unfit could the president go outside it for selection of an officer and then only from the same state.[7] Politically, that was the best that could be done.

Also on the agenda that fall was the restructuring of the army's command system. The lack of effective corps organizations had handicapped Lee during the Seven Days. Now, at last, Congress—with the president's approval—authorized the existence of army corps and created the new rank of lieutenant general for their commanders.[8] This granted legal existence to the ad hoc arrangement of "wings" by which Lee had been operating his army since the middle of August. Indeed, Lee's adoption of this pattern and his success with it, Sharpsburg notwithstanding, probably went far toward persuading both Congress and the president of the propriety of the change.

When it came to giving Lee an adequate staff, however, Davis showed himself far less capable of learning. Senator Louis T. Wigfall, by this time an enemy of the Davis administration, had introduced and pushed through Congress a bill authorizing larger staffs for army commanders. Under its terms, the generals themselves, rather than the president, would choose the members of this new and more efficient staff, and the more important staff officers would have their effectiveness boosted by the added authority that came with the rank of brigadier general. Northern army commanders already had this sort of staff, and its acquisition would have been a distinct boon to their southern counterparts.[9] Inadequate staff work had been one of the chief causes, along with the absence of corps organizations, of the failure of the Army of Northern Virginia to perform as Lee intended during the Seven Days. Now, presented with an opportunity to remedy another of the flaws in the structure of the army, Davis vetoed the bill. The proposed legislation seemed to infringe his prerogatives as president, and he was always very sensitive about such things.[10]

Davis ended the fall season of army structural reform with a distinctly mixed record. He had gained some concessions–though not enough–from Congress regarding the system that produced incompetent regimental officers. He had approved the establishment of corps but scuttled a much needed improvement for the staffs of Lee and other army commanders. If his performance was less than perfect, it would have been more than adequate– if the Confederacy had had a larger margin of error.

The president might not always understand the new aspects of what the military needed, but what he did understand of the army's wants he worked zealously and efficiently to supply. One obvious requirement was additional manpower, and Davis took an intense personal interest in the details of finding it. He sent Lee reports of recruiting efforts as far afield as Kentucky and Louisiana and noted with pleasure that Congress had raised the maximum age for those subject to the draft to 45. So close was the interest he took in recruitment within Virginia that he was aware of which counties had been heavily canvassed for conscripts and which had not and directed special attention to the latter. With equal diligence Davis addressed the issue of supplying Lee's army, giving his attention to such details as the supply of shoes or the shape of the boxes in which the army's hardtack was shipped.[11] The president served as a sort of high-level expediter for seeing that the army in Virginia received as promptly and fully as possible the many small things an army needed in order to function well.

The army also required capable general officers, and seeing to that fell clearly within the more traditional responsibilities of the president. In the selection of the new lieutenant generals, however, the important decisions had already been made for him. Longstreet and Jackson were the senior major generals in the Army of Northern Virginia and for over a month had been functioning in de facto corps command. Davis wrote Lee, "You have two officers now commanding several divisions and may require more. Please send to me as soon as possible the names of such as you prefer for Lt. General."[12] The implication was that the president would, if Lee desired, promote Longstreet and Jackson and as many other corps commanders as the army needed. Equally clear, however, was the president's hint that the occasion of selecting lieutenant generals offered an opportunity, if Lee wished, of escaping reliance on the most senior men in the army and replacing them with the most capable if such were not the same. In a word, either Longstreet or Jackson, or both, could be superseded if Lee was displeased with their performance in their current capacities and preferred other of his major generals in their places. Lee had but to send to Davis the names of whatever officers he might "prefer for Lt. General."

Lee responded promptly. "I can confidently recommend Generals Longstreet and Jackson," he wrote.[13] Yet the president's implication obviously was not lost on Lee, and it was clear which general's shelving the president contemplated. Jackson had been catapulted to fame by his successes in the Shenandoah Valley that spring, but Davis prided himself on being above concern for popular opinion.[14] Jackson had directed the Romney campaign the previous winter. His military dispositions had been characterized as mistaken by Davis and countermanded at his direction. The incident had left strained feelings, and the meeting between the two men the morning after Malvern Hill had been as cold and raw as the weather that day. Davis seems to have undertaken no campaign to get Jackson out of the army, but at least as Lee read it, he was giving the Army of Northern Virginia's commander a convenient opportunity for reducing Jackson's responsibility. In response, Lee felt compelled to affirm his confidence in Jackson in a way he did not in Longstreet's case. "My opinion of the merits of General Jackson has been greatly enhanced during this expedition," he wrote. "He is true, honest, and brave; has a single eye to the good of the service, and spares no exertion to accomplish his object."[15] With that, the unspoken debate was laid to rest. Longstreet and Jackson would receive their promotions in the order of their previous seniority.

As for the additional corps commanders Davis had suggested Lee might need, Lee was of a different mind. "At present," he wrote, "I do not think that more than two commanders of corps are necessary for this army." General A. P. Hill was, Lee explained, the next best officer now serving with him, but for the moment he could remain in division command.[16] Lee was equally undemanding in his response to Davis's request for recommendations for lower-ranking general officers. He had already forwarded to the president a number of names of those whom he believed deserved promotion to major or brigadier general. As far as Lee professed to be concerned, the president could choose from these.[17] The general could not have been ignorant of the political concerns surrounding the issue of selecting general officers. Politicians had been complaining for some time now that this army was led by too many Virginians and too many West Point graduates. If Davis felt the need to ease political pressure by promoting according to the quota system from a pool of at least adequate officers, Lee considerately gave him that much slack.[18]

Far more important to Lee than which of several fairly good officers received a particular promotion was his concern to get out of his army those officers who through defect of temperament, training, or intellect were a threat to its efficiency and, in some circumstances, even its survival. In many cases, Lee was thwarted in this desire to be rid of such men. Davis showed a perverse tendency to interpret unclear laws in the most inconvenient ways possible, and sometimes blocked necessary changes.[19] Still, the president seems to have been sincere in his inconvenient interpretations and devoid of any desire to hinder Lee. Indeed, in some of his more difficult cases, Lee could not have asked for more complete cooperation. The unstable Whiting was one such case. Lee wanted him out of his army in order to make room for the promotion of promising men of lower rank, in this case John Bell Hood. Always courteous and tender of the feelings of others, Lee saw fit to "recommend" Whiting to the secretary of war for service someplace else, preferably far away, where "his services" would be "more valuable than here." Of the two likely posts for a man of Whiting's training, Charleston and Mobile, Lee suggested that Mobile, the more distant of the two, would be the better choice.

As always, the matter was referred to the president. Davis ordered that he should be sent to Richmond pending a decision on what to do with him next.[20] Richmond might not be south Alabama, but Lee apparently considered himself well rid of the troublesome Whiting and began making arrangements for his replacement.[21] A week and a half later, apparently confident that Whiting was gone forever, Lee, discussing the transfer of a couple of other officers whose services he really would miss, generously mentioned that he would miss Whiting too.[22] It was no doubt with some shock that he received from Davis a day or two later a letter in which the president offered to recall the other two officers to the Army of Northern Virginia if Lee wanted them. As for Whiting, the president informed Lee, he was still in Richmond and could return to the front as soon as Lee wanted him.[23] The matter was eventually cleared up, as Whiting departed for North Carolina and Hood rose to division command. Davis, meanwhile, had shown himself extraordinarily eager to meet Lee's desires in matters of personnel whenever he believed in good conscience he could do so.

In other matters as well Davis showed himself ready to meet Lee's requests even when they touched unpleasantly on his own state or his own friends. When the officers of Winfield S. Featherston's Mississippi brigade petitioned to be transferred back to their home state for the winter, Davis referred the matter to Lee and faithfully adhered to his recommendations. His fellow

Mississippians would shiver through another Virginia winter.[24] Even more remarkable was the president's willingness to sacrifice a friend if that was what Lee wanted. Davis displayed an intense loyalty to his prewar friends and a remarkable blindness to their faults. When just a few months earlier Braxton Bragg had hinted at the need to remove an old Davis West Point crony, Leonidas Polk, because of his incompetence and insubordination, Davis had bridled. His stubborn support of Polk was to become one of the significant ingredients in the Confederacy's ultimate defeat west of the mountains. No one as close to Davis as Polk served in Virginia, yet even at that, the deference Davis showed to Lee and the needs of the Army of Northern Virginia in such matters is striking.

This fall Lee faced the problem of what to do with Davis's friend, Brig. Gen. Thomas F. Drayton. The South Carolinian simply could not handle his brigade, and it had gone to pieces in each of the army's last three engagements. After long delay, Lee decided he had no choice but to take the direct approach. Writing to Davis he explained, "I have endeavored for some time to avoid the necessity of pursuing the course I am now about to take," but things had simply come to the point at which Lee believed he could "no longer hesitate." He recited the litany of Drayton's misadventures as a brigade commander and the complaints of every division commander he had ever served under. "I am compelled, therefore," he concluded, "to make a change, and wish to do it in the manner least disagreeable to General Drayton, for whom I feel great friendship." The answer was to be found in the composition of Drayton's brigade. It was composed of Georgia and South Carolina regiments, contrary to the policy of brigading troops by states. Therefore, the various regiments of the brigade would be distributed to other brigades of their own states and Drayton would be given thirty days' leave, "at the end of which," Lee hoped, "some duty may be found for him in the South or Southwest, which he may be able to perform with advantage to the service."[25] Davis made no objection, and it was so ordered.[26]

So Davis and Lee passed the fall of 1862 in tackling the problems of organizing, disciplining, and officering the army. They did not always agree, but Lee was characteristically courteous and patient, while Davis, though limited both by the realities of politics and by the preconceptions of his own mind, made concessions even beyond the considerable ones he had granted previous army commanders. Although hampered as always by poor health, the president had applied himself diligently to the improvement of the army. He had given Lee everything he had asked for in matters of personnel and a fair bit of what he had wanted in matters of organization and law. Through

J. E. B. Stuart (Courtesy of National Archives, 111-BA-1224)

their combined efforts the Army of Northern Virginia was larger, more responsive, and far more combat-ready as winter approached that year than it had ever been before. That was just as well, for the pace of operations, somnolent in the weeks after Sharpsburg, had gradually picked up throughout the fall season, and before the first snows flew it began to build toward another showdown.

Lee had never been fully content with the lull in operations. On October 2, barely two weeks after the carnage of Sharpsburg, he wrote Davis that he had been hoping McClellan "would cross the [Potomac] river and move up the [Shenandoah] valley, where I wish to get him." Sadly, he observed that the northern general did "not seem so disposed."[27] Indeed, to the frustration of Lincoln, McClellan seemed indisposed for any sort of action whatsoever, as week after week went by. The Army of the Potomac sat on the north bank of the Potomac near Harpers Ferry and the Army of Northern Virginia camped over against it some miles up the Valley near Winchester. Both Lee and Davis feared a movement by other Federal troops from either Washington or the Peninsula toward Richmond, but no such threat materialized.[28] Jeb Stuart, Lee's cavalry commander, made use of the pause to make his second spectacular ride around the motionless Union army. Otherwise the month of October was so quiet that Lee, writing to Davis on the twenty-second, was talking of putting the army into winter quarters or even sending some of the troops to "operate in Georgia and South Carolina," a topic on which he sought Davis's direction.[29]

Then things began to change. On October 26, McClellan began to cross the Potomac east of the Blue Ridge. To be sure, he moved with his accustomed deliberation, and two days later he still did not have his entire army on the south bank. Nevertheless, the lead elements of the Army of the Potomac were advancing southward toward Warrenton, and Lee felt compelled to take action lest he find himself cut off from Richmond. Jackson was to remain in the Valley, a potential threat to the right flank of any advancing northern army, while Lee with Longstreet's corps moved eastward into a position to block the northern advance.[30] That same day Davis dispatched Lt. Gen. John C. Pemberton, then between assignments in Richmond, to visit Lee's headquarters. "General Pemberton," Davis wrote in a short note to Lee, was "fully possessed of my views, and charged to communicate them to you."[31] Yet within days even this form of communication failed to satisfy Davis, and he summoned Lee to Richmond for conference. Of special concern at this meeting was the Federal amphibious threat to coastal North Carolina and how many troops that area could spare to reinforce Lee for meeting the current Union offensive in northern Virginia. In the end, a substantial force was left near the coast, although some troops did move north to join Lee.[32] In contrast to his letter less than two weeks before, Lee made clear to Davis that he did not anticipate an idle winter for his army and urged that it would need "every support" in the coming struggle.[33]

Back at his headquarters in Culpeper by the end of the first week in November, Lee grew more convinced than ever than the main Union effort was to be on his front. McClellan continued his slow but steady southward creep—moving, as Lee thought, "more rapidly than usual" and even looking "like a real advance." Lee wrote both Davis and the secretary of war to stress that "the operations south of the James River for the present are intended to divert and distract us." He expected "the whole force of this army" to be needed in northern Virginia at no very distant date.[34] Then on November 9 came the shocking news that Lincoln had replaced McClellan with Maj. Gen. Ambrose Burnside. Some Confederates hailed the departure of the highly regarded McClellan from the enemy camp, but Lee observed wryly to Longstreet, "I fear they may continue to make these changes till they find some one whom I don't understand."[35] Another week passed without action as Burnside gathered in the reins of authority. Clearly, however, a movement was in the works. McClellan had been removed for failure to advance energetically enough, and his successor could entertain no doubts as to what was expected of him. On November 15 the Army of the Potomac moved out, heading east, away from its previous line of advance. Two days later, Lee reported the movement to Davis. He had been expecting a Union move toward Fredericksburg but thought perhaps that the Federals might be drawing back toward Washington to embark on another McClellan-style amphibious operation on the Virginia coast.[36] By the nineteenth, as the lead divisions of Longstreet's corps took up positions behind Fredericksburg just in case, Lee was again convinced that the Federals were planning "to force their way from Fredericksburg."[37] The next day he arrived there in person and wired Davis, "I think Burnside is concentrating his whole army opposite Fredericksburg."[38] Lee took steps to match the move, but that would take time since Jackson was still out at Winchester in the Valley. To the president Lee explained that he had "waited to the last moment" to summon Jackson because he liked the effect the embarrassing presence of Jackson in a flank position was producing on northern operations.[39]

During the three weeks that followed the armies continued to gather on opposite banks of the Rappahannock at Fredericksburg. Burnside was delayed in launching his attack because a crucial pontoon train did not arrive.

Lee, of course, was unaware of this and could only speculate about the Union general's intentions. He kept Davis well informed with a stream of long and detailed letters. The president, for his part, was less communicative than usual, possibly because of preoccupation with the threatening military situation in his home state of Mississippi and possibly because of his poor health and busy schedule. It also may be that he saw little need to send frequent dispatches to Lee since that general kept him well informed and seemed to be proceeding in harmony with his way of thinking. He was far from neglecting the army, however, and when Lee requested heavy guns to counter the northern superiority in artillery, Davis readily dispatched two of the best from the Richmond defenses.[40] More important, in the letters he did send he shared with Lee some of his thoughts on the appropriate Confederate strategy in Virginia. Astutely, Davis deduced that Burnside would not fail to attack. "McClellan having been removed because he did not advance from the Potomac as a base," Davis reasoned, "it is hardly supposable that his successor will fail to attempt that movement." That being the case, Davis had some advice for Lee: "It does not seem likely that he will so divide his forces as to enable you to attack, or to justify you in dividing yours."[41] This amounted to little less than a repudiation of the whole summer's campaign that Lee had finished just a few months before. Only if Federal forces were badly divided, Davis implied, should Lee attack as he had during the Seven Days or divide his own forces after the manner of the Second Manassas and Sharpsburg campaigns. Davis was stating to Lee more clearly than ever before his preference for a more cautious approach to the waging of this war.

For the moment Lee appeared to be falling in with this way of thinking. Speaking of Burnside's suspected intention of advancing overland toward Richmond, Lee wrote, "The longer we can delay him, and throw him into the winter, the more difficult will be his undertaking." He went on to explain that this was the reason he had "determined to resist him at the outset, and to throw every obstacle in the way of his advance" by such means as tearing up the railroad in front of him.[42] This was Davis's attitude entirely. Each day's delay in northern operations without cost to the Confederacy was a success. Harass, delay, obstruct, but avoid risking a major defeat that might prove fatal. Instead, persistent resistance would wear the enemy down and finally bring victory. Lee also seemed to be in agreement when he wrote that "the great attempt now being made to reach our capital, . . . if defeated, may prove the last."[43] That was reassuring reading for the president.

As Lee and Davis discussed strategy by dispatches between Richmond and Fredericksburg, a topic that kept coming up was that of a possible withdrawal closer to Richmond. On November 25 Lee wrote, "should you think it preferable to concentrate the troops nearer to Richmond, I should be glad if you would advise me."[44] Again on December 6 he expressed the hope that Davis would "cause me to be advised when, in your judgment, it may become necessary for this army to move nearer Richmond."[45] Two days later he explained his reasoning in twice suggesting such a move. If the troops presently stationed south of the James could cope with any possible Union threats from that quarter, the Army of Northern Virginia, "if not able to resist General Burnside's advance, can retire upon the capital, and then operate as circumstances may dictate." On the other hand, if the Federals south of the James should prove too much for the defenders there, Lee's army "had better at once approach nearer Richmond," leaving a small covering force at Fredericksburg to delay Burnside's advance. Besides this strategic consideration, another reason for possible retreat loomed unpleasantly large. "I am reluctant to trouble Your Excellency with my wants," Lee wrote near the end of his letter, "but unless the Richmond and Fredericksburg Railroad is more energetically operated, it will be impossible to supply this army with provisions, and oblige its retirement to Hanover Junction."[46] Always alert to matters of supply, Lee wanted Davis to share his own realization that the army's operations could be limited by more than just enemy action.

Davis responded the same day before receiving Lee's explanation. He was quite satisfied to leave the deciding of such matters to Lee. "You will know best," he wrote, "when it will be proper to make a masked movement to the rear, should circumstances require you to move nearer to Richmond."[47] Withdrawal and surrender of territory was not a course Davis relished, since it created political difficulties and gave up additional opportunities to harass and delay the enemy.[48] If Lee believed withdrawal was necessary, Davis would not forbid it but neither would he encourage such a course. Lee took the hint, and apparently the supply situation remained at least tolerable. The Army of Northern Virginia held its ground and awaited the showdown on the low hills just south of Fredericksburg.

Strangely, Lee sounded almost unsure of himself, or at least unsure of his standing with Davis, during these weeks. His requests to be advised in regard to the necessity of falling back on Richmond stand in marked contrast to his announcement two months earlier that he would go into Maryland and even Pennsylvania unless forbidden by the president, who in any case would hardly have had time to respond soon enough to stop the move that Lee began immediately after that notification. Most of what passed between the two men at their early November conference is not recorded, but Lee seemed less inclined to write of offensive matters in his letters to Davis during the following weeks and more inclined to speak in the kind of terms the president more naturally adopted, such as his hope to "delay" the enemy and "throw every obstacle in the way of his advance." The present cautious and hesitating stance, so foreign to the Lee of last summer, seems consistent with the pattern. None of the two men's surviving correspondence suggests anything like an unpleasant exchange between them, but it is possible that Lee sensed the president's discomfort with his aggressive approach and for a time at least strove to conform his philosophy to Davis's. Further contrast to Lee's behavior of the previous summer is provided by his seeking, rather than avoiding, discussion with Davis at the front with battle imminent. "I need not say how glad I should be," Lee wrote in his November 25 letter to Davis, "if your convenience would permit you to visit the army, that I might have the benefit of your views and directions."[49]

Davis, for his part, seemed less impressed than heretofore with the need for such conference and more confident that Lee was acting as his dispatches suggested along the lines of what Davis himself would do. In response to Lee's invitation he replied, "I have been very anxious to visit you, but feeble health and constant labor has caused me to delay until necessity hurries me in an opposite direction."[50] The opposite direction was the sorely threatened Confederate southwest, where Union forces under Ulysses S. Grant were threatening Vicksburg, Mississippi, just a few miles up the river from Davis's old plantation, now in ruins. Davis had just made major command adjustments in that part of the country, assigning Pemberton to command in Mississippi and the lately recovered Joseph E. Johnston to a theater command that included both Pemberton's force and Braxton Bragg's army in Middle Tennessee. "I propose to go out there immediately," Davis explained to Lee, "with the hope that something may be done to bring out men not heretofore in service, and to arouse all classes to united and desperate resistance."[51] Although the president might not be entirely easy about the threat posed by Burnside's massive army, his confidence in Lee's ability as well as in Lee's apparently newfound caution made the Virginia front the least worrisome of the several areas of danger to the Confederacy.

So it was that Davis was in Chattanooga, Tennessee, on his way to points farther west, when news reached him of fighting at Fredericksburg. "About 9 A.M.," read Lee's dispatch forwarded from Richmond by the secretary of war, "the enemy attacked our right, and as the fog lifted the battle ran from right to left; raged until 6 P.M.," but the enemy had been "repulsed along our whole front." Lee's penchant for modest understatement may have been showing again or he may simply have failed to realize the magnitude of what had happened. Although morning attacks against the Confederate right had shaken the lines there briefly, two thirds of the Union army had been hurled against the Confederate left, where a sunken road and a stone wall at the base of Marye's Heights, coupled with terrain features that funneled every Union attack straight into the strongest part of the Confederate defenses, rendered the position impregnable. Before the early winter evening mercifully closed the slaughter, more than 12,000 Federals had fallen, while Confederate casualties totaled less than a third that number. Most of the dead and wounded bluecoats had been shot down while bravely advancing on the stone wall—without the least chance of accomplishing anything at all. Lee had written that he expected "the battle to be renewed at daylight."[52]

Davis was on edge with anticipation to know the issue of the next day's fighting and immediately wired Secretary of War James A. Seddon, who had replaced Randolph a couple of weeks before, for more information.[53] That done, he waited and worried. In a letter to Varina he described the situation and wrote, "You can imagine my anxiety. . . . If the necessity demands I will return to Richmond, though already there are indications of a strong desire for me to visit the further West."[54] And that, in the end, is what he did. The next few days brought telegrams from Lee and Seddon that revealed the stark outlines of what had happened. Contrary to Lee's expectation the battle had not been renewed on the fourteenth or the fifteenth, the armies instead observing a truce that afternoon for the recovery of such of the wounded as might still be alive. That night brought a howling storm of sleet and rain, and under its cover the Army of the Potomac pulled out of its Fredericksburg bridgehead. The morning of the sixteenth revealed the south bank of the Rappahannock void of live, unwounded Federals.[55] Reassured, Davis could complete his morale building and inspection tour of the western theater of the war.

In fact, Lee's old knack for reading his opponent's mind had not failed after all. Burnside himself had been anxious to renew the conflict on the morning of the fourteenth but had been dissuaded by his generals. Another aspect of Lee's generalship, one that might have surprised Davis at the moment, remained unchanged. He still hankered for a crushing victory that would destroy a northern army and sicken northern morale. He had seen an opportunity at Fredericksburg, with the Army of the Potomac crammed into its narrow bridgehead, its back to the unfordable Rappahannock, ripe for destruction. The day of slaughter before the stone wall would have weakened its numbers somewhat and its morale even more. True, the Confederates would still be outnumbered three to two, but if the moral factors really did outweigh the physical ones in war—and Lee never for a moment betrayed a doubt that they did—that might not matter. Once panic took hold in those dense blue-clad ranks it would be so much the worse for the Federals the more men they had crowded onto the south bank of the Rappahannock. Lee seems to have reasoned that an attack might succeed on the evening of the thirteenth or the morning of the next day. Jackson was certainly of that mind. Still, if as Lee confidently expected Burnside was willing to bleed his army another day on the gently sloping plain between Fredericksburg and Marye's Heights, so much the better. The Confederate attack was put off, and the Union subordinate generals disappointed Lee's hopes of seeing substantial additional portions of the Army of the Potomac served up for butchering before the stone wall. The Federal withdrawal took Lee by surprise and closed the door to hopes of a more complete victory. Remarking on the punishment Burnside had taken, Lee observed grimly, "Had I divined that was to have been his only effort, he would have had more of it."[56] To his wife Lee wrote that day, "I had supposed they were just preparing for battle, & was saving our men for the conflict. . . . I . . . could not believe they would relinquish their purpose after all their boasting & preparations. . . . They suffered heavily as far as the battle went, but it did not go far enough to satisfy me."[57]

Davis apparently remained ignorant of Lee's designs at Fredericksburg. None of the general's dispatches from the battlefield indicated any further plans than continuing to hold his ground if he could. Even in his official report of the battle, submitted almost four months later, he contented himself with explaining why he did not see fit to attack on the morning of the fourteenth.[58] Lee was diplomatic and probably saw no purpose in agitating the president with discussions of the might have beens of an otherwise very satisfactory battle. For the moment, the different outlooks of president and army commander were again latent.

As Davis was still absent on his western tour, Lee addressed some strategic reflections to Seddon in a letter he wrote the same day the Federal troops disappeared from the south bank of the Rappahannock. Strangely for a general who had just won a resounding victory, Lee suggested the necessity of retreat. As far back as November 19 he had been contemplating the advantages of a withdrawal to the line of the North Anna River, some thirty miles closer to Richmond.[59] He had not mentioned such speculations to

Davis, merely hinting that he was open to suggestions of withdrawal. Davis's reluctance, Lee's "unwillingness to open more of our country to depredation than possible," and Burnside's surprising cooperativeness in blundering directly into the heart of Lee's defenses rather than turning him out of his position on the Rappahannock had all combined to keep Lee and his troops where they were. Now, however, Lee expressed uneasiness that Burnside might have learned from his mistake. "With the numerous army opposed to me, and the bridges & transportation at its command," Lee explained, "the crossing of the Rappahannock, where it is as narrow & winding as in the vicinity of Fredericksburg, can be made at almost any point without molestation." That meant the potential, at least, that Lee's army could be turned out of its position and placed at a serious disadvantage.

A second reason for the proposed withdrawal Lee mentioned only obliquely. "It will . . . be advantageous to us," he wrote significantly, "to draw him farther away from his base of operations."[60] Fredericksburg had been an incomplete victory in part because the Army of the Potomac had so easily secured itself behind the Rappahannock. Its short supply line to the mouth of Aquia Creek was all but invulnerable to the sort of turning movements at which Lee was a master. Lee preferred to get out of the constricted area of operations in this tight corner of northeastern Virginia and find better ground for maneuver. Still, he would take his cue from Burnside. As the remaining days of 1862 passed with mostly clear skies and dry roads, the Army of the Potomac still did not move and neither did the Army of Northern Virginia.

On Monday, January 5, Davis arrived back in Richmond from his travels. The next day Lee wrote him a cordial letter with warm New Year's wishes for the president's improved health. "Allow me to congratulate you & the country," Lee began, "upon your safe return to Richmond." He went on to "attribute mainly the great victory of Genl Bragg [Murfreesboro] to the courage diffused by [Davis's] cheering words & presence."[61] That was all very nice, but though Lee obviously knew Davis was back at his desk in the capital city, it was to Seddon that four days later Lee addressed an important letter on the subject of the Confederacy's military policy. It may be that Lee judged Seddon the appropriate recipient of such a communication, since the letter's direct subject was the enhancement of recruitment efforts and securing of cooperation from the state governments in boosting the flow of manpower to the army. Yet it was a curious choice of correspondents, for Lee had addressed far more routine and less politically charged appeals directly to Davis, and this letter was extremely revealing of Lee's outlook on the use of battles and the winning of the war. Perhaps that is the reason, after all, that Seddon and not Davis received it.

Lee began by alluding to "the absolute necessity that exists . . . to increase our armies." The people, he suggested, and especially the state governments, needed to be made aware of what was at stake and how badly additional manpower was needed. The "disparity of numbers" between Union and Confederate armies was growing so great that "victory, if attained, can only be achieved by a terrible expenditure of the most precious blood of the country," blood that Lee believed would "be upon the hands of the thousands of able bodied men who remain at home in safety and ease, while their fellow citizens are bravely confronting the enemy in the field." As he warmed to the subject, Lee revealed much about his attitude and intentions in leading an army and trying to win the war. "The country has yet to learn," he continued, "how often advantages, secured at the expense of many valuable lives, have failed to produce their legitimate results by reason of our inability to prosecute them against" the enemy's superior numbers that had spelled the difference "between the defeat of an army and its ruin." Sharpsburg, Second Manassas, and the Seven Days must have flashed through the general's mind as he wrote. "More than once have most promising opportunities been lost for want of men to take advantage of them, and victory itself has been made to put on the appearance of defeat, because our diminished and exhausted troops have been unable to renew a successful struggle against fresh numbers of the enemy." Then came the clearest statement of the goal of battle for which Lee had nearly used up the Army of Northern Virginia the previous summer. "The lives of our soldiers are too precious," he wrote, "to be sacrificed in the attainment of successes that inflict no loss upon the enemy beyond the actual loss in battle. Every victory should bring us nearer to the great end which it is the object of this war to reach." Thus, "if we would save the honor of our families from pollution, our social system from destruction, let every effort be made, every means be employed, to fill and maintain the ranks of our armies."[62]

Lee sought crushing victory. Harassing and foiling the enemy, frustrating his plans, turning back his offensive movements were acceptable only if the army could do no better. A victory like Fredericksburg, in which the Army of the Potomac had suffered no loss "beyond the actual loss in battle" was a disappointment, an inconsequential encounter for the accomplishment of which "the lives of our soldiers are too precious to be sacrificed." What Lee wanted was a decisive victory with a vigorous pursuit that dissolved whole divisions, netted thousands of prisoners, and forced the surrender of a fair-sized chunk or two of the enemy army. When it was over the enemy might still have an army left, might still be able to keep the Rebels out of Washington and Baltimore (or might not), but Lee reckoned that northern morale would not stand many such debacles. Thence came his suggestion that the November Union advance might be the last. It might have been, but only if it could have been crushed and not just stopped. This was fundamentally at variance with Davis's approach to the war. Davis would sacrifice as few lives as possible on each occasion until victory came. Lee would sacrifice as many lives as necessary in order to bring victory, if he could, and end the sacrifices. The fact that Lee addressed this letter to Seddon rather than Davis suggests that Lee, at least, was aware of this difference.

For now though, the armies were dormant, and that issue slept with them. The problem that occupied the thoughts and correspondence of Lee and Davis involved not the great armies in northern Virginia but rather small detachments along the coasts of southern Virginia and North Carolina. The Federals had occupied Suffolk in Virginia and various points on the coast of the Tarheel State. Their presence in these places, and in some of the associated hinterland, potentially threatened both Richmond and its rail supply lines, as well as such vital blockade-running ports as Wilmington, North Carolina. It also alarmed local citizens and stirred up their politicians in Richmond and Raleigh. Equally if not more stirred up was Gustavus W. Smith, now commanding the Richmond and southside Virginia sector. Bitterness at his failure in the quest for glory and promotion had exacerbated the natural tendency to nervous malfunction that had made Smith a failure in the first place. His voice now joined those of panicky politicians in crying for more troops and predicting ruin if they were delayed. Some of the appeals came directly to Lee; others were referred to him by Seddon. Lee resisted the pressure to fritter away troops for such purposes. Although admitting that he was "uneasy at the state of affairs in North Carolina," he argued that the Federals were using the coastal operations as diversions and that the state militia, along with such Confederate detachments as were already within the threatened departments, should be adequate to quell the threat. As insurance he sent one division down to Richmond to be readily available for service south of the James if needed, and he offered to detach North Carolinian D. H. Hill, about whom he was in any case becoming increasingly less enthusiastic, for service in his home state.[63]

North Carolina governor Zebulon Vance was far from satisfied and wrote to Davis requesting that Lee "come down a few days and survey the situation in North Carolina." The president forwarded the request to Lee, commenting, "Your presence there would be important, indeed seems necessary." Still, he left it up to Lee to decide "whether it would be safe to absent yourself for a few days."[64] At the same time, Davis encouraged Vance to do what he could with the militia and assured him that he himself hoped "soon to visit the line."[65] Lee, compliant as always, promised to try to go if he could but cautioned, "As far as I have been able to judge, I have apprehended the movements in North Carolina were intended more as a feint to withdraw troops from this point, when General Burnside could move at once upon Richmond."[66] Several days later Lee wired, "I go to North Carolina as directed," and by January 16 he was in Richmond.[67] He paused there for a few days of discussions with Davis. The president urged Lee to give up additional troops for the defense of North Carolina, and the general agreed to detach two more brigades. Any idea of Lee's own visit to the Tarheel State was quickly given up, however, when word arrived from the Rappahannock of increased activity in the Federal camps.[68]

Lee hurried back to the army on the eighteenth, and by the next day the Army of the Potomac was obviously in motion, taking advantage of the unusually good weather and the firm, dry condition of the roads. "Everything combined seems to indicate a movement," Lee wrote to Davis. Since he believed Burnside's army was larger now than the month before, he informed Davis that he was suspending the scheduled departure of the brigades slated for North Carolina unless the president ruled otherwise.[69] In the days that followed, Lee worried about the possibility of being turned out of his position on the Rappahannock. "We have a long line to watch," he confided to the president, "and, by concealing their movements, a large body of troops might be thrown across before they could be resisted, and might oblige a retrograde movement on our part for concentration." True to form, though, he still hoped in such a case to "be able to deal [the enemy] a successful blow."[70]

Davis agreed with Lee's decision to halt the two brigades earmarked for service south of the James. "My opinion," he told Lee, "is that you would not be justified at this time in making further detachments from your command." In fact, Davis was more worried than Lee, seeing the danger of the army's being turned but not sharing Lee's optimism about dealing the enemy a blow. He fretted that if Lee tried to counterattack, he could be enveloped and destroyed by the larger Union army.[71]

The tension continued through the twenty-third. Lee urged that the army's personnel on leave in Richmond be rounded up and sent to the front along with any other troops that happened to be available. His intelligence on the Union movement remained the same: "It looks as if they intended to concentrate all their forces, and make a vigorous effort to drive us from our position." Rain had fallen the last two days—good weather could hardly be expected to last in January—and Lee speculated on the way this might affect the campaign. "The storm of yesterday and the day before will prove unfavorable for their advance, as the roads have become heavy and the streams swollen." Of course, it was raining on the Confederate side of the Rappahannock as well, potentially hindering any countermovement that might become necessary.[72]

Days passed and nothing happened. On the twenty-ninth, Lee reported the whole sequence of Federal movements in a letter to Seddon, adding the various steps he had taken to counter them. "Whether the storm or other causes frustrated the designs of the enemy," Lee concluded, "I do not know, but no attempt as yet has been made to cross the Rappahannock."[73] And none would be. In fact, the danger had been past even as Davis and Lee exchanged anxious letters a week before. When the rain started on the evening of the twentieth, Virginia's dirt roads had dissolved into muck, and the Army of the Potomac had become hopelessly mired. The long-suffering northern soldiers had dragged themselves and their guns, wagons, and equipment through the mud for the next two days until Burnside at last gave up the attempt and called off what came to be called "the Mud March." Shortly thereafter, Lincoln replaced Burnside with Maj. Gen. Joseph Hooker.

The failure of the Mud March allowed the Confederate high command to shift its attention back to tiresome troubles in southside Virginia and North Carolina. In the midst of it all, the president's health grew worse than ever. Through February, March, and April he suffered with "neuralgia in the head" and then a dental abscess, then more neuralgia and other assorted maladies. The ailments kept him at home, usually in bed.[74] When he did visit his office, War Department personnel noted his "very bad humor."[75] He carried on much of his correspondence through aides who took dictation or turned his briefly expressed thoughts into full letters. Many of these were aimed at Lee, concerned "affairs on our southern and eastern coast," and suggested but did not order that Lee send troops. Lee's belief in decisive victory ran contrary to dispersing forces to guard threatened points. His consistent answer was that he thought it best to keep his army together in hopes of striking a blow at the enemy. Still, he had to admit with frustration that winter weather made battle unlikely in northern Virginia. Thus if Davis thought the coastal threat serious, Lee would send the troops.[76]

Later that month, Lee demonstrated this willingness by detaching Pickett's and Hood's divisions to North Carolina in response to word from Davis that the Union IX Corps had been transferred to the southern coast. Since the troops heading south represented a substantial portion of Longstreet's corps, Lee sent the corps commander as well. Longstreet welcomed the change. He had been growing restless within the Army of Northern Virginia for a number of months.[77] Seeming to resent Lee's authority and desiring a chance to demonstrate his abilities in independent command, he had recently been angling to get Braxton Bragg's job out in Tennessee.[78] The present assignment was not quite as prestigious but still represented the opportunity for operations on his own. An added benefit came several days later when he was officially named the new commander of the Department of Southern Virginia and North Carolina, in place of Smith, who had finally resigned in a huff. After conferring with Davis and Seddon in Richmond, Longstreet proceeded to his new command. His mission was to relieve any possible threat of Federal raids against Richmond and its southern rail connections. At the same time he was to facilitate the gathering of supplies in the region. By early March, he was on the scene and wrote Lee that he had ample troops for the task at hand.[79]

Back on the Rappahannock lines the month of February passed without incident amidst alternating storms of snow and rain.[80] On March 10 Davis wired Lee, "When convenient and practicable, I wish to see you."[81] Within a day or two Lee was in the capital, discussing the present military situation with Davis. Davis wanted Longstreet to attack the Federal outpost at Suffolk, Virginia, if possible. Even if unsuccessful, such a move might open up desirable areas for foraging. Longstreet was not averse but wanted substantial additional resources for the operation, especially more troops. Lee was extremely reluctant to deplete his own numbers further in the face of Hooker's large army and was anxious that Longstreet should keep Hood's and Pickett's divisions handy to a railroad for rapid transportation north if a threat developed.[82]

Ominous news broke up the conference on the eighteenth: the Federals were making cavalry movements along the Rappahannock. Fearing this portended the beginning of Hooker's long-awaited offensive, Lee sent orders for Hood's and Pickett's divisions to return to the army as rapidly as possible and then repaired there himself. On his arrival, he found that this had been another false alarm, so he canceled the orders for the divisions south of the James.[83] Their employment, however, remained uncertain. Throughout the rest of March, Longstreet and Lee debated the issue by letter. Longstreet insisted that he would be unable to accomplish anything in the sector south of the James if the two Army of Northern Virginia divisions should be taken away from him. As for any offensive action on his part, the southside commander now claimed he would need a third or even a fourth division—his entire corps of the Army of Northern Virginia—in addition to the troops that had been in the department before his arrival. Halting and uncertain, Longstreet was finding that independent command was by no means as easy as Lee had made it look. By the end of the month Longstreet had given up and decided that "there are no particular advantages in giving battle at Suffolk."[84]

The whole situation became a good deal more confused and uncertain when on March 28 the Confederates got wind of the movement of the IX Corps away from the base at Newport News on the Peninsula, where it had spent the winter, and westward to operate on the other side of the Appalachians. The presence of the IX Corps in a position to threaten the coastal areas of southern Virginia and North Carolina had been the chief reason for detaching troops from the Army of Northern Virginia in the first place. For Lee there was the added shock that the news came not from Longstreet, in whose front the IX Corps had been stationed and who should have been the first to notice its removal, but rather from a cavalry commander off in the Shenandoah who had learned of the movement from his scouts monitoring the Penn Central and B & O Railroads that had carried the Federals west. Without confirmation from Longstreet, Lee doubted the truth of the report. He wrote to Cooper on the twenty-eighth, passing on the intelligence and adding, "I have inquired of Longstreet." Naturally this dispatch came into the hands of Davis, who failed to understand Lee's desire for confirmation from the southside commander. "Why inquire of General Longstreet?" the president scrawled across the bottom of Lee's telegram. "This may be an error in dispatch, or it may be a suggestion of that which is to my mind indicated—the movements of Longstreet to re-enforce Bragg."[85] The problem was, of course, that what was naturally indicated to the mind of Jefferson Davis—transferring troops to match the northern movement—was not at all the same as what was indicated to the mind of Lee by the same circumstances.

The next few days brought confirmation of the reports. On April 1, Davis put the matter to Lee. Mentioning the IX Corps' movement, the president added incorrectly, "Other troops have been sent from Hooker's army into Tennessee." He concluded, "Would like your views on this."[86] Lee, conceding that the IX Corps "has gone to Kentucky," maintained that a threat to the Atlantic coast might remain. Nor did all promise to remain quiet on the Rappahannock. Lee believed Hooker would cross that stream as soon as the weather cleared. The Virginian's proposed remedy was striking the Union forces in the Shenandoah Valley first. This, he reckoned, would "draw General Hooker out, or at least prevent further re-enforcements being sent to the West." To prevent Federals being shifted away from Longstreet's sector, Lee's solution was similar. "With the same view," he wrote, "I have wished General Longstreet to take the aggressive in North Carolina when the opportunity offers." Unfortunately, Longstreet had now stepped up his complaining to the level of claiming that he could not even carry out his modest supply-gathering activities unless he received both divisions of his corps still remaining with Lee.[87]

Through the first half of April the debate went on. Again and again Davis asked Lee if he could not spare a couple of divisions for the West. Lee's replies explained with increasing fullness why he believed this policy to be wrong. Admitting that "the most natural way to re-enforce General Johnston would seem to be transfer a portion of the troops from this department to oppose those sent west," he nevertheless raised objections. Northern railroads could carry troops east and west faster than the Confederates could move them. "If we rely upon that method we may be always too late." Instead, he averred, "The readiest method of relieving the pressure upon General Johnston and General Beauregard [commanding at Charleston] would be for this army to cross into Maryland." By mid-April he became more specific. "I think it all-important that we should assume the aggressive by the 1st of May. . . . If we could be placed in a condition to make a vigorous advance at that time, I think the Valley could be swept . . . and the army opposite me be thrown north of the Potomac." That meant another of Lee's turning movements and a showdown battle north of the Potomac. Throughout the debate, however, Lee repeated constantly that he was prepared to abide by the president's decision.

Davis made no decision. By this time his neuralgia was threatening to destroy his one remaining usable eye. Confined to his house and described as being "in a very feeble and nervous condition," he continued to handle business almost entirely through Seddon, Cooper, and his various staff officers. Almost no visitors were admitted, and even important political associates were turned away. Poor health probably contributed to his indecisiveness. At any rate, by late April he had fallen silent on the issue.[88]

Lee's talk of going north, however, had been no idle suggestion. Six weeks earlier he had ordered Jedediah Hotchkiss, Jackson's redoubtable topographical engineer, to produce a map of the Shenandoah Valley that would be "extended to Harrisburg, Pa., and then on to Philadelphia." That telling item of preparation was "kept a profound secret" to the extent that Lee did not even apprise Davis of it. To anyone of any military knowledge, the import of such an action would have been obvious. If he could get the supplies and get Longstreet back, Lee meant to invade the North again, and he meant to do it before Hooker could undertake a campaign of his own.[89] Nor was this to be any limited spoiling action, aimed only at throwing Hooker off balance and disrupting his plans for the summer's campaign. Lee intended it to do a good deal more. To Davis he again affirmed that such a campaign would be the best way of relieving pressure on Confederate forces "in Middle Tennessee and on the Carolina coast."[90] Lee intended his 1863 invasion of the North to impact the entire war east of the Mississippi.

For the moment, Davis made no direct response to Lee's projected operations. Despite his severe illness he endeavored to discharge his duties without lapse. When Lee reported he was short of cavalry, Davis promptly gave Cooper specific instructions as to where and how all of the needed mounted troops should be obtained and furnished to Lee.[91] On April 23 Davis wrote to Lee on routine matters and managed so well to disguise his weakness that Lee was led to infer "from the tenor of your letter that you are better."[92] In fact, just the day before, Davis was reported as being "very ill today–dangerously ill–with inflammation of the throat, etc."[93] Yet though he might continue to function bravely, the president seemed little disposed to make major strategic decisions. On the level of commander in chief that spring, Confederate policy was formed by default. Davis neither ordered Lee to send troops west nor forbade him a northward movement nor attempted to provide him with the resources to make such a movement. As May 1 approached, the Army of Northern Virginia remained south of the Rappahannock.

On April 29 Lee telegraphed Davis that Hooker was finally in motion, his army crossing the Rappahannock. "The demand which was looked for has come," Davis wrote in a note to Seddon that day. The president directed that every available man should be sent to Lee at once.[94] A flurry of dispatches flew between Seddon and Cooper and from them to various commanders of small detachments around Richmond and further south. One of the messages from Cooper was for Longstreet and ordered him to "move forward his command to re-enforce" Lee. Despite Longstreet's complaint that he was in the midst of gathering supplies and would need time to gather up his wagons, Cooper believed he could be in Richmond by the evening of

May 2.[95] Meanwhile, Davis telegraphed Lee that reinforcements were on the way.[96] That evening and the next day, further telegrams from Lee revealed that the enemy had stolen a march and while demonstrating in his front at Fredericksburg had gotten a very large force across the Rapidan River beyond the Confederate left. Lee's position was turned. He now would have to retreat or else make a desperate fight. For him that was no choice at all. "I determined," he wrote, "to hold our lines in rear of Fredericksburg with part of the force and endeavor with the rest to drive the enemy back to the Rapidan." Still, if he had Longstreet's troops with him, he assured the president, he "would feel safe."[97]

On May 1 the battle was joined as Lee's troops struck Hooker's advancing columns in hopes of blocking his further advance into the Confederate rear. Then something very strange happened. Contact with the enemy seemed to take all of the fight out of "Fighting Joe" Hooker, at least when it came to exercising the role of army commander. To the surprise and horror of his top subordinates, the Federal general ordered his lead units to pull back into a defensive position just south of the Rapidan, in an area of second-growth timber known as the Wilderness. There he appeared determined to wait for Lee to come to him. Lee, of course, had to do so, but he could have asked for no better place for the encounter than this region of tangled forests where the Union superiority in artillery and numbers would be substantially negated and where heavy advantages would accrue to the side that proved more familiar with the area's confusing terrain and scanty system of roads.

That evening Confederate reconnaissance revealed that Hooker's right flank was "in the air," unsupported and liable to be hit if the Rebels could get a substantial body of troops in position to do so. Lee and Jackson discussed the matter and devised an audacious plan. Lee would divide his outnumbered forces, sending Jackson with the larger portion on a long and daring march around the Union flank, while Lee with the remainder diverted Federal attention. Early next morning Jackson's troops set out on a trek that would take them all day. While he waited, Lee composed a longer dispatch to Davis explaining the situation. "I am now swinging around to my left to come up in [Hooker's] rear," Lee wrote. He spelled out for Davis clearly what was at stake. "It is plain," he noted, "that if the enemy is too strong for me here, I shall have to fall back, and Fredericksburg must be abandoned." On the other hand, if Lee should be victorious in the present battle, "Fredericksburg will be saved and our communications retained." Lee did not expect Longstreet or the other reinforcements from North

Carolina to reach him in time to aid in the present fight, but he hoped they would be in time for struggles he foresaw in the next few days.[98]

Back in Richmond, the intended recipient of this dispatch was having problems of his own. As part of the grand design for defeating Lee, Hooker had dispatched his cavalry under Maj. Gen. George Stoneman on a raid deep into Confederate territory to disrupt communications and threaten Richmond. Stoneman accomplished little of substance but did hover about Richmond long enough to arouse anxiety inside the city, where no regular troops remained to oppose him. Richmond diarist Mary Chesnut related the scene at the Confederate White House, where Varina Davis told her that the enemy was within three miles of Richmond but cautioned her to "be quiet" because "the president is ill."[99] Davis was, indeed, still very sick and still in danger of losing his remaining eye.[100] What rest he could have gotten that night, even if secluded in a room by himself, is hard to imagine. Chesnut described "officers coming and going . . . the excitement of the scene and the constant state of activity and constant change of persons" and much loud talking and laughing to keep everyone's spirits up. Perhaps his exhaustion from days of pain and illness drowned out the noise, or perhaps he simply gave up on sleep. At any rate, Chesnut reported, "Early next morning the president came down. He was still feeble and pale from his illness."[101] He had his aides G. W. C. Lee and James Chesnut, Mary's husband, load his pistols, and then he climbed into "a light open carriage" belonging to a Dr. Garnett, who then drove him out through the city for a bit of fresh air. It seemed to do him good, for one observer noted that he "exhibited the finest spirits" and enjoyed watching the companies of militia–"old men and boys"–drilling at the fortifications surrounding the city.[102]

Davis might well be in high spirits this fine May morning. Longstreet still was not at hand, but Stoneman looked less threatening and from Lee came excellent news. "Yesterday General Jackson, with three of his divisions penetrated the rear of the enemy," Lee had written from the battlefield, "and drove him from all his positions from the Wilderness to within 1 mile of Chancellorsville." Nor was that the end of the good news. "This morning the battle was renewed. He was dislodged from all his positions around Chancellorsville, and driven back toward the Rappahannock, over which he is now retreating. Many prisoners were taken, and the enemy's loss in killed and wounded large."[103] This was premature, as another day's fighting remained before Hooker put his army into retreat. Still the battle of Chancellorsville, as this encounter was to be called, would go down as one of the most amazing against-the-odds victories in the history of warfare. Only one disturbing note marred the otherwise perfect picture presented in Lee's dispatch. "General Jackson," Lee informed the president, "[is] severely . . . wounded."[104] That was bad news, for the disabling of Jackson, even briefly, would cripple the army's leadership. Still, one could always hope for a quick recovery.

On the evening of May 5, Longstreet finally arrived in Richmond but without his troops. The next day he conferred with Davis. By that time Stoneman was already in the process of withdrawing his cavalry raiders, and Davis believed Longstreet should take his troops on to the Army of Northern Virginia without delay. As of the fifth, Hooker had still been lingering on the south bank of the Rapidan, and Lee had planned a massive assault all along the lines to fling him into the river. Two hard-hitting divisions like those of Hood and Pickett would no doubt be most welcome if they could get there in time. Besides, who could say what follow-up and pursuit might be necessary, and fresh divisions would be ideal for such work. But Longstreet had other ideas. He had chafed under Lee's authority last fall and desired independent command. A good deal less than eager to return to Lee's army and Lee's shadow, he had shown little sense of urgency either in finishing up his mission south of the James during the preceding weeks, as Lee more than once urged him to do, or in hastening to join Lee once the call went out. Now he claimed that the real need for his divisions was against Stoneman's raiders and in seeing to it that the railroad they had damaged was set back in order. Remarkably, Davis acceded to this somewhat farfetched request, and Longstreet's divisions did not join Lee until a number of days after the fighting was over.[105] Fortunately for the Confederates, Hooker had pulled out on the night of the fifth, and the big push on the sixth had been unnecessary.[106]

Far from rejoicing at this turn of events, however, Lee was intensely irritated. When Brig. Gen. William Dorsey Pender rode up to him on the morning of the sixth to report that the Federals were gone and the formidable entrenchments before the southerners empty, Lee had exploded, "Why, General Pender! That is the way you young men always do. You allow those people to get away. I tell you what to do, but you don't do it!" The dumbfounded Pender sat speechless in his saddle. "Go after them," Lee snapped, with a gesture of impatience, "and damage them all you can!" The Federals, however, were beyond reach.[107] Once again Lee had sought a crushing victory, though whether a renewed battle on the sixth would have given him what he sought is highly doubtful. Lee would not, of course, have chosen the overall situation of the battle of Chancellorsville. If he had had his

Jefferson Davis's Richmond. (Courtesy of National Archives, 111-B-35, Civil War 16)

way, Longstreet would have hastened to complete his supply-gathering activities south of the James and rejoined the army in time to enable Lee to take the initiative.[108] That hope denied, Lee had had to do what he could under the circumstances. Jackson, too, had striven for the destruction of the Army of the Potomac before his wounding. Late on the evening of the second he had been returning from reconnoitering the possibilities of further attacks—aimed at cutting off the Federals from the river fords—when he was accidentally shot by some of his own troops.

During the week after the battle, however, Jackson had fought a different enemy. Pneumonia had set in after his wounding and the amputation of his left arm, and by Saturday, May 9, his condition was critical. In a small cottage on the Chandler farm near Guiney's Station, Jackson struggled for life, while throughout the Confederacy, as far as the news had had time to travel, his fellow southerners waited and hoped. In Richmond, Jefferson Davis sat in silence that Saturday evening "until twelve or one o'clock." He did no work—an unusual thing for this habitually busy man—and was "unable to think of anything but the impending calamity." In contrast to the gentle lamplight and quiet ticking of a clock at the Confederate White House was the scene at the Richmond train station, where amidst the garish glow of lanterns and the hiss and clang of the steam engines, large crowds of people flocked to meet each new arriving train. "Before the engine slacked up in Broad Street, the crowd shouted to the engineer, 'How is he? Is he better?' "

The Davises made sure one of their servants was among the crowd in order to bring them the latest news of the general's condition, and they kept another at the telegraph office for the same purpose.[109]

Closer to Guiney's Station, at Army of Northern Virginia headquarters, Lee also waited. He dared not leave the army leaderless to visit the wounded general, but being a devout Christian he spent the night in prayer for his recovery. Next morning Lee told a chaplain who was departing to go to Jackson's bedside, "Tell him that I wrestled in prayer for him last night, as I never prayed, I believe, for myself." To one who informed him that the doctors had given up hope for Jackson's survival, Lee seemed shaken, replying, "Surely, General Jackson must recover. God will not take him from us, now that we need him so much. Surely he will be spared to us, in answer to the many prayers which are offered for him!"[110] But God ordained otherwise. That evening Lee sent a dispatch to Seddon, "It becomes my melancholy duty to announce to you the death of General Jackson. He expired at 3:15 p.m. today." Lee asked "that suitable arrangements be made."[111] They were, Davis taking a personal interest in the matter. A few days before, Congress had adopted a new pattern for the national flag. Davis sent the first copy of this new flag to drape the fallen general's casket. The body was brought to Richmond by train on the morning of the eleventh, where it lay in state. In a letter to Lee that day, Davis termed Jackson's death "a great national calamity."[112] In the funeral procession next day, "the President followed near the hearse in a carriage, looking thin and frail in health."[113] Varina reported the emotional impact of these events on the president. That evening, she recalled, "a man came to the mansion and attempted to talk of some business matter to him." Davis "remained silent for a while and then said, 'You must excuse me. I am still staggering from a dreadful blow. I cannot think.' "[114]

The events of the past fortnight seemed to have had an impact on Lee's thinking as well. The Chancellorsville campaign disturbed him deeply. Using a plan drawn up by Union Q.M. Gen. Montgomery Meigs, Hooker had executed a movement that had put Lee in a very tight spot. The Confederate general had had to fight a desperate battle as the only alternative to a headlong retreat that might have taken him all the way to the outskirts of Richmond. That, in turn, would have entailed the loss of vital supply-producing regions. Lee doubted that he could feed his army if he were forced back into the Richmond defenses. He determined therefore that if at all possible he must not wait to see what new and even more threatening move the Federals would try on him next. Instead, he must take the initiative and avoid being placed in a dilemma such as the one he had faced at Chancellorsville.[115] The death of Jackson may also have made an impact on Lee's state of mind. Indeed, it could hardly have failed to do so. The loss of his trusted lieutenant and the South's most beloved general would only have emphasized the attrition that was grinding up the South's ability to continue resisting, much less winning the sort of victories Lee believed would be necessary to break the North's fighting spirit.[116] If Lee had always directed his army as if quick victory were a southern necessity, he could now be expected to move like one who believed time was running out.

Something else may have been at work here too. Lee's behavior and statements during the secession crisis—his denial of the right to secession especially—suggest he may have experienced a certain degree of moral ambivalence about the rebellion. Such ambivalence could well prompt a person to seek a quick resolution of the conflict in order to relieve the tension of moral uncertainty. Even defeat might be preferable to long continuance without knowing if one's course is right or wrong. Whether or not something like this was at work in Lee, he did show a strong desire to press for an early decision to the war. Lee's experiences in early May 1863 were such as could have strengthened such a desire. A man of strong religious conviction, Lee had prayed earnestly for Jackson and been sure that God would answer his prayers in the affirmative. Yet God had not done so. Instead, as Lee termed it in his report, Jackson had been "removed from the scene of his eminent usefulness by the hand of an inscrutable but all-wise Providence."[117] To his son, the president's aide in Richmond, he wrote, "Any victory would be dear at such a price, but God's will be done."[118] A turn of events such as this, however, would almost certainly have shaken Lee's faith that God favored the Confederate cause and would have strengthened any doubts he may have had.[119] In that case the temptation would have been almost overwhelming for Lee to seek a decision, an end to the questions as to whether the cause for which he felt compelled to order thousands of men to their deaths was right or wrong, an appeal to battle that would settle the matter and be done with it.

Even before the death of Jackson, Davis and Lee had moved to get on with the work of reorganizing and supplying the army and directing its movements and Confederate strategy in general. Despite his illness, Davis had not been idle. On May 6, War Department clerk John B. Jones had noted with amazement in his diary, "The President sent to the War Department fifty-five letters today, written to him on various subjects, but mostly asking appointments. He had read them, and several had indorsed on them, in his own hand, what he wished done in the premises. . . . He still attends to business at his dwelling, and has not been in his office for more than a month."[120]

Continuing to do business from his bed with the help of Seddon, Cooper, and his staff, Davis once again took up the tired old issue of sending troops west.[121] This time he seems not to have felt much enthusiasm for the idea, but pleas from western state politicians and perhaps the influence of Seddon led the president to put the matter to Lee yet again. Lee responded as before. This time he added that the Army of Northern Virginia should be strengthened rather than diminished, which should be accomplished by stripping the southern coast of troops, since, as Lee asserted, none would be needed there during the sickly summer season. Beauregard, who commanded in South Carolina, should be brought north with every soldier not needed to man the water batteries at Charleston and Wilmington. "It will be better," he wrote, "to order General Beauregard in with all the forces which can be spared, and to put him in command here, than to keep them there inactive and this army inefficient from paucity of numbers."[122] Lee may have actually been suggesting his own replacement by Beauregard, or, as is indicated by his words and actions during the coming summer, he may have meant that the Army of Northern Virginia would no longer be "here" when Beauregard assumed that command.

In the days that followed, Lee continued his campaign to keep his army intact, writing a series of dispatches arguing against any detachment of troops to the west. Such a course, he asserted, would be "hazardous, and it becomes a question between Virginia and the Mississippi." The distance was too great, the troops might become ill in the Deep South, and they might not be put to good use. This last was a hint that neither Pemberton, the local department commander, nor Johnston, the theater commander, would have the brains and the nerve to employ the troops effectively. Here was his most telling argument, for from the point of view of the Confederate commander in chief it could hardly make sense to put large numbers of the South's best troops into the hands of its least effective commanders. It would have required far less military acumen than Davis undeniably possessed to realize that Lee was likely to accomplish more with an extra division than was either Johnston or Pemberton, provided the strategy to be pursued involved seizing the initiative and forcing the North to fight where and when the South dictated.

Lee pressed his case further. "The strength of this army has been reduced by the casualties in the late battles," he asserted, and Hooker was now receiving massive reinforcements. In this last, as well as his estimate of the

Army of the Potomac's total strength, he overstated the case rather badly, but he was right, of course, in claiming, "We are greatly outnumbered by the enemy now." The battle of Chancellorsville had strengthened Lee's desire to take the offensive. To remain passively on the defensive was to await the Federals' convenience in trying another skillful turning movement like the one that had given Lee an unpleasant glimpse of disaster the week before. Sooner or later, one of those movements had to be successful, throwing Lee backward into the impossible position of holding the Richmond fortifications. As he put it in this letter, "Unless we can obtain some re-enforcements, we may be obliged to withdraw into the defenses around Richmond." Having apparently raised every possible objection, Lee concluded, "You can, therefore, see the odds against us, and decide whether the line of Virginia is more in danger than the line of the Mississippi."[123]

For the moment, Davis was convinced. On one of Lee's first dispatches after Chancellorsville the president had written, "The answer of General Lee was such as I anticipated, and in which I concur."[124] Lee did not know this and so kept up a steady bombardment of dispatches aimed at preventing the transfer. As he did so, he referred increasingly to his proposed invasion of the North. "If I could get in a position to advance beyond the Rappahannock," he wrote, "I should certainly draw their troops from the southern coasts, and give some respite in that quarter." He repeatedly expressed this thought in almost identical words. He was also eager to recover the remainder of the Army of Northern Virginia troops still scattered along the southern coast, where they had been dispatched the previous winter. Four brigades were still detached, two of Pickett's and the two sent down earlier in the winter. Lee wanted them back, and that too became a theme of his correspondence.[125]

This was a more intense barrage of argument than Lee had ever directed at Davis before. Still, the pressure from those concerned with the fate of the Mississippi was also great. Seddon added his voice, doubting that the climate alone, as Lee had suggested, would be enough to stop Grant from taking Vicksburg. Davis seems to have wavered and begun to contemplate again the shifting of troops westward in keeping with his own approach to making war. Uncertain of what to do, he desired further consideration of the issue. Lee himself had mentioned that "there are many things about which I would like to consult Your Excellency, and I should be delighted, if your health and convenience suited, if you could visit the army." He promised to get Davis "a comfortable room in the vicinity of my headquarters." If Davis could not come, Lee added, he would "endeavor to go to Richmond," though he felt that at that moment he could not afford to leave the army.[126] Ordinarily Davis would have jumped at such an invitation to visit the army. Now, however, he was simply too ill. The day after Jackson's death, Lee wrote his son, "if the President cannot visit the army, I must go to him for a day at least."[127] Davis seems to have had the same thought at about the same time and requested that Lee come to Richmond for consultation.

The general arrived on May 14. For the first time in weeks, Davis was "at work again at the Executive Office," though as far as Clerk Jones could tell, he was "not fully himself yet." Lee, who had also been in poor health of late, impressed Jones as looking thin and pale. Along with Seddon, the president and the general spent long, private sessions in discussion that day and the next.[128] The result of these discussions seems to have been a firm decision that Pickett's division, or at least the three brigades of it that were now in Richmond, would be going north to Lee's army rather than west to Pemberton's. "This morning early," Jones noted in his diary on the sixteenth, "the long column marched through the city northward."[129] For Pickett's other two brigades, still in North Carolina, there was no such concrete decision. For the moment, they stayed where they were, and where they would be going remained unclear.

While Pickett's lead brigades marched, and while a thousand miles to the southwest Pemberton was fighting and losing the battle that would doom his army to stand a hopeless siege penned up in Vicksburg, Lee and Davis met again, this time with the full cabinet. The topic now was whether to approve Lee's plan for another invasion of the North. As Postmaster General Reagan remembered it, Lee presented the chief reason for such a movement to be "that army supplies had become scarce south of that river [the Potomac], while they were abundant north of it." This was different from the arguments Lee had used in his letters to Seddon and Davis over the last few weeks, and it sounds remarkably similar to his justification of the 1862 Maryland campaign. Once again, supplies were undoubtedly important to Lee, but he appears to have been understating the scope and ambition of his intended campaign. His eagerness to please—and in this case to cast things in the light most likely to secure the approval of Davis and a roomful of politicians—seems to have led him to present the operation subtly and probably unintentionally as being a much more conservative affair than he actually intended to make it. Reagan believed he saw through Lee. "He favored such a campaign," the postmaster general later wrote, "because he believed he commanded an invincible army, which had been victorious in so many great battles, and in all of them against greatly preponderating numbers and resources."

Reagan, a Texan whose home lay beyond Vicksburg and the contested Mississippi River, spoke up and offered an alternative plan. Why not let Lee feint toward the Potomac, and then when the Federals reacted, detach "25,000 or 30,000 of his army to be sent to reinforce General Pemberton"? Someone objected that this would cost them the Shenandoah Valley. Reagan admitted it might, temporarily, "but added that there would remain with General Lee some 50,000 veteran and victorious troops for the protection of Richmond." Someone else chimed in that "a successful campaign in the territory adjacent to Washington, Baltimore, and Philadelphia might cause the withdrawal of the troops then menacing Vicksburg and Port Hudson." No, insisted Reagan, "General Grant had reached a position which would prevent dealing with him in that way." The only way to stop a man of Grant's bulldog determination would be to destroy his army. But no one else saw it that way. "This view was not favored by any other member of the cabinet," recalled Reagan years later, "and I had to give it up."

As Reagan fell silent, none remained to gainsay Lee. Doing so was no easy task. Mostly quiet, "when he spoke it was in the fullness of conviction." Lee had already "expressed his views on the subject of a campaign north of the Potomac." Now, as he sat calmly listening to the deliberations, his dignified presence and formidable reputation were arguments none could silence. Davis seems to have been one of Lee's earliest converts, though he was reluctant to declare the matter settled. Reagan remarked, "I could not expect, on such a question, to overrule the opinion of great military men like President Davis and General Lee." Apparently the president was expressing enough support for Lee's plan to convince Reagan that he was alone and that further objection was pointless. Still, though the postmaster general gained this impression "early" in the daylong conference, the cabinet continued to discuss "every possible contingency" until after nightfall. Finally, "it was determined that General Lee should cross the Potomac and put himself in a position to threaten Washington, Baltimore, and Philadelphia." Though it is hard to imagine that anyone could have regretted the end of such a marathon discussion session, it was immediately clear that one person, at any rate, was far from happy with the result. Writing his memoirs as a genteel old man many years later, Reagan noted demurely, "I will not now repeat the expression I made when this conclusion was reached."[130]

The conference completed, Lee returned to the army the next day. Reagan, however, was not ready to let the matter rest. He himself had been unable to rest the night before, believing "we had made a great mistake." Rising before daylight he wrote a note to Davis explaining how he felt. Could the cabinet meet again that day to reconsider the matter? Remarkably, Davis agreed. It was still early on that Sunday morning, May 17, when Reagan received a reply from the president stating that the cabinet would reconvene on Monday morning, but the planned meeting never took place. Before Davis could send out the formal summons to the cabinet members, "nearly all" of them happened by his office, and a sort of informal cabinet meeting took place. Davis might be ready for further deliberations, but these men had heard enough and were not about to rehash the whole matter yet again. "It at once appeared that it would be useless to attempt a further consideration of that subject."[131]

Lee commented several days later that he had left the president "in such feeble health."[132] The intense three days of discussions had apparently taken a lot out of the still frail Davis. By Tuesday, May 19, Jones was noting in his diary, "The President is too ill again to come to the Executive Office." Yet as before Davis worked on from his sickbed. "His messenger," Jones continued, "who brought me some papers this morning, says he is in a 'decline.' " The War Department clerk speculated that Davis was "worried at the dark aspects in his own State–Mississippi."[133] Jones may have been right. When little more than a week later Davis related to Lee a favorable assessment of affairs in Mississippi, he added, "My health is steadily improving. And if we can have good news from the West, I hope soon to be quite well again."[134] News from Mississippi, however, had a tendency to be good one day and bad the next two, as did the president's health.

During the week and a half following the cabinet conference that had approved Lee's northward movement, Davis came under more pressure than ever to reinforce Pemberton. Bombarded with pleas for dramatic action to save Mississippi, the president began to waver in his recently confirmed commitment to Lee's strategy. Sending for the members of the cabinet, Davis informed them that he had "received dispatches and letters from both military men and civilians in high authority, urging the reinforcement of Pemberton by sending to his relief a part of General Lee's command." Among those who had written was Mississippi's governor J. J. Pettus. The cabinet members sat glumly about the table as the president read them letter after letter predicting doom if troops were not sent west. Concluding his reading, Davis then "requested the members to meet him on the next day to consider the whole question of the campaign of 1863."[135] The next day was Tuesday, May 26, and the cabinet was in closed-door session "nearly all day."[136] The result was a confirmation of the conclusion already reached in the previous laborious conference.[137] It may be that moral and political support were all Davis sought from the cabinet in the first place, though why that would have required a daylong discussion is hard to understand. When Davis wrote to Lee that evening, he hardly sounded as if he thought operations in Mississippi required disrupting Lee's plans. The news from there, he assured Lee, was "on the whole, encouraging." Pemberton was "stoutly defending the entrenchments" around Vicksburg, while Johnston with an army outside the city should be able at least to raise the siege and possibly, if he could combine with Pemberton, "win a victory."[138] Once again, Davis appeared to be solidly behind Lee's proposed invasion.

Much of the attention Davis gave to Lee's army during the last half of May involved issues of organization and personnel, as Lee strove to make good the gaps created by the battle of Chancellorsville in the army's officer corps. If the army "could be properly organized and officered," Lee told a subordinate about this time, it "would be invincible." Of his soldiers he added, "They will go any where and do anything if properly led. But there is the difficulty—proper commanders. Where can they be obtained?"[139] The greatest gap in the army's officer corps also required the greatest adjustment. Of Stonewall Jackson Lee had written the day after his death, "I do not know how to replace him."[140] His solution finally was not to replace him at all. "I have for the past year," Lee explained to the president, "felt that the corps of this army were too large for one commander." Thus he would reorganize the army's two corps into three, a new III Corps being formed from one division of Longstreet's I Corps, another from Jackson's II Corps, and a third division to be formed primarily from various of the army's brigades now on detached duty in North Carolina. Richard S. Ewell would be promoted to the shadow of Jackson's old position as II Corps commander, while A. P. Hill, described by Lee as the best division commander in the army, would be promoted to take command of the new III Corps. Various other promotions would be needed at lower grades both to replace casualties and to fill the places of others who were moving up. Lee urged Davis that all of these details needed to be dealt with and soon, since "this army has done hard work, and there is still harder before it." That was all the more pressing, Lee maintained, for "It is time I was in motion."[141]

Davis was ready enough to make whatever appointments and approve whatever organizational changes Lee desired. He assured Lee that he was "glad to second your wishes, confiding, as I always do, as well in your judgment as in your information."[142] Some confusion arose, however, as to just what Lee's wishes were in the matter of promotions to the rank of major general. Lee made the matter clear enough in his initial communication, being careful as he always was to leave the president as much room as possible for political maneuver by allowing him to choose from among several qualified men.[143] For some reason Davis misconstrued Lee's letter, and several weeks of confusion ensued. Lee generously took the blame for the misunderstanding.[144] Davis remained fairly even-tempered throughout, and they finally laid the affair to rest with everyone getting the promotion he deserved and all of Lee's divisions led by commanders of whom he approved.[145]

President and general became almost as confused and considerably more irritable in the matter of returning to the Army of Northern Virginia its various detached brigades then in North Carolina. Early on, Lee had explained to Davis that he wanted new North Carolina commander D. H. Hill "to make such disposition of his troops as to give me all the force that can be spared" from that state. Lee was particularly anxious to get the brigades of Jenkins, Ransom, and Cooke, which had previously served with the army, as well as that of Pettigrew, which Lee also believed could be spared.[146] At first, Davis seemed perfectly willing for Lee to have them.[147] Then difficulties arose. Hill became extremely loath to part with any of the troops in his department no matter how little he needed them or how much anyone else did. Never mind that these troops had been components of the Army of Northern Virginia. In departmental tugs of war, possession was indeed nine-tenths of the law. Hill possessed these units and was not about to give them up.

As soon as the cabinet had approved his plan on May 16 for an invasion of the North, even before he left Richmond, Lee had sent Hill discretionary orders to keep only as much force as he absolutely needed to counterbalance the enemy's presence in his department and then send the remainder of his troops to Virginia. Hill balked. He would not take the responsibility of giving up a single man. If Lee wanted troops, then as Hill's superior he would have to send positive orders for such units as he might decide were needed. This was a common ploy of district and department commanders and it usually worked, since few regional commanders at a distance would have the nerve to say what troops the situation in a given department made surplus. Lee, however, was not to be deterred, and the orders were sent. Again Hill objected and declined to send the troops. His considerable patience exhausted at last, Lee turned to Davis. "I cannot operate in this manner," Lee wrote. "I request you to cause such orders to be given him as your judgment dictates."[148]

What was needed at this point was a sharp reprimand of Hill by Davis, admonishing the recalcitrant general to obey orders promptly. What happened instead was that Davis took Lee literally and tried to judge what orders ought to have been given. Hill fed the president a tale of woe about his needs and the threat to his department, and the result was Davis's wiring Lee, "To withdraw Ransom's, Cooke's, and Jenkins' brigades is to abandon the country to the enemy." Besides, Hill claimed Lee had received other troops in place of at least some of the purloined units.[149] By the next day, May 30, the president wrote Lee, "It is embarrassing to be called on for orders, and when they are given to be met with opinions previously invited but withheld"– either commiserating with Lee in his treatment by Hill or reproaching Lee for what Davis may have perceived as that general's treatment of him. At any rate, Davis did admit that he had had only half the facts when he sent the previous day's dispatch, and he promised to "endeavor to have the matter explained."[150]

That same day Lee wrote Davis a lengthy letter that although calm and respectful did betray some of the general's frustration. Explaining again his difficulties with Hill and the falseness of Hill's claims, he repeated, "You will see that I am unable to operate under these circumstances." His solution was to "request to be relieved from any control of the department from the James to the Cape Fear River." Lee had no desire to be saddled with responsibility for a district he could not direct. What bothered him most was that he feared that in all of these petty squabbles he was losing his chance for taking the offensive. "I have for nearly a month," he explained, "been endeavoring to get this army in a condition to move–to anticipate an expected blow from the enemy. I fear I shall have to receive it here at a disadvantage, or to retreat." One more time he tried to make clear to the president his army's need for troops. "This army," he wrote, "has been diminished since last fall by the brigades of Jenkins, Ransom, Cooke, and Evans. It has been increased by Pettigrew's" inexperienced brigade. "General Hooker's army, as far as I can form an opinion, has been increased. I have given Your Excellency all the facts in my possession to enable you to form an opinion as to what is best to be done. I fear the time has passed when I could have taken the offensive with advantage."[151]

When the president answered this letter the next day, it appeared that Lee's persuasion had been effective and that Davis had once more swung over to full support of Lee's program. Yet the program Davis thought he was supporting and the program Lee had in mind were still two very different things. "I had never fairly comprehended your views and purposes until the receipt of your letter yesterday" Davis told Lee, "and now have to regret that I did not earlier know all that you had communicated to others." He assured

Lee that things were not so bad as they seemed. The threat of the Federals downstream on the James was probably exaggerated, and as for the troops Lee sought, Davis promised him another brigade in exchange for those he lost. Somehow, by the president's arithmetic, this made Lee only one brigade short of his previous strength. Unfortunately, the brigade Davis promised in exchange was composed of raw Mississippi recruits led by none other than the president's nephew, Joseph R. Davis, a man whose chief recommendation for military command was his service as his uncle's aide-de-camp. So innocent was the younger Davis of any military qualifications that the Confederate Senate earlier that year had balked at confirming his general's commission in an army peppered with military amateurs. Uncle Jefferson had not, however, served most of a decade and a half in Washington politics for nothing, and he still knew what string to pull to get a job done when he needed it. Accordingly, young Joseph finally got his wreath-and-stars and his brigade too. For whatever comfort it might have been, Lee now could count on having these green-as-grass Mississippians with him when next he went into battle.

Passing on from such reassuring subjects, the president turned to matters of command and strategy. Of Lee's request to be relieved of command south of the James, Davis noted, "This is one of the few instances in which I have found my thought running in the opposite direction from your own." Lee would just have to keep that portion of his department. "I wish," Davis wrote, "I knew how to relieve you from all anxiety concerning movements on the York or James River against Richmond while you are moving toward the north and west." But, Davis concluded regretfully, that was impossible. Did the president still intend Lee to move toward the north and west? "I readily perceive the disadvantage of standing still," he conceded, "and sorely regret that I cannot give you the means which would make it quite safe to attempt all that we desire."[152] In short, the president had, by way of a roundabout journey, come back to the position he had held as early as the fall of 1861, a position consistent with his basically defensive outlook and his confidence that the Confederacy could, if it had to, outlast the North. To him, offensive action was desirable but not necessary. It was to be undertaken when surplus strength made it "quite safe," but when weakness meant that the stake for a chance at national victory would be an equal risk of national ruin, no gambles were to be taken. Instead, limited, harassing offensives might serve to keep the enemy off balance and avoid "the disadvantage of standing still." He had proposed such schemes to Johnston and Beauregard in the fall of 1861, and now this was what he seemed to believe Lee was undertaking.

On June 3, Lee began easing his army out of its positions behind the Rappahannock and sending one division after another sidling off to the west toward the Shenandoah Valley and points north. He did so, however, without the substantial elements that had been detached over the previous months for coastal defense duty. The brigades of Ransom, Jenkins, Corse, Cooke, and Evans—together the equivalent of a large division of crack troops—remained scattered out in driblets from Hanover Junction to South Carolina. Lee never quite gave up on getting at least some of them back. To both Seddon and Davis he expressed his "regret" at losing such "good and tried officers with veteran troops." Under Lee's persistent prodding the Richmond authorities finally did consent to release Corse's brigade in view of the fact that Lee had specifically detached a body of less-experienced troops in its place. Yet it was not allowed to start northwestward from Hanover Junction until June 25, and by that time it was far too late to do Lee any good. No amount of persuasion by Lee could pry so much as an additional corporal's guard out of the region south of the North Anna River. Lee repeatedly suggested that troops should be sent northward wholesale from the Carolina coast. On June 8 he wrote, "I think our southern coast might be held during the sickly season by local troops. . . . This would give us an active force in the field with which we might hope to make some impression on the enemy. . . . Unless this can be done, I see little hope of accomplishing anything of importance." On the twentieth he tried again, "If any of the brigades that I have left behind for the protection of Richmond can in your opinion be spared, I should like them to be sent to me."[153]

On June 23 he repeated these arguments, with many of which he had been plying Davis for months by now, and suggested that "a part, at least, of the troops in North Carolina, and of those under General Beauregard [in South Carolina and Georgia]" come to northern Virginia under the command of that officer. The new army formed by this movement should hover about in the vicinity of Culpeper Court House, "threatening Washington." This would not only make things easier for the Army of Northern Virginia as it elbowed its way into Pennsylvania but should also rule out any chance of a Union threat to Richmond. Additionally, it would draw Federal troops away from the southern coasts and perhaps all the way from the Mississippi Valley as well. "I think it most important that, whatever troops be used for the purpose I have named," Lee continued, "General Beauregard be placed in command, and that his department be extended over North Carolina and Virginia. His presence would give magnitude to even a small demonstration, and tend greatly to perplex and confound the enemy." Obviously, it would be best to have the largest force possible, but even if Davis thought it unwise to remove any of Beauregard's troops from South Carolina, Lee believed "good results would follow from sending forward, under General Beauregard, such of the troops about Richmond and in North Carolina as could be spared for a short time."[154]

It was as clever a proposal for using the services of the flamboyant Creole as anyone came up with during the war. With a command at Culpeper Court House, Beauregard would not really need to do anything. Posturing and grandiose talk would be the chief requirements, and those Beauregard could handle very well indeed. The typical department commander's characteristic reluctance to part with troops, which Lee had encountered in such ugly form in D. H. Hill, would be canceled out by the typical general's desire to command as many troops as he possibly could wherever he might be. Thus although a department commander might have few if any troops to send away, he would likely have a very substantial contingent to bring away should he be transferred as Lee proposed to do with Beauregard. The scheme also played on the well-known propensities of another group of people, the Washington government. Lee referred to "the well known anxiety of the Northern Government for the safety of its capital."[155] He had played on that chord before with gratifying results and now hoped to add it to the symphony of Confederate victory he was composing for the summer of 1863.

The idea was obviously no passing fancy with Lee, as he referred to it several more times in his correspondence to Richmond in the week that remained before Gettysburg cut short his plans. Again and again he mentioned it as the solution to Richmond's worries about Federal forays up the Peninsula. On the twenty-fifth, he suggested the good results that would spring from "organizing an army, even in effigy, under General Beauregard at Culpeper Court House." If even the brigades now being held around Richmond and in southside Virginia "were ordered there at once, and General Beauregard were sent there, [even] if he had to return [soon] to South Carolina," Lee anticipated much benefit.[156] The mystery is why Lee waited until this point to broach the idea to Davis. Naturally, Lee had no idea that his northern excursion would be so unceremoniously curtailed in the first week of July, but that hardly accounts for his failing to inform the government of a major component of his plan for the summer's campaign until that campaign was already three weeks old. The only plausible explanation is that Lee was reluctant to reveal to Davis the full scope of his intentions for the operation prior to the point at which his army was solidly committed to the offensive beyond likelihood of recall. Calling for Beauregard a month earlier, when the northern invasion itself was still being debated by the cabinet, would have made fatally obvious to the cautious president that what Lee had in mind was an all-out end-the-war gamble.

Of course by this time there was no chance of Lee's succeeding in getting Beauregard or any of his troops transferred to Virginia even if Davis had been inclined to send them, and Davis was far from that. As Lee had traveled northward, the transit time for his letters to Richmond had grown proportionately. The June 23 letter in which he first mentioned the possibility of Beauregard's coming north was written in Berryville, Virginia, just east of Winchester in the lower Shenandoah Valley. It did not reach Richmond until the evening of the twenty-eighth and was the last communication that Davis had from Lee until the middle of July.[157] The remainder of Lee's pleas for Beauregard's additional troops were made moot by the battle of Gettysburg.

As disappointed as Lee undoubtedly was at having to make his campaign with no more troops than he had, he had done very well to have as many as that, narrowly avoiding calls from Richmond that he detach even more units. The reason for this was the fear by many in Richmond that the city was sorely threatened by Federal forces somewhere to the east, perhaps at White House Landing on the Pamunkey, perhaps Fort Monroe or Suffolk. No one seemed sure just where the Yankees lurked, but most agreed that they were numerous, barbaric, and bent on sacking Richmond and desolating the surrounding countryside. Ironically, Lee himself was partially to blame for this fear. In late May he had expressed a certain degree of uneasiness about the eastern approaches of the capital. On the thirtieth he recommended to Seddon the "organization of the citizens of Richmond as a local force for the defense of the city" to counter what he considered a probable effort to take the place by certain Federals on the York River.[158] At that time the secretary of war was not inclined to think the danger very great.[159] Given more time to reflect, however, and as distance to Lee's army became greater, Seddon came to see the matter differently.

Lee's view also changed. Although on June 2 he was assuring Davis that he would begin his movement cautiously, keeping an eye on events around Richmond and being sure not to get too far away until it was clear Richmond was safe, a week later he was convinced that the whole Peninsula threat was probably a Yankee hoax intended to make him nervous about Richmond. At any rate, he felt confident no Union movement against the city was brewing at the moment.[160] During the same week, Seddon was making his metamorphosis from complacency to fretfulness. Minor Federal raids in eastern Virginia produced a disproportionate effect both in his mind and in those of others in Richmond. Davis himself seems not to have been as stampeded as most others, but he was distracted enough to approve an order from Richmond garrison commander Maj. Gen. Arnold Elzey that came near to depriving Lee of Pickett's whole division just as it was departing to catch up with the rest of the army.[161] Pickett got away, but many in Richmond came to regret it. Elzey and southside commander D. H. Hill were both wrought up to a high pitch of nervous apprehension and imagined themselves in a desperate situation. Cooper and Seddon were little better. Seddon wrote to Lee on the ninth regarding the "disastrous raids," and on the tenth he fretted, "I press upon your consideration some of the dangers to which our destitution of a covering force to this city and the railroad may expose us." The city, he complained, was "almost defenseless . . . literally without force, should the enemy make a dash with their transports up the James." Worse, that was just what he feared they were about to do.[162] Lee responded by trying to calm Seddon's fears and even dispatched a staff officer to Richmond to "give an exact account of the reported movements of the enemy on the Peninsula."[163] He wrote to Davis as well, emphasizing that he was convinced "that the enemy contemplates nothing important in that region."[164]

The president held remarkably firm in the face of the near panic. Elzey, Cooper, and the others notwithstanding, Davis wrote Lee on the nineteenth that he hoped Richmond could be secured without drawing any more troops from the field army.[165] Nine days later he responded to Lee's final request for his missing brigades by writing, "It has been an effort with me to answer the clamor to have troops stopped or recalled, to protect the city and the railroads communicating with your army." Explaining how each of the various brigades retained around Richmond or in North Carolina was needed at its present post, he added, "Do not understand me as balancing accounts in the matter of brigades; I only repeat that I have not many to send you" and certainly not enough to set up an army for Beauregard to use in threatening Washington.[166]

That letter never reached Lee at all. The courier who carried it was captured at Hagerstown, Maryland, on July 2, providing some very interesting reading for Union Secretary of War Edwin M. Stanton, among others.[167] Its intended recipient might have found difficulty appreciating its slightly self-congratulatory tone. Yet from Davis's point of view, he had done all that could possibly have been expected from him and a great deal more. If the war was to be fought defensively with only such offensive operations as served the purposes of a defensive strategy, if the Confederacy needed only to endure and to stave off military disaster in order to prevail, if time and attrition could be made to serve the South, then the president had shown remarkable willingness to take risks. With his fundamental bent toward a defensive war policy of perseverance and endurance, Davis had undoubtedly been required to call forth tremendous reserves of moral fortitude in order to resist not only the pressure of the inevitable outside clamor but of his own instincts as well, instincts that would have called for restraining Lee's offensive to an operation that risked no more than the Confederacy could afford to lose and that demanded it run no extra risk of disaster on the other fronts whose troops Lee coveted.

But viewed from Lee's perspective, Davis's performance appears less impressive. If the war was steadily grinding down the South's will to resist—if it would do so no matter what strategy was pursued—if the slow exhaustion of Confederate manpower and morale would lead to sure defeat if allowed to go on long enough, then the only hope was a series of crushing battlefield victories that destroyed the will of the North to continue prosecuting the war. No matter how long the odds of achieving such victories might be, they would be desirable odds if time did not favor the South. If that was the case, and Lee's actions and words both tended to suggest he believed it was, the true policy of the Confederacy would be to risk everything on the best chance it could get for battlefield victory.

If Davis had consistently pursued this strategy in May and June 1863, Lee would have taken with him the five veteran brigades he left behind. Beauregard would have been established in Virginia with most of the troops from the southern seaboard and possibly even a few from the West. Two days after Lee wrote his dispatch to Davis requesting this assignment for the Creole, Davis, not yet having received Lee's letter, wrote Beauregard himself, requesting all the troops that general could spare for transfer to Mississippi.[168] This was consistent with a defensive strategy that aimed at avoiding major losses such as that shaping up at Vicksburg, but it flew in the face of a strategy that demanded an all-out bid for victory. If, on the other hand, Davis had consistently pursued his own instinctively defensive strategy during those months, Lee would not have been going north at all, and Pickett, Hood, and perhaps other troops would have been on their way to Vicksburg. Instead, the course actually pursued by the Confederacy during the spring and early summer of 1863 was a hodgepodge of two completely opposite strategies, taking more risks and incurring more losses than Davis's strategy would have entailed while foregoing most of whatever shot at an early victory Lee's might have gained. That it was so was partially the fault of Davis, who shied away from making hard decisions and so did not opt clearly for one path or the other. Partially it was the fault of Lee, whose habit of modestly understating what he hoped to accomplish, along with his manipulating of the president by telling him only what he wanted to hear, gave Davis an incorrect notion of just what sort of campaign he was approving.[169]

As the campaign progressed, Lee's intentions became increasingly clear. During the first week of June he was still writing in terms of forcing the enemy to draw troops away from the Atlantic coast and avoiding the probability that if the army did not advance, the enemy would ultimately succeed in driving it back into the Richmond entrenchments to stand a siege the result of which was certain. Yet at the same time he warned that "there is always hazard in military movements" and that the Confederacy had simply a choice between the "positive loss of inactivity and the risk of action." He also mentioned the desirability of drawing the enemy army "out into a position to be assailed."[170]

By the next week he had become more explicit. On June 10 he wrote Davis regarding "the manner in which the demonstration of a desire for peace at the North has been received in our country." Lee was concerned that southern editors and politicians were making pronouncements that would tend to discourage northerners seeking a compromise peace. He, for one, did not think the Confederacy could afford to "make nice distinctions between those who declare for peace unconditionally and those who advocate it as a means of restoring the union, however much we may prefer the former." The goal was to end the fighting with the Confederacy still in existence. If that meant allowing misguided northerners to indulge the mistaken belief that a compromise peace would restore the Union, so be it. "Should the belief that peace will bring back the Union become general, the war would no longer be supported, and that, after all, is what we are interested in bringing about. When peace is proposed to us, it will be time enough to discuss its terms, and it is not the part of prudence to spurn the proposition in advance, merely because those who wish to make it believe, or affect to believe, that it will result in bringing us back to the Union." Once again, Lee was moving north while suggesting that peace feelers should or might soon be extended by one side or the other.

His apology for addressing Davis on a subject primarily political was "its connection with the situation of military affairs." The enemy, Lee pointed out, was superior in numbers and resources, and "we have no right to look for exemptions from the military consequences of a vigorous use of these advantages. . . . While making the most we can of the means of resistance we possess, . . . it is nevertheless the part of wisdom to carefully measure and husband our strength, and not to expect from it more than in the ordinary course of affairs it is capable of accomplishing." This might almost sound like a renunciation of the costly campaigns Lee had waged during the past year as well as the one he was now bent on carrying out, but Lee saw it otherwise. A slow war of attrition would doom the South; what was needed was to use crushing victories to raise the North's level of discouragement to the point at which the government in Washington could no longer prosecute the war. What Lee now asked of Davis was that he use his influence with those seen as spokesmen for the South to ensure that they did not, through heated rhetoric, raise the threshold of demoralization at which the northern will to win would collapse, thus making Lee's job that much harder. "We should not, therefore," Lee wrote, "conceal from ourselves that our resources in men are constantly diminishing, and the disproportion in this respect between us and our enemies, if they continue united in their efforts to subjugate us, is steadily augmenting." This Lee illustrated by pointing to the declining manpower within his own army, as battle losses were not made good.[171] Such a discussion amounted to little less than a thinly veiled suggestion that if the war was to be won, it must be this year. Davis would hardly have been at fault in reading into Lee's letter a hint that he ought to make the best terms he could before snow flew. Nothing, of course, could have been further from the president's mind, and he probably never suspected Lee of thinking so either. Lee, for his part, was not yet ready to give up. He seems to have hoped through the combination of decisive battlefield victory on northern soil and cunning manipulation of public opinion by the South's political leaders to achieve that summer the goal for which he had fought so long.

As with his suggestion for Beauregard's transfer to Virginia, Lee continued to mention his hopes for peace in his correspondence as the campaign progressed. "It is plain to my understanding," Lee told Davis in a June 25 letter, "that everything that will tend to repress the war feeling the Federal States will inure to our benefit."[172] Lee could not possibly have avoided thinking that another Chancellorsville—or, better still, a more complete victory—on northern soil would go far toward that end. Just how complete Lee wished the Confederacy's effort to achieve victory to be that summer is revealed by his suggestions for other theaters of the war. Not only did he desire troops on the southeastern coast to be added to his army or thrown into Virginia to threaten or take Washington, but he also wanted Confederate forces to advance against the enemy in southwestern Virginia as well as in East and Middle Tennessee.[173] Without such diversions, he pleaded, his army would become the Federals' only target, and "it would result in our accomplishing nothing, and being compelled to return to Virginia."[174] That was not at all what he intended. "I think I can throw General Hooker's army across the Potomac," he wrote in the same letter, "and draw troops from the south, embarrassing their plan of campaign in a measure, if I can do nothing and have to return."[175] To return to Virginia having merely gathered supplies and disrupted Federal operations, to have strung the war along successfully through another campaigning season, was to "do nothing." Lee had more in mind.

He seems to have left open the question of whether he would develop this penetration as a raid or whether he would endeavor to maintain a supply line through the Shenandoah as he had the year before. On June 19, while still in the Shenandoah Valley, he informed Davis, "The difficulty of securing supplies retards and renders more uncertain our future movement."[176] Davis and Seddon seemed to assume right on into July that Lee would be maintaining a supply line, and Davis expressed regret at not having available at Richmond a force of cavalry that he could use in protecting such a line.[177] On June 25, however, with his headquarters and A. P. Hill's corps about to cross the Potomac, Ewell's corps already well up into Pennsylvania and headed for the Susquehannah, and Longstreet's divisions just crossing into the Shenandoah Valley far to the south, Lee decided to change his policy. Tersely, he explained the matter to the president, "I have not sufficient troops to maintain my communications, and, therefore, have to abandon them."[178] This may have been at least partly due to the fact that the Federals, as they had the summer before, were maintaining a force at Harpers Ferry, threatening any Confederate supply line through the Valley. Lee had already made the experiment of reducing such a garrison while a Union army bore down on his rear and may not have been enthusiastic about trying it again.

Another reason for cutting loose of his supply line may have been that he simply wanted to have every available man present in the ranks rather than guarding wagons full of hardtack. He could live off the land all summer in Pennsylvania as long as he kept moving and was not bothered by an enemy army. The appearance of the Army of the Potomac would, of course, put a stop to his foraging, but an encounter with the Army of the Potomac was precisely what he had come north to provoke. When the time came, Lee, as a raider dependent on foraging, would now be forced to attack at once. A prolonged halt or even close maneuvering in the presence of the enemy was impossible without starving his army, but that was the gamble Lee chose to take in order to have the largest possible army available for the showdown, a further indication that Lee sought not to delay and disrupt the Federals but to defeat them decisively. At first glance his statements that to return to Virginia would be to fail seem to contradict his choice to make the campaign a raid that must ultimately end in his returning to Virginia. The answer lies in the fact that Lee sought decision that year. He did not plan to stay in Pennsylvania indefinitely or even until winter, but he did hope to be there when peace was concluded.

His hopes were to be disappointed. The Army of the Potomac that he met in Pennsylvania was under the command of Maj. Gen. George G. Meade, who had replaced Hooker only a few days before the collision at Gettysburg. Meade was a far more able commander than Lee had previously encountered. The usually reliable J. E. B. Stuart, Lee's cavalry commander, failed to provide reconnaissance. When the Army of Northern Virginia did make contact with the enemy, more or less by surprise, Lee's previous decision to opt for a raiding policy without a supply line meant he would have to fight here and defeat the enemy quickly. Longstreet seemed incapable of grasping this and insistently pressed his own unrealistic operational ideas on Lee. When Lee declined to be guided by Longstreet's advice, the corps commander became sulky and contrary. Still, Lee's other two corps commanders were inexperienced, so Lee chose to rely on his "Old Warhorse" notwithstanding. The assaults Lee ordered Longstreet to make might have failed in any case, but Longstreet clearly withheld his cooperation and obstructed Lee's plans to some degree.[179]

Lee too had failed. Placed at a disadvantage and forced to attack, he had pressed his assaults far beyond the point at which reason would have demanded that he cut his losses and withdraw. Lee had always been combative, but this was extreme. To have acted in this way would almost have required a belief that the Confederacy had, absent decisive victory here, no tomorrow. The decision had to be now, both for the South and perhaps for Lee. If the death of Jackson had shaken Lee's confidence and inclined him to an even stronger desire to decide matters immediately and once and for all, he hardly could have been expected to act any differently than he did at Gettysburg. Interestingly, some observers noted that at this battle Lee was not himself and seemed emotionally agitated.[180] Whatever may have been behind the general's actions, they were an unhappy caricature of the most unfortunate aspects of his tactics. The determined Army of the Potomac under its new cautious but competent leader might have defeated Lee and his lieutenants even had they performed up to their usual standard, but their various failings made the defeat enormously costly in southern lives. Indeed, like the Sharpsburg campaign of the previous year, this threatened to end the Army of Northern Virginia's existence altogether.

When Lee's beaten army reached the Potomac on its retreat back into Virginia, it faced a stream far different from what it had forded a couple of weeks earlier. Recent rains had brought the river to flood stage and made crossing an impossibility. Trapped against the north bank of the river with Meade's victorious Federals closing in, Lee wrote in a letter to Davis, "I shall therefore have to accept battle if the enemy offers it, whether I wish to or not." This might be the answer to Lee's desires for a decisive outcome to the summer's campaign, though not the one he had sought. "The result," he wrote, "is in the hands of the Sovereign Ruler of the Universe and known to Him only."[181] This time, however, the decision was once again postponed indefinitely. Meade, whose army had suffered almost as badly as Lee's, approached slowly and gingerly, and by the time he was finally ready to take definite action, the river had fallen and Lee and his Confederates escaped back into Virginia.

Back in Richmond, Davis waited day after day for news from Lee. The last dispatch he had received from Lee had been the general's letter of June 23, written near Berryville, Virginia. Vague reports and rumors from various sources had brought news that Lee had indeed crossed the Potomac and was operating in the North, but from the general himself came no word at all. This was a factor of the difficulty of getting couriers through rather than any lack of communicativeness on Lee's part, for he continued to write lengthy letters to Davis almost every day and sometimes twice a day. Yet even by July 9, Davis still had not received Lee's two letters of June 25.[182] The nervous tension, coupled with his concern for Vicksburg, seem to have taken their toll on his health. He had enjoyed improving health and growing strength early in June, as relief of Vicksburg seemed possible and Lee's army swung north with high hopes.[183] Now under the strain of suspense he suffered a relapse. By July 2 he was confined to bed, and the Richmond rumor mills began to grind on the possibility of his imminent demise.[184] For several days he had been too sick even to meet with the secretary of war.[185] By the sixth, he had rallied enough to rise from his bed, but John B. Jones confided in his diary that Davis's "health is apparently gone, and it may be doubtful whether he will ever be quite well again."[186] Ironically, that was the day that brought the first unofficial reports of the fall of Vicksburg. Perhaps, even for Davis, bad news was better than the unendurable suspense.

With Lee's army, however, such relief was not yet at hand. As always when military events hung in the balance, Davis wished he could take a hand in them himself. Several times during the campaign he expressed his frustration to Varina. "If I could take one wing and Lee the other," he told her wistfully, "I think we could between us wrest a victory from those people."[187] In their own ways others seemed as little able to bear the waiting and not knowing as was Davis. On the eighth, Seddon caught what Jones called "the prevailing alarm at the silence of Lee." The secretary of war wrote a note to Davis passing along some wildly optimistic rumor, which he hoped might be true, and asking what was to be done. For the moment, of course, nothing could be done, and so Davis responded. In his diary that night Jones wrote, "If Lee falls back again, it will be the darkest day for the Confederacy we have yet seen."[188] By the ninth, rumors were flying thick and fast. A great victory had been won, Meade was defeated.[189] Or, alternately, Federals had been sighted somewhere in the vicinity of Williamsport, dangerously close to what everyone in Richmond still assumed to be Lee's line of supply.[190] Still, noted Jones at the War Department, "We get nothing from Lee himself." That afternoon Davis, still obviously very sick, summoned Cooper, Seddon, and D. H. Hill to meet him in his office at 1:00 P.M. "They seemed in haste, and excited," Jones observed and speculated further that the excitement might kill the ailing president.[191] The topic of the meeting, of course, was what to do about Lee. For some days now Davis had been fishing for troops to send to his aid. The day before, Hill had allowed that he might be able to spare a brigade or two, especially if the rumor about Meade's defeat turned out to be true.[192] On the ninth, Davis, presumably with the counsel of his subordinates summoned to the 1:00 P.M. meeting, directed southeastern Virginia commander Samuel Jones to send 3,000 men and a couple of batteries of artillery to Winchester, where they would await orders from Lee and be available as a force to cover his threatened communications.[193] It was not much, but then Jones possessed only a very small force to begin with, and at least it allowed Davis to do something, however small, to help Lee.

That evening the suspense was broken by the arrival of a dispatch from Lee dated July 4.[194] A three-day battle had been fought, and though Lee strove to put the best face on it, the Confederates had obviously not been victorious and were retreating. The full measure of the disaster began to break through the restrained wording of Lee's dispatch in the final paragraph when the general turned his attention to a casualty list that sounded like a roster of the army's general officers. "Gen. Barksdale is killed, Gen. Garnett and Armistead are missing and it is feared that the former is killed and the latter wounded and a prisoner. Genl. Pender and Trimble are wounded in the leg, Genl. Hood in the arm and Gen. Heth slightly in the head." And so the list went on, concluding with the terse observation that the South had lost "many other valuable officers and men."[195] Further casualty reports followed in the days afterward as well as the alarming news that Lee was trapped north of the Potomac and at the mercy of the Federals. Again, Davis did what he could, dispatching a pontoon train to help Lee get back across the river, though as events developed the river had receded and Lee made good his escape before the bridging equipment could arrive.[196]

During the weeks that followed Davis and Lee corresponded frequently and at length. Their topics often were matters of recruiting and reorganizing the Army of Northern Virginia in the wake of its crippling Gettysburg losses. They worked together smoothly on these matters, each man sharing his assessments and suggestions and readily taking up those of the other. Neither mentioned a single area of disagreement between them.[197]

This harmony extended as well to decisions regarding military operations. On July 29 Lee speculated as to whether the enemy would again seek to advance in the vicinity of Fredericksburg as both Burnside and Hooker had tried within the previous eight months. If they did, Lee doubted "the policy of our resuming our former position in rear of Fredericksburg." Unless the enemy general would, like Burnside, be so accommodating as to confine himself to a frontal attack, a Confederate army on the line of the Rappahannock was very likely to be put at a disadvantage. "I therefore think it better to take a position farther back," he explained to Davis. He also wanted to know what Davis thought in the matter.[198] The president replied promptly. "You are so much better able to judge of the propriety of resuming your former position in rear of Fredericksburg than myself," he wrote Lee on August 2, "that I hesitate to express an opinion." Still, since Lee had specifically asked for one, Davis complied. "The facility with which your former position [on the Rappahannock] may be turned if approached from the rear, and its proximity to the enemy's base" made it "more advisable to take a position further to the rear before accepting . . . battle." The ideal situation, Davis felt, would be a well selected and fortified position close enough to Richmond to allow troops in the vicinity of the city to join Lee in time for the battle "without exposing the capital to attack by a hostile force on the Peninsula."[199] Even in the immediate aftermath of the debacle at Gettysburg with its apparent discrediting of Lee's strategy, Davis was still ready to allow Lee virtually complete freedom to choose his strategy and direct his operations.

Indeed, Gettysburg seems not to have damaged Davis's regard for Lee in the least. While the president grew increasingly bitter at Joseph E. Johnston after his failure even to attempt the relief of Vicksburg, he remained friendly toward Lee. The general, of course, was careful as always in what he asked of Davis, but it is still significant that Lee's every request in the areas of supply, organization, recruitment, and operations during these weeks promptly elicited Davis's best efforts to fulfill it. The president signed his letters to Lee during this period, "With cordial regards," "As ever truly your friend," and "With prayers for your health, safety and happiness, I am as ever, your friend." Davis still valued Lee's military acumen and missed having him in his old role as commanding general in Richmond. On July 28 he wrote, "I have felt more than ever before the want of your advice during the recent period of disaster." Five days later he told Lee, "You were required in the field and I deprived myself of the support you gave me here. I need your counsel but must strive to meet the requirements of the hour without distracting your attention at a time when it should be concentrated on the field before you."[200]

Not everyone, however, was pleased with Lee's performance in the Gettysburg campaign. "Gettysburg has shaken my faith in Lee," wrote one diarist, who considered the battle "a great military blunder." A Confederate politician wrote of Lee's "blunder at Gettysburg, his wretched handling of his troops, & his utter want of generalship." Even an officer in Lee's own army professed to be "thoroughly disgusted." As for the newspapers, "the tone of the public press," as Varina delicately phrased it many years later, "indicated dissatisfaction with the result of the campaign."[201] Other individuals and papers were more favorable to Lee and the campaign. On the whole, opinion appears to have been mixed but definitely included an undertone of censure.[202] Davis never took the negative assessment of Lee's 1863 invasion of the North. For one thing, he had always had a more conservative concept of what the campaign was to be and a more limited set of objectives that he expected it to accomplish. It had, he believed, been meant for the purpose of disrupting Federal offensive plans for the summer. That it seemed to have done. Therefore, the campaign could be viewed as a success, if a rather expensive one. "The wisdom of the strategy," Davis wrote in his memoirs, "was justified by the result." True, "the battle of Gettysburg was unfortunate," but only in that the Confederacy with its limited pool of manpower could not afford the casualties that the North could. In general, Davis, at least in this latter day account, defended Lee against most charges made against him in connection with the battle and merely conceded "that it would have been better to withdraw than to renew the attack on the third day."[203]

Still, Davis would need to have been blind in both eyes, rather than just one, and deaf too if he were not to notice the "mutterings of discontent," as he called them. In a July 28 letter to Lee he mentioned the matter in a reassuring tone. "Misfortune," he noted, "often . . . makes men complain. It is comfortable to hold some one responsible for one's discomfort." He noted specifically that some "find an appropriate remedy in the removal of officers who have not succeeded." These Davis believed were badly misguided since they could not, or at least did not, name "substitutes who would be better than the officers displaced." No doubt thinking of the criticism presently being heaped on Lee, and much more so on Bragg and Pemberton as well as on Davis himself, the president wrote, "If a victim would secure the success of our cause I would freely offer myself, and there are many of those most assailed who would I am sure contend for the place if their sacrifice could bring such reward."[204]

Though Davis almost certainly intended this to reassure Lee of his continued support, it may well be that Lee interpreted it as a roundabout hint that his resignation might be in order. Besides that, Lee was tired and no longer in good health, and the public criticism, mild though it was compared to what was being ladled out to Pemberton, Bragg, and Davis, would still have been extremely unpleasant. Willing perhaps to allow Davis to pursue his policy of sinewy endurance with the aid of a more defensive-minded general in Virginia, Lee moved to step aside. In an August 8 letter to Davis, he offered his resignation.[205] In words that sounded strange when coming from his pen, Lee asserted of the southern people that "nothing is wanted but that their fortitude should equal their bravery, to insure the success of our cause." This was a new tone for Lee, whose whole policy in the war to this point had proclaimed his belief that southern bravery must triumph before southern fortitude failed. Now sounding like an echo of the president himself, he wrote, "Our people have only to be true and united, to bear manfully the misfortunes incident to war, and all will come right in the end." Coming then to the point, he continued, "The general remedy for want of success in a military commander is his removal. This is natural, and in many instances proper." If a general lost the "confidence of his troops, disaster must sooner or later come." Lee believed this rule applied in his present case, thus he continued, "I have been prompted by these reflections more than once since my return from Pennsylvania to propose to your excellency the propriety of selecting another commander for this army." He had, he explained, "seen

and heard of expressions of discontent in public journals," and these probably reflected feeling within the army as well. "I, therefore, in all sincerity,
request your excellency to take measures to supply my place. I do this with
the more earnestness because no one is more aware than myself of my
inability for the duties of my position. I cannot even accomplish what I
myself desire. How can I fulfill the expectations of others?" Besides, poor
health was preventing his being the sort of active commander he believed
was needed. "A younger and abler man . . . can readily be obtained," and
Lee urged Davis to do so. In conclusion, he assured the president, "I have no
complaints to make of anyone but myself. . . . To your excellency, I am
specially indebted for uniform kindness and consideration. You have done
everything in your power to aid me in the work committed to my charge."[206]

The letter came as a shock to Davis, and he replied immediately. Not failing
to notice Lee's new emphasis on a war policy of endurance, Davis began, "I am
glad that you concur so entirely with me as to the want of our country in this
trying hour." He was happy to assure Lee of his belief that "our people will
exhibit that fortitude which we agree in believing is alone needful to secure
ultimate success." Davis could well sympathize with Lee in the criticism he was
receiving. "There has been nothing," the president wrote, "which I have found
to require a greater effort of patience than to bear the criticisms of the
ignorant." Davis went on to admit the truth of Lee's assertions that "success is
the test of merit" for generals and that a general "who loses the confidence of
his troops should have his position changed." There the agreement stopped.
"When I read [that] sentence I was not at all prepared for the application you
were about to make." Then Davis proceeded point by point to dispute Lee's
grounds for resignation. The newspapers were "partisan" and "venal," so much
for their carping. Next, no doubt thinking of his present controversy with
Johnston and certain of his facile-penned staff officers, Davis added, "Were you
capable of stooping to it, you could easily surround yourself with those who
would fill the press with your laudations." Speaking again from personal
experience, Davis suggested that Lee's physical condition might improve, and
even if it did not, Lee would get used to it. Passing on from such objections,
Davis came then to his conclusion. "But suppose, my dear friend, that I were to
admit, with all their implications, the points which you present, where am I to
find that new commander who is to possess the greater ability which you
believe to be required? . . . To ask me to substitute you by someone in
my judgment more fit to command, or who would possess more of the
confidence of the army, or of the reflecting men of the country, is to demand
an impossibility."[207]

Thus Jefferson Davis, for whom decision making always came exceptionally hard, made one decision firmly, clearly, and irrevocably. For the rest of the war, for victory or defeat, his lot was cast with Lee. Very few Confederates knew at that time that Lee had offered his resignation, but none ever had cause to doubt the president's commitment to the commander of the Confederacy's largest army. That in itself probably did much to steady southern morale in the bleak months that followed. Retaining Lee would, of course, do nothing to alleviate the ambiguity of Confederate strategy, for Lee knew but one way to make war and had but one hope of achieving Confederate victory, even if that hope now seemed a forlorn one. He would defend if he had to, but strike when he could. Yet from now on the case would increasingly be the former, as necessity finally compelled Lee to the course that had always seemed most obvious to Davis.

The Confederate president had indeed done all he could, within the limits of his own strategic point of view, to help Lee along to victory. For one whose approach to the war was defensive, Davis had skirted the boundaries of recklessness in supporting Lee's 1863 offensive. That the often hesitant and uncertain Confederate president found the nerve to take such steps is a measure of his confidence in Lee despite the difference in outlook that made Davis view as tempting fate what Lee saw as the South's only hope of safety. That confidence in Lee remained unshaken despite Gettysburg and now became more than ever the one fixed point in Davis's direction of the war in Virginia.

7
VICTORY OR SUBJUGATION

One of the first things Davis and Lee had to deal with in the aftermath of Gettysburg was the problem of desertion from the army. As had been the case during and after the previous summer's hard campaigning, thousands of Confederate soldiers left their units and either hung about the army avoiding duty and danger or else set out for their more or less distant homes. This time, however, the case involved more than just an army that had been used too hard and soldiers who had seen too many of their comrades fall in too short a time. Along with such causes worked other more sinister factors, for the morale of the whole Confederate people was beginning to crack. The realization began to creep through the hearts and minds of southerners after July 1863 that they might lose this war. It was not so much Gettysburg that began to stir these doubts as the string of other Confederate disasters that summer. Vicksburg fell, and with it a 30,000–man army was lost. The Army of Tennessee was driven out of the state whose name it bore, and Charleston faced a massive seaborne onslaught by the Federals. As southern morale began to decline, almost imperceptibly at first, soldiers deserted, and their civilian relatives encouraged them to do so.[1]

Desertion became such a problem after Gettysburg that Lee urged Davis to issue a proclamation of amnesty to all deserters who would return to their units.[2] So on August 1 Davis issued a lengthy proclamation, alluding floridly to the enemy's supposed "malignant rage" that aimed "at nothing less than the extermination of yourselves, your wives, and children." After expanding at some length on the evils of the foe in a tone little short of snarling, the president came to the point. "Fellow-citizens, no alternative is left you but victory or subjugation." Thus it was of the utmost importance that southerners fight on, that deserters return to the ranks, and that southern women "take care that none who owe service in the field shall be sheltered at home from the disgrace of having deserted their duty." Every soldier who would return to his regiment within twenty days would be immune from prosecution for his absence.[3] The badly overheated rhetoric was a further indication of the slippage of southern morale, and Davis seems to have felt that stronger exhortations were necessary to hold the southern people to their task.[4] Whether scare tactics—or an amnesty for deserters—would work remained to be seen.

Lee at first thought the proclamation was having a good effect. "Our absentees are returning," he wrote on August 8, "and I hope the earnest and beautiful appeal made to the country in your proclamation may stir up the whole people."[5] Less than two weeks later, however, he was of a different opinion entirely. "The number of desertions from this army is so great, and still continues to such an extent," he wrote on the seventeenth, "that unless some cessation of them can be caused, I fear success in the field will be endangered." The worst of it was that the amnesty seemed to have produced the opposite of the intended effect. "Immediately on the publication of the amnesty, which I thought would be beneficial in its effects," Lee continued, "many presumed on it, and absented themselves from their commands, choosing to place on it a wrong interpretation." The amnesty thus had been taken by many Confederate soldiers as an indication that desertion would no longer be punished at all. Lee therefore proposed a very different solution. "I would now respectfully submit to your excellency the opinion that all has been done which forbearance and mercy call for, and that nothing will remedy this great evil which so much endangers our cause excepting the rigid endorsement of the death penalty in future in cases of conviction."[6] Events were to prove Davis less amenable to Lee's desires in this respect than he had been in the matter of the amnesty. Over the next year and a half, the Confederate president would show himself consistently less willing to shoot deserters than was Lee, and the matter would become one of the few items of irritation between them. For now, Lee had no one on hand to shoot, and Davis had before him no application for clemency, and so the matter remained dormant.

Lee's thoughts on operations during the month of August remained in theory as different from the president's ideas as they had ever been. After reporting on the twenty-second the quiescence of the Army of the Potomac, Lee added, "As soon as I can get the vacancies in the army filled, and the horses and men recruited a little, if General Meade does not move, I wish to attack him."[7] That was vintage Lee. A couple of days later he was writing, "Nothing prevents my advancing now but the fear of killing our artillery horses."[8] As it turned out, another obstacle stood in the way of Lee's resuming the offensive, and that was the much different mind of the Confederate president. The same day Lee wrote of the weakness of his artillery horses, Davis sent a dispatch to him. "For some days," the president informed him, "I have hoped to be able to visit you, wishing to consult you on military questions of a general character. Events in the South and West continue to detain me here. If circumstances will permit your absence, I wish you to come to Richmond."[9]

Leaving Longstreet to mind affairs along the Rappahannock, Lee hurried immediately to Richmond. There for the next two weeks he discussed with Davis the various military problems that plagued the Confederacy: what was to be done about desertion, how was an adequate supply of fodder to be obtained for the Army of Northern Virginia's horses, and, most important, what was to be done about the steadily worsening military situation in Tennessee? There, during the summer months, the Federal Army of the Cumberland under Maj. Gen. William S. Rosecrans had maneuvered Braxton Bragg's Army of Tennessee all the way back to Chattanooga and was threatening to force it out of that key city as well. At the same time, another smaller Federal army under Burnside was moving into East Tennessee, threatening the vital railroad between Virginia and Tennessee and leading Confederates to believe he planned to unite with Rosecrans to form an unstoppably large army. As Davis and Lee debated possible responses to the threat, the old disagreement arose again as to whether the Confederacy should shift troops to threatened areas or force the Union to respond by threatening its vital areas. Lee, in keeping with his still generally offensive outlook, favored the former course and urged that he be allowed to attack Meade. He nearly prevailed, as Davis was at first inclined to acquiesce. Lee even went so far as to send Longstreet orders to get the army ready for an advance. Then, however, the president's own instincts, and perhaps the pressure of western politicians, took the upper hand.

By the end of Lee's first week in Richmond, Davis had decided against offensive action in Virginia and in favor of the basically defensive policy of shifting troops to heavily threatened Tennessee.[10] Indeed, Davis wanted not only some of the Army of Northern Virginia's soldiers to go west but its commander as well. Respectfully, however, he asked rather than ordered Lee to take command of the Army of Tennessee. Lee assured the president that he was willing to do whatever might be for the good of the Confederacy, but that if the matter was put to him, he did not believe his transfer to the West would help matters much. Reluctantly, Davis agreed, and their remaining discussions focused on the manner of sending troops to Bragg. A good deal of their talking seems to have been done while riding around the Richmond area inspecting the fortifications. In the course of their horseback conferences, they decided that Longstreet and his corps should go to Tennessee, though the pitiful remnant of Pickett's division would be left near Richmond. In exchange Longstreet would take a couple of large brigades that had been guarding the capital and its approaches. The original plan was for Longstreet to proceed down the railroad directly into East Tennessee to aid Bragg by opposing Burnside and preventing his junction with Rosecrans. On September 2, however, Burnside's army marched into Knoxville, cutting the railroad and thus ensuring that should Longstreet advance by that route the Federals would in no way be hindered from uniting their forces while easily holding Bragg and Longstreet apart and defeating them each in turn. Consequently, Davis and Lee decided that Longstreet's divisions should take a roundabout rail journey through the eastern tier of states, then around to Atlanta and back north again to join Bragg's army near Chattanooga.[11]

Lee returned to the Army of Northern Virginia on September 7 but before leaving Richmond wrote a brief note explaining his preparations for the movement and expressing his willingness to go west himself if that was really what Davis thought best. "I did not intend to decline the service," Lee explained, "but merely to express the opinion that the duty could be better performed by the officers already in that department."[12] A reply from the president followed Lee back to the army's camps around Orange Court House. Davis believed Lee's "presence in the western army would be worth more than the addition of a corps, but fear[ed] the effect of your absence from Virginia." He assured Lee that he "did not doubt your willingness to do whatever was best for the country" and suggested that Lee help to determine just what that might be. In the past, Lee had frequently expressed his views to Davis and added that the president, with fuller information from all fronts, would know best what needed to be done. Now Davis undertook to send Lee detailed information about the situation on other fronts in hopes that Lee might aid him in making decisions.[13] A month earlier Davis had expressed his regret at having had to give up Lee's support as a counselor in order to give him command of an army in the field. As the Confederacy's military situation became increasingly grim, Davis sought more and more to lean on Lee's wisdom.

By September 9, Lee could wire Davis that "troops are on march."[14] Despite his disagreement with the president's decision, he had complied more promptly than most department commanders would to a call for some of their troops. Yet he was uncomfortable with the new situation and continued to think in terms of either forcing the enemy back or being forced back himself. In one September letter to the president he asserted, "If I was a little stronger, I think I could drive Meade's army under cover of the fortifications of Washington before he gathers more re-enforcements." Yet in the same letter he suggested the importance of strengthening the fortifications around Richmond and moving some of the Confederacy's government-run manufacturing efforts "in[to] the interior, so that if Richmond should fall we would not be destitute." When the Federals advanced again, Lee feared, "I may be forced back to Richmond."

Throughout his letters to Davis this month ran the theme of Longstreet's return. "The blow at Rosecrans should be made promptly, and Longstreet returned," he wrote just two days after the first of that general's troops moved south.[15] "Should General Longstreet reach General Bragg in time to aid him in winning a victory, and return to this army, it will be well, but should he be detained there without being able to do any good, it will result in evil," he added three days after that. Nor had he completely given up on his preferred strategy of striking in Virginia to take pressure off Bragg rather than sending troops to him. "If General Bragg is unable to bring General Rosecrans to battle," he wrote in the same letter, "I think it would be better to return General Longstreet to this army, to enable me to oppose the advance of General Meade with a greater prospect of success."[16] Indeed, Lee's correspondence during the absence of the I Corps reads like an ongoing lament for the decision that was made. Longstreet's troops, Lee opined, would reach Bragg too late to be of any use, they would not be in condition to fight when they arrived, and they might not do any good anyway. On the other hand, Lee never tired of reminding Davis how much he needed the troops, what he could accomplish with them, and how without them "it is probable we may be forced back."[17]

The president commiserated with Lee and expressed regret that affairs in Tennessee were not working out as they had envisioned during their long rides around Richmond. Even Bragg's hard-fought victory at Chickamauga did little to change his general opinion or relieve him of "vain regrets at the detachment of troops" to Bragg when they might have been sent to East Tennessee instead and thus have been more readily available to Lee. He invited Lee's advice about what to do next but explained that recalling Longstreet would have to wait. To Lee's claim that with more men he could have handled Meade, Davis responded, "I deeply regret your want of an adequate force to avail yourself of the opportunity afforded by the present condition of the enemy, but hope before he is prepared to attack that you will be re-enforced." The president was not opposed to offensive action but was little inclined to make further grand gambles. He believed Lee would be able to hold Richmond with his present force. "Like the people generally," he wrote, "I feel secure in the confidence you and your army inspire; that, in the meantime, nothing worse can befall us than a temporary withdrawal to a more interior line."[18]

Lee hoped to do better than that. On September 27 he received the first of a number of reports from scouts indicating the Army of the Potomac had detached its two smallest corps to reinforce the beleaguered Union army in Chattanooga. Lee immediately forwarded the news to Davis, along with other information that came in during the following days. By October 1, Lee was certain the movement had taken place and correctly estimated it as involving some 12,000 troops. This, too, he reported to Davis but said nothing of what he intended to do about it.[19] Disturbed by the speed at which Longstreet's transfer had become known to the enemy, Lee took great pains to keep his next movement secret, even going so far as to not notify Davis, a very unusual step for Lee.[20] In deep secrecy he made preparations to take advantage of Meade's decreased numbers by launching another offensive. Not everyone was oblivious to Lee's intentions. In Richmond, a War Department functionary wrote in his diary on October 4, "It is pretty certain that General Lee meditates a forward movement this week. Hard bread and bacon in large quantity have been sent up to him in the last three days."[21]

The week passed while Lee continued to write bland letters to the president discussing anything but the planned offensive movement.[22] Davis, apparently less well informed than some of the bureaucrats in town, had no inkling of Lee's plans and made plans of his own for a trip to the western theater in hopes of straightening out some of the tangled personnel problems within the high command of the Army of Tennessee. On the sixth, Davis left town.[23] The next day, Federals along the Rapidan noticed unusual movements in the Confederate camps, and the Army of the Potomac was on the alert for a possible move by Lee—so much for the elaborate security measures. On the ninth, the Confederates finally marched out of their camps, crossing the Rapidan and swinging west to attempt to duplicate the turning movement of the Second Manassas campaign over a year before by passing around Meade's right flank. Much had changed, however, since August 1862. This time the flanking march was led by A. P. Hill, an adequate corps commander but a far cry from the hard-driving Stonewall Jackson. Lee was not exactly his former self, making a good part of the trip in a wagon rather than on horseback, because of a relapse of his malady of the previous spring, in all probability the early stages of the heart disease that would take his life seven years hence. Perhaps the most important difference was that George Meade was no John Pope. Though the move did force Meade to drop back temporarily to the neighborhood of the old Manassas battleground—demonstrating that whichever army moved first could generally force the other back a few miles if it used a turning movement—the northern general skillfully parried Lee's efforts to gain an advantage. On the fourteenth, Hill's troops blundered up against solid Union lines at Bristoe Station and in an affair that was wretchedly handled on the Confederate side lost 1,300 men and four guns while accomplishing nothing. For the next few days Lee regarded the well-positioned Federal front unhappily while his men did such damage as they could to nearby railroads. Then, with nothing else to do, on October 18 he headed the Army of Northern Virginia south again, and by the twentieth he had taken up a position back on the south bank of the Rappahannock near where the Orange and Alexandria Railroad had crossed that stream before its bridge had been burned many months ago. For Lee it was a bitterly disappointing nine days.[24]

During these days Davis had been busy with his efforts to inspire confidence and determination among the people of the Confederate West and cooperation and harmony into the generals tasked with defending the region. The former effort met with uncertain success; the latter was a marked failure. Nevertheless, the undertaking was to occupy the Confederate president until the second week of November. On the ninth, Davis arrived back in Richmond, just in time to receive more bad news from the Army of Northern Virginia. After returning from Bristoe Station, Lee had put the army into winter quarters on the south bank of the Rappahannock, maintaining a fortified bridgehead north of the river to facilitate a future offensive move should he be able to make one and to complicate the situation for Meade should he endeavor to approach the north bank. Somehow, things failed to work out as Lee had envisioned, and on November 10 he was compelled to write a letter to Davis, welcoming the president back to the capital and explaining that three days before a rapid and well executed offensive movement by Meade had caught the Confederates flat-footed, overrun the Confederate bridgehead, and established a far more threatening Federal one on the south bank. Lee had had no choice but to retreat, and the Army of Northern Virginia, turning its back on its enemies, had abandoned its winter quarters and taken refuge behind the Rapidan, a dozen or so miles further south.[25]

Once again in his old position behind the Rapidan—the same he had left to open the Bristoe Station campaign six weeks earlier—Lee's greatest problem for the moment was not Federal action but lack of supplies and the complications that might arise should this problem remain unremedied when next the Army of the Potomac took the offensive. The lack of adequate supply directly affected the army's mobility. Many of its infantrymen were barefooted in the mid-November chill and most of its horses so underfed that Lee feared, "We shall lose many horses and mules this winter."[26] Indeed, should it become necessary for the army to begin maneuvering again, forcing the weakened animals to haul wagons, guns, and caissons, Lee did not know "how they will survive two or three days' march without food." The prospect loomed of the army becoming completely immobilized three days into a mid-November campaign that Lee suspected Meade was preparing to launch.[27] Lee put the matter bluntly to Seddon. Unless the Virginia Central Railroad, his main conduit of supplies, could be operated more efficiently, "the only alternative will be to fall back nearer to Richmond."[28] To Davis, Lee specifically suggested what amounted to little less than a government takeover of the railroad, forbidding anything to be transported on it save supplies for the army.[29]

Davis responded promptly, assuring Lee that he was taking steps to see that supplies got through and quickly.[30] He also seems to have lit a fire under the Richmond bureaucracy, which may have fallen into a bit of complacency during the president's western tour. Seddon quickly wrote Lee, "I owe you an apology for not sooner acknowledging the receipt of your letter calling my attention to the deficiency of the supplies, both of shoes for the soldiers and of forage for the animals of your command." After explaining the steps that were being taken to provide for the army's needs, Seddon promised, "Supplies in future will be more regular and abundant."[31] Commissary Gen. Northrop was also stirred to write to Lee, urging that Lee should give orders for the agents of Northrop's own Subsistence Department, operating in Lee's part of Virginia, to begin impressment—seizing from Confederate civilians, by force if necessary, needed supplies at arbitrarily set prices far below market values. This Lee was reluctant to do and notified Seddon that he would take such a step only on positive orders from Richmond.[32] The secretary of war was no more enthusiastic about Northrop's idea, and the matter was allowed to drop.[33]

Lee was apparently eager to speak personally with Davis, probably about the supply issue and possibly also about the army's future operations that winter. When Lee's son, the president's aide G. W. C. Lee, arrived in camp carrying a message from Davis, the general had him write to the president suggesting a visit to the army. Lee still believed that Meade could move any day and was reluctant to leave the front himself, but he had his son assure Davis that "a visit to this army would be of great service to the army and not without interest for yourself. By giving a little notice you can be well provided for, and can have a quiet visit." The elder Lee had "many subjects on which he desires to have your opinion."[34] This time Davis responded to the invitation with his usual alacrity. Two days later, November 21, he was in Lee's camp near Orange Court House. For the next several days Lee and Davis discussed the military and supply situation, though no dramatic decisions or changes in policy seem to have been made. Davis and Lee also discussed military affairs outside Virginia, particularly the critical situation at Chattanooga. Davis was then less than two weeks back from his journey aimed at setting to rights the high command of the Confederate army there. Yet he probably already realized that his efforts along those lines had been less than entirely successful. He suggested to Lee, therefore, that he try his hand at the matter, going west on some sort of temporary assignment in the role of a troubleshooter. They came to no firm conclusion on this matter, though Lee, with memories of his miserable West Virginia sojourn two years before, could hardly have been enthusiastic about the idea. He apparently begged off by pointing to the probability of an imminent Union advance in Virginia.[35] If the president was hoping for a "quiet visit," he was disappointed, being serenaded by a regimental band upon his arrival and making various speeches. On the twenty-fourth, the president braved a cold rain to review A. P. Hill's III Corps, made a highly complimentary speech, and headed back for Richmond.[36]

If Davis thought the problems with supply in Lee's army had been solved, he was sadly mistaken. No sooner had the president left the army's camps below the Rapidan than Lee became aware that the promised improvement in the flow of supplies had not occurred. He wired Davis that on some days his army was still receiving pitiful amounts of grain for the horses and on other days none at all.[37] Once again the president made inquiries and tried to get the much-needed forage on the road to Lee's suffering animals.[38]

It was just as well, too, for that same day, Wednesday, November 25, Lee's scouts brought reports that Meade's troops north of the Rapidan had filled their haversacks and received their marching orders.[39] Their information proved correct when the next day the Army of the Potomac moved across the Rapidan and southeastward toward Lee's right flank.[40] Meade hoped to maneuver Lee out of his position by turning that flank and getting between the Army of Northern Virginia and Richmond. This time, however, it was Lee's turn to maneuver skillfully and present the enemy with a solid defensive front in a strong position, just behind a little stream named Mine Run. Once again the two armies had maneuvered to a stalemate, and this time Meade had to recognize that his plan had been foiled and ordered his troops back to their camps north of the Rapidan. By December 2 the last of the Federals were gone from the south bank.

The day before Meade's Federals had first crossed the Rapidan in this abortive late-fall offensive, Union troops under Maj. Gen. Ulysses S. Grant had won a devastating victory over Braxton Bragg and the Confederate Army of Tennessee at Chattanooga. That city, the gateway to Georgia, was now firmly in Federal hands, and the thoroughly whipped rebel army retreated all the way to Dalton, Georgia, some twenty miles to the south. Bragg asked to be relieved, and Davis readily complied.[41] Leadership of the unhappy Confederate force still bearing the name "Army of Tennessee" though it no longer held a single square inch of that state passed temporarily into the hands of corps commander William J. Hardee, who let it be known he would not accept the job on a permanent basis.[42] Up on the Rapidan line, Lee heard of all this and pondered it "with some anxiety." The day after the Mine Run campaign ended, he wrote Davis with his thoughts in the matter. At present, he believed the Federal army at Chattanooga posed a threat to "penetrate Georgia." For commander of the army at Dalton, Lee had an even more radical suggestion. "I know the difficulties that surround this subject, but if General Beauregard is considered suitable for the position, I think he can be replaced at Charleston." Above all, "every effort should be made to concentrate as large a force as possible, under the best commander, to insure the discomfiture of Grant's army."[43]

Davis too had been much in thought about the problems of the Army of Tennessee. Reading Lee's statement that that force should be placed "under the best commander," Davis apparently drew a conclusion that Lee had not intended. On December 6 he wired Lee to ask if the general was any more amenable to the suggestion he had raised two weeks ago when he was with the army. "Could you now," the president asked, "consistently go to Dalton as heretofore explained?"[44] Lee's reply the next day was not encouraging. "I can if desired," he wrote, "but of the expediency of the measure you can judge better than I can." Lee saw no value in a temporary role in the western army and was not sure he could do any good even if given permanent command. In view of the bickerings of subordinates that had ruined Bragg's career, Lee remarked, "I also fear that I would not receive cordial co-operation." A final problem with the proposed transfer would be finding a new commander for the Army of Northern Virginia. Ewell, the senior corps commander, was in Lee's opinion definitely not up to the challenge. Having placed all the obstacles he could think of in the way of the measure, Lee assured Davis, "I hope Your Excellency will not suppose that I am offering any obstacles to any measure you may think necessary. I only seek to give you the opportunity to form your opinion after a full consideration of the subject. I have not that confidence either in my strength or ability as would lead me of my own option to undertake the command in question."[45]

The president's reply was just as swift: "Your letter of yesterday received. If convenient to you and not objectionable for military reasons, I wish you would come to Richmond for full conference."[46] Lee figured he knew what that meant. To Stuart he wrote, "I am called to Richmond this morning by the President. I presume the rest will follow. My heart and thoughts will always be with this army."[47] Convinced that he was to be transferred to Georgia despite his wishes, Lee set out for Richmond the day he received the president's telegram. The evil he feared, however, did not come upon him. He remained in Richmond until December 21, and by the fifteenth, Davis had given up on sending him west. Lee had steadfastly urged that others could do the job better than he, and he was not backward about saying who he thought they were. When he perceived that Beauregard was completely unacceptable to Davis, he apparently shifted his recommendation to Johnston, and it was to him that the appointment went.[48]

That winter the armies in Virginia remained idle. Week after week, supplying the Army of Northern Virginia remained a constant struggle. Lee frequently found himself compelled to write to Seddon or Northrop about "our crying necessity for food," and when letters to these officials failed to produce the desired results, he did not hesitate to write to the president himself on the subject. "I beg leave to apologize to Your Excellency for troubling you with subjects which properly ought not to come under your notice," Lee explained, "but sometimes I find it impossible to accomplish what is desirable without invoking the aid of all in authority, even including yourself." Davis never suggested this was anything but appropriate and always prodded Richmond officials to provide what was necessary or at least explain why it could not be done. He also advised Lee that "the emergency justifies impressment" from the stores that local families had laid up to tide them through the winter.[49] Somehow soldiers and horses—and, presumably, the civilians—were kept alive through the cold months.

Another issue during these months was the continuing problem of coast defense, particularly the coast of North Carolina. Whiting had been sent to command the defenses there, and for months he had been bombarding Richmond with pleas for troops and dire predictions of what would occur if a large army were not kept constantly at his beck and call in eastern North Carolina. The frantic general's appeals went to Davis himself, to Seddon, to Cooper, even to Davis's aide Col. William Browne: "I beg you will call the attention of the President . . ."[50] The port of Wilmington was important to the Confederacy, but Whiting's constant crying was out of all proportion to the potential threat or the Confederacy's means of countering it. Confronted with one of Whiting's numerous letters forwarded to him for comment, Lee came as close as he ever did to venting some of his feelings about the stationing of troops on the coast. "If the defenses of Wilmington require 'the constant presence of an army,' " he wrote, "I do not see where it is to come from." Lee believed the problem could be dealt with in other ways. Besides, to him the whole system of rushing troops around the Confederacy was mistaken. "The custom of the enemy when he wishes to attack one point," Lee continued, "is to threaten a distant one. The troops are rushed to the threatened points and the real point is exposed. I could at this time send some troops from here, but when should I get them back? Then, it would be seen that it was impossible to withdraw them. Three divisions of this army, and they of the best, are now scattered over the country, and I see no prospect of recovering them." In matters such as this, even Lee could sound like a typically myopic department commander. Having recommended the previous summer that troops from southern departments come north for action in Virginia rather than remain idle through the summer, he now maintained of his Virginia army, "The troops want some rest, some time for reorganization and recruiting their ranks." The second opinion was probably more nearly correct, but in fairness Lee had been determined to gamble everything the summer before in hopes of securing final victory but was not free to say as much to Davis lest the president disapprove the venture. Now, however, hearing reports of steady northern preparations for the next summer's campaign, Lee was dismayed by the contrast with the constant pressure for the Confederate authorities to disperse troops. Grimly, he concluded, "I fear the spring will open upon us and find us without an army."[51]

Davis remained concerned about the situation in North Carolina and hopeful that the Confederates might be able to eliminate certain Federal lodgments along the coast. In January 1864 he approached Lee about going temporarily to North Carolina to supervise the limited coastal counter-offensive. "You could give it form," the president urged, "which would insure success, but without your personal attention I fear such failures as have elsewhere been suffered. . . . If circumstances permit, you had better go down; otherwise, I will go myself, though it could only be for a very few days."[52] Once again, Lee was not receptive. Little of lasting value would be accomplished there, he warned, unless the Confederates could complete and put into service the ironclad gunboats they had been working on for some time. There was no telling when they might be ready, and until that time an expedition would probably be fruitless. "I would go to North Carolina myself," Lee added, "but I consider my presence here always necessary, especially now, when there is such a struggle to keep the army fed and clothed." Still, he would of course go if the president insisted.[53] As usual Davis did not. He recognized Lee as his best general, indeed as the Confederacy's chief military asset, and he sought to employ him more extensively. Lee, however, remained convinced that the main show would be in northern Virginia and that he should remain there.

Lee still retained his aggressive instincts despite the weakness of his army and his health. "If we could take the initiative and fall upon them unexpectedly," he wrote Davis on February 3, "we might derange their plans and embarrass them the whole summer."[54] A little more than two weeks later he lamented that if only he had adequate supplies and strong horses, "I think I could disturb the quiet of the enemy and drive him to the Potomac."[55] He had neither, however, and so remained on the defensive.

On the twenty-second, Lee again visited Richmond for a week of conference with Davis.[56] While Lee was in town, Davis finalized his plans to assign "General Braxton Bragg to duty at the seat of Government as commanding general in accordance with the Act of Congress approved March 25th, 1862." Cooper suggested that it would be better to frame the order much like the one that had assigned Lee to the same post nearly two years before, avoiding mention of the act of Congress. Davis approved of this change and thus the order was issued.[57] It was a highly controversial move, since Bragg had been extremely unpopular as commander of the Army of Tennessee.[58] Yet Davis realized that Bragg had been undermined by criticism within the army and unfairly vilified by denunciations throughout the country. Davis knew Bragg to be a better officer than his reputation indicated and was determined not to let public clamor prevent him from using a good man. Indeed, had Davis been inclined to accept the judgment of most of those demanding Bragg's banishment from military affairs, he would have been obliged to remove himself from office as well.

Braxton Bragg. (Courtesy of National Archives, 111-B-35, Civil War 16)

Bragg's new position was rather vaguely defined, but he soon staked out an area of responsibility. Indeed, he tended to supplant Seddon as the president's chief military assistant in the capital. He was clearly very powerful, but that power did not extend to directing operations of the Army of Northern Virginia. Lee outranked Bragg and in any case still possessed far more influence with Davis. When the two gave conflicting counsel even on matters not directly pertaining to the Army of Northern Virginia, Lee's opinion invariably prevailed with the president.[59] Nor did Davis himself surrender to Bragg any part of his initiative or direct control over Confederate military policy. As the Richmond *Whig* commented on the appointment several weeks later, "The President never for a moment relinquished his rights as Commander-in-Chief, and never entertained the first thought of doing so. This earth holds not the human being more jealous of his constitutional rights than Mr. Davis, and among those rights that to which he clings with death-like tenacity is well-known to be the supreme and exclusive control of military operations."[60] The editor framed his statement in uncomplimentary terms, but the basic fact was true. Davis believed it his duty. The Confederate president might at times be indecisive, but he would never concede that the decision was anyone's but his to make. Thus Bragg, much like Lee two years earlier, wound up with a post that amounted essentially to a supervisory authority over most Confederate forces in the field except the main army in Virginia. In all things, it was well understood, he would have the president looking over his shoulder.

Davis spent the last week of February discussing the military situation, particularly the troublesome Army of Tennessee, with Bragg and Lee. On the last day of the month, word of another approaching Yankee cavalry raid broke up the meeting, as Lee hastened back to his army in case the Federal mounted foray should prove a precursor of more serious action. It did not, and although Lee narrowly missed encountering the raiders in person during his return by train to the Army of Northern Virginia and there were a few tense moments for those still in Richmond as well, this raid, like the one of the preceding May, fizzled out without accomplishing much of anything.[61] Those of the raiders who escaped death or capture at the hands of rapidly converging Confederate forces made their way back to Federal lines as best they could.

On March 12, Lee was back in the capital city again, this time with a more specific mission. Longstreet had left his corps in East Tennessee, where it had been serving during the fall and winter in a thoroughly ineffective attempt first to take and then at least to threaten Knoxville. With the question of how to recoup the Confederacy's sagging fortunes in Tennessee foremost on the mind of everyone among the Confederate brass, Longstreet had a plan of his own. It involved the government's somehow providing him with enough mules to mount his entire command for a raid into Tennessee. At a time when the Quartermaster Bureau's best efforts could not provide enough strong and healthy horses to pull Lee's artillery and supply wagons, Longstreet might just as well have suggested putting his infantrymen on the backs of war elephants. Around March 10, Longstreet brought his idea to Orange Court House and pitched it to Lee. Lee suggested that Longstreet travel on to Richmond and present the plan to Davis. This did not appeal to Longstreet, since he had over the past fall and winter thoroughly alienated the president by his churlish behavior toward a large number of the other officers whose misfortune it had been to serve with him, not least of all the president's new right-hand man, Braxton Bragg. Longstreet tried to get Lee to go to Richmond himself and present the bizarre plan as his own. Now it was Lee's turn to balk. The compromise solution they finally worked out was for both of them to go.[62]

They arrived in Richmond on Saturday, March 12, attended church and rested the next day, and met with Davis on the fourteenth. Davis rejected Longstreet's plan. In its place, Davis, Bragg, and Lee further worked out the plan for Johnston to take the offensive northward from Dalton that they had developed during Lee's last visit. In any event, Johnston proved no more receptive to their plans than they had been to Longstreet's. Despite persistent urging from Davis and Bragg, the new Army of Tennessee commander resisted every suggestion that he pursue any other course but the passive defensive.

By March 25, Lee was back at Orange Court House and considering the prospects for the spring campaign. On this subject his thoughts went through a radical transformation during the last week of March. When Davis forwarded to him some papers regarding probable Federal actions that spring, Lee replied on the twenty-fifth that he was "not disposed to believe . . . that the first important effort will be directed against Richmond." Instead, he considered Johnston's army a likely target.[63] Just five days later, however, he had taken an entirely different view. More and more information reached him from his scouts indicating that Virginia would indeed be the scene of a major Federal effort as soon as the roads were dry.[64] Reports during the following days were of the same nature, and Lee was soon urging "that all available re-enforcements be sent to this army."[65] Bit by bit more information flowed in during the following weeks until by the middle of

April, Lee was predicting that a Federal landing at City Point, on the James River east of Richmond, followed by a movement toward Drewry's Bluff would accompany the major southward thrust by the Army of the Potomac, still under Meade's command but now under the direct supervision of new Union commanding general Ulysses S. Grant. To counter the threat on the James, Lee proposed that Beauregard, with at least a portion of the troops then serving under him at Charleston, be brought up to cover North Carolina and southside Virginia and be handy in case of any Federal move by way of the James. "If Richmond could be held secure against the attack from the east," Lee explained to Davis, "I would propose that I draw Longstreet to me and move right against the enemy on the Rappahannock. Should God give us a crowning victory there, all their plans would be dissipated." The alternative, of course, was that Lee wait and receive the Federal attack passively, with the strong possibility that he would be turned and forced backward, something he characterized as fraught with "great injury" for the Confederacy.[66]

Yet beyond the danger from Grant's skillful maneuvering or the appearance of Federals down the river from Richmond was the ever present problem of supply, threatening disaster even when the enemy's thrusts might otherwise be parried by the troops in the field. As usual when the supply situation was critical, Lee wrote directly to Davis. "My anxiety on the subject of provision for the army is so great that I cannot refrain from expressing it to your Excellency," Lee explained. "I cannot see how we can operate with our present supplies." More was at stake now than a mere retreat into the Richmond defenses. If anything should happen to interrupt the flow of supplies, it would "render it impossible for me to keep the army together and might force a retreat into N[orth] C[arolina]." Lee urged that "every exertion" be made to get the needed supplies to the troops.[67] In subsequent dispatches he continued to stress the same theme.[68] With this exception, however, Lee remained optimistic about the coming campaign. If supplies could be brought up, and Lee seemed to believe they would be if he prodded Davis hard enough, and if the Federals he expected on the James could be held at bay, "I have no uneasiness as to the result of the campaign in Virginia."[69]

Lee was right to be confident in Davis, as the president did indeed put forth "every exertion" to send Lee both the supplies and the reinforcements he requested. Bragg assured Lee that "the President is keenly alive to the necessity," and over in the War Department a bureaucrat noted, "The President and Bragg are very anxious to make Lee as strong as possible."[70]

They were indeed. On April 7, Longstreet, with 12,000 men in two divisions and a battalion of artillery, was ordered to "proceed immediately" to join Lee, moving "as rapidly as possible by rail." The next day Bragg assured Lee that "every effort is being made to increase the supplies here" and that "the best efforts of the Government are being used to prepare you for an emergency."[71] The measure of the success of these efforts is visible in the fact that when the spring campaign finally did begin in early May, Lee's army was not significantly handicapped for lack of supplies and was as numerous as it had been at any time since Gettysburg.

A final aspect of Davis's compliance with Lee's wishes for the defense of Virginia against the 1864 Union campaign was his transfer of Beauregard. Having declined to bring the Charleston commander or any of his forces northward the previous summer in support of Lee's grand offensive gamble, Davis now readily complied with Lee's request to bring Beauregard and most of his troops into the Virginia theater of the war in hopes of shortening the odds in an almost equally desperate defensive effort. That, after all, was more consistent with the president's unarticulated, probably even unconscious, defensive approach to the war.

Early in April Bragg telegraphed Beauregard to ask if he thought he could come north for service in North Carolina and southern Virginia. The Creole, who was far from content with presiding over the sideshow in Charleston, readily agreed, and on April 15 Cooper issued the order for his transfer.[72] A week later Beauregard arrived in Weldon, North Carolina, and the next day he officially assumed command. At the moment, the only activity in the department involved more Confederate attempts to dislodge the Federals from their enclaves on the coast. Beauregard was unenthusiastic about such ventures, questioning whether it was "prudent to leave longer the forces in the department so scattered. Is the object in view worth the great risk incurred?" Like Lee, Beauregard anticipated a Federal move up the James and wanted to be ready for it. He also entertained thoughts of possibly serving in the scenes of his old glory in northern Virginia. Suggesting this possibility, he requested Bragg to prepare "maps of that part of the country" and to make other preparations. "I take this opportunity to remark," Beauregard concluded, "that should the operations of the coming campaign make it necessary that I should be placed under immediate command of that distinguished officer, General R. E. Lee, I would take pleasure in aiding him to crush our enemies and to achieve the independence of our country." The letter was passed from desk to desk until it landed on the president's. Davis noted rather uncharitably on it, "I did not doubt the readiness of General

Beauregard to serve under any general who ranks him. The right of General Lee to command would be derived from his superior rank." So much for any gracious gestures Beauregard might be inclined to make. Meanwhile, the Richmond authorities, presumably with Davis's approval, were still eager to see the coastal ventures carried out. Reluctantly Beauregard took over the supervision though not the actual command of the expeditions and waited for something else to turn up.[73]

Clearly, he would not have to wait long. By this time it had become unmistakably obvious that the Federals were building up to the biggest offensive yet launched at the Confederacy. Up on the Rapidan, Lee could not understand why Grant had not moved as early as April 25. The Army of Potomac's preparations appeared to be complete, and it sat poised to advance.[74] On the twenty-fourth Lee suggested to Davis, "Should the enemy remain quiet this week and the weather good," he might want to come up to the Rapidan to confer with Lee and inspire the troops.[75] The president, it turned out, was "unable to visit the army" that week, probably because of poor health. Varina mentioned that at this point his "health [had] declined from loss of sleep so that he forgot to eat."[76] Lee expressed his regret. "I know it would have afforded the troops great pleasure," he told Davis, "and I think it would have been attended with benefit."[77] Even as Davis was hindered in the function of commander in chief by his physical infirmities, personal disaster struck and added emotional distraction to the difficulties he had to overcome. On the last day of April, the president's five-year-old son, Joseph, fell to his death from a second-story balcony at the Confederate White House. That day, at least, the president found it impossible to proceed with the business of war and government.[78] Yet there was little time to grieve. Two days later he was firing off a dispatch to Lee acknowledging the general's warnings of impending Federal action and promising to push reinforcements north "as soon as possible."[79] Then events began to move rapidly.

"Soon after midnight, May 3d-4th, the Army of the Potomac moved out from its position north of the Rapidan, to start upon that memorable campaign, destined to result in the capture of the Confederate capital and the army defending it." So wrote Ulysses S. Grant in his memoirs twenty years later.[80] Early the next morning, Lee had his army in motion to counter the Union advance. Pausing to write to Davis, Lee noted, "The long-threatened effort to take Richmond has begun." He predicted that the Federals on the Peninsula would soon be moving and observed, "Under these circumstances I regret that there is to be any further delay in concentrating our own troops." He had made reference to those limited offensives

Richmond had been pressing Beauregard to undertake on the North Carolina coast. Such operations were all well and good, Lee conceded, "but they will not compensate us for a disaster" on the main fighting fronts in Virginia and Georgia. "Success in resisting the chief armies of the enemy will enable us more easily to recover the country now occupied by him." The reverse was obvious and too unpleasant to state. Lee thus urged that the operations in North Carolina be called off and the troops there sent to the Army of Northern Virginia, while Beauregard and whatever forces could be drawn from his old department be brought up to hold Richmond.[81]

The situation was awkward for Davis. Lee was obviously right, but Beauregard had telegraphed just the day before that the planned assault on New Bern, North Carolina, had started "with all available forces" on May 2 under the command of Maj. Gen. Robert F. Hoke. Hoke had orders to "use the utmost dispatch," but Beauregard, not known for his pessimism in such things, estimated he might need four or five days to finish the job.[82] Now Davis lost no time in reversing the previous policy. "Unless Newberne [sic] can be captured by coup-de-main," he wired Beauregard, "the attempt must be abandoned, and the troops returned with all possible dispatch to unite in operations in N[orthern] Virginia. There is not an hour to lose. Had the expedition not started, I would say it should not go." He concluded by ordering Beauregard to make arrangements to ship the troops north "with the greatest dispatch."[83] The general's reply, at 4:00 that afternoon, was reassuring. "All necessary orders are already being given to carry out your instructions. One of my aides will leave this evening with special orders to General Hoke. Utmost dispatch will be used."[84]

Throughout the day Lee continued to report the progress of the Army of the Potomac as it swung toward his right flank.[85] That evening Davis sent a longer dispatch, bringing Lee up to date on the various efforts he was making to speed reinforcements to the Army of Northern Virginia. He also passed on various reports tending to confirm that the Federals were indeed landing in large force at Bermuda Hundred, the peninsula formed by the confluence of the James and Appomattox Rivers, a scant dozen miles by land—more by the meanderings of the river—from Drewry's Bluff, the riverside fortress in the outer ring of Richmond defenses that for two years had more or less alone kept Federal warships from ascending the James and shelling Richmond.[86] Though both Davis and Lee were thus aware of this threat—indeed, both had been expecting it—they did little at first to counter it. Lee's attention was taken up with the Union army in his front; Davis seems to have been so taken up with Lee's requests for more troops as to ignore other areas. For the moment, the James River front had no such forceful and influential advocate as the Rapidan front had in Lee.

The next day the Army of Northern Virginia clashed with its opponent in the tangled forests of the Wilderness, where Lee and Jackson had bested Hooker a year and three days before. Jackson was not here this time and neither was Hooker, and the ensuing battle of the Wilderness was a far cry from Chancellorsville. When Lee wrote to the War Department at 11:00 P.M. he could report only bloody and inconclusive fighting.[87]

Meanwhile down along the James and Appomattox Rivers, the Federal offensive, under the command of cockeyed Massachusetts politician Benjamin F. Butler, had finally come to the notice of a Confederate general. Having served an unhappy winter in North Carolina with his brigades scattered over most of two states, George Pickett was now in Petersburg on his way north to rejoin his reunited division at Hanover Junction and then Lee in the Wilderness. Nothing could have pleased Pickett better. A simple-minded man whose rise to division command owed much to his close friendship with James Longstreet, Pickett was anxious to get back to simpler, if far more deadly, duties with the Army of Northern Virginia. The appearance of Butler's Federals ruined this bright prospect, as Beauregard ordered Pickett to remain in Petersburg and coordinate the defense of the place.[88]

Butler's move threatened to ruin a great deal more than George Pickett's long-desired change of duty. From their position at Bermuda Hundred these troops could within a day or two seize either Petersburg, scarcely ten miles distant, or the railroad that connected that city with Richmond. Either way, they would make the supply situation for the Confederate capital, not to mention Lee's army, completely impossible. For that matter, no Confederate force of comparable size stood between this Union army, the Army of the James, and Richmond itself. Butler's 39,000 Yankees were for practical purposes about a half day's march from the end of the war. In their path was a single Confederate division of not more than 5,000 men in Richmond, while at Petersburg there were a couple of weak brigades, perhaps 1,000 rifles all told, and Pickett. The latter now found himself in the midst of a nightmare that made even service in North Carolina seem easy by comparison. Frantically he wired Beauregard for reinforcements. Sixty miles to the south at Weldon, North Carolina, that general had at the moment none to send him, though he was "using all possible dispatch to push the troops forward" from points south and east. Beauregard authorized Pickett to communicate directly with the authorities in Richmond and repeatedly telegraphed Bragg for permission to have Pickett divert troops passing through Petersburg on their way to northern Virginia or at least to keep the small force already there, also slated to go north. Bragg showed at least one of the dispatches to Davis, who readily agreed to allow the two brigades at Petersburg to remain. Only after repeated urging by Beauregard, however, was authorization given to stop the northbound units.[89]

Pickett, meanwhile, was about to come unstrung, sending telegram after telegram to Richmond faster than the harassed authorities there could hope to answer them. "I have telegraphed you four times this morning and received no answer," he fretted. "Please answer this." This did not inspire confidence, of which Davis and his advisers possessed little enough in Pickett as it was. Believing that he was grossly exaggerating the magnitude of the threat, they complacently filed away his numerous dispatches without taking action. By nightfall several more telegrams and a dispatch hand-carried by a staff officer had been added to the files.[90] While Pickett stewed at Petersburg, Beauregard had nervous problems of his own at Weldon. It was an unfortunate but by no means unique characteristic of Beauregard—one that he shared with G. W. Smith, among others—that when confronted with situations of extreme tension and high responsibility, he reported himself sick. He had done so when first transferred to the West in the desperate situation of February 1862 and repeated the performance the following summer when things looked bad after the fall of Corinth. Things looked bad now, and the Creole duly reported to Bragg at 10:00 that evening that he was "unfortunately too unwell to go to Petersburg tonight." Pickett would have to shift for himself, and Beauregard would go to the threatened area "tomorrow evening, or next day."[91]

May 6 brought more furious fighting in the gloomy Wilderness below the Rapidan as both Lee and Grant slashed aggressively at each other, and the tide of battle flowed back and forth through the smoky undergrowth. Thousands fell on each side, among them Longstreet, severely wounded in a "friendly fire" incident much like Jackson's of the year before. With all his faults, and they were many and serious, Longstreet possessed a competence in handling troops and a reassuring battlefield presence that made his place hard to fill. For the present, his corps would be led by Maj. Gen. Richard H. Anderson. Though Lee had gained local advantages twice during the day's confused fighting, the final result had been inconclusive. The most striking incident of the day had come when a threatened Federal breakthrough seemed to promise final disaster for the Army of Northern Virginia. As Confederate reinforcements double-timed forward to plug the breach, Lee, straight-backed, tall, and conspicuous astride his large gray horse, had made as if to lead their desperate charge. His troops would have none of it. Shouting promises to restore the broken line if only he would go to the rear, they and his frantic staff officers at last succeeded in dissuading him from so rash a course of action.[92] That night Lee once again sat down by lamplight to write out a brief account of the day's action. He dispatched it to the War Department, and there it arrived the following afternoon.[93]

Down on the James, May 6 saw the president and his advisers begin to show an awareness of the danger they faced southeast of the city. In a stark reversal of the previous day's attitudes, Cooper wired Beauregard to "urge forward by rail the troops ordered from the south to Petersburg, which is much threatened."[94] This was true, of course, and Beauregard knew it very well. He quickly replied that "every effort is being made to transport the troops as rapidly as possible."[95] This was also true, with brigades moving up both from the North Carolina coast and from Beauregard's old South Carolina command as well.[96] By midday, however, concern in Richmond had reached the level at which Davis himself sent a wire to Beauregard. Referring the general to previous dispatches from Bragg and others for information on events around Richmond and to the north, Davis expressed his hope that Beauregard would "be able at Petersburg to direct operations both before and behind you, so as to meet necessities."[97] The first problem with this view, of course, was that Beauregard was not at Petersburg and had only vague plans of going there. "Am still confined to my tent by sickness," he replied by telegraph at 4:00 that afternoon, "but hope to leave tomorrow morning for Petersburg." He assured the president, however, that he was already "concentrating as rapidly as possible all available troops" at Petersburg and that once in the threatened city he would "then do all in my power to meet successfully present emergencies."[98] While remaining in Weldon, however, Beauregard sent duplicate messages to Cooper, Seddon, and Bragg, inquiring about the extent of his authority. "Am I authorized," he asked, "to control to best advantage I may think proper all troops now in this department or arriving?"[99] This amounted to little less than a bid for complete autonomy within his department, something no Confederate officer, with the possible exception of Trans-Mississippi commander E. K. Smith, would ever have. For an officer operating, or at least proposing to operate, on the very doorstep of the capital to give notice that he wanted no interference from his superiors was, even by Beauregard's standards, uncommonly cheeky.

On that day and the next, Butler made halfhearted probes toward the railroad between Richmond and Petersburg. On the sixth, a single Union brigade advanced but was turned back by the first of the Confederate brigades Pickett had been authorized to detain at Petersburg. The next day Federals in division strength actually seized a stretch of tracks briefly before retreating in the face of one-third their number of Confederates. Pickett, with intense activity little short of nervous frenzy, was everywhere, riding the lines to encourage the troops, organizing a scratch force of mounted and more or less armed civilians for emergency service, and having empty trains run up and down the tracks south of town to simulate the arrival of additional troops. Those troops that were on hand he got to the right places at the right times. The result, when added to the incompetence of Butler and timidity of his subordinates, was that Petersburg was saved for the Confederacy, at least for the time being, and George Pickett, now on the verge of coming apart emotionally, was the unlikely hero of the episode.[100]

In northern Virginia, May 7 was quiet after the carnage of the Wilderness, but the eighth saw renewed action as Grant again tried to turn Lee's right, lunging for the strategic crossroads hamlet of Spotsylvania Court House. Lee's men got there first, though by the narrowest of margins, and held on through a day of disjointed attacks by the exhausted troops of the Army of the Potomac. After a day's rest on the ninth, Grant renewed his assaults on the tenth, but with no better results. Contemplating how he might break Lee's seemingly unshakable lines, Grant determined to slash at the Confederate lines of communication by dispatching Maj. Gen. Philip H. Sheridan with the Army of Potomac's powerful cavalry corps on a raid aimed at the vicinity of Richmond. Stuart's Confederate horsemen gave chase, while Lee, waiting for the next round of Federal assaults, kept Richmond posted on the progress of the fighting.[101] For the Confederate president such reports were especially welcome as bits of good news in the midst of an increasingly distressing situation around Richmond.[102]

While Pickett continued to resist Butler's intermittent, feeble pushes against Petersburg and its railroad connection with Richmond, the authorities there began to doubt that he was quite up to the job. On the seventh Seddon shared his doubts with Bragg. He felt "some distrust of Pickett's adequacy to the load upon him" and wished Beauregard would hurry up and relieve him by going to Petersburg himself.[103] As the Creole still showed no inclination of doing so by the eighth, Davis himself began to lose patience. "We have a strong incentive," he wrote in a note to Bragg that day, "to make a prompt and earnest attack" against Butler as soon as all the Confederate forces available could be brought up. After suggesting ways in which the rail movement of the needed troops could be expedited, the president

directed, "If General Beauregard's health disqualifies him for field operations, it would be well to order Hoke to proceed in advance of his troops and
take command of the forces in front of Petersburg."[104] Hoke was a young but
promising officer with a good reputation in Richmond. As for Pickett, he
would be adequate as long as operations on the Petersburg front remained
strictly defensive.

Bragg promptly telegraphed Beauregard to ask if he were too sick to go to
Petersburg and to pass along the president's suggestion regarding alternate
rail routes. Beauregard, sensing that he was in danger of removal, made a
remarkable recovery, which he attributed to the salubrious North Carolina
water. He repeated that "all troops are being urged forward rapidly as
possible" but rejected as impractical the president's plan for moving them
along faster. His own move to Petersburg seemed less urgent. First he
telegraphed Bragg that he hoped "to leave today for Petersburg." Then it was
"by first train" that evening. Later he promised, "Will leave here at 11 P.M.
for Petersburg." Finally, he admitted, "I should have started today for
Petersburg." Still, in the morning he would "run through and assume
command as desired."[105] Somehow the president's patience stretched to
accommodate all of this, and Beauregard remained in command.

Finally, on the morning of May 10, Beauregard arrived in Petersburg. By
that time, however, the city on the banks of the Appomattox was no longer the
Union target. On the ninth, Butler had decided to shift his thrust northward
toward Richmond itself. Even as Beauregard had traveled toward Petersburg,
troops of the Richmond garrison had begun skirmishing with the advancing
Federals on the south bank of the James not far from Drewry's Bluff. Though
Butler's approach was timid and halting, so little Confederate force stood
between him and Richmond that he still presented an appalling threat to the
city. By now Davis was taking a very direct interest in the affair and was present
on the Drewry's Bluff lines until almost 9:00 P.M. on the ninth. Returning to
his office, the president apparently directed Bragg to order up reinforcements
from Petersburg. For some reason the Richmond authorities believed Hoke to
be in that city already, and so to him Bragg addressed an order, sent about
10:00 that night, to move north immediately with his whole force. In fact,
however, Hoke did not arrive in Petersburg until 2:30 the next afternoon,
some five and a half hours after Beauregard. This produced a considerable
amount of confusion, with the final result being that Beauregard inquired of
Bragg and suspended execution of the order.[106]

Back in Richmond, Davis kept an anxious watch on the progress of the
garrison's skirmish with Butler's advancing troops. Desperate for information

of the battle, the president sent a dispatch to the major commanding the fort at Drewry's Bluff, asking what he could see from there, but there was little enough he could pass on—only that Maj. Gen. Robert Ransom, the Richmond garrison commander, was still holding his own and "the fight is progressing."[107] As if the gradually approaching Federal force on the south bank of the James was not enough, word began to come in during the course of the day about the approach of Sheridan's cavalry from the north. Stuart was still skirmishing with the Union horsemen but as yet had been unable to stop them. This was particularly serious since the entire Richmond garrison was now engaged south of the James in trying to hold Butler at bay. Davis decided that the best course was for Beauregard, with the by now sizable force he had collected at Petersburg, to dispose of Butler quickly so that troops could be released to face the threat from the north.[108] At 3:30 that afternoon Bragg apprised Beauregard of the situation, ordering him to prepare to attack. As soon as he was ready, he should inform the Richmond authorities so that Ransom could cooperate by making a simultaneous assault. This must be done quickly, Bragg stressed. "Every hour is now important." Later Bragg followed up this wire with another one even more forceful. "We are seriously threatened here from above," he wrote. The situation required that Beauregard demonstrate immediately against Butler's southern flank in order to distract the Federals from the thin Confederate lines in front of the capital. Then, "at an early hour in the morning," Bragg directed Beauregard to "go over to the offensive."[109]

Upon arriving in Petersburg that morning, Beauregard had assured Bragg that he would "take the offensive as soon as practicable."[110] His idea of "practicable," however, differed considerably from Bragg's. Ten hours later and with the necessity for action much stronger, he still moved with surprisingly little urgency. He had ten brigades in Petersburg by this time but was determined to wait for various odds and ends of troops still trickling in from their dispersed posts. He told Bragg in a 7:15 P.M. dispatch that he hoped "to be in position for offensive tomorrow night."[111] Since night attacks were generally not practicable during the Civil War, this meant no offensive action would be taken until the morning of May 12. That prospect proved unacceptable to Davis and his advisers, none of whom probably got much sleep that night. Twenty minutes after midnight, Bragg wired Beauregard to advance with his whole force straight up the road for Drewry's Bluff. He was to leave as soon as possible, and if he found Federals between him and the James, he was to cut his way through them. Beauregard received the dispatch about 3:00 A.M. and thirty minutes later sent back one of his own in protest.

He was now concerned about organizing his various brigades into provisional divisions. "Would it not be preferable," he wrote, "to complete the organization . . . and then make a crushing attack on enemy?" He asked for an answer that would authorize him to set aside the previous order, but receiving none, felt compelled to obey–after a fashion.[112]

At 7:00 A.M. Beauregard telegraphed Bragg, "Offensive movement against enemy has commenced. General Hoke's division in the advance supported by Pickett's division. Give necessary orders to Major-General Ransom."[113] In fact, this was not really true even at the time Beauregard sent it. He had meant to organize his brigades into two divisions, as explained in the dispatch, but Pickett had finally suffered the nervous breakdown he had been working on ever since finding himself in command at Petersburg in the face of an oncoming Union juggernaut. On the evening of the tenth he reported himself sick and took to his room. The next day he showed no inclination of coming out.[114] Rather than assign any one of his ten brigade commanders to temporary divisional command, Beauregard decided to wire his friend W. H. C. Whiting, now serving at Wilmington, to come over to Petersburg for a visit if possible without telling Whiting what he had in mind.[115] As for that day's advance, Beauregard had Hoke prepare to lead off with six brigades and simply decided to keep the rest in Petersburg and stay there himself. Once again the Creole found reason to stay away from the place of greatest responsibility. This time it was that two more brigades were expected, and he simply had to be in Petersburg when they arrived.[116]

Thus Beauregard's next dispatch was also misleading. "My forces are being united soon as practicable. You may then rely on my hearty co-operation in defense of Richmond." From Beauregard's point of view this all may have been true but produced in the minds of the Richmond authorities the impression that things on the Petersburg front were proceeding much differently than they in fact were. Only the telegram's last two sentences might have raised some doubts in the minds of its recipients. "Appearances here this morning are that the enemy is about withdrawing from this point to re-enforce elsewhere. I will try to strike him a severe blow before he leaves."[117] This was curious because the Federals in front of Drewry's Bluff appeared to have no interest in going anywhere at the moment except–if they could–into Richmond. As for striking the enemy before he escaped, this did not sound like the direct march on Drewry's Bluff that had been ordered.

It was not. The Creole's next dispatch made that clear at least. He had somehow picked up an entirely unfounded rumor that Butler was withdrawing and now proposed to act upon it. At 8:00 A.M. he sent word that he was

James Seddon. (Courtesy of National Archives, 111-BA-1224)

having Hoke make a forced reconnaissance toward Bermuda Hundred, to be turned into an all-out attack if the rumor should prove true. In that event, Beauregard somehow proposed to send some of the troops left in Petersburg around by the south side of the Appomattox to strike simultaneously at City Point. Thus Beauregard would have his army divided by a broad tidal river controlled by the enemy's warships. He concluded by suggesting that if Bragg did not approve of this remarkable plan, he respond at once to have the movement stopped.[118] Bragg and Seddon had been working together closely, in consultation with Davis, in dealing with the present crisis. Now it was Seddon who responded to Beauregard's twisting of the plan he had been ordered to carry out. "Division of your forces is earnestly objected to," the secretary of war wrote. "It is decidedly preferred that you carry out the instructions given last night, and endeavor to unite all forces."[119] Beauregard received this message about noon and replied forty-five minutes later, "My division of force is only temporary to meet present emergency." He protested that he was "carrying into effect to best of ability instructions received" and said that the movement was already in progress. Seddon should state his objections, the general maintained, and then Beauregard would comply with the secretary's wishes "if practicable."[120] This was not only insolent, it was also untrue—at least with respect to the movement already being in progress—as Hoke did not march until 1:00 P.M.[121]

Seddon, meanwhile, had gotten tired of waiting for Beauregard's reply. At 1:00 he fired off another dispatch that revealed the tension inside the Confederate capital. "This city is in hot danger," the secretary raged. "It should be defended with all our resources to the sacrifice of minor considerations. You are relied on to use every effort to unite all your forces at the earliest practicable time with the troops in our defenses, and then together either fight the enemy in the field or defend the intrenchments."[122] The reason for Seddon's alarm was the continued approach of Sheridan's horsemen. At Yellow Tavern, just six miles from Richmond, Stuart was fighting a desperate engagement against Sheridan in order to buy time for the authorities to put some troops into the city defenses. That could not be done until the threat to Drewry's Bluff was contained at least enough to allow the position to be held securely with only a portion of the available troops. Under these circumstances, Beauregard's constant delays were hard to stomach.

Beauregard was nevertheless irate when he received Seddon's second dispatch that afternoon. He shot back an angry response, insisting that the troops were "being pushed forward as rapidly as possible." He complained about the sacrifice he had made by giving up a sick leave in order to take the North Carolina and Virginia assignment and indulged in some self-pity about his "shattered health." He was willing to sacrifice all this and more for the cause, he asserted, "but if my course be not approved by the War Department I wish to be relieved at once."[123] Seddon had no time for such childishness. Acknowledging Beauregard's telegrams, he expressed "pain and surprise." This was not the time to respond to them fully, perhaps later, but at present he would content himself with admonishing Beauregard to do his duty and "use every effort in your power with all your forces to carry out the instructions of the Department and accomplish the junction of all our forces to fight the enemy or defend the capital."[124]

Davis had been busy that day. The sounds of battle carried southward from Yellow Tavern, where Stuart's men fought desperately to hold off the Union cavalry. Varina remembered, "At the Executive Mansion, the small-arms could be distinctly heard like the popping of fire-crackers." Davis had been working in his office that morning, writing a letter to Lee. "We have been sorely pressed by enemy on south side," he wrote. "Are now threatened by the cavalry on the Brooke turnpike and Westham road. I go to look after defence." He meant it, too. That morning, as Varina recalled, "Mr. Davis came hurriedly in from the office for his pistols, and rode out to the front." He was too late, though, to see—or take part in—the battle and so rode back to Richmond.[125] As a result of all this, he had been out of touch with Bragg and Seddon most of the day, and though he knew of Bragg's orders just after midnight for Beauregard to advance, he was unaware of Beauregard's substantial disobedience of them. At 2:15 P.M. he sent a telegram to "Commanding Officer, Petersburg," asking, "What forces have you today to unite with General Ransom? When did General Beauregard leave?"[126] To this, Beauregard himself replied, "I have not left here, my presence being still absolutely necessary." He explained his day's activities in a somewhat different light than they appeared in his correspondence with Bragg and Seddon. The part of his original plan about dividing forces on either side of the broad Appomattox River disappeared. Instead, Beauregard now asserted that he had promised to join Hoke if he was needed. He also claimed to have obeyed the secretary of war promptly but to have received belated approval for his scheme from Bragg.[127] Having thus tried to win over the president, at least to some degree, Beauregard a few minutes later made a bid for Bragg's support. Sending copies of his correspondence with Seddon that day, he stated, "I must insist on receiving orders only from one source, and that from the general commanding."[128] That was Bragg, whom Beauregard probably considered to be the most favorably inclined toward him of those in authority in Richmond.

The end of the day brought a gradual return to calmness and stability, both in the military situation and in the relations between Beauregard and his Richmond superiors. Nothing having come of the forced reconnaissance, Hoke finally did make his way to Drewry's Bluff and link up with Ransom.

Since Butler and his lieutenants had once again shown great timidity, the Confederates still held Drewry's Bluff and had suffered no disastrous consequences from Beauregard's strange ideas. To the north, at Yellow Tavern, Stuart's cavalry had bought a vital day of delay in Sheridan's approach to the city. The price had been high though, and now Stuart lay dying in Richmond, where he had been carried after falling with a Federal cavalryman's bullet in him. By nightfall Beauregard had settled down enough to write a civil dispatch to Seddon reporting on the general situation in his front and expressing his intention at last to go in person to Drewry's Bluff the next day.[129] Back in Richmond, a very weary secretary of war and commanding general could at least take satisfaction that the enemy had been kept out of the city that day and that a sizable force was finally at hand with which to fend off the two Federal threats. In his final note to Bragg that evening, a discussion of how best to get supplies through to Lee's hard-pressed army, Seddon advised the commanding general to "endeavor to secure some quiet and repose at home tonight."[130]

"Thunder, lightning, and rain all day," wrote John B. Jones in his diary for May 12.[131] Through the rain-swept streets of Richmond marched the troops of the now reinforced garrison division on their way to man the fortifications north of the city and foil Sheridan's last menacing effort, while most of Hoke's brigades held the line at Drewry's Bluff. Once again Davis headed for the front, and this time was present to see Sheridan driven off.[132] Later, about noon, Davis paid a visit to the dying Stuart and spent a quarter hour chatting with the young general.[133] Down in Petersburg, Beauregard again promised to come north to take charge at Drewry's Bluff as soon as his last two brigades arrived. They came in that day, but he went nowhere.[134] In northern Virginia the battle of Spotsylvania raged with renewed fury, but along the Drewry's Bluff lines no major action took place.

On May 13, Whiting finally arrived at Petersburg, expecting a short visit for discussions with Beauregard and then an early return to Wilmington. The discussion with Beauregard was short, to be sure, but it was a briefing on the role that Beauregard was assigning him. Whiting was to have command at Petersburg with two brigades while the Creole went north to fight at Drewry's Bluff. Then, about noon, Beauregard finally rode north in company with his staff and a brigade of troops. Taking a roundabout route that brought him just clear of the extended Union left flank, he was all day and most of the night getting to the Confederate lines south of the James.[135] Bragg had hoped he might be there sooner and with his added force help Hoke to dispatch the Federals in his front. "We must destroy this force between here and Petersburg," he urged Beauregard. The reason was obvious. As long as Butler continued in his threatening position on the outskirts of Richmond, watching him would tie down substantial Confederate forces badly needed elsewhere, particularly if Sheridan's cavalry, now resting at Haxall's Landing on the north bank of the James below the city, should decide to make another swipe at Richmond. On this day, however, Bragg was to be disappointed. Beauregard was long in coming, and Hoke, outnumbered two to one and with the Federals threatening his right flank from the south, was forced out of the first ring of fortifications and back into the intermediate entrenchments.[136]

Meanwhile, Davis was giving thought to the needs of Lee's army. "The President has had the Secretary of War closeted with him nearly all day," noted Jones.[137] Their topic of discussion, if the content of Davis's correspondence that day is any indication, was the Army of Northern Virginia. The day before, a massive Union assault had shaken Lee's army, temporarily broken its lines, and taken 4,000 prisoners and 20 guns. In a bloody, daylong battle the Confederates had hung on and prevented their army from being broken in two. All of this Lee reported in dispatches that reached Davis by the thirteenth.[138] Lee did not report to Davis that as the breach was opened in the Confederate line at the height of the battle, Lee had once again endeavored to lead a counterattack himself and had only been dissuaded by the uproarious protests of his troops. What Davis did have before him, however, were a number of requests from Lee for additional troops, both from South Carolina and from specific units formerly part of the Army of Northern Virginia that had been serving that winter in North Carolina.[139] Although Davis could explain that "every organized brigade in the Department of So. Carolina and Georgia has been ordered on and is supposed to have reached Petersburg," the problem was in explaining why none of them had passed north of the James. The same was true for former Army of Northern Virginia units such as Hoke's old brigade. "I have been painfully anxious to send your troops to you," Davis explained, "but unaccountable delays have occurred." Expecting Beauregard to arrive on the twelfth with the two brigades he was supposed to bring up from Petersburg and with Sheridan's cavalry having pulled back to Haxall's Landing, the president had hoped to be able to send at least Hoke's old brigade to Lee and had even given orders for it to move. In fact, the troops had actually marched to the railroad depot in Richmond and were awaiting transportation when word of the continued pressure at Drewry's Bluff–and Beauregard's nonarrival–forced their recall. "I anticipated your want of fresh troops," the president assured

Lee, "and have earnestly watched for an opportunity to send them. I dare not promise any thing now."[140] The hard fact remained that until Butler's southside force was dealt with, Lee's hard-pressed Army of Northern Virginia would be receiving no reinforcements.

At 3:00 A.M. on May 14, Beauregard finally arrived at Drewry's Bluff. He was all activity from the very outset, but instead of directing his attention to the immediate problem before him, and the ever more pressing need to solve it quickly, he devoted his efforts to the creation of strategic pipedreams. That was in character, at least, and little had changed since Beauregard last served in Virginia in the first springtime of the war. At Drewry's Bluff he found a couple of engineer officers and after chatting with them for an hour or so, he ordered one of them, Col. Walter H. Stevens, to go at once to Richmond, obtain an audience with the president, and present a plan that Beauregard had thought up on the spur of the moment. Not taking time to write out the scheme, he simply trusted Stevens's memory and understanding of it. As Beauregard himself finally committed it to writing later that day, it went something like this. Lee would retreat to the outer or even the intermediate line of fortifications on the northern outskirts of Richmond. This would allow him to detach 15,000 men to reinforce Beauregard who would then assail Butler in front while Whiting, with the two brigades left at Petersburg, would hit him from behind. Thus, "in two days at futherest" from the time Beauregard got his reinforcements, "Butler must necessarily be crushed or captured." When this happened, the Confederates would capture his entire vast stock of supplies intact, so the plan went, and that would allow them to thumb their noses at every consideration of logistics for a few days. Then, with 25,000 men Beauregard would join Lee in attacking the Army of the Potomac, "and Grant's fate could not long remain doubtful." The result would be a victorious end to the war.[141]

With this modest proposal, or some presumably reasonable facsimile thereof, committed to memory, Stevens rushed off and arrived at the Confederate White House at an hour that was still so early that he was not permitted to disturb the sleeping president, whose intense activity during recent days belied the fact that he was still a very sick man. Instead, the best he could do was Braxton Bragg, who listened intently but would not issue the immediate orders that Beauregard had directed Stevens to request. Bragg probably thought that the young staff officer had somehow garbled the plan and may have assumed that Beauregard could not seriously be suggesting something so farfetched. So he had his own horse saddled up and rode down to Drewry's Bluff to hear what this was all about. There he heard the whole thing again from the general's own mouth. Beauregard gave it his best pitch. "Bragg," he said, "circumstances have thrown the fate of the Confederacy in your hands and mine; let us play our parts boldly and fearlessly! Issue those orders and I'll carry them out to the best of my ability. I'll guarantee success!" Bragg was polite, so much so that in later years Beauregard went so far as to claim he had actually agreed with the plan. He did not, of course, and the one thing everyone agreed on in recalling the incident was that he refused to issue any such orders without the president's approval.[142]

Bragg apparently talked the matter over with Davis once he got back into the city. At 10:00 that morning the president cabled Beauregard to ask about the situation at Drewry's Bluff at that time, and the Creole responded that aside from a little desultory firing all was quiet on his front.[143] That afternoon Davis rode down to confer with Beauregard himself. The general still had not given up in his efforts to get his strategic plan approved and not long before had written it all up and sent it off to Bragg for further consideration.[144] Now he made his pitch to Davis. With Butler threatening Richmond, Sheridan in a position to renew his threat at any time, and Lee desperately in need of reinforcement in northern Virginia, the president and commanding general had no time for such things, and Davis apparently took very little time to make clear to Beauregard that the scheme was not going to be implemented.

The discussion now turned to the question of how best to deal with Butler. The president offered to let Beauregard have the use of Ransom's garrison division of about 5,000 men presently holding the city's northern defenses against the possibility of a return visit from Sheridan. This Beauregard readily accepted. Davis also wanted Whiting and his troops brought up from Petersburg—indeed, he had already had Bragg issue such an order to Whiting—and he wanted Beauregard with the combined force to crush Butler as soon as possible. Beauregard insisted that Whiting's movement toward Butler's rear while Beauregard engaged him in front was "an essential feature to the entire success" of the plan. "To this," the president later recalled, "I offered distinct objection, because of the hazard during a battle of attempting to make a junction of troops moving from opposite sides of the enemy." Davis was not overestimating the difficulty of such a movement. Combining two such forces separated by miles of territory as well as the enemy army itself was the sort of thing dreamed of by people like Beauregard and almost never successfully carried out.

Instead of this unrealistic measure, Davis proposed that Whiting's troops make a night march, which in contrast to a night attack was a very practical thing for a Civil War army. If orders were sent to them at once and they made no worse time than had Beauregard and his brigade of infantry over the same route the night before, they should be at Drewry's Bluff "by or soon after daylight." "The next day being Sunday," Davis continued, "they could rest, and, all the troops being assigned to their positions, could move to make a concerted attack at daylight on Monday," May 16. When Davis remained firm in this opinion, Beauregard complained that no reliable courier could be found who knew the roundabout route necessary to get to Petersburg and could carry word of the operation to Whiting. This was hardly a point in favor of attempting to coordinate maneuvers over such a distance nor as it turned out was it a good choice of excuses, as just then a courier arrived from Whiting. With persuasion ineffective and his last excuse removed, Beauregard "reluctantly yielded," as he put it, to Davis's point of view. He did, however, have one trick left to him. As Davis recalled, "He then said the order would have to be drawn with a great deal of care, and that he would prepare it as soon as he could." That satisfied the president, and he returned to Richmond.[145]

He had not been gone long before Beauregard telegraphed Bragg regarding Bragg's previous order to Whiting to join Beauregard at Drewry's Bluff. "I have already sent General Whiting his instructions to co-operate with me," he wrote. "Please telegraph him to follow them as delivered by Colonel Logan. Yours may conflict with mine."[146] This might have aroused in a suspicious mind, or in one familiar with Beauregard, a doubt as to Beauregard's intention of obeying the president's instructions. Bragg was apparently not so naive as to comply with this request, or at least no record of his doing so has remained. The fact was that Beauregard had not yet dispatched Col. T. M. Logan of his staff to carry a message to Whiting, but he planned to do so the next day. It would be a message much different from that which Davis had expected when he left Drewry's Bluff that afternoon.[147]

Early the next morning, Davis instructed Bragg to send another order to Whiting directing him to march to join Beauregard at the "earliest moment with his whole force." He also had Bragg send a telegram to Beauregard informing him of the action and stating, "It is hoped you may receive him [Whiting] in time to attack tomorrow. Time is all important to us."[148] Perhaps the president had some inkling that Beauregard might not be strictly carrying out his wishes. If so, he was very perceptive, for Beauregard had no intention of drawing Whiting to Drewry's Bluff before the start of the planned battle. Beauregard apparently responded to Bragg's notification with some sort of protest, for Bragg in turn telegraphed him, "My dispatches of this morning to you and General Whiting were by direction of the President, and after his conference with you."[149] At 6:15 A.M., Beauregard telegraphed Bragg, reporting affairs quiet on his front and then blandly stating, "Whiting cannot be here until Tuesday afternoon. Attack will commence Wednesday morning." This two-day postponement of the attack was exactly what Davis and Bragg had been endeavoring to avoid. Submitting the dispatch to the president, Bragg noted on it, "May I be pardoned for saying that this proposed delay seems to me fatal. By Wednesday our fate will in all probability be settled. . . . I cannot conceive why General Whiting could not have moved yesterday or may not today." Bragg's conclusion was that "the attack has been already too long delayed, and should now be made at the earliest practicable moment." Davis agreed. He still hoped Whiting could make Drewry's Bluff by nightfall "so as to take part in the attack tomorrow," and he ordered Bragg to instruct Beauregard accordingly.[150] Just what had moved Whiting not to obey either of Bragg's orders to march for Richmond, or indeed what moved Whiting to do any number of the strange things he did this day and the next, is unclear, but he definitely did not want to go to Drewry's Bluff and was probably receiving contrary directions from Beauregard.[151]

The Creole, for his part, had probably been expecting Davis and Bragg to react as they did to the outrageous announcement of the postponement of the assault. Immediately upon receipt of Bragg's order, he dispatched Col. Samuel Melton of his staff to the executive mansion with a letter for Davis and additional oral explanations.[152] In the dispatch he reiterated his claim that Whiting would take two days to march from Petersburg to Drewry's Bluff, passing around the Federal flank, and he relayed Whiting's nervous apprehension that such a move would leave Petersburg open to seizure by the Federals during the interval. Then announcing as if it were his own conception that "further delay" in attacking Butler "might be fatal to success," Beauregard advised the president, "I have determined to attack him in my front at day break tomorrow morning" and had "ordered Major-General Whiting to co-operate with all his forces by attacking the enemy in rear."[153] This was precisely the scheme Davis had forbidden the previous afternoon, and he said as much to Melton. The staff officer replied that "General Beauregard had directed him to explain to [Davis] that upon a further examination he found his force sufficient; that his operations, therefore, did not depend upon making a junction with Whiting."[154] By this curious turnabout, Beauregard passed—in the space of about eighteen hours—from claiming that Whiting should strike the Federal rear because such a move was essential to the success of the attack to claiming that Whiting should strike the Federal rear because such a move was not essential to the success of the attack.

By this time, Davis had little option but to acquiesce. Simultaneous with his sending of Melton to see Davis, Beauregard had sent Logan to see Whiting and give him the orders he preferred.[155] To have changed this now would probably have entailed most if not all of the delay Beauregard had threatened in order to get his way. And so the president gave in. Beauregard made preparations that afternoon, and the attack went in at 5:00 A.M. the next day, Monday, May 16. The troops Butler had been forced to detach to cover his base and supply line had changed the ratio of the two forces to the point that the Confederates now enjoyed a modest superiority in numbers. Beauregard planned to hold Butler in position with attacks all along the line while he would strike hardest at the Federal right, tearing that flank loose from the James River and separating the Union force from its base at Bermuda Hundred. The arrival of Whiting in the Federal rear was to complete Butler's undoing.

The attack began as scheduled and met with initial success. By 8:30 Beauregard could write to Bragg that "our progress is very satisfactory." The Confederate left was driving the Federal right while the rest of the line held solidly and firing had been heard from the direction of Whiting's anticipated approach.[156] His reports continued to be favorable until at 9:45 he noted that his troops had halted to regroup and replenish ammunition.[157] Some further sounds had been heard from Whiting, and Beauregard hoped soon to see the effects of that officer's planned assault on the Union rear. To be sure of this and to speed Whiting along, he sent several messages urging him to "press on and press over everything in your front, and the day will be complete." By 10:00 A.M., with resistance stiffening in front and some of his troops badly fatigued, Beauregard decided to suspend the offensive pending the arrival of Whiting. More might well have been accomplished, but Beauregard was counting on Whiting's arrival to finish the task. Thus when Bragg wrote to suggest a movement around the enemy's right, Beauregard declined, still expecting at every moment to hear the swelling roar of battle from the Federal rear that would tell him Whiting was engaged. When that happened, he wanted to have the troops of his main body well rested and organized and with full cartridge boxes.[158] And so he waited—and waited. At 1:15 P.M. he wrote Bragg, "I hear nothing yet of Whiting's movements." Indeed, it had been a long time now, well over four hours, since any sound at all had been heard from the direction of Petersburg.[159]

That morning Davis had ridden out to the battlefield and had witnessed the latter stages of the actual fighting in front of Drewry's Bluff. Now he found Beauregard standing near the place where the turnpike to Petersburg crossed the Confederate lines. To the president's query, Beauregard replied that "he was waiting to hear Whiting's guns and had been expecting him for some time to approach on the Petersburg road."[160] They had not been there long before they were joined by a number of politicians, including Postmaster General Reagan. About 1:45 P.M. a sputter of small-arms fire came from the south. "At last," said the president with grim satisfaction. Yet as minute after minute passed, no further sound came from the direction of Petersburg. The afternoon wore on with the boredom relieved by the heavy fire of Federal artillery and sharpshooters. Among their targets was the collection of Confederate officers and officials near the turnpike. A shell struck the earth near Davis's feet but failed to explode. Officers standing nearby were hit by sniper fire. Presently, it began to rain, and Reagan recorded that Davis took shelter under a leaning silver maple tree and a waterproof cape loaned to him by a young officer. Beauregard suggested they take shelter—from the rain at least—in a nearby shanty. As they were going in, however, a soldier standing nearby had one of his arms blown off by a shell. "Beauregard suggested that the enemy seemed to have the range of that place, and that they had better go across the turnpike to the open ground." A few minutes there convinced them the change had been no improvement with respect to the Yankee artillery, which Beauregard suggested "seemed to have the range everywhere."[161]

By 4:00 P.M. word arrived that Whiting would not be coming that day. Inexplicably, he had ordered first a halt and then a retreat after an insignificant contact with the enemy. Many both inside and outside the army attributed this to drunkenness, but whatever his problem, such movements rarely worked. Davis had been right all along.

At about the same time that word of Whiting's strange failure reached Beauregard, Butler, unnerved by the Confederate attack and fearful for his flanks, began to fall back toward Bermuda Hundred. Beauregard still hoped to launch a final assault, without Whiting, against the retreating Federals, but as darkness came on he at last gave up the effort. Similarly, he entertained hopes of a coordinated attack the next day, but this too came to nothing. In the end, Butler drew himself back into the peninsula of Bermuda Hundred, and Beauregard drew a defensive line across the neck of the peninsula, leaving the Federal Army of the James, in the words of Ulysses S. Grant, "as completely shut off from further operations directly against Richmond as if it had been in a bottle strongly corked."[162] Yet from the Confederate point of view the results were not entirely satisfactory. The moral impact of a major victory was lacking, and the soldiers of the Army of the James were still available for use elsewhere. Worse, a substantial number of Confederate troops would still be required in order to keep the cork in the bottle at a time when Lee needed every additional man he could get.

In the days after the battle of Drewry's Bluff, Beauregard did not give up his strategic ideas. First he proposed to Davis a plan almost identical to what he had proposed earlier. Lee was to detach to him 15,000 troops with which to crush Butler; then Beauregard would go to Lee with that many troops and more and finish off Grant. This met with a predictable response. Next he proposed, in writing this time, that he take 15,000 men to Lee, who would in the meantime have fallen back to the Chickahominy. They would destroy Grant, and if they could do so within three or four days, they might be able to get some troops back to the southside in time to prevent Butler from taking Petersburg or the railroad. Bragg and Seddon both strongly disapproved of the plan, believing it would entail the loss of Petersburg and with it Richmond's supply lines. Further, it would sacrifice considerable territory needed for the production of supplies, including the valuable Shenandoah Valley. Finally, a sudden sixty-mile retreat by Lee's army while in contact with a powerful enemy and with Sheridan's cavalry potentially operating in its rear areas was a desperate undertaking. Davis shared their reservations but liked the idea of Beauregard sending to Lee such reinforcements as he could without exposing Petersburg. Accordingly he ordered Beauregard to pull about 5,000 of his troops out of line and send them to Lee, a movement that the president felt compelled to assure Lee was "not in accordance with" Beauregard's plan.[163] Beauregard, to be sure, was not at all pleased with Davis's action. He complained that he had been planning to undertake a limited offensive to shorten his lines and allow them to be held with fewer troops. He would march the force thus made available down the south bank of the James and seize a position that would allow him to cut off Butler's supplies. The last part was more of Beauregard's dreaming, and the first part, shortening his lines, was accomplished within a couple of days even without the transferred troops.[164] Davis wrote to Beauregard to stress "the importance which I attach to the defeat of Grant" and to admonish him to keep a sharp lookout for any possible transfer of troops from Butler to Grant.[165]

Lee's army, meanwhile, had continued its deadly grapple with the Army of the Potomac. After the bloodbath of May 12, five days of relatively minor skirmishing had followed along the Spotsylvania line while Grant had sidled around gradually to the east and south, constantly threatening Lee's right flank. On the eighteenth and nineteenth heavy fighting flared up again, and then Grant swung his army into motion, once again moving east and south.[166] As Lee explained it to Davis two days later, the Union movement had started at night and "was not discovered until after daylight." The problem was that "in a wooded country like that in which we have been operating . . . a day's march can always be gained." Grant having thus got the jump on him, Lee was forced to drop back behind the North Anna River, just twenty-three miles from Richmond. "I should have preferred contesting the enemy's approach inch by inch; but my solicitude for Richmond caused me to abandon that plan."[167] Another stolen march by Grant could mean the loss of the capital, and that was something Lee would not risk. Lee repeatedly asked for whatever reinforcements Richmond could spare him, and he suggested that there would be little point in keeping troops around Richmond should his own army prove unable to stop Grant. "The question is whether we shall fight the battle here or around Richmond," he wrote. "If the troops are obliged to be retained at Richmond I may be forced back."[168] Throughout the operations, whether momentous events were transpiring or not, Lee kept Davis constantly informed with daily dispatches. Indeed, on some days two or even three letters and telegrams went to Richmond from Lee's headquarters.

Davis naturally wrote less often, but he kept Lee posted on military developments in the Richmond area and gave what aid he could.[169] He also admonished Lee not to place himself in personal danger. "I have been pained to hear of your exposure of your person in various conflicts," the president wrote. "The country could not bear the loss of you, and, my dear friend, though you are prone to forget yourself, you will not, I trust, again forget the public interest dependent on your life."[170] When Lee commented that the Federal artillery was superior to his both in range and in weight of metal, Davis promptly responded with a list of all the mobile heavy artillery in the Richmond defenses and offered to let Lee have any and all of it if he wanted.[171] Nor was Davis slow or hesitant in forwarding infantrymen to Lee. He followed Lee's suggestions aggressively whenever they offered promise of freeing up more troops for the Army of Northern Virginia, and he pursued such other ideas of his own as might serve the same purpose. By the time Lee reached the North Anna, Davis had managed to add several thousand more troops to his army, making good a fair percentage of the campaign's already shocking losses.[172] This purely defensive campaign displayed Davis's qualities to best advantage. It was a type of warfare he understood and that fit his ideas of what the South needed to do in order to win the war. During these weeks he proved steadfast, resourceful, and quite capable of weighing the dangers on one front against those on another and making shrewd and sometimes necessarily ruthless decisions about the allocation of Confederate forces. When a May 15 victory at New Market in Shenandoah Valley by a scratch Confederate force under John C. Breckinridge eased pressure in that sector, Davis brought Breckinridge and many of his troops east to bolster Lee. It was only a few thousand men, but it helped. By late May Lee's army included practically all of the regular organized Confederate forces on the eastern seaboard with the exception of those in Beauregard's Bermuda Hundred force.

It was therefore to Beauregard that both Davis and Lee looked for the additional troops that seemed to be needed to stop Grant. Davis passed along to Lee Beauregard's proposals for a grand concentration, and while Lee shared Davis's disapproval of any unforced retreat on the part of the Army of Northern Virginia, the plan began to look more and more realistic as Grant maneuvered Lee closer and closer to Richmond. Beginning on May 20, Lee began to mention regularly the possibility of a major accession of troops from Beauregard. On the twenty-third he wrote that he was now "near enough Richmond . . . to combine the operations of this army with that under General Beauregard." The wisest course, he suggested, would be to unite against Grant's army "and endeavor to crush it," and Lee would thus "be very glad to have the aid of General Beauregard in such a blow, and if it is possible to combine, I think it will succeed." Still, he believed this should be done on the Pamunkey rather than the Chickahominy, surrendering as little territory as possible.[173] By the twenty-eighth he was even more anxious for Beauregard's help. Noting again that he was close enough for this purpose he added, "Should any field nearer to Richmond be more convenient to him and he will designate it, I will endeavor to deliver battle there."[174]

By this time the scene of the conflict had shifted even closer to Richmond, to the very Chickahominy River that Lee had written five days earlier he wanted to keep the enemy away from. He had successfully blocked Grant by taking up an excellent position behind the North Anna and had even had a favorable opportunity to strike a counterblow at the Federal army. This opportunity had been lost, however, as Lee had been for several days all but incapacitated by severe illness. The army's senior corps commander, Ewell, was little better off himself. The next ranking officer, A. P. Hill, was not equal to the occasion, and Longstreet's replacement, R. H. Anderson, had been in corps command for less than a month. The result was that the Army of Northern Virginia was all but leaderless for several days. Halted by Lee's strong position, Grant swung east and again turned the Confederates. The move was detected just in time, and by the twenty-eighth Lee's army had just won the race to interpose itself between Grant and Richmond. The race had taken it, however, to the very outskirts of the city, the old Peninsula battlefields of two years before, and a small crossroads called Cold Harbor.[175] Cooperation with Beauregard was more important than ever.

Davis forwarded Lee's suggestions to Beauregard along with a report, all too true, that large numbers of Butler's troops were being transferred to Grant, making it all the more vital for Beauregard to reinforce Lee.[176] Beauregard, however, had been claiming to be outnumbered two to one and in need of every man he had. For once, the president seemed to be taken in by this.[177] On the morning of May 29 Lee invited Beauregard to his head-quarters to discuss the matter, but that evening he could report to Davis only that Beauregard claimed to have hardly enough troops for his own needs "and can spare none." Grimly Lee concluded, "If Genl Grant advances tomorrow I will engage him with my present force."[178] The next day Beauregard emphasized his unwillingness to give up troops by writing Lee, "War Department must determine when and what troops to order from here."[179] As far as he was concerned, none would be going. Lee immediately relayed this information to Davis and then stated bluntly, "The result of this delay will be disaster. Butler's troops . . . will be with Grant tomorrow. Hoke's division, at least, should be with me by light tomorrow."[180] Davis responded to this with remarkable speed. Just three and a half hours after Lee had written his telegram, Davis was writing a reply in which he promised Hoke's division would move at once and that "every effort will be made . . . to place it with you early tomorrow."[181] For Beauregard there was to be no discretionary order this time. "By direction of the President," wrote Bragg, "you will send Hoke's division . . . immediately to this point."[182] When Grant's army attacked, on June 1 rather than May 31 as Lee had feared, Hoke's 7,000 men were in Lee's lines.[183]

Though only minor skirmishing took place along the lines at Cold Harbor on May 31, Davis could hear the firing clearly from his office. To Lee he wrote, "But for duties in the office I would have gone out to see you this morning."[184] The next day the first serious fighting took place around Cold Harbor but with inconclusive results. Davis began to be suspicious that Grant would make another of his moves by his left flank and cross to the south bank of the Chickahominy for a lunge toward Richmond. A false report on the evening of June 1 convinced him that such a move was in progress, and he directed Ransom to have the Richmond garrison ready to stop it. He also continued trying to persuade Beauregard to part with additional reinforcements for Lee.[185] Although no heavy fighting occurred on June 2 and the Army of Northern Virginia easily repulsed the massive Union attacks of the third with great slaughter, Lee too continued to believe that the magnitude of transfers from Butler to Grant required further reinforcements from Beauregard.[186] The result was the transfer of an additional brigade from Bermuda Hundred to Lee's lines.

Monday, June 6, brought news of Confederate disaster out in the Shenandoah Valley. A small force there under Brig. Gen. W. E. Jones had tried to stop an advancing Union army under Maj. Gen. David Hunter at Piedmont. They had been routed and Jones killed, and then the Federals had proceeded to occupy Staunton. This debacle drew the attention of Davis and Lee, and over the next week various options were considered.[187] At Lee's recommendation, Breckinridge, who had recently joined Lee with his force, was again detached for service in the Valley, taking 2,000 men west with him. Bragg advised that enough additional force be sent to clear the Shenandoah Valley, and Davis referred the matter to Lee for his opinion. True to form, Lee initially resisted the move because it would draw troops away from his hard-pressed Army of Northern Virginia. Equally true to form, Davis accepted his recommendation. The next day Bragg wrote a second note to Davis to plead his case again. "It seems to me a pressing necessity," he concluded, "to send at least 6,000 good troops to re-enforce Breckinridge." Far more powerful was the news received that day that Hunter's army out in the Valley had penetrated all the way to Lexington and burned the Virginia Military Institute. From Lexington, Hunter was in a position to turn east into central Virginia and do even more damage to the state's ability to supply Lee's army. Faced with this threat, Lee required no further prodding from Davis. He immediately dispatched Maj. Gen. Jubal Early with another 8,000 men to defeat Hunter and if possible clear the Valley and even threaten Washington.[188]

The next morning Grant's army was gone. Without a clue or a sound to betray its movement, the Federal host of nearly 100,000 men had simply disappeared in a night. Confederate skirmishers went forward but found no foes even well beyond the enemy's former entrenchments. Clearly, Grant was up to something, but for the moment Lee was at a loss to know what. Several days earlier, Davis, who had been monitoring the situation with Lee's army closely enough to have visited some of its outposts, had warned him, "The indications are that Grant, despairing of a direct attack, is now seeking to embarrass you by flank movements."[189] Now with Lee transferring Early and his troops to the Shenandoah and with Grant's army on the march for points unknown, Davis rode down to Lee's headquarters on the afternoon of June 13 in hopes of discussing the situation with him. Lee was out on his lines at the time, and Davis had to go back to Richmond without seeing him. Nevertheless, when Lee wrote Davis the next day he revealed the same sort of hunch about Grant's likely movements. "I think the enemy must be preparing to move South of James River," but where, how, and when still remained a mystery. On the evening of the thirteenth, the Confederates probing for the missing Army of the Potomac had clashed with a Federal screening force of cavalry and infantry. Lee made plans to strike it again in the morning, "but it disappeared from before us during the night."[190] For the rest of that day and the next, reports continued to suggest that Grant was heading for the James, and Lee even speculated that Petersburg was his probable objective. Yet Lee remained uncertain enough to delay drawing his army back any closer to Richmond, though he did make preparations to return to Beauregard the troops he had received from him over the past fortnight.[191]

In the midst of all this uncertainty, Early's troops began their march toward the Shenandoah—"in motion this morning at 3 o'clock & by daylight . . . clear of our camps," Lee explained to Davis in a dispatch written on the evening of June 15. "If you think it better to recall him," Lee added, "please send a trusty messenger to overtake him tonight." Lee admitted that having Early's men with the army in the present crisis "would make us more secure here, but," he concluded, "success in the Valley would relieve our difficulties that at present press heavily upon us."[192]

This was a return to Lee's gambling strategy. Sending Early north might be a risk, but defeat would be a certainty, Lee believed, unless he could contrive somehow to take the initiative away from Grant.[193] Early's move was his best chance of doing that. Of course, this strategy was contrary to Davis's, but this time the president deferred to Lee's judgment and made no move to call Early back from his march to the Valley. The worse the Confederacy's prospects became, the more Davis came to lean on Lee's judgment. This applied to matters beyond Virginia as well. When on June 14 Army of Tennessee corps commander Leonidas Polk was killed far away at Pine Mountain, Georgia, Davis appealed to Lee—in the midst of the confusion surrounding the disappearance of the Army of the Potomac—to suggest a good successor, something Lee was very much at a loss to do.[194]

At the same time that he might burden Lee with such requests for advice, Davis did his best to aid Lee in facing the military necessities of the present moment. Thus, for example, the president arranged with engineer officers to have a new pontoon bridge laid down on the James River "at any point designated, by daybreak tomorrow," he explained to Lee on the fifteenth.[195] He would help as much as he could with the details of army support, but far from giving strategic direction to the general, he moved perhaps unwittingly toward more complete dependence on Lee's opinions.

That same day, June 15, there had been ominous developments south of the James. Beauregard had found himself defending Petersburg with barely 3,000 men against Federals who by the end of the day numbered upwards of 16,000, with more coming all the time. Although Beauregard and his Confederate troops had performed their desperate task with commendable valor, nothing could have prevented their being overrun and Petersburg taken but the appalling confusion and disorganization that existed among the commanders of the lead units of the Army of the Potomac. During the night Beauregard pulled all but a handful of his troops off the Bermuda Hundred line and managed to scrape together perhaps 14,000 men for the defense of Petersburg. He would need every one of them as even larger numbers of Federals hastened to the scene of the fighting.

At 2:00 A.M. on the sixteenth, Beauregard simply notified Lee that the Bermuda Hundred lines would be left practically undefended and suggested that Lee had better look to them himself. Lee did so, but still mistakenly believed that Grant had substantial forces north of the James. Thus, he would not take the risk of rushing his entire force to the defense of the vital rail junction on the Appomattox despite a stream of dispatches from Beauregard begging for help. "The enemy is pressing us in heavy force." Beauregard wrote on the morning of the sixteenth. "Can you not send for the re-enforcements asked for [earlier] this morning?" Further telegrams that day and early the next were much the same, as Beauregard correctly reported himself to be engaging at least two corps of the Army of the Potomac.[196] Finally, on the seventeenth, the fog of war parted enough to allow Lee to grasp Grant's purpose. Moving his army quickly over the James, he had his veteran troops in the Petersburg trenches, most of which Beauregard had been able to hold, in time to repulse attacks by the full Army of the Potomac on June 18.[197] Across the lines, Grant came to the decision that a siege was the only course left to him. From now until the last week of the war, the great armies in Virginia were through with maneuver, as the battle was to be fought out in the trenches.

Through the campaign from Cold Harbor to Petersburg, Davis had taken very little active role in the direction of Confederate movements, leaving such matters entirely up to Lee. With Lee fighting in a purely defensive mode, indeed with this the only possible strategy at this point, Davis seemed completely comfortable leaving to the general the freedom to follow his own judgment. Early's northward movement was an exception to Lee's passive defense but could be overlooked by Davis in his growing reliance on Lee. Given that Lee was acting mostly within Davis's strategic framework for the prosecution of the war, the president's consistent support was entirely appropriate. At the same time, the Confederate president had shown himself active and resourceful during the months of April, May, and June 1864, in endeavoring to provide Lee both the supplies and the reinforcements he needed. When necessity demanded and in order to shore up the kind of defensive grand strategy he instinctively followed, Davis was prepared to make bold moves and take large risks, ruthlessly stripping troops from the southern coasts and from North Carolina in order to bolster Lee's outnumbered army. Thus the 1864 campaign represents in many ways the brightest chapter in Davis's function as commander in chief. During these months the president had worked together with Lee more effectively and harmoniously than with any other general or at any other time during the war. Now, with Lee solidly fixed in a defensive role, though that was entirely by Grant's doing rather than his own, Davis once again found himself in substantial harmony with his chief Virginia general's operational ideas, and as the outlook for the Confederate cause grew darker the president came to rely on Lee as never before.

8
A QUESTION OF TIME

"We must destroy this army of Grant's before he gets to the James River," Lee had told Jubal Early that June. "If he gets there, it will become a siege, and then it will be a mere question of time."[1] Lee had believed for some time that a siege, the ultimate in passive defensive warfare, would be the doom of his army.[2] Now, penned into the Richmond and Petersburg fortifications, he faced just that. With chances of final Confederate victory fading, Lee continued to expend his best efforts on disproving his own prophecy or failing that at least making the siege a matter of as much time as possible. History might offer examples of causes apparently lost that had somehow prevailed through eleventh-hour reversals of fortune, and besides that, Lee was a soldier, and his duty was to go on resisting until his government told him to stop or until he could resist no more.

By contrast, Jefferson Davis was the chief political executive officer of his republic, the commander in chief of its armies. If the moment should ever come at which further resistance by those armies offered no further hope of national survival, no one else but Davis could well be expected to perceive it or act upon it. No government could reasonably include in its organic law a provision for its own extinction by surrender to an opposing government that denied its right to exist. No official could possibly have the constitutional authority to surrender unconditionally and in so doing dissolve his own government. Yet when resistance became futile, and the people—if in no other way than by their declining willingness to remain in the ranks of the army—showed their own readiness to give up the fight, whose responsibility was it to cut the best deal that could be obtained with the victors while some leverage for negotiation, at least the threat of inflicting more casualties in a bitter, last-ditch defense, still remained? If Davis ever pondered this question or reflected that he might himself be the answer to it, he left no record of it. He stated again and again that the only requirement for Confederate victory was continued steadfast resistance no matter what happened. That was the course he took, and so, although for different reasons, he and Lee continued to work together in a common endeavor if not toward a common goal.

Lee's first concern as the siege got under way was obtaining adequate supplies. "My greatest apprehension at present," he wrote to Davis on the third day of the siege, "is the maintenance of our communications south." While the Confederates still held the Weldon Railroad, connecting Petersburg with Weldon, North Carolina, and points south, it was not presently operational and Lee believed it would be almost impossible to prevent Grant from breaking or seizing it sooner or later. Even the Southside Railroad, running southwest out of Petersburg, Lee believed to be vulnerable. Only the Richmond and Danville could be relied on, and every effort should be made to improve its efficiency, prepare for mending possible breaks, and stockpile supplies against probable interruptions in the flow of foodstuffs from the south.[3] A few days later Lee wrote, "I am less uneasy about holding our position than about our ability to procure supplies for the army." If the supply position became desperate, Lee suggested that he would have to assault Grant's entrenchments, a move that would be costly beyond imagination and in which "a want of success would . . . be almost fatal." He asked for "the benefit of Your Excellency's good judgment and views upon this subject."[4]

In the meantime, he did what he could to make such counsels of desperation unnecessary, using the army's wagons to draw what supplies he could beyond the flanks of Grant's army.[5] In July, he got the Weldon Railroad back in operation and was able to accumulate a reserve of four or five days' rations, but that was as far ahead as he could get. Surpluses had accumulated at the Weldon's southern depots while service had been interrupted, but once these stocks had rattled up the tracks to Petersburg, the Confederate system for procuring and transporting supplies simply failed to push enough victuals into the line's southern branches to do more than provide Lee's army its scant daily rations—sometimes not even that—despite all Lee's enterprise in operating it within a few miles of the Federal left flank. The army's reserve food stock began to dwindle again, and Lee appealed to Davis for remedy. "I dislike to add to the troubles and labors of your Excellency," Lee wrote, "but deem this subject sufficiently important to be brought directly to your attention."[6] Davis did not grudge it that and promptly wrote back explaining some of the difficulties in gathering the necessary supplies further south.[7]

Although the president was willing to give his personal attention to the supply issue, he carried a misplaced faith in his Old Army crony Commissary Gen. Lucius B. Northrop. Northrop's inefficiency and his ignorance of the first principles of economics assured that the situation would not improve.

In August Grant rendered that particular question of supply moot by seizing and holding a section of the Weldon Railroad. Lee went back to the cumbersome expedient of hauling by wagon on the roundabout route beyond the now extended Federal left flank. Even then, he remained optimistic that he could "accumulate a surplus to provide against those occasional interruptions" in the flow of supplies, but he had to admit that the little reserve he had built up so laboriously the month before was all gone. "I trust," he wrote almost wistfully, "your Excellency will see that the most vigorous and intelligent efforts be made to keep up our supplies, and that all officers concerned in the work be required to give their unremitting personal attention to their duty."[8] Once again Davis wrote back immediately with details of the government's efforts to procure and transport supplies. He too was optimistic, expressing confidence that if only the Army of Tennessee could deal with Sherman, "we shall be better able to sustain an army here than we were the first year of the war."[9] Seddon also wrote in response to Lee's supply concerns and in the same positive vein. Since the railroads farther south were rapidly being repaired, and "there is no real deficiency of supplies existing in the south," it followed theoretically that "there should be soon a decided increase in the quantity forwarded." The secretary did admit, however, that the artificially low schedule of prices the government would pay for supplies, with its disdain for true market values, was "operating very seriously to prevent deliveries." This was all too true, and Seddon went on to admit "that there may be very serious strain within the next few months in providing adequate supplies." "Still," he concluded, "I believe it can and will be done, and certainly no exertion shall be spared on my part to accomplish it."[10] For all that, the Army of Northern Virginia continued to experience a supply situation that was never better than hand-to-mouth.

Along with his worries about supplies, and almost more intense, was Lee's concern for the problem of finding and maintaining adequate manpower for the army. By August he was concerned enough to write to Seddon on the matter. "Unless some measures can be devised to replace our losses, the consequences may be disastrous." He went on to suggest a rigorous tightening of the loopholes of the conscription law. "Our numbers are daily decreasing, and the time has arrived in my opinion when no man should be excused from service, except for the purpose of doing work absolutely necessary for the support of the army." If this was not done Lee was not sanguine as to the final outcome. "Without some increase of strength," he concluded, "I cannot see how we are to escape the natural military consequences of the enemy's numerical superiority."[11] Seddon assured Lee that he had been "endeavoring, by all the means in my power, to give activity to the conscript service" but promised to step up efforts even further in keeping with Lee's suggestions.[12]

Still, by early September Lee's concern had grown enough to prompt him to write directly to the president, calling attention "to the importance of immediate and vigorous means to increase the strength of our armies, and to some suggestions as to the mode of doing it." The suggestions were extensive, running to well over 1,200 words. Lee wanted most draft exemptions revoked, and if the officials of the Conscript Bureau proved unsuccessful at routing out sufficient numbers of draft-eligible men, he was for putting muskets in their hands and putting them in the ranks too. Slaves should be requisitioned for fatigue duties, thus freeing white men for combat, and reserve forces composed of those too old or too young for conscription into the regular armies should be used to man "trenches, forts, &c.," leaving the regular troops "free for active operations." Again Lee pointed out the direction in which things were heading. "Our ranks are constantly diminishing by battle and disease, and few recruits are received; the consequences are inevitable."[13] Even then, Lee had not yet entirely eased his mind of the subject and just one week later wrote another lengthy letter to Davis with further suggestions on getting more men into the army.[14] These matters, especially the need for getting as many slaves as possible requisitioned for "labor on the fortifications," became a constant theme in Lee's correspondence for the rest of the month.[15]

By October Lee was prepared to make the consequences of his situation exceedingly plain to the Richmond authorities. On the fourth he wrote to Seddon, "I beg leave to inquire whether there is any prospect of my obtaining any increase to this army. If not, it will be very difficult for us to maintain ourselves." He reiterated the points he had been making for the past two months and added that these things needed to be done "unless we would see the enemy reap the great moral and material advantages of a successful issue of his most costly campaign." His prognosis in the event that the skulkers were harried into the ranks was almost more shocking. If "our entire arms-bearing population in Virginia and North Carolina" could be gotten out, "we may be able . . . to keep the enemy in check to the beginning of winter. If we fail to do this the result may be calamitous."[16] Seddon responded the next day, admitting the "grave anxiety" Lee's letter caused him and assuring the general, "I have been employing, and, under the warning of your letter, shall, if possible, with zeal and energy strain the powers and means of the Department to accomplish an efficient recruitment."[17] Seddon did try, but the problem was insoluble, and Lee's army continued to decline in numbers. Early in November after riding his lines and inspecting the condition of the defenses Lee wrote to Davis, "the greatest necessity I observed . . . was the want of men."[18]

Part of the problem with the army's declining numbers was due to something besides poor recruitment and was, if anything, even more alarming. The rate of desertions was beginning to rise ominously by the end of the summer. In August Lee wrote to Seddon about it, urging various steps to make desertion less attractive to the men of the Army of Northern Virginia, and Seddon promised to do his best. They had ample cause for concern when Lee was forced to relate that in a single night a lieutenant and twenty-four men of one regiment had gone over even while ten men from a single artillery battery crossed the lines to the enemy.[19] Yet their efforts proved unavailing. In a speech in late September, Davis exhorted his fellow citizens to renewed efforts and promised that "if one-half the men now absent without leave will return to duty, we can defeat the enemy."[20]

Yet Davis was part of the problem. When it came to shooting deserters, he was too tender-hearted. During the past year the number of pardons Davis had issued to deserters had been on the rise. On the contrary, Lee had favored taking a hard line with deserters ever since the amnesty he had suggested to Davis after Sharpsburg had backfired. As early as October 1863, Lee had expressed to Seddon his "serious apprehension of the consequences of a relapse into that lenient policy which our past experience has shown to be so ruinous to the army." Nevertheless, the pardons went on, and in March 1864 Davis had written Lee to suspend executions altogether "to give time to examine all the cases of men sentenced to death in your army now before me."[21] In November a message came across Lee's camp desk that summed up the problem. A staff officer reported, "Major-General Pickett [who had returned to duty] reports about 100 men from his command in the guardhouse charged with the crime of desertion. He accounts for this state of things by the fact that every man sentenced to be shot for desertion in his division for the past two months has been reprieved." Lee sent the report to the secretary of war along with a note that "desertion is increasing in the army notwithstanding all my efforts to stop it." He recommended "a rigid execution of the law." Seddon passed the paper along to the president, who was not at all pleased with it. "When deserters are arrested," he penned across the bottom of it, "they should be tried, and if the sentences are reviewed and remitted that is not a proper subject for the criticism of a military commander."[22] For the time being Lee would have to content himself with forwarding reports of the growing desertion rate without editorial comments by himself or his officers.

Throughout the months of the summer and autumn, while Lee, Davis, and Seddon wrestled with the problems of filling the army's ranks as well as its haversacks, the deadlock in the trenches continued. The threat of defeat on the battlefield did not worry Lee as much as those to his army's continuing viability posed by the growing shortages of manpower and supply, but even in this he was not optimistic. To Davis he wrote a few days after the siege began, "I hope your Excellency will put no reliance in what I can do individually, for I feel that will be very little. The enemy has a strong position, & is able to deal us more injury than from any other point he has ever taken. Still we must try & defeat them."[23] Although he hoped to be able to deal with any direct assaults Grant might launch in the immediate future–and believed such moves on the part of the northern commander to be unlikely–he entertained no illusions about the likely results of an extended siege. His hopes turned increasingly to various Confederate moves aimed at drawing northern attention away from the South's desperate situation around Richmond. "I still think it is our policy to draw the attention of the enemy to his own territory." Thus, in late June, when Early had driven off but not destroyed the Federal force in the Shenandoah Valley Lee recommended to Davis that the partial success be followed up by an advance down the Valley and across the Potomac. That would get Grant's attention and possibly force him either to attack Lee in his entrenchments or to weaken his army by detaching troops to stop Early.[24]

Such a small raid across the Potomac was in keeping with Davis's ideas and was not very different from what he had proposed to Johnston and Beauregard during the first autumn of the war. He readily gave his support to Lee's plans. These included another scheme, for which both of them had high hopes, involving a projected lightning-fast amphibious raid on the Federal prisoner-of-war camp at Point Lookout, Maryland, on the lower Potomac. Freed, armed, and organized, the prisoners were envisioned as a powerful fighting force that would then join up with Early. Davis and Lee corresponded frequently and extensively on the matter that summer.[25] In the end, however, both expeditions failed of their intended purposes. The Point Lookout raid depended on surprise, and this element was obviously lost by

July 8, when Davis had to inform Lee that it was "spoken of on the streets." He gave Lee authority to cancel the mission, and Lee in turn left the decision up to the officers who had been slated to lead it. It was never attempted.[26] Early's troops did cross the Potomac, and after scattering a few home guards and militia, actually appeared outside the fortifications of Washington, creating a stir within the city but posing little real threat to take it. A division of troops from Grant's army had arrived in time to man the defenses and bar further progress by the Confederates. While two more divisions were on the way from the Army of the Potomac—ample force to deal with Early—the detachment resulted in no significant reduction of pressure around Petersburg, where the grinding trench warfare went on. Regretfully, Lee wrote Davis, "I had hoped that General Grant, rather than weaken his army, would have attempted to drive us from our position. I fear I shall not be able to attack him to advantage." By the middle of July no further prospect of relief existed from Early's expedition than from the abortive Point Lookout raid, though Lee continued to hope that with additional reinforcements from the Army of Northern Virginia, Early might be able to accomplish something in the Shenandoah.[27]

Davis supported Lee's efforts in these matters, but his primary attention was focused elsewhere. In Georgia, Johnston had steadily retreated before Sherman until in mid-July it became apparent that the Confederate general was going to abandon Atlanta without a fight. At the last minute Davis sought to avert the calamity of Atlanta's loss by replacing Johnston with a commander of more nerve. At this point he sought Lee's advice in the matter. Lee counseled caution, hinting that it might be best not to make such a momentous change at the present time. If a change were nevertheless to be made, Lee subtly suggested that of Johnston's two senior corps commanders, Joseph Hardee would be preferable to John B. Hood.[28] For once Davis passed over Lee's advice and proceeded to give the job to Hood. With his back to Atlanta, Hood was forced to fight three desperate battles within eight days during late July. In each of them he got much the worse of the exchange, but when they were over he continued to hold Atlanta in a deadlock that came increasingly to resemble the present siege of Richmond and Petersburg far to the north.

When he did turn his attention to operations in the Virginia theater, Davis took an interest in the Richmond and Petersburg lines themselves and in how possible Confederate moves on this front might break the Federal stranglehold. He took frequent, long horseback rides to inspect the fortifications, often riding alone, to the dismay of his wife and staff. When he found affairs in a given sector not to his liking, he was quick to inform Lee, gently, of the perceived problem.[29] In August he gave orders for John C. Pemberton, lately lieutenant general and unsuccessful defender of Vicksburg and now a field officer of artillery, to set up mortar batteries for the purpose of "dislodging the enemy by rendering his pontoon bridge [over the James] useless to him." It was an unlikely expedient with the means available, but, as Pemberton said of Davis, "he nevertheless desires the experiment to be tried."[30]

Lee sought other means of ending the deadlock around Richmond, looking farther afield and continuing to place much hope in what Early might do in the Valley. When intelligence reports revealed that the Federal force opposing Early had been strengthened, Lee responded with his old audacity by recommending to Davis that two more divisions of the Army of Northern Virginia be sent to the Valley. After a consultation in Richmond during the first part of August, Davis and Lee were agreed in the matter and ordered the movement, despite the fact that it "would leave not a man out of the trenches for any emergency which might arise" along the Richmond and Petersburg lines.[31] For Lee this was the only logical course of action, for he still held to his old assessment of what would be required for Confederate victory. In a letter to Davis that summer he wrote, "I have no idea that Grant will evacuate his position unless forced." In another letter he was even more explicit. "If we can defeat or drive the armies of the enemy from the field," he wrote, "we shall have peace."[32]

Nothing could have seemed farther away, however, as the summer of 1864 declined into fall, and the Confederacy's hopes seemed to decline with it. In mid-August Grant induced Lee to shift some of his forces north of the James by feinting an attack in that sector. Then the Federals slashed at Lee's weakened southern flank, successfully taking control of the Weldon Railroad southwest of Petersburg. Lee rushed troops back across the James, but his efforts to dislodge the northerners proved unavailing. Davis spent the day watching the inconsequential skirmishing north of the James that had prompted Lee to overbalance in that direction.[33] Back in his office several days later, he expressed to Lee his dismay at the present turn of events. "I cannot say I was surprised that the enemy have been able to break through the Weldon railroad," Davis wrote, "though I regret they should have had time to fortify themselves as a consequence of feeble attacks made upon them at the time of their first occupation of it."[34]

September brought more bad news. Atlanta fell. In hopes of repairing the South's drooping western fortunes, Davis traveled to Georgia and Alabama later that month. He took Beauregard with him. Now that Lee's army was concentrated in the Richmond-Petersburg area, the Creole was reduced in practice to little more than a corps commander, a role with which he was dissatisfied. Lee was willing to part with his services, and Davis hoped he might do some good in a supervising and coordinating role in the western theater. In speeches in Macon, Montgomery, and elsewhere, Davis had high praise for Lee. He spoke of his own preference for the role of a general to that of commander in chief and of his "faith in his capacity for arms." He deprecated the prospect of a compromise peace or of what influence might be exerted on the present northern election campaign by an apparent southern willingness to enter into such an arrangement. "Victory in the field is the surest element of strength to a peace party," he proclaimed. This sounded much like Lee's belief in driving "the armies of the enemy from the field," but Davis had a different concept of "victory in the field." "We have beaten Grant," he boasted in the same speech, "and still defiantly hold our lines before Richmond and Petersburg." Such a victory was purely defensive and fully consistent with Davis's sense that for the Confederacy, anything short of final defeat was in fact a triumph. In this sense he concluded, "Let us win battles and we shall have [peace] overtures soon enough."[35]

Yet while he was gone, Grant drove Lee out of crucial sectors of Richmond's outer line of fortifications north of the James. Lee managed to stabilize the situation on the inner lines, but his army had been stretched that much closer to the breaking point. Out in the Shenandoah, Early had been defeated the day before Davis started south and was whipped again and driven far southward up the Valley before the president returned to Richmond. Arriving back in the capital early in October, Davis was just in time to confer with Lee on an attempt to retake the lost entrenchments, but like every other trial of arms this month, it too proved a failure for the Confederates.[36] Another blow came on October 19, when a battle that began with promise of victory for Early ended with crushing defeat. The southern forces in the Valley were reduced to mere nuisance status, unable to accomplish anything further of significance. Even more important, this battle, Cedar Creek, provided an added morale boost for the North less than three weeks before northern voters went to the polls in an election that was little less than a referendum on the continuation of the war. After the string of Union victories through the late summer and fall, such a boost was hardly needed. On November 8, northern voters resoundingly reelected Abraham Lincoln and in so doing determined that the Union would continue to prosecute the war for at least another four years if necessary. By this time nothing could have been clearer to most observers than the fact that nothing like four years was going to be necessary. With the Union elections of 1864, the Confederacy's last flickering flame of hope finally guttered out once and for all.

Lee knew it, and evidence suggests that ever increasing numbers of his fellow southerners were coming to recognize it as well.[37] Davis would never admit it as long as he personally remained at liberty to dispute it. No one was eager to surrender, and in the face of Davis's steadfast refusal to consider such a course, none ventured to press it upon him. Thus the South was required to endure such additional months of slaughter and destruction as might be necessary to render it—or at least its organized authorities—incapable of further resistance. The slaughter began within the month, as Hood hurled his army in a series of vain assaults against entrenched Federals at Franklin, Tennessee, on November 30. Some of the Federals were equipped with repeating rifles, and the execution among Hood's troops was ghastly. Little more than two weeks later, Hood's army was even more decisively defeated just outside Nashville. The destruction of property took other forms but proceeded with even less delay. On November 18 Davis asked Lee to "please give me your views as to the action proper under the circumstances of Sherman's movement on Macon."[38] The march to the sea had begun two days before, and no significant Confederate force remained available to stop Sherman from fulfilling his promise to Grant to "make Georgia howl." Davis and Lee conferred in Richmond for several days but could find no solution to the hopeless military situation to the south. Over the weeks that followed, Davis referred to Lee suggestions from Beauregard and Bragg that he send troops from the Army of Northern Virginia to stop Sherman from reaching Savannah, but with his own lines pressed almost to the breaking point, Lee had to decline.[39] Sherman reached the sea on December 13, and eight days later occupied Savannah as Confederate forces fled northward up the coast.

During the month of December, Davis suffered from a return of his neuralgia, and although he was far from the dying condition rumors assigned him, he was sufficiently incapacitated to be confined to his house for a number of days. Once again he continued to transact business from his sickbed, and more than ever he turned to Lee for advice on all manner of military matters throughout the length and breadth of the Confederacy. In his illness he was unable to continue his previously frequent practice of riding out to the lines to confer with Lee in person, and he summoned Lee to Richmond for conference even more frequently than before. The meetings were informal and friendly, though the trips may have been a strain on Lee. Davis seems to have relied on the general as much for moral support as for military counsel. On one occasion, Varina recalled, Lee arrived "evidently worn out and worried, to find Mr. Davis lying quite ill on a divan, in a little morning-room in which we received only our intimate friends." Apologizing for "coming in on the white carpet with his splashed boots," Lee "sat down and plunged at once into army matters." A long conversation followed, "until both were worn out."[40]

Davis's emotional dependence on Lee, coupled with the absence from Richmond of Braxton Bragg—sent to look after affairs on the southern coast some weeks before—led Davis to continue his frequent summons to Lee for conference. Lee, of course, was a busy man, and such demands on his time could not always be met to the president's satisfaction. By far the most unpleasant incident between the two men involved just such a problem. Davis wrote Lee early in February that rumors about his opinions were holding up the passage of necessary legislation. "Come over," the president instructed, "I wish to have your views on the subject." Lee had his hands full at the moment and explained this in his reply. "Send me the measures," he offered, "and I will send you my views."[41] This was far from satisfying the president, who probably desired Lee's sympathetic ear in the midst of the problems created by a contrary and contentious Congress as much as he did Lee's opinions on matters of policy. In a long and angry reply, Davis wrote, "Rest assured I will not ask your views in answer to measures. Your counsels are no longer wanted in the matter." Lee immediately went to Richmond, and the affair seems to have been patched up.[42]

The continuing good relations between Davis and Lee are all the more remarkable in view of the mood then taking hold of the Confederate capital. An insistent undertone of murmuring among politicians and people alike made Davis a scapegoat for the Confederacy's troubles and vaunted Lee as the best solution for them. "There is supposed to be a conspiracy on foot to transfer some of the powers of the Executive to Gen. Lee," John B. Jones wrote in his diary on the last day of 1864. The next day he noted that "the disaffection is intense and wide-spread" and that "consternation and despair are expanding among the people." "Nearly all desire to see Gen. Lee at the head of affairs; and the President is resolved to yield the position to no man during his term of service. Nor would Gen. Lee take it."[43] Several days later, another bureaucrat reported a rumor of "an entire change of the Executive by the resignation of the President and Vice-President," a move that despite constitutional provisions would, he thought, result in making "Lee commander-in-chief."[44] Elsewhere, there was talk of an equally extraconstitutional congressional "no-confidence" vote against the president.[45] On January 17 the Virginia legislature unanimously passed a secret resolution stating its opinion that "the appointment of General Robert E. Lee to the command of all the Armies of the Confederate States would promote their efficiency and operate powerfully to reanimate the spirits of the Armies, as well as of the people of the several States, and to inspire increased confidence in the final success of our cause." The legislators also threw in a few kind words for Davis, making the whole slightly easier to swallow.[46] No sugarcoating, however, could have made palatable their action the next day in calling for the resignation of the president's cabinet. This was especially hard for Seddon to take, since Virginia was his own state. He at once submitted his resignation, which Davis reluctantly accepted on February 1.[47]

To the demand for Lee's appointment as general in chief, Davis returned a gracious reply, assuring the Virginians that only Lee's reluctance to assume the role while still retaining direct command of the Army of Northern Virginia was preventing such an assignment.[48] The same day Davis wrote to Lee. "It has been reported to me," he explained, "that you had changed your opinion in regard to the extension of your command, while retaining command of the Army of N. Virginia." Therefore, Davis renewed his offer, first made back at the time of the Gettysburg campaign, for Lee to add the Department of South Carolina, Georgia, and Florida to his present command of Virginia and North Carolina. Or, if Lee were willing, he could have command of all Confederate forces east of the Mississippi or even resume his role as "Commander of all the Armies of the Confederacy," so long as he retained direct command of the Army of Northern Virginia.[49] Lee hastily replied that he had not changed his mind and that he did "not know how such a report originated." Even if he had the ability, he would not have the time to direct affairs on so many fronts, and although he was "greatly gratified" at the confidence Davis showed in him by offering him so much responsibility, he did not think he could "accomplish any good" with it. "I am willing to undertake any service to which you think proper to assign me," he concluded, "but I do not wish you to be misled as to the extent of my capacity."[50]

Meanwhile, even more trouble was brewing in the Confederate Congress. On January 15, the Senate passed by a fourteen-to-two vote a joint resolution calling on the president to make Lee general in chief and to restore Johnston to command of the remaining fragments of the Army of Tennessee. On the nineteenth, the House of Representatives gave its assent to the measure.[51] This was wormwood and gall to Davis, for Johnston was anathema to him, and the elevation of Lee, though something he himself had sought, was when pushed by Congress in this manner a clear repudiation of his own cherished role as commander in chief. Inwardly he seethed with the injustice and unconstitutionality of it all, and those close to him knew it.[52] Yet in what was in some ways his finest hour as the political leader of the Confederacy, he maintained his outward demeanor. "The President is calm," Jones wrote in his diary. Davis apparently succeeded in working out a compromise with Congress by which a bill would be passed, and receive his signature, creating the post of general in chief to have "command of the military forces of the Confederate States."[53] On February 1, Davis fulfilled the legislators' expectation by naming Lee to the newly created post.[54] Several days later, official orders were issued by the Adjutant and Inspector General's Office, and on February 9 Lee formally assumed his new duties.[55]

Smooth cooperation between the president and his new general in chief would now be that much more difficult. Davis could not possibly be ignorant of the fact that Lee's new title represented Congress' rejection of Davis's own conduct of the war, or that Congress now intended that Lee should be not quite subject to Davis's direction in the future conduct of the war. Others expected Lee to dispense with Davis's military role entirely. Longstreet wrote Lee anticipating he would "proceed to handle the Confederate armies and affairs under his own good judgment" and urging the restoration of Johnston. Others agreed, but to Longstreet's intense disgust, "instead of exercising authority on a scale commensurate with the views of Congress and the call of the crisis," Lee continued his deferential manner of dealing with the president.[56]

As always, Lee handled the president's feelings gently. Writing to notify Davis of his assumption of command, he stated, "I know I am indebted entirely to your indulgence and kind consideration for this honorable position," and he begged Davis to continue such kindness "and allow me to refer to you at all times for counsel and advice." He hoped he could relieve the president "from a portion of the constant labor and anxiety which now presses upon you." Having thus endeavored to assuage Davis, Lee got down to business. First, he mentioned briefly that as commanding general he would need to depend greatly on subordinate generals and that if any of these men failed in his duty, "I must ask for their removal."[57] Although still deferential, this was a somewhat different tone from what Lee had previously been wont to use on Davis.

His next concern was of even greater significance. As winter had settled in that year, the rate of desertion had risen steadily and was now at a disastrous level. Lee had consistently attributed the exodus of troops to "scant fare, light clothing, [and] constant duty."[58] Now he proposed to Davis another proclamation of amnesty to all deserters who would return promptly to their units, "with the assurance that this will be the last act of amnesty extended for such offenses." Most important, however, the proclamation would include the "promise that hereafter offenders will receive the full sentence of the courts upon their conviction, without suspension, remission, or delays, from which there need be no appeal for clemency." Lee was trying to stop the president's habit of pardoning convicted deserters so frequently that it was hard to convince soldiers that a firing squad awaited them should they be apprehended after deserting. "All who may desert after the publication of the order," Lee stated hopefully, "shall receive quick and merited punishment."[59] In this last endeavor, Lee was unsuccessful. Davis wrote back the next day, approving the new proclamation of amnesty, but protesting that he had not been too free in issuing pardons. "Sentences have been rarely remitted except upon new evidence which if it had been before the Court would have changed their finding." He also observed that there appeared to be a tendency to hasten convicted deserters to execution in order to prevent their having time to appeal to the president for clemency.[60] This was probably as true as it was understandable, and it was to remain the only sure method of punishing convicted deserters.

Nevertheless, Lee was successful in retaining the kind feelings of the president. On the same day he wrote to deny Lee's request for a curtailment of pardons, Davis wrote another letter praising Lee's "patriotic devotion" and admitting that "the burden already imposed on you [was] too heavy to enable an ordinary man to bear an additional weight." He assured Lee that the promotion had "been so fully won, that the fact of conferring it can add nothing to your fame," and he acknowledged that Lee had been too busy to come up to Richmond for conference but expressed his wish to see him "when circumstances will permit." He signed the letter, "With sincere regard, I am, as ever your friend."[61]

Lee soon was forced to turn to the president again for solution of another of the army's nagging problems. The supply situation had been growing steadily worse during the winter. On February 8 Lee had reported to the secretary of war that a large portion of his army had been three days in the line of battle in "the most inclement" weather of the winter and that "some of the men had been without meat for three days" while "all were suffering from reduced rations and scant clothing, exposed to battle, cold, hail, and sleet." The chief commissary of the Army of Northern Virginia reported that he had not one pound of meat on hand. "If some change is not made and the commissary department reorganized, I apprehend dire results," Lee wrote. "The physical strength of the men, if their courage survives, must fail under this treatment." After reading the dispatch Davis endorsed it, "This is too sad to be patiently considered, and cannot have occurred without criminal neglect or gross incapacity. Let supplies be had by purchase, or borrowing or other possible mode."[62] The problem, however, was to some extent the fault of Northrop. Even in the face of the president's demand that he beg, borrow, or steal the means of feeding the troops, Northrop seemed less concerned with remedying the problem than with explaining why all would have been well if his directions had been carried out. He even had the temerity to suggest that the problem was at least partially Lee's fault.[63] Davis rarely overcame his loyalty to old friends, no matter how miserably they failed. This time, however, was one of the rarities. Within the week Northrop was gone, and the office of the commissary general was filled by Isaac St. John, who had functioned successfully in the Confederacy's Nitre and Mining Bureau.[64]

Davis's confidence in Lee was shortly to be tested even further. Pressure for the assignment of Joseph E. Johnston to some military command continued to grow.[65] In response, on February 18 Davis wrote a lengthy paper to Congress, explaining his reasons for not assigning Johnston. In well over 3,000 words, the president recounted the military career—and repeated failures of nerve—of the controversial general. "My opinion of Gen. Johnston's unfitness of command," Davis concluded, "has ripened slowly and against my inclination into a conviction so settled, that it would be impossible for me again to feel confidence in him as the commander of an army in the field. The power to assign Generals to appropriate duties is a function of the trust confided to me by my countrymen . . . ; while I hold it, nothing shall induce me to shrink from its responsibilities or to violate the obligations it imposes."[66] Having gone to the trouble of preparing such a paper, Davis thought twice about sending it. To do so might imply that Congress legitimately had something to say about the selection and assignment of generals. To avoid giving color to such an inference, Davis felt he would have to accompany the paper with an explicit protest against congressional meddling. That would create controversy that he did not need at the moment, so he filed the lengthy paper away unsent.[67] His restraint paid off in a way he had not anticipated, saving him considerable embarrassment in the turn events took next.

The situation in South Carolina had gone beyond critical. While Davis composed his examination of Johnston's failings, Columbia went from stately city to raging inferno to smoldering ruins. Burning cotton, ignited by fleeing Confederates and fanned by high winds, had touched off an enormous conflagration as the city changed hands. Sherman's army, having completed the destruction of the military and industrial installations there and having at least tried to fight the flames in the business and residential districts, was preparing to continue its irresistible northward progress. The scant Confederate forces opposing its advance were under the command of Beauregard, but neither he nor anyone else could have stopped Sherman's tough, resourceful, confident–and numerous–midwesterners. In desperation, Davis wrote to Lee on the eighteenth, "Reports from So. Carolina induce me to suggest that you go to General Beauregard's Headquarters for personal conference and observation as soon as the circumstances in your front will permit."[68] Lee, who found it difficult to spare himself from direction of his own army long enough to ride the twenty or so miles into Richmond, was hardly in a position to make the trip to South Carolina. His solution, instead, was apparently both to provide senior advice for Beauregard and to silence a substantial segment of public unrest by appointing Johnston to take command of Beauregard and all of the Confederate troops south of the Petersburg trenches. Davis could not have been enthusiastic about the move, but he permitted it. As he explained it to a friend several days later, "General Lee has asked that General Johnston should be ordered to report to him for duty, and . . . I have complied with his wish, in the hope that Genl. Johnston's soldierly qualities may be made serviceable to his country when acting under General Lee's orders, and that in his new position those defects which I found manifested by him when serving as an independent command will be remedied by the control of the General in Chief."[69]

Late in February, Longstreet, in the course of a routine flag-of-truce conversation, was approached by Federal Gen. E. O. C. Ord with the suggestion that perhaps the war might be ended by a military convention negotiated between Grant and Lee. Longstreet discussed the matter that evening in a conference with Davis, Lee, and Breckinridge, who had replaced Seddon as secretary of war. Several days later, Longstreet met Ord a second time, and they decided that Grant and Lee should definitely open up communications.[70] Davis directed Lee to go ahead with the meeting if he saw any value in it. He readily granted the general "all the supplemental authority you may need in the consideration of any proposition for a military convention, or the appointment of a commission to enter into such an arrangement as will cause at least temporary suspension of hostilities."[71] Lee was not optimistic. "My belief is that he will consent to no terms, unless coupled with the condition of our return to the Union." Then remarkably

Lee continued, "Whether this will be acceptable to our people yet awhile I cannot say—I shall go to Richmond tomorrow or next day to see you, & hope you will grant me an hour's conversation on the subject."[72] On the same day, Lee wrote to Grant proposing that they meet "to submit the subjects of controversy between the belligerents to a military convention."[73]

Lee had known the likely outcome of the war for some months now. He had said that the beginning of the Richmond siege made defeat a matter of time, and only the possibility of Lincoln's defeat in the November elections could have held out the hope that the North might not be willing to invest as much time as would be needed. Now Lee was ready to seek peace even at the price of giving up the dream of a Confederate nation. The next day, March 3, he talked with his subordinate General John B. Gordon, who urged that the best course now was to "make terms with the enemy, the best we can get." Otherwise, "abandon Richmond and Petersburg, unite by rapid marches with General Johnston in North Carolina, and strike Sherman before Grant can join him." When Gordon asked his commander's opinion, Lee replied, "I agree with you fully." The conversation continued, with Lee explaining that he was a soldier and this question was political and he had, therefore, no rightful say in it with the government. Gordon was insistent—Lee must use his influence to bring about peace negotiations. Lee could not, of course, inform Gordon that he had, just the day before, written Grant for precisely that purpose, but he did tell him he was going to Richmond the next day to talk with Davis on the subject.[74] Lee's letter to Davis as well as his conversation with Gordon strongly suggest that when he did go to Richmond on March 4, he probably went with the intention of presenting to the president the case for making the best possible terms at once, even at the cost of reunion. If he tried, he probably did not get far. Davis was utterly closed to the idea of any peace short of Confederate independence. Lee later reported to Gordon that "nothing could be done at Richmond." Congress seemed to have no appreciation of the seriousness of the situation; Lee had high praise for Davis's steadfastness and amazing continued faith in the Confederacy's hopes of victory, but he did remark pointedly, "You know that the President is very pertinacious in opinion and purpose."[75] The whole question of Lee's entering into any immediate negotiations with Grant was rendered moot even before Lee's return to Petersburg by Grant's reply to his note of the second. The Federal government forbade him, he informed Lee, to enter into negotiations on any political questions.

Davis and Lee had more to talk about during their March 4 conference than peace negotiations. Lee had told Gordon he agreed with him, and

Gordon's second course of action had been abandoning Richmond. As Davis later recalled this "long and free conference," Lee "stated that the circumstances had forced on him the conclusion that the evacuation of Petersburg was but a question of time." Richmond would naturally follow. Davis suggested that if this were the case, perhaps it would be better to move at once rather than wait until the last minute to be driven out in desperate condition. Lee explained that this was impossible because the army's artillery and draft horses were too weak to haul their loads over the still muddy roads. When it did become possible to move, Lee specified that their retreat should be southward, toward Danville, Virginia, where they would link up with Johnston to defeat Sherman. Then they hoped that "Grant, drawn far from his base of supplies into the midst of a hostile population . . . might yet be defeated." In the meantime, Lee's horses were to get extra rations of corn to strengthen them for the hard pulling ahead.[76]

A week or two later, as Davis recalled, Lee presented to him a plan that might yet, he hoped, avert the fall of Richmond. Lee would strike the Union lines near Petersburg and try to roll them up. If he could, it would force Grant to pull in the long westward extension of his lines and allow Lee to hold Richmond and Petersburg while detaching a large force to join Johnston and defeat Sherman.[77] It was at best a forlorn hope, but it was all that remained. Added urgency came from a telegram from Johnston on March 23. It concluded, "Sherman's course cannot be hindered by the small force I have. I can do no more than annoy him. I respectfully suggest that it is no longer a question whether you leave present position. You have only to decide where to meet." For once, this was not Johnston's habitual pessimism but the sober truth, and Lee sensed it. He transmitted the wire to Davis, adding, "Please give me your counsel."[78] Davis seems to have made no immediate reply.

On March 25 Lee launched his last offensive, aimed at a part of the Union fortifications known as Fort Stedman. The assault went in just before daylight, and by 8:00 A.M. the fighting was over and the surviving attackers swarmed back into Confederate lines. The operation had cost Lee one-third of the troops committed and one-tenth of his total strength. It had accomplished nothing, and in terms of available Union troop strength northern casualties had been negligible. Lee reported the results, as optimistically as he could, to the secretary of war that day, and the next day he wrote to Davis, explaining the situation. "I fear now it will be impossible to prevent a junction between Grant and Sherman," he wrote, "nor do I deem it prudent that this army should maintain its position until the latter shall approach too near." Enumerating the weakness of Johnston's and his own forces and the strength of Grant's and Sherman's, he concluded, "I have thought it proper to make the above statement to your Excellency of the condition of affairs, knowing that you will do whatever may be in your power to give relief."[79]

But relief was now beyond the power of Davis or any other Confederate. Congress had adjourned with all but indecent haste a week before, as the members hurried to leave the doomed city. It was apparently about the time of Lee's attack on Fort Stedman that Davis informed Varina "gently, but decidedly" that she and the children would be leaving Richmond. "If I live," he told her, "you can come to me when the struggle is ended, but I do not expect to survive the destruction of constitutional liberty."[80] On April 1 Davis wrote a lengthy letter to Lee, discussing his attempts to boost the army's numbers and the problems presented by growing public distrust of the Confederate government. "Last night we had rumors of a general engagement on your right," the president noted. "Your silence in regard to it leads to the conclusion that it was unwarranted."[81]

In fact, it was all too true. Grant had now begun his last offensive, and it was an entirely different affair than Lee's effort of the week before. A powerful combined force of infantry and cavalry under Maj. Gen. Philip Sheridan swung west beyond the two armies' flanks to Dinwiddie Court House, whence he could drive north against Lee's position and the vital Southside Railroad. The rumor of action that had reached Richmond on the last day of March had reflected the clash between this force and some 12,000 Confederates under Pickett, whom Lee had deployed to block the move. Pickett was compelled to fall back to Five Forks that evening, closer to Confederate lines. There Sheridan struck him the next afternoon. Pickett himself seems to have been absent from his lines, having chosen this of all times to attend a shad bake some miles to the rear. He probably could have done little in any case to stop the Union juggernaut. The Army of Northern Virginia's entire right flank had crumbled by nightfall, and nothing could be more certain than that Grant would press his advantage in the morning. While Lee waited that day for news of the engagement, he wrote a grim letter to Davis. Even if Pickett held at Five Forks, the situation was desperate. "The movement of Gen. Grant to Dinwiddie C[ourt] H[ouse] seriously threatens our position, and diminishes our ability to maintain our present lines in front of Richmond and Petersburg," Lee informed the president. "This in my opinion obliges us to prepare for the necessity of evacuating our position on James River at once." Once again, Lee felt the need of direction from his civilian superiors. He was just playing out the string now, continuing to fight because he believed it his duty to carry out the will of the civil authorities. Understandably, he wanted to be very sure what that will was. "I should like very much to have the views of your Excellency upon this matter as well as counsel," he wrote, "and would repair to Richmond for the purpose, did I not feel that my presence here is necessary. Should I find it practicable I will do so, but should it be convenient for your Excellency or the Secretary of War to visit Hd Qrs, I should be glad to see you."[82]

Next morning several anxious officials gathered at the War Office to await news from the front. At 9:30 a dispatch arrived from Lee announcing that Grant's assault that morning had broken his lines in several places and urging immediate preparations to evacuate Richmond. A copy of the telegram was sent to Davis, but Postmaster General Reagan, rushing off immediately with the news, reached the president first, meeting him as he was on his way to St. Paul's Church. Around 11:00 A.M. another dispatch from Lee painted an even grimmer picture. His army would be pulling out that evening, and Richmond must be evacuated by then. A messenger took this wire to Davis as he sat in his pew at worship. Quietly and without tumult he rose and left the church. The news that the evacuation was to be carried out this very day came as a shock to him. "It was not believed to be so near at hand," he later confessed.[83] Davis's first reply to Lee was to question the necessity of such haste. "To move tonight will involve the loss of many valuables," the president complained in a telegram that day.[84] Lee was in no mood for such remonstrance and in a rare outburst of temper tore up the message, muttering savagely, "I am sure I gave him sufficent notice."[85] As usual, however, Lee managed to control himself and replied respectfully, "Your telegram rec[eive]d. I think it will be necessary to retire tonight. . . . The Enemy is so strong that they will cross above us to close us in between the James & Appomattox Rivers—If we remain."[86] That same busy afternoon he managed to reply to Davis's letter of the previous day, adding an explanation of the army's recent actions and of how he planned to move it in the retreat. "I regret to be obliged to write such a hurried letter to your Excellency," he concluded, "but I am in the presence of the enemy, endeavoring to resist his advance."[87] Davis failed to receive this letter and so was to be handicapped in his efforts to support the army and make decisions during the days that followed.[88]

Davis spent the afternoon packing up papers at the executive office, then went home and packed his personal things. "Then," as he later recalled, "leaving all else in care of the housekeeper, I waited until notified of the time when the train would depart; then, going to the station, started for

Richmond after its capture by Federal troops. (Courtesy of National Archives, 111-B-562, Civil War 117)

Danville," toward which Lee was supposed to be retreating.[89] "It was near midnight," recalled Reagan, when the "frightfully overcrowded" train bearing the president and cabinet, among many others, left Richmond. The postmaster general remembered the long night journey to Danville as one of oppressive sorrow.[90] The train pulled into Danville on the morning of the third, and with almost bizarre efficiency under the circumstances, "rooms were obtained, and," as Davis described it, "the different departments resumed their routine labors." Davis set himself to the task of supervising the collection of "supplies of various kinds for General Lee's army."[91] He was in communication with Johnston and Beauregard to the south but despite repeated efforts was unable to get any information about Lee.[92] On both the fifth and sixth of April he wrote Varina that he was uncertain as to what course to take until he heard from the Army of Northern Virginia. "I am unwilling to leave Va.," he told her, but "cannot decide on my movements until those of the army are better developed."[93]

While in Danville the president also hoped to revive civilian morale. Seemingly unaware that he was by this time all but alone in his desire to prolong the conflict and his hope of achieving anything thereby, Davis issued on April 5 a proclamation to "The People of the Confederate States of America." "The General-in-Chief of our Army has found it necessary to make such movements of the troops as to uncover the Capital," he began, "and thus involve the withdrawal of the Government from the city of Richmond." He admitted that this was a serious blow but maintained that

Lee's army would now be free to maneuver more aggressively. The North, Davis asserted, was nearly spent and could not keep up the fight much longer. "It is for us, my countrymen, to show by our bearing under reverses, how wretched has been the self-deception of those who have believed us less able to endure misfortune with fortitude, than to encounter danger with courage." He said that the war was now entering "a new phase" in which "relieved from the necessity of guarding cities and particular points" the Confederate army would be "free to move from point to point, and strike in detail the detachments and garrisons of the enemy," with the advantage of operating in familiar and friendly country against a foe far from his base. In short, "nothing is now needed to render our triumph certain, but the exhibition of our own unquenchable resolve. Let us but will it, and we are free."[94] Speaking of this proclamation years later, Davis admitted, "Viewed by the light of subsequent events, it may fairly be said it was over-sanguine.[95]

He had been right, of course, in his claim that southerners could win their independence if as one man they determined to continue the fight until they succeeded or were all dead, though it might have taken decades. That, however, was out of the question. The resolve of the southern people had been thoroughly quenched and too few of them willed any longer the sort of freedom of which Davis spoke. The "self-deception" had been on his part in not seeing this, and as for the Army of Northern Virginia, it was free to maneuver in precisely one direction, west, and in one manner, as rapidly as possible, while overwhelming Union forces closed in for the kill from the north, east, and south.

On Sunday, April 9, a full week after Davis had last heard from Lee and had left Richmond, the president received his first news from the Army of Northern Virginia. It was a dispatch from Lee, short almost to the point of being cryptic, sent three days before and informing Davis that the army would be at Farmville that night.[96] This at least revealed that Lee had been unable to maintain his southwest course toward Danville but had been forced, presumably by enemy action, to bear due west toward Lynchburg. If the Army of Northern Virginia had continued on that course at about the same pace it had kept up since leaving the Richmond and Petersburg lines under duress one week before, it should now be perhaps twenty miles or so from Lynchburg, somewhere in the vicinity of the little town of Appomattox Court House. Davis immediately replied to Lee's brief message and made arrangements for setting up a line of couriers to provide for rapid communication. He wrote of the military preparations being made at Danville and of Johnston's situation in North Carolina. He mentioned the fall of the vital

McLean House, Appomattox Court House. (Courtesy of National Archives, 165-SB-99, Civil War 111)

manufacturing center at Selma, Alabama, to Union forces driving southward into that state. "I had hoped to have seen you at an earlier period," Davis continued, "and trust soon to meet you. . . . You will realize the reluctance I feel to leave the soil of Virginia, and appreciate my anxiety to win success north of the Roanoke" River. "I hope soon to hear from you at this point," he concluded, "where offices have been opened to keep up the current business, until more definite knowledge would enable us to form more permanent plans."[97]

While Davis penned his dispatch, Lee, sixty-five miles to the northeast at Appomattox Court House, rode through the lines under flag of truce to the trim and pleasant home of Wilmer McLean, designated as the appointed place for a meeting with Grant. By 4:00 P.M. it was all over. Lee had surrendered the Army of Northern Virginia. Back in Danville, Davis's first hint of disaster came the next day, from a young lieutenant who had fled the army the night before the surrender when he began to suspect such action was imminent. Other fragments of information drifted in throughout that Monday, all pointing to the same thing. Davis passed the grim news along to

Johnston and then as scouts brought word that Union cavalry was ranging southward uncomfortably close to Danville directed that the government should move on to Greensboro, North Carolina. Additional stark evidence of the disintegration of Confederate morale came with the news received as Davis and his cabinet were boarding the train that a civilian mob was looting the Confederate supply stocks in Danville.[98]

On April 11, the fugitive government reached Greensboro, where Beauregard had his headquarters. The president promptly telegraphed Johnston. "As your situation may render best, I will go to your Head Quarters . . . or you can come here." The latter would be preferable, he explained, since Beauregard then could also take part in the conference. Davis still had "no official report from General Lee." The problem at hand, however, as Davis saw it, was to decide where and how to concentrate the remaining Confederate forces so as to deal with Sherman and Grant. "Your more intimate knowledge of the date for the solution of the problem deters me from making a specific suggestion on that point."[99] Johnston left Raleigh by train about midnight and arrived in Greensboro the next morning, Wednesday, April 12, around 8:00 A.M. An hour or two later, Davis summoned both generals and the cabinet to a meeting at the house where he had been staying. After some discussion of the military situations faced by Beauregard and Johnston, Davis spoke at some length about what he considered to be the Confederacy's prospects. According to Johnston, the president claimed he would soon boost troop strength by bringing deserters back to the ranks and routing out those subject to conscription who had hitherto evaded service. The generals expressed skepticism but left the meeting disgusted that their opinions had not been sought on the issue they wanted most to address—surrender.

That afternoon, Secretary of War Breckinridge, absent from the morning's meeting because he had accompanied Lee's army almost up to the surrender, arrived in Greensboro with the first official confirmation of what had happened at Appomattox. In separate conversations with Breckinridge and Secretary of the Navy Stephen Mallory, Johnston expressed his belief that the war was over. "The only power of government left in the President's hands," Johnston later put it, "was that of terminating the war, and . . . this power should be exercised without more delay." Both agreed, and Mallory pressed Johnston to say as much to Davis. Breckinridge promised to secure for him the opportunity. He was apparently as good as his word, for Davis shortly sent word to the various officers and officials to meet him again at 8:00 P.M. Present were Davis, Johnston, Beauregard, Breckinridge, Mallory, and Reagan. Secretary of the Treasury George Trenholm was too ill to attend.

John C. Breckinridge. (Courtesy of National Archives, 111-BA-1215)

Davis opened the gathering as if it were the most routine of cabinet meetings, rambling on about unrelated matters for perhaps as much as two hours. Finally, he brought the discussion around to what was obviously the reason of their return to the president's quarters that evening. "I have requested you and General Beauregard, General Johnston, to join us this evening, that we may have the benefit of your views." As for himself, he realized the situation was bad but not hopeless. "I think we can whip the enemy yet if our people will turn out." When the president ceased speaking, the various dignitaries sat silently as if waiting for one of the others to speak first. "We should like to have your views, General Johnston," Davis prompted. "My views," began Johnston, "are that our people are tired of the war, feel themselves whipped, and will not fight." The country was overrun, its military resources all but gone, and the foe stronger than ever and gaining power daily. Johnston's army, by now the last Confederate force of any size east of the Mississippi, was "melting away like snow before the sun" as soldiers deserted en masse and even made off with the artillery horses to speed them back to long neglected homes. "Under such circumstances it would be the greatest of human crimes for us to attempt to continue the war," since "the effect of our keeping the field would be, not to harm the enemy, but to complete the devastation of our country and ruin of its people." Johnston delivered this speech with an intensity Mallory thought smacked of spite, while Davis sat in silence, head down, "eyes fixed on a scrap of paper, which he was folding and refolding abstractedly." When the general stopped speaking silence fell again over the assembly that Reagan called "one of the most solemnly funereal I ever attended." Davis continued to fiddle nervously with the piece of paper through what seemed like several minutes of painful silence. Then, without looking up, he said, "What do you say, General Beauregard?" "I concur in all General Johnston has said," the Creole replied.

Still the president folded and refolded his piece of paper. Without raising his head, he asked the opinions of the other cabinet members. Each in turn agreed with the generals save Benjamin, who having made his career in the Confederacy by knowing and saying what Davis wanted to hear now made an eloquent little speech for fighting on. More silence followed. Davis spoke again. "Well, General Johnston, what do you propose?" As Johnston recalled his answer nearly a decade later, "I . . . urged that the President should exercise at once the only function of government still in his possession, and open negotiations for peace." Davis was annoyed at this. It was idle, he maintained, to talk about negotiations. The failure of various roundabout attempts at negotiation during the past several months had made clear that the Federal government would accept no peace without the preservation of the Union, what Davis called "a surrender at discretion." Besides, the U.S. government would not negotiate with him because it did not recognize the legitimacy of his government or office. Johnston suggested that in such cases the military commanders might be the proper ones to open negotiations. There was another of those unpleasant silences. "Well, sir, you can adopt this course," Davis said at last, "though I confess I am not sanguine as to its ultimate results." Davis dictated a brief message for Johnston to sign and send to Sherman. Then he turned to what he held to be more practical considerations: what line of retreat would Johnston be taking after Sherman rejected his proposal, and where should supplies be stockpiled for the use of his army. Johnston "declared a preference for a different route from that suggested by me," Davis later recalled, "and, yielding the point, I informed him that I would have depots of supplies for his army placed on the route he had selected."[100]

This business accomplished, Johnston returned to his army, which had in the meantime left Raleigh to continue its retreat before Sherman. A day or two later, Davis and his cabinet took up their own retreat again, leaving Greensboro and heading for Charlotte. The strange cavalcade, some officials on horseback, others in carriages, reached Lexington, North Carolina, the next evening and there Davis received a dispatch from Johnston informing him that Sherman had agreed to meet with him the next day, April 16, and requesting that Breckinridge be sent back to attend the meeting. Davis sent both the secretary of war and Postmaster General Reagan to represent the Confederate government. Continuing southward the president and his entourage reached Charlotte on April 18 and about the same time received news that Johnston, Breckinridge, and Sherman had come to some sort of agreement. He had to wait four days to find out the substance of that agreement. Then, on the twenty-second, Breckinridge arrived to give his report. The settlement called for cessation of all hostilities, disbanding of all Confederate forces, deposit of their arms at the various state capitals, and recognition of the exiting state governments as soon as their members took the oath of allegiance. It was much better than the South could well have expected, indeed better than it would get once the northern government, now in the aftermath of the assassination of Lincoln, learned of it. Still, Davis did not approve. Once again, however, he faced the united opposition of his cabinet, every one of whom now believed the convention should be accepted. Again Davis yielded. The next day, however, brought news that the

Washington authorities had denounced the agreement and ordered Sherman to secure the surrender of Johnston's army. Sherman gave Johnston forty-eight hours' notice that he would be resuming hostilities if a Confederate surrender was not forthcoming. Johnston passed the news along to Davis, who ordered him to "retire with his cavalry, and as many infantry as could be mounted upon draught-horses, and some light artillery." He was to disband the rest of his infantry, with orders to rendezvous at some designated point safely beyond Federal reach. This order Johnston simply disobeyed, quickly negotiating a simple surrender of his army.[101]

During the two weeks that followed, Davis and his dwindling group of followers made their way farther south and west, sometimes only just ahead of probing Federal cavalry. There was talk of joining Confederate forces west of the Mississippi and continuing the fight, but Davis seems to have been the only one who took it seriously. One by one the various members dropped off either as sickness incapacitated them to go further or as their instincts for self-preservation prompted them to seek to make their escapes individually. After crossing into Georgia on May 4, Davis paid off the remnant of troops that had stuck with him thus far with the last funds of the Confederate treasury, laboriously dragged all the way from Richmond. He "temporarily" disbanded the Confederate government–to reconvene west of the Mississippi some day–and went on with Reagan and a handful of personal aides. On May 9 he caught up with Varina, the children, and their servants and wagons, also fleeing to the west. The next morning, their camp was surprised by troopers of the Fourth Michigan Cavalry. Davis made off on foot through the gray dawn toward a nearby swampy thicket and the chance to continue his progress toward the Mississippi, but a blue-jacketed rider headed him off. The Confederate president's war was finally over.[102]

Davis had failed to realize that his fellow southerners were through with fighting and ready to give up the war because he had from the outset refused to admit the nature of the cause for which the Confederacy was fighting. Whether for the preservation of slavery or simply to keep the northern "invaders" away from home and family, continued resistance offered no reward once the Confederacy's conventional armies had broken down to the point of allowing Union forces to overrun the country at will. Davis had insisted on imagining that he was fighting for an idea, "constitutional liberty," while his countrymen were in fact fighting for a place and a social system. Davis's misconception about southerners' motives in defending the Confederacy led to his bizarre overestimate of their willingness to fight on after Appomattox.

This overestimate also produced Davis's final disagreement with his generals. Johnston and Beauregard had not demonstrated themselves during this war to be men of great nerve or moral courage, but their insistence that the war was over in the wake of Appomattox had less to do with their own inherent reluctance to commit armies to battle than it did with their recognition of the fact that the southern people simply were not going to fight any longer. By a strange irony, these generals, who had more than once during this war shown less military acumen than their civilian commander in chief, now demonstrated in their final interaction with him a dramatic superiority in their grasp of political reality. Their alertness to that of which Davis was willingly blind produced a final episode in the Confederate commander in chief's war-long inability to find generals in basic agreement with him on the goals to be pursued and methods to be used in the South's military policy and to direct those generals in a systematic implementation of his ideas on such matters. While Davis had sought to prolong the war, Johnston and Beauregard had aimed at ending it. Once again, Jefferson Davis and his generals had been working at cross-purposes.

On a lesser scale the same had been true of Davis's relations with Lee over the past eleven months since the beginning of the Richmond siege. Though he had continued to play out his opportunities as advantageously as he could, prolonging the Confederacy's life and maximizing its all but vanishing chances of victory, Lee had believed that defeat was only a matter of time since the beginning of the siege, an immediate certainty after the reelection of Lincoln. He had fought on because he considered it his duty as a soldier, and for the same reason he probably did not fully communicate his misgivings to Davis. After all, the articles of war provided for court-martial for officers advising their superiors to surrender. He undoubtedly did present his views to the president at least a full month before Appomattox, but Davis would entertain no suggestion of peace without independence. Thus although Lee fought to obtain the best terms possible and simply because it was his duty, Davis remained intent on continuing a war that the rapidly rising desertion rates in Confederate armies—if nothing else—demonstrated that his people no longer supported.

Davis's inability to find and direct generals in such a way that they would carry out his ideas in the operation of southern armies forms the main theme in his relations with his generals in Virginia. Davis's instincts as to the South's true strategy for the war were sound, offering one of the two viable methods by which the Confederacy might have won its independence and the method that many modern scholars believe to have been the only rational course.[103] Davis proceeded on the assumption that to win the war the South need only to avoid losing. Interior lines and the inherent advantages of the defender would allow the weaker Confederacy to fend off Union attacks until the North wearied of the contest. He thus favored a defensive grand strategy that held such key points as the South would need to enable it to endure a long war. Offensive action, because it might lower enemy morale and raise that of southerners, was desirable but only within the bounds of well calculated risks. Since victory could be won–eventually–without such actions, Davis was ordinarily prepared to risk on them only such resources as he thought the South could afford to lose without jeopardizing its chances of enduring to the point of northern exhaustion.

The problem came in finding generals to carry out this grand strategy in Virginia and directing them in how to do so. Davis's efforts along these lines break down rather neatly into four chronological periods, each about a year in length. The first began with his arrival in Virginia and the direction of his energies to command of the theater where the war's most important battles were expected to be fought. Bypassing Lee by leaving him in the purely organizational job that he had held before Virginia's official annexation to the Confederacy, Davis selected Johnston and Beauregard as his chief Virginia generals. Both men proved to be failures, and both showed themselves in one way or another incompatible with the president's approach to the war. Beauregard was a man of pipedreams. Though by no means devoid of military skill, he was given to the concoction of farfetched plans such as his wildly unrealistic schemes for Confederate offensives before Manassas and in the fall of 1861. He also possessed an outsized ego and a nasty propensity for meddling in politics when he was not getting his way from his superiors. Davis quite properly squelched the Creole's ill-advised plans but proved incapable of getting Beauregard to use his military talents, which were considerable within certain limits, for the good of the Confederacy without at the same time doing it even greater harm by giving rein to his vices. In fairness to Davis, that task may well have been utterly impossible. The Confederate president transferred Beauregard out of Virginia early in 1862, had astutely taken his measure as a general by the middle of that year, and found the ideal spot for the exercise of the Creole's special talents and curious personality by assigning him to the defense of Charleston.

The other prominent Confederate general during the first year of Davis's direction of the Virginia theater was Joseph E. Johnston. Like Beauregard a commander of some military ability, Johnston clashed with the president's grand strategy in precisely the opposite way. While Beauregard envisioned wild offensive schemes and incalculable risks, Johnston could hardly be induced to fight even on the defensive and apparently would sooner accept certain Confederate defeat than risk his own reputation. If he had a grand strategy beyond his own instinctive dread of the decision of battle, it seems to have been a purely Fabian policy that would refuse to hold any fixed points at all, no matter how important they might be to Confederate supply, manufacturing, or morale. Davis would eventually come to this position, but only as a matter of necessity when no fixed points could be held. As it turned out, by that time further prosecution of the war itself was impossible. In this first year of the war, Davis was anxious to avoid the tremendous damage that would be produced by northern occupation of vital centers of war production and supply. In retreating from Harpers Ferry in June 1861, from northern Virginia in March 1862, and from the Peninsula during the next two months, Johnston was going counter to Davis's program for the defense of Virginia. Diagnosing his problem proved more difficult than that of Beauregard, and here Davis's indecision and unwillingness to change prewar opinions worked against him. He did not fully realize Johnston's unsuitability for army command until July 1864, and then it was too late even to save Atlanta. Johnston was removed from the Virginia theater long before that by several pieces of northern lead and iron. His wounding at the botched battle of Seven Pines on the last day of May 1862 ended a long and trying period of increasingly acrimonious conflict between general and commander in chief as to how the war in Virginia should be waged, a period during which the general's views had been put into practice more than the president's.

Davis's choice of Robert E. Lee to succeed the fallen Johnston was his best of the war. Indeed, it probably deserves to be ranked with the few most brilliant command decisions of military history. Nor was it as obvious a choice at that time, even to Davis, as its subsequent stupendous success makes it appear in retrospect. Davis and Lee became one of the most potent high-command collaborations of this or any other war. Yet their cooperation was hindered by fundamentally different concepts of what was needed to win the war. Like Davis, Lee realized that the Confederacy was at a serious disadvantage in terms of men, money, and materiel. His solution, however, was just opposite that of Davis. Since the South was weaker, it must strike hard and fast, winning victories that would at least demoralize the North and perhaps even temporarily paralyze its military strength. If the war dragged on for years, if the North's military and industrial potential were given time for complete mobilization, the weaker South would be doomed. In a long, grinding war of attrition, the arithmetic was all against the poorer and less populous Confederacy. Thus Lee was prepared to take massive gambles, not because the South could afford to lose them but because it could not afford failure to win them, even by refraining from taking them. Lee's approach to the Civil War was aggressive, audacious, and aimed at a quick victory. This was no foolish grand strategy. Alongside Davis's much different vision, it was probably the only other viable course for the Confederacy, and the eventual collapse of southern resources and especially southern morale suggest it may have been the better of the two. Either policy, pursued consistently, gave some hope of success. The trouble was that neither was so pursued.

Lee presented an entirely different set of problems for his commander in chief than did either Johnston or Beauregard. He was one of the handful of individuals within the Confederacy whose military acumen matched or exceeded the president's. Genuinely brilliant, he could win battles and gain both public reputation and a claim to powerful influence in the Confederacy's strategic counsels. Having disciplined himself for years to be courteous and kind, he also understood the need to deal wisely with the president in order to bring him around to his point of view. All this made it extraordinarily difficult for Davis to resist Lee's counsel or to refuse him anything he requested, particularly during the second major chronological segment of the war in Virginia, the time from Lee's accession to command to his defeat at Gettysburg thirteen months later. During this year Lee seemed all but invincible, his requests all but undeniable. On the other hand, Lee presented opportunities for his commander in chief that neither Beauregard nor Johnston had afforded. Unlike those two egotists, Lee endeavored to rein in his pride. His devotion to duty was literally religious. He undoubtedly would have followed conscientiously such strategic guidelines as Davis laid down plainly for him, though he would also stretch ambiguities in order to do what he believed was best for the Confederacy.

Presented with the astonishing gift of a general of Lee's brilliance, no commander in chief could rightly consider declining to give him the nation's most crucial field command. If Lee's talents were then to be used in commanding the Confederacy's largest army, the question was how best to direct and support his efforts. In this Davis had essentially two options. He could watch Lee closely, keeping him on a short leash and using his tactical brilliance to win indecisive but hopefully inexpensive victories while keeping the foe out of Richmond and conserving Confederate manpower. On the other hand, he could throw over his own strategic conception in favor of making maximum use of the gift Providence had made to him in Lee. He could steel himself to make the same sort of dizzying gambles on the national scale–in delivering Lee maximum troops and supplies–as Lee himself was making on the roads and battlefields of northern Virginia, Maryland, and Pennsylvania. This would mean an all-out bid for victory in 1862 or early 1863, with a quick end of the war assured one way or the other. It might have failed, but few military pundits could fault a commander in chief who chose to lay his country's never very robust hopes of victory on the shoulders of the likes of Robert E. Lee in the spring of 1863, ably seconded as he was, until Chancellorsville, by Stonewall Jackson.

Neither of these two courses did Davis pursue, and in this he failed to extract from his remarkable collaboration with the remarkable Lee all the benefits that might have accrued to the Confederacy by it. Impressed by Lee's victories, moved by Lee's persuasiveness, the president gave way to his general's designs only far enough to stretch his basically defensive grand strategy. He supported Lee's ventures to an extent that was all but reckless within his defensive framework, but he clung to the notion of taking no risk that would preclude the Confederacy's ability to go on enduring should the gamble fail. That prevented him from giving Lee the maximum possibility of success in his great bid for Confederate victory in the summer of 1863. Meanwhile, allowing Lee to force battles and assail his opponents beyond the necessities of holding his ground undermined Davis's enduring strategy by hemorrhaging Confederate manpower at a rate the South could not possibly sustain in a long war. Either strategy might still have failed. Neither got a fair chance.

Gettysburg was the bitter fruit of mixed strategies. Lee, sensing the fading of opportunity for decisive victory and possibly shaken by the death of Jackson and the recurrence of doubts–known to have plagued him earlier–about the rightness of his cause, moved with desperation into the worst-run battle of his career. None of his lieutenants turned in his best performance in Pennsylvania that summer; few were up to even their average quality. Lee faced his toughest opponent to date and in the midst of these disadvantages showed little of the brilliance that had already made him the idol of his countrymen and terror of his foes. Still the affair was a near-run thing, and the additional troops Davis held back might have made a difference. At any rate, if they were not to go, Lee should not have been in Pennsylvania sustaining over 20,000 casualties in desperate assaults.

The defeat at Gettysburg opened the third period of relations between Davis and his generals in Virginia. In the eleven and a half months between

Gettysburg and the beginning of the Richmond-Petersburg siege, Davis and Lee worked as harmoniously together as at any time during the war. Davis was still highly supportive of Lee but more assertive of his own strategic ideas. Thus he insisted on transferring troops from Lee's army to the West, reducing Lee's ability to wage offensive warfare. One is tempted to speculate that Davis deliberately withheld manpower from Lee for the purpose of preventing his squandering it in another offensive battle after the manner of Gettysburg, but nothing in the Confederate president's correspondence or postwar writings suggests such an attitude on his part. Instead, Davis expressed intense continued confidence in Lee. The president apparently still did not fully recognize the difference between his and Lee's approaches to the war. That, in turn, suggests that Davis not only refrained from enunciating an explicit, clearly defined grand strategy but also neglected to think such a policy through even within his own mind.

Lee had undergone no change of mind about the requirements for southern success but was largely limited in his ability to carry out the type of audacious warfare he had waged the previous year. The Bristoe Station campaign in the fall of 1863 and Early's raid in the summer of 1864 were both contrary to Davis's implicit grand strategy but only in one sense. Though these were offensive movements, Lee's opportunities were so limited in the first and his resources so limited in the second that the resulting operations were less in the style of Lee's grand gambles and more in the style of Davis's limited harassing offensives. Early's movement was in some ways a special circumstance. Although the number of troops involved was very small in comparison with the Gettysburg campaign, the risk involved was extremely high due to the desperate situation of Lee's army facing Grant before Richmond. Sending any troops away at such a time was another act of sublime audacity. That Davis permitted it with so little demure is a measure of the extent to which he was coming to depend entirely on Lee for strategic direction. Strategically, Lee was coming to control the war to an ever increasing degree, though Davis would have been loath to admit it.

The last period of Davis's direction of the war in Virginia, the Richmond-Petersburg siege, the Appomattox campaign, and its aftermath, reveals the president and his chief Virginia general still working effectively together but separated in outlook by Davis's increasingly unrealistic faith in the continued possibility of Confederate victory, especially after the reelection of Lincoln. By late winter of 1865, the difference between Davis's and Lee's assessments of the Confederacy's prospects led the president to while away, in steadfast and increasingly irrelevant performance of old duties, the last few weeks that Lee's skill–and the endurance of his men–could buy for him to seek to end the war with the best deal possible. Such a deal would mean acceptance of the enduring union of the states as well as the necessity of negotiating as a mere influential citizen rather than as president of a sovereign nation, but during those same months Lincoln indicated his willingness to treat on those terms and to give a far better deal than the South ultimately received. That it received no worse was the result of Lincoln's magnanimity rather than any lingering ability of the Confederacy to extort favorable terms from its conquerors. Davis's inability–or refusal–to see the obvious meant that peace would come only when the South was utterly prostrate and thoroughly devastated. That and the deaths and maimings of thousands of young men, northerners and southerners alike, while the issue was no longer in doubt might indeed be characterized, as Joseph E. Johnston asserted, a "crime."

"I have cherished and long ago expressed," Ordnance Bureau Chief Josiah Gorgas wrote in his diary on January 15, 1865, "that the President is not endowed with military genius, but who would have done better?"[104] The question has come down to modern historians, and none can suggest a likely candidate. Davis was the best the South could offer, and he demonstrated by his impressive performance that this was no mean distinction. He was close to possessing the military genius Gorgas rightly denied him, and his eloquence and political savvy appear to disadvantage only by comparison with the unexcelled and scarcely equaled measure in which his opponent Lincoln possessed both those traits. Only defeat exposed his weaknesses: indecisiveness, pride, and reluctance to change an opinion or admit an error. The product of these in Virginia was failure to delineate and direct a consistent strategy. The resolute fortitude he displayed amid the decline of a failing cause undoubtedly prolonged the struggle six months to a year beyond the point at which collapse would have come under any other conceivable leadership. Though his determination grew out of a refusal to accept the cause for what it was and though its misguided application in the war's closing months was a tragedy, yet Davis's steadfastness prior to that can still excite admiration. It was worthy of a better cause, indeed worthy of the cause for which he claimed–and perhaps believed–he was fighting, "constitutional liberty." Had every southerner–or even a slim majority–displayed Davis's devotion to the Confederacy, had most southern generals manifested his skill and nerve, independence would have been won. It was not, of course, and stretched to his limit in the reach for it Davis is measured against the exacting standard of perfection. That fact, though hard for his reputation, offers valuable lessons to those who would learn from the past.

NOTES

PREFACE

1. A classic example is Douglas Southall Freeman, *R. E. Lee: A Biography* (New York: Scribners, 1934), and *Lee's Lieutenants: A Study in Command* (New York: Charles Scribner's Sons, 1944), in which Davis plays a bit part. The most recent is Alan T. Nolan, *Lee Considered: General Robert E. Lee and Civil War History* (Chapel Hill: University of North Carolina Press, 1991), 112–33, in which the author taxes Lee for failing to make strategic decisions rightfully belonging to Davis.

2. Steven E. Woodworth, *Jefferson Davis and His Generals: The Failure of Confederate Command in the West* (Lawrence: University Press of Kansas, 1990).

3. Russell F. Weigley, *The American Way of War: A History of United States Military Strategy and Policy* (New York: Macmillan, 1973), 92–127; Nolan, *Lee Considered,* 59–106.

4. Archer Jones, *Civil War Command and Strategy: The Process of Victory and Defeat* (New York: Free Press, 1992), 227–28.

5. Jefferson Davis to Varina Davis, January 24, 1866, in Dunbar Rowland, ed., *Jefferson Davis, Constitutionalist: His Letters, Papers, and Speeches,* 10 vols. (Jackson: Mississippi Department of Archives and History, 1923), 7:64–65.

CHAPTER 1

1. Edward Porter Alexander, *Military Memoirs of a Confederate* (New York: Charles Scribner's Sons, 1907), 42; Jefferson Davis, *The Rise and Fall of the Confederate Government,* 2 vols. (New York: Appleton, 1881), 1:349–51.

2. J. Davis, *Rise and Fall,* 1:348–49.

3. Ibid.

4. Alexander, *Military Memoirs,* 41–42; Jedediah Hotchkiss Papers, microfilm reel 49, frame 166, Library of Congress Manuscript Division.

5. J. Davis, *Rise and Fall,* 1:349–51, 357; Joseph E. Johnston, *Narrative of Military Operations* (New York: Appleton, 1874), 53–54, and "Responsibilities of the First Bull Run," in Robert U. Johnson and Clarence C. Buel, eds., *Battles and Leaders of the*

Civil War, 4 vols. (New York: Thomas Yoseloff, 1956), 1:244–45. The account given here seems to be the best way to reconcile the conflicting claims of Davis and Johnston.

6. Douglas Southall Freeman, *Lee's Lieutenants: A Study in Command,* 3 vols. (New York: Charles Scribner's Sons, 1944), 1:76; Lynda Lasswell Crist and Mary Seaton Dix, eds., *The Papers of Jefferson Davis,* 7 vols. to date (Baton Rouge: Louisiana State University Press, 1971–), 7:258 (hereafter cited as *Davis Papers*).

7. J. Davis, *Rise and Fall,* 1:230.

8. Varina Howell Davis, *Jefferson Davis: Ex-President of the Confederate States of America, A Memoir by His Wife,* 2 vols. (New York: Belford, 1890), 2:12, 163, 498.

9. William C. Davis, *Jefferson Davis: The Man and His Hour* (New York: Harper Collins, 1991), 3–298.

10. John H. Reagan, *Memoirs,* ed. Walter F. McCaleb (New York: Neale, 1906), 120. W. C. Davis offers an interesting explanation of this trait in *Jefferson Davis,* 82–84.

11. Dunbar Rowland, ed., *Jefferson Davis, Constitutionalist: His Letters, Papers, and Speeches,* 10 vols. (Jackson: Mississippi Department of Archives and History, 1923), 5:136–37.

12. W. C. Davis, *Jefferson Davis,* 227–31.

13. V. H. Davis, *Jefferson Davis,* 2:163.

14. Freeman, *Lee's Lieutenants,* 1:4–5.

15. *Davis Papers,* 7:258.

16. Hudson Strode, ed., *Jefferson Davis, Private Letters, 1823–1889* (New York: Harcourt Brace, 1966), 124.

17. Albert Taylor Bledsoe to Davis, May 10, 1861, Manuscript Department, Perkins Library, Duke University.

18. John Janney to Davis, April 27, 1861, in Rowland, *Jefferson Davis Constitutionalist,* 5:67.

19. Slidell to Davis, April 24, 1861, by permission of the Houghton Library (Dearborn Collection), Harvard University.

20. Bledsoe to Davis, May 10 and 11, 1861, by permission of the Houghton Library (Dearborn Collection), Harvard University.

21. Pryor to Walker, May 2, 1861, U. S. War Department, *The War of the Rebellion: A Compilation of the Official Records of the Union and Confederate Armies,* 128 vols. (Washington, D.C.: Government Printing Office, 1880–1901), 2:797 (hereafter cited as O.R.; except as noted, all volumes cited are from series 1).

22. Walker to Letcher, May 1 and 5, 1861; and Letcher to Walker, May 1, 1861, O.R. 2:792, 805.

23. Letcher to Davis, May 12, 1861, by permission of the Houghton Library (Dearborn Collection), Harvard University.

24. Ruffin to Davis, May 16, 1861, O.R. 51, pt. 2:92.

25. Reagan, *Memoirs,* 136.

26. Rowland, *Jefferson Davis, Constitutionalist,* 5:102–4; Alvy L. King, *Louis T. Wigfall* (Baton Rouge: Louisiana State University Press, 1970), 127–29; W. C. Davis, *Jefferson Davis,* 337.

27. John B. Jones, *A Rebel War Clerk's Diary,* ed. Earl Schenck Miers (New York: Sagamore, 1958), 21.

28. V. H. Davis, *Jefferson Davis*, 2:74–75.

29. Steven E. Woodworth, *Jefferson Davis and His Generals: The Failure of Confederate Command in the West* (Lawrence: University Press of Kansas, 1990), 315.

30. W. C. Davis, *Jefferson Davis*, 112, 348, 353, 355–56, 389, 480, 494, 499, 506, 577.

31. *Davis Papers*, 7:183; V. H. Davis, *Jefferson Davis*, 2:74–75; Rowland, *Jefferson Davis Constitutionalist*, 5:102–4.

32. Rowland, *Jefferson Davis, Constitutionalist*, 5:102–4.

33. Ibid.

34. *Davis Papers*, 7:183; W. C. Davis, *Jefferson Davis*, 338.

35. W. C. Davis, *Jefferson Davis*, 339.

36. William C. Davis, *"A Government of Our Own": The Making of the Confederacy* (New York: Free Press, 1994), 174–75; George C. Rable, *The Confederate Republic: A Revolution Against Politics* (Chapel Hill: University of North Carolina Press, 1994), 72.

37. Archer Jones, *Civil War Command and Strategy: The Process of Victory and Defeat* (New York: Free Press, 1992), 12.

38. Ibid., 16, 113–14.

39. Grady McWhiney, "Jefferson Davis and Confederate Military Leadership," in Roman J. Heleniak and Lawrence L. Hewitt, eds., *Leadership During the Civil War: The 1989 Deep Delta Civil War Symposium* (Shippensburg, Pa.: White Mane, 1992), 29.

40. Walker to Letcher, May 1, 1861, O.R. 2:792.

41. Letcher to Walker, May 1, 1861, ibid.

42. Walker to Letcher, May 6, 1861, ibid., 805.

43. Alan T. Nolan, *Lee Considered: General Robert E. Lee and Civil War History* (Chapel Hill: University of North Carolina Press, 1991), 29.

44. Ibid., 34–35.

45. Ibid.

46. Ibid., 32–39.

47. Letcher proclamation and General Orders no. 1, April 23, 1861, O.R. 2:775–76.

48. Nolan, *Lee Considered*, 37–45, 51–52.

49. Steven Harvey Newton, *Joseph E. Johnston and the Defense of Richmond* (Ann Arbor: UMI, 1991), 250.

50. Craig L. Symonds, *Joseph E. Johnston: A Civil War Biography* (New York: W. W. Norton, 1992), 20.

51. Newton, *Joseph E. Johnston*, 250; Symonds, *Joseph E. Johnston*, 34.

52. Newton, *Joseph E. Johnston*, 250.

53. Ibid., 251–52; Johnston to Davis, July 11, 1855, *Davis Papers*, 5:440.

54. Newton, *Joseph E. Johnston*, 251–52; Symonds, *Joseph E. Johnston*, 75.

55. Symonds, *Joseph E. Johnston*, 90–91.

56. General Orders no. 3, April 26, 1861, O.R. 2:783; Gilbert E. Govan and James W. Livingood, *A Different Valor: The Story of General Joseph E. Johnston, C.S.A.* (Indianapolis: Bobbs-Merrill, 1956), 30.

57. Douglas Southall Freeman, *R. E. Lee: A Biography*, 4 vols. (New York: Scribners, 1934), 1:515–16.

58. Lee to Davis, May 7, 1861, in Clifford Dowdey and Louis H. Manarin, eds., *The Wartime Papers of R. E. Lee* (New York: Bramhall House, 1961), 21.

59. Ibid.

60. Freeman, *R. E. Lee,* 3:533–34.

61. Lee to Jackson, May 10 (two dispatches) and 12, 1861, O.R. 2:824–25, 836.

62. Alf J. Mapp, *Frock Coats and Epaulets* (New York: Thomas Yoseloff, 1963), 159.

63. Govan and Livingood, *A Different Valor,* 31.

64. Johnston, *Narrative,* 13.

65. Samuel Cooper to Johnston, May 15, 1861, O.R. 2:844; Johnston, *Narrative,* 13.

66. The men's wartime animosity led to stories claiming to reveal the cause of a quarrel between them going back, in some versions, to their West Point days. However, no solid evidence exists to substantiate such claims. To the contrary, Davis's correspondence with Johnston, up until September 1861, seems remarkably cordial, even friendly.

67. Johnston, *Narrative,* 13.

68. Johnston to Lee, May 18, 1861, O.R. 2:856.

69. Johnston, *Narrative,* 15.

70. G. F. R. Henderson, *Stonewall Jackson and the American Civil War,* 2 vols. (New York: Longmans, Green, 1909), 1:24–102.

71. Letcher to Lee, April 27, 1861, Lee to Jackson, April 27, 1861, O.R. 2:784.

72. Frank E. Vandiver, *Mighty Stonewall* (College Station: Texas A&M University Press, 1957), 144.

73. Lee to Jackson (2 dispatches), May 10, 1861, Jackson to Lee, May 11, 1861, O.R. 2:824–25, 832.

74. Lee to Jackson, May 12, 1861, ibid., 836.

75. Johnston to Jackson, May 24, 1861, ibid., 871.

76. Jackson to Johnston, May 24, 1861, ibid.

77. Freeman, *R. E. Lee,* 1:514–15.

78. Davis to Lee, May 28, 1861, *Davis Papers,* 7:179.

79. Garnett to Davis, May 28, 1861, ibid., 180.

80. Alfred Roman, *The Military Operations of General Beauregard in the War Between the States, 1861–1865,* 2 vols. (New York: Harper and Brothers, 1884), 1:64. This work is in fact Beauregard's military autobiography, written in the third person. Roman's collaboration was obtained merely to relieve the general of appearing to praise himself so highly.

81. Beauregard to Davis, February 10, 1861, Beauregard Papers, Perkins Library, Duke University.

82. Mary Boykin Chesnut, *Mary Chesnut's Civil War,* ed. C. Vann Woodward (New Haven, Conn.: Yale University Press, 1981), 33.

83. Francis W. Pickens to Davis, *Davis Papers,* 7:181; Roman, *Military Operations,* 1:66.

84. Roman, *Military Operations,* 1:66.

85. J. Davis, *Rise and Fall,* 1:340.

86. Ibid., 309.

87. Freeman, *Lee's Lieutenants,* 1:7.

88. Roman, *Military Operations,* 1:66.

89. Ibid., 66–67.

90. Freeman, *Lee's Lieutenants,* 1:7.

91. Roman, *Military Operations,* 1:66–67; Beauregard to Davis, June 3, 1861, *Davis Papers,* 7:186–87.

92. Freeman, *R. E. Lee,* 1:518–19.

93. Beauregard to Davis, June 3, 1861, *Davis Papers,* 7:186–87.

94. Johnston, *Narrative,* 17.

95. Newton, *Joseph E. Johnston,* 117–18.

96. James Longstreet, *From Manassas to Appomattox,* ed. James I. Robertson, Jr. (Bloomington: Indiana University Press, 1960), 113.

97. Clement Eaton, *Jefferson Davis* (New York: Free Press, 1977), 157.

98. Johnston, *Narrative,* 17.

99. Freeman, *Lee's Lieutenants,* 1:13.

100. Johnston to Garnett, May 26, 1861, O.R. 2:880–81.

101. Johnston to Garnett, May 28, Johnston to Lee, May 31 and June 6, 1861, O.R. 2:889, 895–96, 907–8; Symonds, *Joseph E. Johnston,* 107.

102. Lee to Johnston, May 30 and June 1 and 3, 1861, O.R. 2:894, 897, 901; Lee to Johnston, June 1, 1861, in Dowdey and Manarin, *Wartime Papers,* 42.

103. Johnston to Lee, June 6, 1861, O.R. 2:907–8.

104. Lee to Johnston, June 7, 1861, ibid., 910.

105. Ibid.

106. Jeffrey N. Lash, *Destroyer of the Iron Horse: General Joseph E. Johnston and Confederate Rail Transport, 1861–1865* (Kent, Ohio: Kent State University Press, 1991), 7; Cooper to Johnston, June 13, 1861, O.R. 2:923–25.

107. A. Jones, *Civil War Command and Strategy,* 222.

108. Cooper to Johnston, June 13, 1861, O.R. 2:923–25.

109. Freeman, *R. E. Lee,* 1:531.

110. Symonds, *Joseph E. Johnston,* 107; Johnston to Davis, June 14, 1861, O.R. 51, pt. 2:139.

111. Robert G. Tanner, *Stonewall in the Valley: Thomas J. "Stonewall" Jackson's Shenandoah Valley Campaign, Spring 1862* (Garden City, N. Y.: Doubleday, 1976), 34.

112. Lash, *Destroyer of the Iron Horse,* 15, 39–40.

113. Johnston, *Narrative,* 24; Johnston to Cooper, June 15, 1861, O.R. 2:929–30; Symonds, *Joseph E. Johnston,* 109.

114. Johnston to Cooper, June 17, 1861, O.R. 2:934.

115. Cooper to Johnston, June 18 and 19, 1861, O.R. 2:934–35, 940. That Davis was fully responsible for the content of these dispatches there can be no doubt. The matters dealt with views expressed are typical of the president's known interests and concerns and are well outside the realm of what Cooper would conceivably have sent on his own responsibility. Johnston recognized Davis as the source in his *Narrative,* 24.

116. Davis to Johnston, June 22, 1861, *Davis Papers,* 7:208–9.

117. Johnston to Davis, June 26, 1861, Davis to Johnston, June 22, 1861, ibid., 208–9, 212–13.

118. George C. Rable (*The Confederate Republic,* 83) takes a remarkably different view of this entire exchange. Of Johnston's suggestion that Davis "appear in the

position General Washington occupied during the revolution," Rable asserts: "Davis probably dismissed this suggestion as flattery or sycophancy because his distrust of Johnston quickly became obvious. Rather than trying to work with and use this difficult subordinate, Davis seemed determined to alienate him." Obviously my research has led to a different conclusion.

119. J. B. Jones, *Rebel War Clerk's Diary*, 27–28.

120. Proclamation of Governor Letcher, June 8, 1861, in Dowdey and Manarin, *Wartime Papers*, 44–45; General Orders no. 25, June 8, 1861, O.R. 2:911–12.

121. Freeman, *R. E. Lee*, 1:527.

122. Lee to wife, June 9, 1861, in Dowday and Manarin, *Wartime Papers*, 46.

123. Freeman, *R. E. Lee*, 1:528–30.

124. J. B. Jones, *Rebel War Clerk's Diary*, 27.

125. Chesnut, *Mary Chesnut's Civil War*, 80.

126. Ibid., 62.

127. Beauregard to Davis, June 12, 1861, *Davis Papers*, 7:197–98.

128. T. Harry Williams, *P. G. T. Beauregard: Napoleon in Gray* (Baton Rouge: Louisiana State University Press, 1955), 71.

129. William C. Davis, *Battle at Bull Run: A History of the First Major Campaign of the Civil War* (Garden City, N. Y.: Doubleday, 1977), 64.

130. Davis to Beauregard, June 13, 1861, *Davis Papers*, 7:199–200.

131. Beauregard to Davis, June 16, 1861, ibid., 7:201–2; Roman, *Military Operations*, 1:432–33. Each contains parts of the letter.

132. A. C. Myers to Beauregard, June 17, 1861, in Roman, *Military Operations*, 1:435.

133. W. C. Davis, *Jefferson Davis*, 345.

134. Chesnut, *Mary Chesnut's Civil War*, 62.

135. Ibid., 80.

136. Ibid.

137. J. B. Jones, *Rebel War Clerk's Diary*, 28.

138. Ibid., 27.

139. Jefferson Davis to Joseph E. Davis, June 18, 1861, *Davis Papers*, 7:203–4.

140. Beauregard to Wigfall, July 8, 1861, in Roman, *Military Operations*, 1:81–82; King, *Louis T. Wigfall*, 130–31.

141. Beauregard to Davis, July 9, 1861, O.R. 2:969; Roman, *Military Operations*, 1:202.

142. Beauregard to Davis, July 11, 1861, *Davis Papers*, 7:234–35.

143. Williams, *P. G. T. Beauregard*, 74.

144. Beauregard to Johnston, July 13, 1861, in Roman, *Military Operations*, 1:87.

145. Roman, *Military Operations*, 1:84.

146. Ibid., 1:85–87, 438; W. C. Davis, *Battle at Bull Run*, 66–67; Freeman, *Lee's Lieutenants*, 1:42 and *R. E. Lee*, 1:535–36; Chesnut, *Mary Chesnut's Civil War*, 100; Williams, *P. G. T. Beauregard*, 75, 94. George C. Rable in *The Confederate Republic* (82) astutely points out the political constraints that influenced Davis in favor of the defense policy he maintained at this time. "The president stuck to a defensive strategy," Rable writes. "This decision reflected the government's cautious approach

to building a Southern nation: a costly offensive, even if partly successful, might further strain both the economy and the political system."

147. P. G. T. Beauregard, "The First Battle of Bull Run," in Johnson and Buel, *Battles and Leaders,* 1:198; Roman, *Military Operations,* 1:89.

148. Williams, *P. G. T. Beauregard,* 76; Roman, *Military Operations,* 1:203–4; Beauregard to Davis, July 17, 1861, *Davis Papers,* 7:249.

149. Davis to Beauregard, July 17, 1861, *Davis Papers,* 7:249; Cooper to Johnston, July 17, 1861, J. Davis, *Rise and Fall,* 1:346; Cooper to Holmes, July 17, 1861, O.R. 2:980.

150. Beauregard to Davis, Beauregard to Johnston, July 17, 1861, in Roman, *Military Operations,* 1:90, 438; Beauregard to Cooper, July 17, 1861, O.R. 2:980.

151. Holmes to Cooper, June 15, 1861, in Roman, *Military Operations,* 1:435; Lee to Holmes, June 17, 1861, O.R. 2:932.

152. Freeman, *R. E. Lee,* 1:532.

153. Johnston to Davis, July 8 and 15, *Davis Papers,* 7:225–26, 242–43; Johnston to Cooper, July 8 and 9, ibid., 227, and O.R. 2:969; Davis to Johnston, July 10 and 13, *Davis Papers,* 7:227, and O.R. 2:973–74.

154. Cooper to Johnston, July 17, 1861, in J. Davis, *Rise and Fall,* 1:346.

155. Ibid., 346–47.

156. Ibid.

157. Ibid., 345–46.

158. Johnston to Beauregard, July 17, 1861, in Roman, *Military Operations,* 1:193.

159. Johnston to Cooper, July 18, 1861, O.R. 2:982.

160. Beauregard to Davis, July 18, 1861, *Davis Papers,* 7:251.

161. Davis to Beauregard, July 18, 1861, in Rowland, *Jefferson Davis, Constitutionalist,* 5:111.

162. Chesnut, *Mary Chesnut's Civil War,* 102.

163. Davis speech, July 16, 1861, *Davis Papers,* 7:244–45.

164. Cooper to Beauregard, July 19, 1861, O.R. 2:983.

165. Beauregard, in Johnson and Buel, *Battles and Leaders* 1:202.

166. J. Davis, *Rise and Fall,* 1:348.

167. Davis to Johnston, July 20, 1861, *Davis Papers,* 7:254.

168. J.Davis, *Rise and Fall,* 1:348.

169. Lash, *Destroyer of the Iron Horse,* 17, 190 n. 13; Lucius B. Northrop to Davis, April 29, 1879, in Rowland, *Jefferson Davis, Constitutionalist,* 8:385–89. Lash (15–16) asserts that Davis himself had not previously contemplated a movement by rail. Davis to Beauregard, June 13, 1861 (*Davis Papers,* 7:199–200), however, seems to imply that Davis had expected use of the railroad as a matter of course and thus had said nothing about it.

170. Williams, *P. G. T. Beauregard,* 77: Johnston, *Narrative,* 37–38.

171. Roman, *Military Operations,* 1:192–99.

172. Freeman, *Lee's Lieutenants,* 1:48; Williams, *P. G. T. Beauregard,* 79.

173. Freeman, *Lee's Lieutenants,* 1:50–72; Williams, *P. G. T. Beauregard,* 80.

CHAPTER 2

1. *Davis Papers,* 7:261; William C. Davis, *Battle at Bull Run: A History of the First Major Campaign of the Civil War* (Garden City, N.Y.: Doubleday, 1977), 243–44,

250; Jefferson Davis, *Rise and Fall of the Confederate Government,* 2 vols. (New York: Appleton, 1881), 1:351–56; Jefferson Davis to Varina Davis, July 21, 1861, O.R. 2:986; Edward Porter Alexander, *Fighting for the Confederacy: The Personal Recollections of General Edward Porter Alexander,* ed. Gary W. Gallagher (Chapel Hill: University of North Carolina Press, 1989), 57.

2. W. C. Davis, *Battle at Bull Run,* 244.

3. John B. Jones, *A Rebel War Clerk's Diary,* ed. Earl Schenck Miers (New York: Sagamore, 1958), 34–35; Mary Boykin Chesnut, *Mary Chesnut's Civil War,* ed. C. Vann Woodward (New Haven, Conn.: Yale University Press, 1981), 105.

4. Davis to Cooper, July 21, 1861, O.R. 2:987.

5. J. Davis, *Rise and Fall,* 1:354–56; Alexander, *Fighting for the Confederacy,* 58.

6. Edward Porter Alexander, *Military Memoirs of a Confederate* (New York: Scribners, 1912), 43. Johnston either was unaware of Whiting's action or, very much in character, chose to suppress information about it in his postwar accounts. Joseph E. Johnston, *Narrative of Military Operations* (New York: Appleton, 1874), 52–53.

7. William Garrett Piston, *Lee's Tarnished Lieutenant: James Longstreet and His Place in Southern History* (Athens: University of Georgia Press, 1987), 14.

8. Alexander, *Military Memoirs,* 43–45; Alfred Roman, *The Military Operations of General Beauregard in the War Between the States, 1861–1865,* 2 vols. (New York: Harper and Brothers, 1884), 1:109–10; P. G. T. Beauregard, "The First Battle of Bull Run," in Robert U. Johnson and Clarence C. Buel, eds., *Battles and Leaders of the Civil War,* 4 vols. (New York: Thomas Yoseloff, 1956), 1:215–16.

9. J. Davis, *Rise and Fall,* 1:356.

10. Ibid., 1:352–56.

11. Ibid.; Alexander, *Military Memoirs,* 49–50, and *Fighting for the Confederacy,* 58; Roman, *Military Operations,* 1:114; T. Harry Williams, *P. G. T. Beauregard: Napoleon in Gray* (Baton Rouge: Louisiana State University Press, 1955), 89–90.

12. Roman, *Military Operations,* 1:115–16; J. Davis, *Rise and Fall,* 1:356.

13. J. Davis, *Rise and Fall,* 1:356.

14. Johnston, *Narrative,* 59.

15. Beauregard, in Johnson and Buel, *Battles and Leaders,* 1:216; J. Davis, *Rise and Fall,* 1:359.

16. J. Davis, *Rise and Fall,* 1:359.

17. Johnston, *Narrative,* 59.

18. Ibid.

19. O.R. 51, pt. 2:190.

20. Davis to Cooper, *Davis Papers,* 7:260.

21. J. Davis, *Rise and Fall,* 1:357.

22. Ibid., 359–60.

23. Ibid.; Johnston, *Narrative,* 62. Johnston ("Responsibilities of the First Bull Run," in Johnson and Buel, *Battles and Leaders,* 1:252) denies ever having been a party to such a conference. Beauregard (Roman, *Military Operations,* 1:117) denies having spoken as Davis described. In this case, Davis's assertion seems more convincing than the general's diverse denials. Though Davis was not above bending the truth to make himself look better or, for example, claiming he had "always believed" one

thing or "never intended" another when such was obviously not the case, he was not given to making things up out of whole cloth. Furthermore, Davis's testimony is corroborated by Alexander (*Fighting for the Confederacy*, 57–58). It is more likely that each general chose to deny something that, in retrospect, was embarrassing to him.

24. William C. Davis, *Jefferson Davis: The Man and His Hour* (New York: Harper Collins, 1991), 352.

25. *Davis Papers*, 7:261–63.

26. J. B. Jones, *Rebel War Clerk's Diary*, 36.

27. Chesnut, *Mary Chesnut's Civil War*, 109.

28. J. B. Jones, *Rebel War Clerk's Diary*, 35.

29. Chesnut, *Mary Chesnut's Civil War*, 105.

30. Martin Van Creveld, *Supplying War: Logistics from Wallenstein to Patton* (Cambridge: Cambridge University Press, 1977), 200; R . B. Lee to Davis, July 23, 1861, in Roman, *Military Operations*, 1:121.

31. W. C. Davis, *Jefferson Davis*, 61–70.

32. Johnston to Cooper, July 28, 1861, O.R . 51, pt. 2: 203–4.

33. Beauregard to Davis, July 29, 1861, ibid., 204.

34. Roman, *Military Operations*, 1:121–22; on the growing discontentment with the failure to take Washington, see J. B. Jones, *Rebel War Clerk's Diary*, 37, and *Davis Papers*, 7:394 n.1.

35. Williams, *P. G. T. Beauregard*, 97; Lucius B. Northrop, "The Confederate Commissariat at Manassas," in Johnson and Buel, *Battles and Leaders*, 1:261; Douglas Southall Freeman, *Lee's Lieutenants: A Study in Command*, 3 vols. (New York: Charles Scribner's Sons, 1944), 100.

36. Jeffrey N. Lash, *Destroyer of the Iron Horse: General Joseph E. Johnston and Confederate Rail Transport, 1861–1865* (Kent, Ohio: Kent State University Press, 1991), 20; Williams, *P. G. T. Beauregard*, 70.

37. Freeman, *Lee's Lieutenants*, 1:100.

38. Davis to Beauregard, August 4, 1861, Dunbar Rowland, ed., *Jefferson Davis, Constitutionalist: His Letters, Papers, and Speeches*, 10 vols. (Jackson: Mississippi Department of Archives and History, 1923), 5:120–21.

39. Freeman, *Lee's Lieutenants*, 1:81.

40. Miles to Beauregard, August 6, 1861, in Roman, *Military Operations*, 1:128.

41. Ibid.; Miles to Beauregard, August 8, 1861, ibid., 126.

42. Beauregard to Davis, August 10, 1861, ibid., 123–24.

43. J. B. Jones, *Rebel War Clerk's Diary*, 41: Chesnut, *Mary Chesnut's Civil War*, 164, 167, 182; Davis to Leonidas Polk, September 2, 1861, Leonidas Polk Papers, Southern Historical Collection, Library of the University of North Carolina at Chapel Hill.

44. J. B. Jones, *Rebel War Clerk's Diary*, 40.

45. Chesnut, *Mary Chesnut's Civil War*, 129–30.

46. William C. Davis, *"A Government of Our Own": The Making of the Confederacy* (New York: Free Press, 1994), 156, 179, 185, 380–81. Davis goes so far as to hint that Benjamin may have been homosexual.

47. J. B. Jones, *Rebel War Clerk's Diary*, 40–43; Roman, *Military Operations*, 1:52; William C. Harris, *Leroy Pope Walker: Confederate Secretary of War* (Tuscaloosa, Ala.:

Confederate Publishing, 1962), 110–11; Eli N. Evans, *Judah P. Benjamin: The Jewish Confederate* (New York: Free Press, 1988), 121, 128, 134.

48. Davis to Johnston, August 1, 1861, in Rowland, *Jefferson Davis, Constitutionalist,* 5:119–20.

49. Johnston to Davis, August 3, 1861, *Davis Papers,* 7:272–74, and August 10, 1861, O.R. 5:777.

50. Johnston to Davis, August 10, 1861, O.R. 5:777; Davis to Johnston, August 13 and 20, 1861, O.R. 5:784, 789; Johnston to Davis, August 16, 17, and 19, ibid., 789–90, 797–98; Johnston to Davis, August 21 and 23, 1861, *Davis Papers,* 7:296, 304.

51. Johnston to Davis, September 3 and 10, 1861, *Davis Papers,* 7:320–22, 334–35.

52. Davis to Johnston, September 5, 1861, in Rowland, *Jefferson Davis, Constitutionalist,* 5:135–36; Davis to Johnston, September 13, 1861, O.R. 5:850–51.

53. George C. Rable, *The Confederate Republic: A Revolution Against Politics* (Chapel Hill: University of North Carolina Press, 1994), 117.

54. Davis to Johnston, September 8, 1861, O.R. 5:833–34.

55. Steven Harvey Newton, *Joseph E. Johnston and the Defense of Richmond* (Ann Arbor: UMI, 1991), 16–17.

56. Rowland, *Jefferson Davis, Constitutionalist,* 8:232, 9:206, 270, 292.

57. Francis W. Pickens to Davis, August 11, 1861, O.R. 50, pt. 1:566.

58. Dabney Maury, *Recollections of a Virginian* (New York: Charles Scribner's Sons, 1894), 144–45.

59. Johnston to Cooper, July 24, 1861, quoted in Varina Howell Davis, *Jefferson Davis: Ex-President of the Confederate States of America, A Memoir by His Wife,* 2 vols. (New York: Belford, 1890), 2:138–39.

60. Ibid.

61. Johnston to Cooper, July 29, 1861, ibid., 139–40.

62. *Davis Papers,* 7:254.

63. In his *Narrative* (72–73), Johnston stated that he held his letter to Davis for two days before sending it, and the letter itself (O.R. 52, pt. 2:605–8) is dated September 12. Davis received it in Richmond on or before September 14 (Davis to Johnston, September 14, 1861, in Rowland, *Jefferson Davis, Constitutionalist,* 5:132, something that would have been impossible had Johnston mailed it that same day. Therefore, September 12 was the date Johnston mailed the letter, not the day he wrote it, which must have been the tenth, the same day that Johnston wrote and sent his other letter to Davis, also reflecting a knowledge of his actual rank.

64. Johnston to Davis, September 10, 1861, *Davis Papers,* 7:334–35.

65. Davis to Johnston, September 13, 1861, O.R. 5:850–51.

66. Johnston to Davis, September 12, 1861, ibid. 52, pt. 2:605–8.

67. Newton, *Joseph E. Johnston,* 519.

68. Ibid., 17–18.

69. Davis to Johnston, September 14, 1861, in Rowland, *Jefferson Davis, Constitutionalist,* 5:132.

70. Newton, *Joseph E. Johnston,* 18.

71. Newton (ibid., 13, 18–20) argues that "the disagreement over rank may not have been the primary cause" of estrangement between Davis and Johnston, pointing

out that after the incident, "Johnston and Davis kept working together in harness." This is true, and their relationship was not nearly as bad as it came to be later in the war, for example, after Vicksburg. However, it seems clear that the disagreement over rank in September 1861 constituted the greatest single change in the relationship and poisoned Johnston's mind, at least, to the point of ensuring future troubles. Richard Taylor wrote in *Destruction and Reconstruction: Personal Experiences of the Late War,* ed. Richard B. Harwell (New York: Longmans, Green, 1955), 44–45, "General Johnston's mind was so jaundiced by the unfortunate disagreement with President Davis [over rank] . . . as to seriously cloud his judgement and impair his usefulness."

72. Many students of the war have made the mistake of asserting that Davis made almost no political appointments at all, a school of thought of which the following statement is an example: "To [appointments] Davis applied military criteria only, knowingly depleting some political capital by refusing to give recognition to generals whose military ability did not match their political prominence" (Archer Jones, *Civil War Command and Strategy: The Process of Victory and Defeat* [New York: Free Press, 1992], 113). The fact is that Davis was a good deal more political in his appointments than has often been recognized. Gideon Pillow, Felix Zollicoffer, Leonidas Polk, John B. Floyd, Henry A. Wise, Robert Toombs, Leroy Pope Walker, and John C. Breckinridge are examples.

73. Grady McWhiney, "Jefferson Davis and Confederate Military Leadership," in Roman J. Heleniak and Lawrence L. Hewitt, eds., *Leadership During the Civil War: The 1989 Deep Delta Civil War Symposium* (Shippensburg, Pa.: White Mane, 1992), 23.

74. Mason Matthews to Davis, September 19, 1861, O.R. 5:864.

75. Douglas Southall Freeman, *R. E. Lee: A Biography,* 4 vols. (New York: Scribners, 1934), 1:541–42.

76. Davis to Johnston, August 1, 1861, O.R. 5:119–20.

77. Freeman, *R. E. Lee,* 1:542.

78. J. Davis, *Rise and Fall,* 1:434.

79. Walter H. Taylor, *Four Years with General Lee* (Bloomington: Indiana University Press, 1962), 33–34.

80. Freeman, *R. E. Lee,* 1:541–42.

81. Benjamin to A. C. Myers, September 20, 1861, O.R. 5:867; Capt. W. L. Powell to Davis, September 20, 1861, ibid. Myers to Benjamin, September 21, 1861, ibid., 871; Benjamin to Myers, September 22, 1861, ibid., 871; Johnston to Davis, September 22, 1861, ibid., 872; Johnston to Benjamin, September 22, 1861, ibid., 873; Myers to Benjamin, September 23, 1861, ibid., 875; Benjamin to Johnston, September 24, 1861, ibid., 877.

82. Roman, *Military Operations,* 1:131; Johnston to Benjamin, September 26, 1861, O.R. 5:881–82.

83. Johnston, *Narrative,* 77.

84. Johnston to Beauregard, September 6, 1861, in Roman, *Military Operations,* 1:477.

85. Freeman, *Lee's Lieutenants,* 1:162–63.

86. Smith to Davis, September 3, 1861, *Davis Papers,* 7:323–24.

87. Freeman, *Lee's Lieutenants,* 1:162–63; Johnston and Beauregard to Davis, September 14, 1861, *Davis Papers,* 7:340.

88. Special Orders, no. 157, Adjutant and Inspector General's Office, September 19, 1861, O.R. 5:866; John Cheves Haskell, *The Haskell Memoirs,* ed. Gilbert E. Govan and James W. Livingood (New York: G. P. Putnam's Sons, 1960), 9.

89. General Orders no. 31, Headquarters, Army of the Potomac (Confederate), September 25, 1861, O.R. 5:881; Haskell, Memoirs, 13.

90. In fact, Johnston and Beauregard seem to have pioneered the practical establishment of army corps on the North American continent. These large, combined-arms organizations, capable of maneuvering and fighting independently if need be, were indispensable to the effective use of armies of the size that would be contending in the major theaters of the Civil War. Europeans had dealt with armies that size and had utilized corps organizations. Napoleon's pioneering use of the army corps had been a significant element of his army's superiority to other European armies during the early years of the Napoleonic Wars. Americans had never fielded an army as large as a single one of Napoleon's corps. Thus corps organization was as new to American officers as it was necessary to the scale of warfare they were setting out to wage. Beauregard, with his affinity for French military practices, was probably primarily responsible for this extremely positive innovation in the Confederate army. See Robert M. Epstein, "The Creation and Evolution of the Army Corps in the American Civil War," *Journal of Military History* 55 (January 1991): 21–46, and Epstein, *Napoleon's Last Victory* (Lawrence: University Press of Kansas, 1994).

91. Gustavus Woodson Smith, *Confederate War Papers* (New York: Atlantic Publishing and Engraving, 1884), 14, 31–32.

92. Smith to Davis, September 26, 1861, *Davis Papers,* 7:350.

93. Smith, *Confederate War Papers,* 14.

94. Johnston to Benjamin, September 26, 1861, O.R. 5:881–82.

95. Benjamin to Johnston, September 29, 1861, ibid., 883.

96. Davis speech, September 30, 1861, *Davis Papers,* 7:351.

97. *Davis Papers,* 7:352; Clement Eaton, *Jefferson Davis* (New York: Free Press, 1977), 146–47.

98. Jefferson Davis to Varina Davis, October 2, 1861, *Davis Papers,* 7:352; quote from *Charleston Daily Courier,* October 7, 1861, ibid., 353.

99. Jefferson Davis to Varina Davis, October 2, 1861, ibid., 352–53.

100. Smith, *Confederate War Papers,* 34–36.

101. Roman, *Military Operations,* 1:137–38.

102. Smith memorandum, January 31, 1862, O.R. 5:884–87.

103. Beauregard, in Johnson and Buel, *Battles and Leaders,* 1:221–22; Roman, *Military Operations,* 1:137.

104. W. C. Davis, *Jefferson Davis,* 363.

105. Beauregard, in Johnson and Buel, *Battles and Leaders,* 1:221–22; Roman, *Military Operations,* 1:137.

106. Smith memorandum, O.R. 5:884–87.

107. Ibid.

108. Smith, *Confederate War Papers,* 34–36.

109. Smith memorandum, O.R. 5:884–87.

110. J. Davis, *Rise and Fall,* 1:449.

111. Smith, *Confederate War Papers,* 34–36.

112. Ibid.
113. Smith memorandum, O.R. 5:884–87.
114. Ibid.
115. Ibid.
116. Jefferson Davis to Varina Davis, October 2, 1861, *Davis Papers,* 7:352–53.
117. Jefferson Davis speech, October 3, 1861, *Davis Papers,* 7:354.
118. W. C. Davis, *Jefferson Davis,* 366.
119. Ibid.
120. Chesnut, *Mary Chesnut's Civil War,* 208.
121. W. C. Davis, *Jefferson Davis,* 367.
122. J. B. Jones, *Rebel War Clerk's Diary,* 37.

CHAPTER 3

1. Benjamin to Johnston, October 7, 1861, Davis to Smith, October 10 and 24, 1861, O.R. 5:893–95, 918–19; Davis to Beauregard, October 16, 1861, *Davis Papers,* 7:358–60; Special Orders no. 419, October 12, 1861, O.R. 5:896.
2. Davis to Smith, October 10, 1861, O.R. 5:893–95.
3. Davis to Beauregard, October 16, 1861, *Davis Papers,* 7:358–60.
4. Benjamin to Johnston, October 7, 1861, O.R. 5:892; Johnston to Benjamin, October 11, 1861, ibid. 51, pt. 2:340; Joseph E. Johnston, *Narrative of Military Operations* (New York: Appleton, 1874), 78–79.
5. Smith to Davis, October 8, 1861, Gustavus Woodson Smith, *Confederate War Papers* (New York: Atlantic Publishing and Engraving, 1884), 20.
6. Ibid.; Davis to Beauregard, October 16, 1861, *Davis Papers,* 7:893–95; Alfred Roman, *The Military Operations of General Beauregard in the War Between the States, 1861–1865,* 2 vols. (New York: Harper and Brothers, 1884), 162–63.
7. Davis to Braxton Bragg, October 29, 1863, Rosenbach Museum and Library, Philadelphia, AMs 530/7.
8. John Cheves Haskell, *The Haskell Memoirs,* ed. Gilbert E. Govan and James W. Livingood (New York: G. P. Putnam's Sons, 1960), 13.
9. Smith to Davis, October 8 and 14, 1861, *Davis Papers,* 7:355, 357; Davis to Smith, October 24, 1861, O.R. 5:918–19.
10. Smith to Davis, October 25, 1861, *Davis Papers,* 7:381; Davis to Smith, October 29, 1861, in Dunbar Rowland, ed., *Jefferson Davis, Constitutionalist: His Letters, Papers, and Speeches,* 10 vols. (Jackson: Mississippi Department of Archives and History, 1923), 5:154–56.
11. Smith endorsement, November 2, 1861, *Davis Papers,* 7:382.
12. Davis to Smith, November 22, 1861, in Rowland, *Jefferson Davis, Constitutionalist,* 5:174–75.
13. Davis to Smith, November 30, 1861, ibid., 178; G. W. C. Lee to Smith, December 17, 1861, ibid., 181.
14. Beauregard to Davis, October 20, 1861, O.R. 51, pt. 2:255–56; Davis to Beauregard, October 25, 1861, ibid. 5:920.
15. Beauregard to Benjamin, October 9, 1861, ibid. 51, pt. 2:339.
16. Ibid.

17. Beauregard to Davis (telegram), October 20, 1861, *Davis Papers*, 7:364.

18. Beauregard to Davis, October 20, 1861, ibid., 365.

19. Davis to Beauregard, October 17, 1861, O.R. 5:903–4.

20. Benjamin to Beauregard, October 17, 1861, ibid., 904–5.

21. Beauregard to Davis, October 22, 1861, *Davis Papers*, 7:368–70. This letter mentions one of the president's of the sixteenth but is clearly a reply to the letter that O.R. 5:903–4 dates October 17.

22. Beauregard to Davis, October 21, 1861, *Davis Papers*, 7:366–67.

23. Beauregard to Davis, October 22, 1861, ibid., 368–70.

24. Davis to Beauregard, October 25, 1861, O.R. 5:920.

25. Roman, *Military Operations*, 1:448–49.

26. T. Harry Williams, *P. G. T. Beauregard: Napoleon in Gray* (Baton Rouge: Louisiana State University Press, 1955), 106; Douglas Southall Freeman, *Lee's Lieutenants: A Study in Command*, 3 vols. (New York: Charles Scribner's Sons, 1944), 1:102–4.

27. Beauregard to Cooper, August 25, 1861, in Roman, *Military Operations*, 1:448–49.

28. Davis to Beauregard, October 30, 1861, ibid., 165.

29. Davis to Chesnut, November 11, 1861, in Rowland, *Jefferson Davis, Constitutionalist*, 5:164–66.

30. Davis endorsement, October 30, 1861, *Davis Papers*, 7:384–85.

31. Beauregard to Davis, November 7, 1861, ibid., 399–401.

32. Beauregard to the editors of the Richmond *Whig*, November 3, 1861, in Roman, *Military Operations*, 1:163–64.

33. Williams, *P. G. T. Beauregard*, 108.

34. George C. Rable, *The Confederate Republic: A Revolution Against Politics* (Chapel Hill: University of North Carolina Press, 1994), 116.

35. John B. Jones, *A Rebel War Clerk's Diary*, ed. Earl Schenck Miers (New York: Sagamore, 1958), 53.

36. Beauregard to Davis, November 5, 1861, *Davis Papers*, 7:397.

37. Davis to Beauregard, November 10, 1861, O.R. 5:945.

38. Beauregard to Davis, November 7, 1861, *Davis Papers*, 7:399–401.

39. Williams, *P. G. T. Beauregard*, 108.

40. Davis to Johnston, November 3, 1861, *Davis Papers*, 7:393–94; Davis to Cooper and Lee, November 4, 1861, in Rowland, *Jefferson Davis, Constitutionalist*, 5:158; James Chesnut to Davis, November 2, 1861, *Davis Papers*, 7:388–92.

41. James Chesnut to Davis, November 2, 1861, Cooper to Davis, November 9, 1861, *Davis Papers*, 7:388–92, 405–6.

42. James Chesnut to Davis, November 2, 1861, ibid., 388–92; Davis to James Chesnut, November 11, 1861, in Rowland, *Jefferson Davis, Constitutionalist*, 5:164–66.

43. Davis to Fontaine, November 9, 1861, Johnston to Davis and Smith to Davis, November 12, 1861, *Davis Papers*, 7:405, 411; Davis to Beauregard, November 9, 1861, O.R. 5:944; Davis to Smith and Davis to Johnston, November 9, 1861, in Rowland, *Jefferson Davis, Constitutionalist*, 5:159, 161; Johnston to Davis, November 10, 1861, *Davis Papers*, 7:407.

44. *Mary Chesnut's Civil War*, 235–37.

45. Johnston to W. H. C. Whiting, November 9, 1861, O.R. 5:944.

46. Davis to Johnston, November 10, 1861, ibid., 945–47.

47. Haskell, *Memoirs,* 13; Wirt Armistead Cate, *Lucius Q. C. Lamar: Secession and Reunion* (New York: Russell and Russell, 1935), 85; James B. Murphy, *L. Q. C. Lamar: Pragmatic Patriot* (Baton Rouge: Louisiana State University Press, 1973), 66–67.

48. Cooper to Johnston, December 3, 1861, O.R. 52, pt. 2:402.

49. Benjamin to Johnston, December 9, 1861, ibid. 5:987–88.

50. Johnston to Cooper, December 6, 1861, Johnston to Benjamin, December 13, 1861, ibid., 985, 993–94.

51. Richard Taylor, *Destruction and Reconstruction: Personal Experiences of the Late War,* ed. Richard B. Harwell (New York: Longmans, Green, 1955), 23–24; T. Michael Parrish, *Richard Taylor: Soldier Prince of Dixie* (Chapel Hill: University of North Carolina Press, 1992), 142–43.

52. Benjamin to Johnston, December 27, 1861, O.R. 5:1011–12.

53. Johnston to Benjamin, January 1, 1862, ibid., 1015–16.

54. Benjamin to Johnston, January 5, 1862, Johnston to Benjamin, January 14, 1862, ibid., 1020–21, 1028; Gilbert E. Govan and James W. Livingood, *A Different Valor: The Story of General Joseph E. Johnston, C.S.A.* (Indianapolis: Bobbs-Merrill, 1956), 84–85.

55. Whiting to Davis, February 4, 1862, Dearborn Collection, Houghton Library, Harvard University.

56. Davis to Whiting, February 10, 1862, Louisiana Historical Association, Davis Papers, microfilm reel 17, frames 261–63.

57. Kemper to Beauregard, January 9, 1862, in Roman, *Military Operations,* 1:173.

58. Freeman, *Lee's Lieutenants,* 1:108–9; Williams, *P. G. T. Beauregard,* 111.

59. Roger A. Pryor to Beauregard, January 1862, O.R. 5:1048; Beauregard to Benjamin, January 29, 1862, Beauregard to "Soldier of the First Corps, Army of the Potomac," January 30, 1862, O.R. 51, pt. 2:455.

60. Williams, *P. G. T. Beauregard,* 113–15.

61. Douglas Southall Freeman, *R. E. Lee: A Biography,* 4 vols. (New York: Scribners, 1934), 1:602–3; Stephen W. Sears, *To the Gates of Richmond: The Peninsula Campaign* (New York: Ticknor and Fields, 1992), 155.

62. Cooper to Lee, September 4, 1861, O.R. 5:828–29, Jefferson Davis, *The Rise and Fall of the Confederate Government,* 2 vols. (New York: Appleton, 1881), 1:436; Freeman, *R. E. Lee,* 1:603, 606–7.

63. Johnston, *Narrative,* 81; General Orders no. 15, October 22, 1861, Adjutant and Inspector General's Office; Benjamin to Jackson, October 21, 1861, Jackson to Benjamin, October 25, 1861, O.R. 5:913, 921–22.

64. Jackson to Benjamin, November 20, 1861, with endorsement by Johnston, November 21, O.R. 5:965–66.

65. Benjamin to Loring, November 24 and December 3, 1861, Loring to Benjamin, November 29, 1861, Cooper to Loring, December 5, 1861, ibid., 968–69, 983–84, 978, 982.

66. Frank E. Vandiver, *Mighty Stonewall* (College Station: Texas A&M University Press, 1957), 185.

67. Loring to Benjamin, November 29, 1861, O.R. 5:983–84.

68. Lt. Col. G. W. Lay to Johnston, January 31, 1862, O.R. 51, pt. 2:461; Jackson to Maj. Thomas G. Rhett, February 21, 1862, ibid. 5:389–95.

69. Lay to Johnston, January 31, 1862, ibid. 51, pt. 2:461.

70. Loring to Benjamin, January 26, 1862, Johnston to Cooper, February 7, 1862, ibid. 5:1046–48, 1065–66.

71. Samuel V. Fulkerson to Walter R. Staples, January 23, 1862, Taliaferro to Staples, January 23, 1862, ibid., 1040–42; Robert G. Tanner, *Stonewall in the Valley: Thomas J. "Stonewall" Jackson's Shenandoah Valley Campaign, Spring 1862* (Garden City, N.Y.: Doubleday, 1976), 84.

72. Benjamin to Johnston, January 26, 1862, O.R. 5:1049.

73. Davis to Johnston, February 14, 1862, ibid., 1071–72.

74. Johnston to Benjamin, January 29, 1862, ibid., 1059; Johnston to Cooper, February 4, 1862, ibid. 51, pt. 2:460.

75. Vandiver, *Mighty Stonewall*, 193.

76. Davis to Benjamin, January 29, 1862, O.R. 5:1050.

77. Benjamin to Jackson, January 30, 1862, ibid., 1053.

78. Jackson to Benjamin, January 31, 1862, ibid.

79. Letcher to Benjamin, February 3, 1862, ibid., 1060.

80. Jackson to Letcher, February 6, 1862, ibid., 1062–63.

81. Steven Harvey Newton, *Joseph E. Johnston and the Defense of Richmond* (Ann Arbor: UMI, 1991), 110.

82. Johnston to Jackson, February 3, 1862, O.R. 5:1059–60.

83. Johnston to Davis, February 5, 1862, ibid., 1062.

84. Jackson to Thomas G. Rhett, February 1, 1862, ibid., 1056.

85. Johnston endorsement, February 7, 1862, on Jackson to Benjamin, January 31, 1862, ibid., 1053.

86. Tanner, *Stonewall in the Valley*, 87.

87. Jackson to Letcher, February 6, 1862, O.R. 5:1062–63.

88. Benjamin to Johnston, February 3, 1862, ibid., 1059.

89. Johnston to Benjamin, February 7, 1862, ibid., 1064–65.

90. Davis to Johnston, February 14, 1862, ibid., 1071–72.

91. Freeman, *Lee's Lieutenants*, 1:127.

92. Johnston to Cooper, February 7, 1862, O.R. 5:1065–66.

93. Benjamin to Davis, February 13, 1862, with Davis endorsement, ibid. 51, pt. 2:488–89.

94. Benjamin to Johnston, February 9, 1862, ibid. 5:1066–67.

95. Davis to Congress, February 17, 1862, National Archives, Records Group 109.

96. Davis to Van Dorn, October 25, 1861, in Rowland, *Jefferson Davis, Constitutionalist,* 5:153–54; William Garrett Piston, *Lee's Tarnished Lieutenant: James Longstreet and His Place in Southern History* (Athens: University of Georgia Press, 1987), 16–17.

CHAPTER 4

1. For Davis's reaction to the fall of Forts Henry and Donelson and his attempts to restore the Confederacy's fortunes west of the Appalachians in the late winter and

spring of 1862, see Steven E. Woodworth, *Jefferson Davis and His Generals: The Failure of Confederate Command in the West* (Lawrence: University Press of Kansas, 1990), 71–108.

2. Steven Harvey Newton, *Joseph E. Johnston and the Defense of Richmond* (Ann Arbor: UMI, 1991), 79–80, 84–85. Newton argues that up to this point Davis had maintained a policy of bluffing by keeping weak Confederate forces pushed as far forward as possible all along the frontier. Although this strategem was undoubtedly used by Albert Sidney Johnston in Kentucky, it is difficult if not impossible to make any connection between it and a deliberate policy of the president.

3. Joseph E. Johnston, *Narrative of Military Operations* (New York: Appleton, 1874), 96; Newton, *Joseph E. Johnston,* 29–31.

4. That Davis intended some urgency in this summons is not disproved by the fact that he sent it by mail—a three-day process—rather than by telegraph. Extremely concerned with secrecy in this case, Davis was also habitually distrustful of telegraph operators.

5. Johnston to Davis (telegram), February 16, 1862, Earl Gregg Swem Library, College of William and Mary.

6. Johnston to Davis, February 16, 1862, O.R. 5:1074.

7. Davis to Johnston, February 19, 1862, ibid., 1077.

8. Newton, *Joseph E. Johnston,* 63–68.

9. Ibid., 153.

10. Ibid., 154–55.

11. Ibid., 88.

12. Ibid., 154–55.

13. Ibid., 92–93.

14. Ibid., 93–94; Johnston, *Narrative,* 97.

15. Newton, *Joseph E. Johnston,* 90.

16. Davis to Johnston, February 28, 1862, in Dunbar Rowland, ed., *Jefferson Davis, Constitutionalist: His Letters, Papers, and Speeches,* 10 vols. (Jackson: Mississippi Department of Archives and History, 1923), 5:208–10. Davis's reference to Johnston's "opinion" that his position could be easily turned must indicate a statement made by Johnston at this conference, since, as Johnston points out in "Responsibilities of the First Bull Run" (Robert U. Johnson and Clarence C. Buel, eds., *Battles and Leaders of the Civil War,* 4 vols. [New York: Thomas Yoseloff, 1956], 1:256), none of his letters to Davis included such a statement. Yet had Johnston not believed it true and known that he had made such a statement to the president, he undoubtedly would have immediately repelled the assertion in Davis's February 28 letter. By the time Davis wrote *The Rise and Fall of the Confederate Government,* 2 vols. (New York: Appleton, 1881) nineteen years later, he had apparently forgotten the general's oral statement but knew from copies of his own correspondence that Johnston had somewhere expressed such an opinion to him (1:462).

17. Newton, *Joseph E. Johnston,* 90.

18. Ibid., 95–96.

19. Davis to Johnston, February 18, 1862, in Rowland, *Jefferson Davis, Constitutionalist,* 5:208–10.

20. Davis to Johnston, March 6, 1862, ibid., 211–12.

21. Johnston to Benjamin, February 1 and 14, 1862, O.R. 5:1057–58, 1072; Johnston, *Narrative*, 90–91; Hal Bridges, *Lee's Maverick General: Daniel Harvey Hill* (Lincoln: University of Nebraska Press, 1991), 31; Craig L. Symonds, *Joseph E. Johnston: A Civil War Biography* (New York: W. W. Norton, 1992), 134–37.

22. Johnston to Benjamin, February 16, 1862, O.R. 5:1075.

23. Symonds, *Joseph E. Johnston*, 138: Newton, *Joseph E. Johnston*, 99–100.

24. Symonds, *Joseph E. Johnston*, 138.

25. William C. Davis, *Jefferson Davis: The Man and His Hour* (New York: Harper Collins, 1991), 402: Newton, *Joseph E. Johnston*, 99–100.

26. Johnston, "Responsibilities," in Robert U. Johnson and Clarence C. Buel, eds., *Battles and Leaders of the Civil War*, 4 vols. (New York: Thomas Yoseloff, 1956), 1:256.

27. John B. Jones, *A Rebel War Clerk's Diary*, ed. Earl Schenk Miers (New York: Sagamore, 1958), 67–68.

28. W. C. Davis, *Jefferson Davis*, 394.

29. Jones, *Rebel War Clerk's Diary*, 67–68.

30. Johnston, *Narrative*, 97; Johnston to Davis, February 23, 1862, O.R. 5:1079.

31. Lucius B. Northrop to Davis, January 26, 1881, in Dunbar Rowland, ed., *Jefferson Davis, Constitutionalist: His Letters, Papers and Speeches*, 10 vols. (Jackson: Mississippi Department of Archives and History, 1923), 8:580–86.

32. Johnston to Davis, February 22, 1862, O.R. 5:1079.

33. Johnston to Davis, February 23, 1862, ibid.

34. Johnston to Davis, February 25, 1862, ibid., 1081.

35. Johnston to Davis, February 28, 1862, ibid., 1082.

36. Johnston to Davis, March 5, 1862, ibid., 1088.

37. Johnston to Davis, February 22, 23, 25, and 28, and March 5, 1862, ibid., 1079, 1081–82, 1088.

38. Newton, *Joseph E. Johnston*, 63–101.

39. Davis to Johnston, February 28, 1862, in Rowland, *Jefferson Davis, Constitutionalist*, 5:208–10.

40. Davis to Johnston, March 6, 1862, ibid., 5:211–12.

41. Johnston to Davis, March 1, 1862, O.R. 5:1086–87.

42. Davis to Johnston, March 4, 1862, in Rowland, *Jefferson Davis, Constitutionalist*, 5:210–11.

43. Johnston, *Narrative*, 100–101.

44. Davis to Johnston, March 5, 1862, O.R. 51, pt. 2:487.

45. Newton, *Joseph E. Johnston*, 22, sees this, rather than the previous fall's dispute over rank, as the chief cause of dissension between Davis and Johnston.

46. Ibid., 176.

47. Ibid., 176–77; Douglas Southall Freeman, *R. E. Lee: A Biography*, 4 vols. (New York: Scribners, 1934), 2:4; Davis, veto message, March 14, 1862, O.R., series 4, 1:997.

48. Davis to Lee, March 2, 1862, O.R. 6:400.

49. Lee to Davis, March 2, 1862, in Clifford Dowdey and Louis H. Manaris, eds., *The Wartime Papers of R. E. Lee* (New York: Bramhall House, 1961), 123.

50. Freeman, *R. E. Lee*, 1:628.

51. General Orders no. 14, Adjutant and Inspector General's Office, March 13, 1862, O.R. 5:1099.

52. Newton, *Joseph E. Johnston,* 166–67.

53. Davis to Johnston, March 10, 1862, O.R. 5:1096.

54. W. C. Davis, *Jefferson Davis,* 411.

55. Davis to Johnston, March 15, 1862, O.R. 5:527–28.

56. W. C. Davis, *Jefferson Davis,* 411.

57. Davis to Johnston, March 15, 1862, O.R. 5:527–28.

58. Davis to Johnston (telegram), March 15, 1862, ibid., 527.

59. Johnston to Cooper, March 12, 1862, ibid., 526–27.

60. Johnston to Davis, March 13, 1862, ibid. 51, pt. 2:1073–74.

61. Jefferson Davis, *The Rise and Fall of the Confederate Government,* 2 vols. (New York: Appleton, 1881), 1:464–65.

62. Davis to Johnston (telegram), March 15, 1862, O.R. 5:527.

63. Davis to Johnston, March 15, 1862, ibid., 527–28.

64. A. C. Meyers to Davis, March 7, 1862, ibid., 1093; Lucius B. Northrop, "The Confederate Commissariat at Manassas," in Johnson and Buel, *Battles and Leaders,* 1:261; Jeffrey N. Lash, *Destroyer of the Iron Horse: General Joseph E. Johnston and Confederate Rail Transport, 1861–1865* (Kent, Ohio: Kent State University Press, 1991), 28, 31–32, 34; Johnston to Davis, March 17, 1862, O.R. 51, pt. 2:504; J. Davis, *Rise and Fall,* 1:468; Douglas Southall Freeman, *Lee's Lieutenants: A Study in Command,* 3 vols. (New York: Charles Scribner's Sons, 1944), 1:140–41.

65. Lee to Holmes, March 16, 1862, in Dowdey and Manarin, *Wartime Papers,* 130.

66. Widely divergent views have been expressed regarding the extent of Lee's power and influence as commanding general. These range from the assertion that Lee was severely limited by Davis (Freeman, *R. E. Lee,* 2:6–7; Robert G. Tanner, *Stonewall in the Valley: Thomas J. "Stonewall" Jackson's Shenandoah Valley Campaign, Spring 1862* [Garden City, N.Y.: Doubleday, 1976], 155) to more recent claims that Lee had wide-ranging powers and an influence powerful enough to create a major change in Confederate strategy (Newton, *Joseph E. Johnston,* 179–80, 191–92).

67. J. Davis, *Rise and Fall,* 1:465–66.

68. Newton, *Joseph E. Johnston,* 188–89, argues that the defensive line had nothing to do with Davis's visit, the purpose of which was in fact to discuss the possibility of shifting forces to meet threats to coastal Virginia and North Carolina. Although these issues were discussed in Fredericksburg, Davis's behavior patterns throughout his presidency give ample reason to believe that the original purpose of the trip was as he stated. Johnston was apparently embarrassed enough about the purpose of Davis's visit to deny after the war that it had ever taken place. Johnston, "Responsibilities of the First Bull Run," in Johnson and Buel, *Battles and Leaders,* 1:257.

69. J. Davis, *Rise and Fall,* 1:465–66.

70. Ibid.; J. T. Doswell to William S. Barton, August 10, 1885, and W. S. Barton to ?, August 17, 1885, in Varina Howell Davis, *Jefferson Davis: Ex-President of the Confederate States of America, A Memoir by His Wife,* 2 vols. (New York: Belford, 1890), 2:195–97.

71. Newton, *Joseph E. Johnston,* 190–91.

72. J. Davis, *Rise and Fall,* 1:465–66; Doswell to Barton, August 10, 1885, in V. H. Davis, *Jefferson Davis,* 2:195–96.

73. J. Davis, *Rise and Fall,* 1:465–66.

74. Lee to Davis, March 21, 1862, O.R. 51, pt. 2:512.

75. Lee to his wife, March 22, 1861, in Dowdey and Manarin, *Wartime Papers,* 133–34.

76. Davis to Johnston, March 22, 1861, O.R. 9, pt. 3:392.

77. Newton, *Joseph E. Johnston,* 191.

78. Magruder to Lee, March 21, 1862, O.R. 11, pt. 3:389–90.

79. Lee to Johnston, March 25 and 28, 1862, ibid., 397, 408–9.

80. Lee to Johnston, March 25, 1862, ibid., 397. Considerable difference of opinion exists as to just what was being attempted here and in the following days and who was trying to do it. Freeman (*R. E. Lee,* 2:16–17) surmised that Lee was trying to bring about an early strategic concentration on the Peninsula and was carrying Davis with him. Perceiving that Johnston would not willingly part with troops, Lee then is supposed to have modified his plan to a more gradual buildup on the Peninsula, but this simply does not fit with the correspondence between Lee and Johnston. Newton, on the other hand (*Joseph E. Johnston,* 198–203), argues that Davis favored rapid concentration, while Lee wanted to wait until northern intentions were more apparent. Thus Lee actually tried to discourage Johnston from sending the troops. This would seem to be nearer the truth, but on the whole a far more likely explanation is that Lee was doing just what he said, acting on behalf of Davis, and that Davis, acting very much in character, was hesitating and even waffling between reinforcing the Peninsula and keeping his lines strong on the Rappahannock and Rapidan.

81. Johnston to Lee, March 27, 1862, O.R. 11, pt. 3:405–6.

82. Johnston to Lee, March 26, 1862, ibid., 400–401.

83. Johnston to Lee, March 27, 1862, ibid., 405–6.

84. Lee to Johnston, March 28, 1:00 A.M., ibid., 408.

85. Lee to Johnston, March 28, ibid., 408–9.

86. Ibid.

87. Freeman, *Lee's Lieutenants,* 1:166–67; Hamilton J. Eckenrode and Bryan Conrad, *James Longstreet: Lee's War Horse* (Chapel Hill: University of North Carolina Press, 1986), 29.

88. Johnston to Davis, April 4, 1862, Davis Collection, Emory University.

89. Johnston to Lee, April 4, 1862, O.R. 11, pt. 3:419–20.

90. William J. Miller, "The Grand Campaign: A Journal of Operations in the Peninsula Campaign, March 17–August 26, 1862," in *The Peninsula Campaign of 1862: Yorktown to the Seven Days,* 1 vol. to date (Campbell, Calif: Savas Woodbury, 1993), 1:183.

91. Lee to Johnston, April 4, 1862, O.R. 11, pt. 3:420.

92. Johnston to Lee, April 6, 1862, ibid., 423.

93. Miller, *Peninsula Campaign,* 183.

94. Stephen W. Sears, *To the Gates of Richmond: The Peninsula Campaign* (New York: Ticknor and Fields, 1992), 37–43.

95. Miller, *Peninsula Campaign,* 184.

96. Freeman, *R. E. Lee,* 2:20; Newton, *Joseph E. Johnston,* 217; J. Davis, *Rise and Fall,* 2:86–87; Johnston, *Narrative,* 110.

97. Special Orders no. 6, April 12, 1862, in Dowdey and Manarin, *Wartime Papers,* 145.

98. J. Davis, *Rise and Fall,* 2:86–87; Johnston, *Narrative,* 110.

99. Johnston, *Narrative,* 11–14.

100. Sears, *To the Gates of Richmond,* 46.

101. Bridges, *Lee's Maverick General,* 7.

102. Johnston, *Narrative,* 111–14.

103. Gilbert E. Govan and James W. Livingood, *A Different Valor: The Story of General Joseph E. Johnston, C.S.A.* (Indianapolis: Bobbs-Merrill, 1956), 110–11.

104. Johnston, *Narrative,* 114–15; J. Davis, *Rise and Fall,* 2:86–87; Freeman, *R. E. Lee,* 2:21–22.

105. Newton, *Joseph E. Johnston,* 239–40; Gustavus Woodson Smith, *Confederate War Papers* (New York: Atlantic Publishing and Engraving, 1884), 41–42.

106. Smith, *Confederate War Papers,* 41–42.

107. Johnston, *Narrative,* 114–15.

108. J. Davis, *Rise and Fall,* 2:86–87; Johnston, "Manassas to Seven," in Johnson and Buel, *Battles and Leaders,* 2:203.

109. Newton, *Joseph E. Johnston,* 256.

110. Ibid., 260.

111. James Longstreet, *From Manassas to Appomattox,* ed. James I. Robertson, Jr. (Bloomington: Indiana University Press, 1960), 66.

112. Sears, *To the Gates of Richmond,* 47.

113. Longstreet, *From Manassas to Appomattox,* 66.

114. Smith, *Confederate War Papers,* 42.

115. Newton, *Joseph E. Johnston,* 246–47, 253, 255, suggests Lee envied Johnston's fame and field command.

116. Ibid., 242–43; Johnston, *Narrative,* 114–15.

117. Johnston, "Manassas to Seven Pines," in Johnson and Buel, *Battles and Leaders,* 2:203.

118. W. C. Davis, *Jefferson Davis,* 414.

119. Johnston, "Manassas to Seven Pines," in Johnson and Buel, *Battles and Leaders,* 2:203.

120. J. Davis, *Rise and Fall,* 2:86–87.

121. Newton, *Joseph E. Johnston,* 261.

122. Freeman, *R. E. Lee,* 2:21–22.

123. Newton, *Joseph E. Johnston,* 244, 263, 273–74.

124. J. Davis, *Rise and Fall,* 2:87.

125. Johnston, *Narrative,* 116.

126. Lee to Johnston, April 21, 1862, O.R. 11, pt. 3:452.

127. Johnston to Lee, April 22, 1862, ibid., 455.

128. Johnston to Lee, April 22, 1862, ibid., 456; Lee to Johnston, April 23, 1862, ibid., 458.

129. Johnston to Lee, April 27, 1862, ibid., 469.

130. Lee to Johnston, April 30, 1862, ibid., 476.

131. Johnston, *Narrative,* 118, 127, and "Manassas to Seven Pines," in Johnson and Buel, *Battles and Leaders,* 2:204.

132. Johnston to Lee, April 29, 1862, O.R. 11, pt. 3:473.

133. Johnston to Lee, April 30, 1862, ibid., 477.

134. Lee to Johnston, May 1, 1862, ibid., 484–85.

135. Davis to Johnston, May 1, 1862, ibid., 484–85.

136. Ibid.

137. Johnston, *Narrative,* 119; J. Davis, *Rise and Fall,* 2:93.

138. J. Davis, *Rise and Fall,* 2:92–93; Lee to Johnston, May 2, 1862, in Dowdey and Manarin, *Wartime Papers,* 164.

139. J. Davis, *Rise and Fall,* 2:94; Freeman, *Lee's Lieutenants,* 1:155.

140. V. H. Davis, *Jefferson Davis,* 2:265; Jones, *Rebel War Clerk's Diary,* 63.

141. Joseph Davis to Jefferson Davis, April 20, 1862, Davis Papers, no. 220, Transylvania University.

142. That Davis must have directed Lee to exercise some degree of supervision over the forces in northern Virginia is indicated by the fact that such action—coordinating the various forces defending Richmond—was precisely the purpose for which he had brought Lee to Richmond. Davis also had a known propensity to give his attention to what he considered the main front while leaving the sideshows to Lee's direction, and, as will shortly be seen, Davis did not trust Jackson to operate independently.

143. Longstreet, *From Manassas to Appomattox,* 65; Eckenrode and Conrad, *James Longstreet,* 29–30; Freeman, *Lee's Lieutenants,* 1:166–67.

144. Newton, *Joseph E. Johnston,* 286, 313–23, 376–77.

145. Lee to Ewell, April 17, 25, and 27, 1862, Lee to Jackson, April 21, 25, and 29, and May 1, 1862, in Dowdey and Manarin, *Wartime Papers,* 146, 151–52, 155–57, 159–61, 163.

146. Tanner, *Stonewall in the Valley,* 143.

147. Freeman, *Lee's Lieutenants,* 1:371; Frank E. Vandiver, *Mighty Stonewall* (College Station: Texas A&M University Press, 1957), 238.

148. T. Michael Parrish, *Richard Taylor: Soldier Prince of Dixie* (Chapel Hill: University of North Carolina Press, 1992), 153.

149. Davis to Johnston, May 1, 1862, O.R. 11, pt. 3:485.

150. Johnston to Lee, May 9, 1862, ibid., 502–3; Parrish, *Richard Taylor,* 153.

151. Tanner, *Stonewall in the Valley,* 130.

152. Jefferson Davis to Varina Davis, May 31, 1862, in Rowland, *Jefferson Davis, Constitutionalist,* 5:264.

153. Johnston to Lee, April 22 and 23 and May 8, 9, and 10, 1862, O.R. 11, pt. 3: 455, 458–59, 499–500, 502–4, 506; Johnston to Lee, May 7, 1862, ibid. 51, pt. 2: 552–53.

154. Lee to Johnston, May 8, 10, and 12, 1862, W. H. Taylor to Johnston, May 10, 1862, ibid. 11, pt. 3: 500–501, 505–6, 510–11; Lee to Johnston, May 9, 1862, ibid. 51, pt. 2:553–54.

155. Lee to Johnston, May 3, 1862, ibid. 11, pt. 3:491.

156. Davis to Johnston, May 11, 1862, ibid., 507–8. Rowland, *Jefferson Davis, Constitutionalist,* 5:242–43, dates this letter May 10.

157. Symonds, *Joseph E. Johnston*, 158.

158. Mary Boykin Chesnut, *Mary Chesnut's Civil War*, ed. C. Vann Woodward (New Haven, Conn.: Yale University Press, 1981), 268.

159. Newton, *Joseph E. Johnston*, 339–40; John B. Hood, *Advance and Retreat: Personal Experiences in the United States and Confederate States Armies* (Bloomington: Indiana University Press, 1959), 153–55.

160. Newton, *Joseph E. Johnston*, 346, 352–53, 354 n. 64, 363.

161. Ibid., 364; Freeman, *Lee's Lieutenants*, 1:192.

162. Freeman, *Lee's Lieutenants*, 1:193–95. Johnston's overreaction to the small Federal landing at Eltham's Landing seems best explained by Edward Porter Alexander's claim that he was planning offensive–not defensive–operations there. Alexander, *Fighting for the Confederacy: The Personal Recollections of General Edward Porter Alexander*, ed. Gary Gallagher (Chapel Hill: University of North Carolina Press, 1989), 82.

163. Alexander, *Fighting for the Confederacy*, 82–83.

164. Lee to Johnston, May 8, 1862, in Dowdey and Manarin, *Wartime Papers*, 166–67.

165. W. H. Davis, *Jefferson Davis*, 2:268.

166. Randolph to Cooper, Gorgas, Northrop, Moore, and Myers, May 10, 1862, O.R. 11, pt. 3:504.

167. Freeman (*Lee's Lieutenants*, 1:210) thinks it probable that Davis learned of the loss of the *Virginia* the same day he visited Johnston's headquarters, but puts this on or about (but no later than) May 14. Letters from Davis to Varina (Rowland, *Jefferson Davis, Constitutionalist*, 5:245) and from Robert Toombs to his wife (William Y. Thompson, *Robert Toombs of Georgia* [Baton Rouge: Louisiana State University Press, 1966]) fix the date of Davis's visit at May 12. As the *Virginia* was destroyed on the eleventh, it is not unlikely that Davis had received the news by the next day.

168. Jefferson Davis to Varina Davis, May 13, 1862, in Rowland, *Jefferson Davis, Constitutionalist*, 5:245; J. Davis, *Rise and Fall*, 2:101–2.

169. Thompson, *Robert Toombs*, 184.

170. Jefferson Davis to Varina Davis, May 13, 1862, in Rowland, *Jefferson Davis, Constitutionalist*, 5:245.

171. J. Davis, *Rise and Fall*, 2:101–2.

172. Jefferson Davis to Varina Davis, May 13, 1862, in Rowland, *Jefferson Davis, Constitutionalist*, 5:245.

173. Lee to Johnston, May 13, 1862, O.R. 11, pt. 3:512–13.

174. Cole to Johnston, May 13, 1862, ibid., 513.

175. Freeman, *R. E. Lee*, 2:47–48; Randolph to Huger, May 14, 1862, O.R. 11, pt. 3:515.

176. Freeman, *R. E. Lee*, 2:47–48; John H. Reagan, *Memoirs*, ed. Walter F. McCaleb (New York: Neale, 1906), 139.

177. Jefferson Davis to Varina Davis, May 16, 1862, in Rowland, *Jefferson Davis, Constitutionalist*, 5:245–46.

178. Reagan, *Memoirs*, 137–38.

179. Davis to Johnston, May 17, 1862, in Rowland, *Jefferson Davis, Constitutionalist*, 5:247–48.

180. J. Davis, *Rise and Fall*, 2:101–2.

181. Davis to Johnston, May 17, 1862, in Rowland, *Jefferson Davis, Constitutionalist*, 5:247–48.

182. Lee to Johnston, May 17, 1862, O.R. 11, pt. 3:523.

183. Reagan, *Memoirs*, 138.

184. Ibid.

185. Ibid., 138–39; J. Davis, *Rise and Fall*, 2:103.

186. Sears, *To the Gates of Richmond*, 109–10.

187. Johnston, "Manassas to Seven Pines," in Johnson and Buel, *Battles and Leaders*, 2:207.

188. Johnston to Cooper, May 19, 1862, O.R. 11, pt. 1:275–76.

189. This point is as controversial as any in the Peninsula campaign. The preponderance of historians, including Freeman (*Lee's Lieutenants*, 1:212n) and Newton (*Joseph E. Johnston*, 414 n. 70) have taken Johnston's side, accusing Davis of a weak memory or worse. William C. Davis (*Jefferson Davis*, 421–22) takes the opposite view. Direct evidence for the fact that Davis was unaware of the army's proximity to Richmond prior to his afternoon ride on May 18 is found in the memoirs of both Davis (*Rise and Fall*, 2:103) and Reagan (*Memoirs*, 138–39). Circumstantial evidence is provided by Davis's sending of his aide the day before. Had he realized Johnston was or soon would be so close, Davis undoubtedly would have gone himself. Finally, it strains credulity to suggest that both Davis and Reagan fabricated substantially the same story. The simplest, and thus most sensible, solution is that Lee–for whatever reason–did not inform Davis of the army's position.

190. Reagan, *Memoirs*, 138–39; J. Davis, *Rise and Fall*, 2:103.

191. Reagan, *Memoirs*, 138–39.

192. Lee to Johnston, May 18, 1862, O.R. 11, pt. 3:526.

193. Jefferson Davis to Varina Davis, May 19, 1862, in Rowland, *Jefferson Davis, Constitutionalist*, 5:248.

194. Jones, *Rebel War Clerk's Diary*, 77.

195. Ibid., 78; V. H. Davis, *Jefferson Davis*, 2:271.

196. Davis passport, Davis Collection, Museum of the Confederacy, Richmond.

197. Randolph to Johnston, May 19, 1862, O.R. 11, pt. 3:526.

198. Johnston to Cooper, May 19, 1862, ibid., pt. 1:275–76.

199. Johnston to Cooper, May 20, 1862, ibid., pt. 3:527.

200. Lee to Johnston, May 21, 1862, in Dowdey and Manarin, *Wartime Papers*, 176–77.

201. Lee to Johnston, May 22, 1862, ibid., 177.

202. Davis to Johnston, May 23, 1862, O.R., 11, pt. 3:536.

203. J. Davis, *Rise and Fall*, 2:120–21.

204. Freeman, *Lee's Lieutenants*, 1:212–13.

205. Johnston to Lee, May 25, 1862, O.R. 11, pt. 3:543.

206. Davis to Johnston, May 25, 1862, Schoff Collection, Clements Library, University of Michigan.

207. Davis to Johnston, May 26, 1862, in Rowland, *Jefferson Davis, Constitutionalist*, 5:251–52.

208. Freeman, *R. E. Lee*, 2:61; *Lee's Lieutenants*, 1:213–14; and J. Davis, *Rise and Fall*, 2:120–21.

209. Johnston, *Narrative*, 120–32.

210. Johnston to Lee, May 28, 1862, O.R. 11, pt. 3:555.

211. Newton, *Joseph E. Johnston*, 425–26.

212. Sears, *To the Gates of Richmond*, 117–18.

213. J. Davis, *Rise and Fall*, 2:121–22; Smith, *Confederate War Papers*, 155.

214. Johnston to Davis, May 19, 1862, Davis Collection, Emory University Library.

215. Jefferson Davis to Varina Davis, May 31, 1862, in Rowland, *Jefferson Davis, Constitutionalist*, 5:264.

216. Jones, *Rebel War Clerk's Diary*, 79–80.

217. J. Davis, *Rise and Fall*; 2:122.

218. Ibid.; Edward Porter Alexander, *Military Memoirs of a Confederate* (New York: Scribners, 1912), 92.

219. Johnston's motive in riding away from his headquarters at this moment has been debated. His highly sympathetic biographers Govan and Livingood (*A Different Valor*, 154) denied that his purpose was to avoid the president. Freeman (*R. E. Lee*, 2:69–71, and *Lee's Lieutenants*, 1:238) left it an open question. However, both observers at the time (Alexander, *Military Memoirs*, 92) and the best modern scholars (Symonds, *Joseph E. Johnston*, 170; Newton, *Joseph E. Johnston*, 489–93) suggest that the general's reason was indeed to escape Davis.

220. Sears, *To the Gates of Richmond*, 118–23; Newton, *Joseph E. Johnston*, 436–38.

221. Among those who tend to exonerate Longstreet is his close friend Edward Porter Alexander (*Fighting for the Confederacy*, 85–86), who claims Longstreet made an honest mistake for which Johnston was "solely" responsible. Longstreet's sympathetic modern biographer Jeffrey D. Wert (*General James Longstreet: The Confederacy's Most Controversial Soldier—A Biography* [New York: Simon and Schuster, 1993], 123) agrees the mistake was honest but allows Longstreet to share a small portion of the blame still belonging primarily to Johnston. Freeman (*Lee's Lieutenants*, 1:234) leaves open the question as to whether Longstreet's error was the result of mistake or willfulness. Govan and Livingood (*A Different Valor*, 149–50), Bridges (*Lee's Maverick General*, 39–40), and Symonds (*Joseph E. Johnston*, 165) take much the same position.

222. Sears, *To the Gates of Richmond*, 121; Newton, *Joseph E. Johnston*, 450–52, 503; Eckenrode and Conrad, *James Longstreet*, 53, 55–56.

223. Govan and Livingood, *A Different Valor*, 148; Sears, *To the Gates of Richmond*, 121–23; Newton, *Joseph E. Johnston*, 469–70; Bridges, *Lee's Maverick General*, 39; Eckenrode and Conrad, *James Longstreet*, 45–46; Freeman, *Lee's Lieutenants*, 1:234–35; Symonds, *Joseph E. Johnston*, 167.

224. Eckenrode and Conrad, *James Longstreet*, 52; Johnston to Cooper, June 24, 1862, O.R. 11, pt. 1:933–35; Bridges, *Lee's Maverick General*, 55; Hill's report, O.R. 11, pt.1:943–46; Huger's endorsement on Longstreet's Seven Pines report, June 21, 1862, ibid., 942; Longstreet's report, June 10, 1862, ibid., 939–41; Huger to Johnston, September 20, 1862, ibid., 935–36; Smith, *Confederate War Papers*,

167–70; Johnston to Randolph, October 4, 1862, O.R. 11, pt. 1:938–39; Huger to Davis, September 21, 1862, ibid., 936–37; Huger to Randolph, September 22, 1862, ibid., 936; Randolph to Johnston, October 2, 1862, ibid., 936.

225. Sears, *To the Gates of Richmond,* 121.

226. Newton, *Joseph E. Johnston,* 464.

227. Freeman, *Lee's Lieutenants,* 1:238.

228. Symonds, *Joseph E. Johnston,* 169; Freeman, *Lee's Lieutenants,* 1:223, Newton, *Joseph E. Johnston,* 454–55, 465–66.

229. Bridges, *Lee's Maverick General,* 44–45, 54–57; Eckenrode and Conrad, *James Longstreet,* 55.

230. Wert, *General James Longstreet,* 152.

231. Sears, *To the Gates of Richmond,* 130; Symonds, *Joseph E. Johnston,* 169; Newton, *Joseph E. Johnston,* 470–72.

232. Sears, *To the Gates of Richmond,* 136–38.

233. J. Davis, *Rise and Fall,* 2:122–23; W. P. Johnston to Rosa, June 1, 1862, the Mrs. Mason Barret Collection of Albert Sidney and William Preston Johnston Papers, Tulane University Library; Freeman, *R. E. Lee,* 2:69–71; Reagan, *Memoirs,* 140–41.

234. J. Davis, *Rise and Fall,* 2:122–23; W. P. Johnston to Rosa, June 1, 1862, the Mrs. Mason Barret Collection of Albert Sidney and William Preston Johnston Papers, Tulane University Library; Freeman, *R. E. Lee,* 2:71–73.

235. Reagan, *Memoirs,* 140–41.

236. Johnston, *Narrative,* 138–39.

237. W. P. Johnston to Rosa, June 2, 1862, the Mrs. Mason Barret Collection of Albert Sidney and William Preston Johnston Papers, Tulane University Library.

238. Smith, *Confederate War Papers,* 180–82; Freeman, *R. E. Lee,* 2:71–72; Sears, *To the Gates of Richmond,* 141.

239. That this was Davis's assessment of Lee can be inferred from Davis's letters to Varina of May 31 (Rowland, *Jefferson Davis, Constitutionalist,* 5:264) and June 23, 1862 (Museum of the Confederacy, Richmond) as well as his reaction to Lee's experiences in West Virginia (*Rise and Fall,* 1:436) and his opinion of engineer officers, of which Lee had been one (*Rise and Fall,* 2:132).

CHAPTER 5

1. W. P. Johnston to Rosa, June 1, 1862, the Mrs. Mason Barret Collection of Albert Sidney and William Preston Johnston Papers, Tulane University Library.

2. Davis to Lee, June 1, 1862, O.R. 11, pt. 3:568–69. That the note was sent "early that morning" is borne out by Gustavus Woodson Smith, *Confederate War Papers* (New York: Atlantic Publishing and Engraving, 1884), 211.

3. Douglas Southall Freeman, *R. E. Lee: A Biography,* 4 vols. (New York: Scribners, 1934), 2:76.

4. Archer Jones, *Civil War Command and Strategy: The Process of Victory and Defeat* (New York: Free Press, 1992), 113.

5. Davis to Lee, June 1, 1862, O.R. 11, pt. 3:568–69.

6. Douglas Southall Freeman, *Lee's Lieutenants: A Study in Command,* 3 vols. (New York: Charles Scribner's Sons, 1944), 1:252.

7. Jefferson Davis, *The Rise and Fall of the Confederate Government,* 2 vols. (New York: Appleton, 1881), 2:128.

8. Smith, *Confederate War Papers,* 211–13. That Smith's account of this incident is more accurate than Davis's (*Rise and Fall,* 2:128–29) is argued persuasively in Hal Bridges, *Lee's Maverick General: Daniel Harvey Hill* (Lincoln: University of Nebraska Press, 1991), 51–53.

9. Bridges, *Lee's Maverick General,* 51–52.

10. Freeman, *R. E. Lee,* 2:75.

11. Freeman, *Lee's Lieutenants,* 1:242–43, 262–63; Hamilton J. Eckenrode and Bryan Conrad, *James Longstreet: Lee's War Horse* (Chapel Hill: University of North Carolina Press, 1986), 49.

12. J. Davis, *Rise and Fall,* 2:128–29; John H. Reagan, *Memoirs,* ed. Walter F. McCaleb (New York: Neale, 1906), 142–43; Johnston to Rosa, June 2, 1862, the Mrs. Mason Barret Collection of Albert Sidney and William Preston Johnston Papers, Tulane University Library.

13. Jefferson Davis to Varina Davis, June 2, 1862, in Dunbar Rowland, ed., *Jefferson Davis, Constitutionalist: His Letters, Papers, and Speeches,* 10 vols. (Jackson: Mississippi Department of Archives and History, 1923), 5:264–65.

14. Freeman, *R. E. Lee,* 2:86; James M. McPherson, *Battle Cry of Freedom: The Civil War Era* (New York: Oxford University Press, 1988), 462; Shelby Foote, *The Civil War: A Narrative,* 3 vols. (New York: Random House, 1958), 1:465.

15. William Garrett Piston, *Lee's Tarnished Lieutenant: James Longstreet and His Place in Southern History* (Athens: University of Georgia Press, 1987), 20.

16. James Longstreet, *From Manassas to Appomattox,* ed. James I. Roberston (Bloomington: Indiana University Press, 1960), 112.

17. Freeman, *Lee's Lieutenants,* 1:485–86.

18. J. Davis, *Rise and Fall,* 2:132.

19. Davis to Lee, June 2, 1862, O.R. 11, pt. 3:569–70.

20. Freeman, *Lee's Lieutenants,* 1:264.

21. Davis to Lee, June 2, 1862, O.R. 11, pt. 3:569–70.

22. J. Davis, *Rise and Fall,* 2:130–31; Longstreet, *From Manassas to Appomattox,* 112–13; Freeman, *R. E. Lee,* 2:88–89.

23. Longstreet, *From Manassas to Appomattox,* 113–14.

24. J. Davis, *Rise and Fall,* 2:130–31.

25. Lee to Davis, June 3, 1862, in Douglas Southall Freeman and Grady McWhiney, eds., *Lee's Dispatches: Unpublished Letters of General Robert E. Lee, C.S.A. to Jefferson Davis and the War Department of the Confederate States of America, 1862–1865* (New York: G. P. Putnam's Sons, 1957), 3–5.

26. Lee to Davis, June 7, 1862, in Freeman and McWhiney, *Lee's Dispatches,* 10–12.

27. Stephen W. Sears, *To the Gates of Richmond: The Peninsula Campaign* (New York: Ticknor and Fields, 1992), 155.

28. Lee to Davis, June 5, 1862, in Freeman and McWhiney, *Lee's Dispatches,* 5–10.

29. W. P. Johnston to Rosa, June 7, 1862, the Mrs. Mason Barret Collection of Albert Sidney and William Preston Johnston Papers, Tulane University Library.

30. Ibid.

31. Lee to Davis, June 5, 1862, in Freeman and McWhiney, *Lee's Dispatches,* 5–10.

32. Jefferson Davis to Varina Davis, June 11, 1862, in Rowland, *Jefferson Davis, Constitutionalist,* 5:272–73.

33. Ibid.

34. Ibid.; Lee to Davis, June 5, 1862, in Freeman and McWhiney, *Lee's Dispatches,* 5–10.

35. Sears, *To the Gates of Richmond,* 151–52.

36. Davis to Jackson, June 4, 1862, in Rowland, *Jefferson Davis, Constitutionalist,* 5:207–8.

37. Lee to Davis, June 5, 1862, in Freeman and McWhiney, Lee's Dispatches, 5–10.

38. Lee to G. W. Randolph, June 5, 1862, O.R. 11, pt. 3:575.

39. Lee to Davis, June 10, 1862, in Clifford Dowdey and Louis H. Manarin, eds., *The Wartime Papers of R. E. Lee* (New York: Bramhall House, 1961), 188.

40. Jefferson Davis to Varina Davis, June 11, 1862, in Rowland, *Jefferson Davis, Constitutionalist,* 5:272–73.

41. O.R. 11, pt. 3:582–83.

42. Jackson to Lee, June 13, 1862, with endorsements by Lee and Davis, in Dowdey and Manarin, *Wartime Papers,* 193.

43. Sears, *To the Gates of Richmond,* 152, 176.

44. J. Davis, *Rise and Fall,* 2:132.

45. W. P. Johnston to Rosa, June 9, 1862, the Mrs. Mason Barret Collection of Albert Sidney and William Preston Johnston Papers, Tulane University Library.

46. John B. Jones, *A Rebel War Clerk's Diary,* ed. Earl Schenck Miers (New York: Sagamore, 1958).

47. Jefferson Davis to Varina Davis, June 19, 1862, National Archives, Records Group 109.

48. Edward Porter Alexander, *Military Memoirs of a Confederate* (New York: Scribners, 1912), 110–11.

49. Jefferson Davis to Varina Davis, June 21, 1862, in Rowland, *Jefferson Davis, Constitutionalist,* 5:283–84.

50. Jefferson Davis to Varina Davis, June 23, 1862, ibid., 284.

51. Ibid.

52. Lee to Davis, June 24, 1862, in Freeman and McWhiney, *Lee's Dispatches,* 12–13.

53. Lee to Davis, June 25, 1862, ibid., 14; Lee to wife, June 25, 1862, in Dowdey and Manarin, *Wartime Papers,* 200–201; Jefferson Davis to Varina Davis, June 25, 1862, Confederate Museum, Richmond.

54. Lee to Davis, June 26, 1862, in Freeman and McWhiney, *Lee's Dispatches,* 15–17.

55. Lee to G. W. Randolph, June 26, 1862, O.R. 11, pt. 3:617.

56. R. H. Chilton to Davis, June 26, 1862, in Freeman and McWhiney, *Lee's Dispatches,* 18.

57. Freeman, *R. E. Lee,* 2:129; Sears, *To the Gates of Richmond,* 200.

58. Alexander, *Military Memoirs,* 118.

59. Sears, *To the Gates of Richmond*, 200.

60. Ibid.

61. James I. Roberston, Jr., *General A. P. Hill: The Story of a Confederate Warrior* (New York: Random House, 1987), 69–70.

62. Sears, *To the Gates of Richmond*, 201–3.

63. Daniel Harvey Hill, "Lee's Attacks North of the Chickahominy," in Robert U. Johnson and Clarence C. Buel, eds., *Battles and Leaders of the Civil War*, 4 vols. (New York: Thomas Yoseloff, 1956), 2:352.

64. Freeman, *R. E. Lee*, 2:131–32.

65. Mary Boykin Chesnut, *Mary Chestnut's Civil War*, ed. C. Vann Woodward (New Haven, Conn.: Yale University Press, 1981), 410–11.

66. Alexander, *Military Memoirs*, 119; Longstreet, *From Manassas to Appomattox*, 124; Freeman, *Lee's Lieutenants*, 1:515; Hill, "Lee's Attacks North of the Chickahominy," in Johnson and Buel, *Battles and Leaders*, 2:381.

67. Varina Howell Davis, *Jefferson Davis: Ex-President of the Confederate States of America, A Memoir by His Wife*, 2 vols. (New York: Belford, 1890), 2:317, 324; Jones, *Rebel War Clerk's Diary*, 86.

68. Lee to Huger, June 27, 1862, in Freeman and McWhiney, *Lee's Dispatches*, 18–19; Lee to Davis, June 27, 1862, O.R. 11, pt. 3:622; Lee to Davis, June 29, 1862, in Freeman and McWhiney, *Lee's Dispatches*, 19–22; Jones, *Rebel War Clerk's Diary*, 86.

69. Jones, *Rebel War Clerk's Diary*, 86; V. H. Davis, *Jefferson Davis*, 2:317.

70. Jones, *Rebel War Clerk's Diary*, 86.

71. J. Davis, *Rise and Fall*, 2:140.

72. Jones, *Rebel War Clerk's Diary*, 86.

73. Freeman, *R. E. Lee*, 2:172.

74. V. H. Davis, *Jefferson Davis*, 2:316–17.

75. James Longstreet, " 'The Seven Days,' Including Frayser's Farm," in Johnson and Buel, *Battles and Leaders*, 2:400; Freeman, *R. E. Lee*, 2:181–82.

76. Longstreet, " 'The Seven Days,' " in Johnson and Buel, *Battles and Leaders*, 2:400–401; Longstreet, *From Manassas to Appomatox*, 134; Alexander, *Military Memoirs*, 140; Freeman, *Lee's Lieutenants*, 1:574, and *R. E. Lee*, 2:181–82; Sears, *To the Gates of Richmond*, 290; Robertson, *General A. P. Hill*, 88.

77. J. Davis, *Rise and Fall*, 2:144.

78. Richard Taylor, *Destruction and Reconstruction: Personal Experiences of the Late War*, ed. Richard B. Harwell (New York: Longmans, Green, 1955), 99.

79. J. Davis, *Rise and Fall*, 2:143–44.

80. Bridges, *Lee's Maverick General*, 79.

81. Sears, *To the Gates of Richmond*, 313–14.

82. D. H. Hill, "McClellan's Change of Base and Malvern Hill," in Johnson and Buel, *Battles and Leaders*, 2:391.

83. Eckenrode and Conrad, *James Longstreet*, 80–81.

84. Sears, *To the Gates of Richmond*, 317–18. Sears doubts that Lee so much as saw the order before it was sent to the subordinate commanders.

85. D. H. Hill, "McClellan's Change of Base and Malvern Hill," in Johnson and Buel, *Battles and Leaders*, 2:394.

86. William W. Averell, "With the Cavalry on the Peninsula," in Johnson and Buel, *Battles and Leaders*, 2:432.

87. Bridges, *Lee's Maverick General*, 79.

88. Lee to Davis, July 2, 1862, in Freeman and McWhiney, *Lee's Dispatches*, 22–24.

89. Hunter McGuire to Jedediah Hotchkiss, May 28, 1896, Jedediah Hotchkiss Papers, Library of Congress, Manuscript Division, microfilm reel 34, frame 125.

90. J. Davis, *Rise and Fall*, 2:149–50.

91. Russel F. Weigley, *The American Way of War: A History of United States Military Strategy and Policy* (New York: Macmillan, 1973), 108.

92. Jefferson Davis to Varina Davis, July 6, 1862, in Rowland, *Jefferson Davis, Constitutionalist*, 5:290–91.

93. J. Davis, *Rise and Fall*, 2:149.

94. Lee to Davis, July 3, 4, and 9, 1862, in Freeman and McWhiney, *Lee's Dispatches*, 24–32; Lee to Davis, July 6, 1862, O.R. 11, pt. 3:634–35.

95. Davis to Lee, July 5, 1862 (two dispatches), O.R. 11, pt. 2:631–34; Samuel Cooper to John C. Pemberton, July 15, 1862, ibid., 642.

96. V. H. Davis, *Jefferson Davis*, 2:320; Piston, *Lee's Tarnished Lieutenant*, 20–21.

97. Jones, *Rebel War Clerk's Diary*, 88.

98. Bridges, *Lee's Maverick General*, 72.

99. Freeman, *Lee's Lieutenants*, 1:628–29.

100. Jefferson Davis to Varina Davis, July 6, 1862, in Rowland, *Jefferson Davis, Constitutionalist*, 5:290–91.

101. Frank E. Vandiver, *Mighty Stonewall* (College Station: Texas A&M University Press, 1957), 329; Freeman, *Lee's Lieutenants*, 1:661–62.

102. William J. Miller, "The Grand Campaign: A Journal of Operations in the Peninsula Campaign, March 17–August 26, 1862," in Miller, ed., *The Peninsula Campaign of 1862: Yorktown to the Seven Days*, 1 vol. to date (Campbell, Calif.: Savas Woodbury, 1993), 1:197.

103. Davis to Lee, July 31, 1862, in J. Davis, *Rise and Fall*, 2:315–17.

104. Foote, *The Civil War*, 1:589.

105. Vandiver, *Mighty Stonewall*, 330; Freeman, *R. E. Lee*, 2:273.

106. Lee to Davis, July 18, 1862, O.R. 51, pt. 2:1074–75.

107. Richard E. Beringer, Herman Hattaway, Archer Jones, and William N. Still, Jr., argue in *Why the South Lost the Civil War* (Athens: University of Georgia Press, 1986) that "as a result of the Seven Days' Battles, Lee resolved to avoid further battles, using instead strategic turning movements to force the enemy back" (474; see also 181). Jones, in *Civil War Command and Strategy*, makes much the same case (134–35, 227–28). In fact, though Lee sometimes spoke of avoiding battles, he as often spoke of "striking a blow." His actions, too, remained those of one seeking victory on the battlefield.

108. Foote, *The Civil War*, 1:592.

109. Ibid., 605.

110. Lee to Davis, August 15, 1862, with Davis endorsement, O.R. 11, pt. 3:678; Special Orders no. 190, Adjutant and Inspector General's Office, August 15, 1862, ibid., 679.

111. Lee to Davis, August 16, 1862, in Freeman and McWhiney, *Lee's Dispatches,* 49–51.

112. Randolph to Davis, August 17, 1862, O.R. 11, pt. 3:680.

113. Lee to Davis, August 17, 1862, ibid. 51, pt. 2:1075–76.

114. Davis to Lee, August 21, 1862, in Rowland, *Jefferson Davis, Constitutionalist,* 5:327.

115. Lee to Davis, August 17, 1862, O.R. 51, pt. 2:1075–76.

116. Longstreet, *From Manassas to Appomattox,* 162.

117. Lee to Davis, August 21, 1862, O.R. 51, pt. 2:609.

118. Alan T. Nolan, *Lee Considered: General Robert E. Lee and Civil War History* (Chapel Hill: University of North Carolina Press, 1991), 89.

119. Lee to Davis, August 25, 1862, in Freeman and McWhiney, *Lee's Dispatches,* 52.

120. Ibid.; Davis to Lee, August 28, 1862, in Rowland, *Jefferson Davis, Constitutionalist,* 5:332.

121. Davis to Lee, August 21, 1862, in Rowland, *Jefferson Davis, Constitutionalist,* 5:327.

122. Davis to Lee, August 26, 1862, ibid., 330.

123. Lee to Davis, August 27, 1862, in Freeman and McWhiney, *Lee's Dispatches,* 54.

124. Davis to Lee, August 28, 1862, in Rowland, *Jefferson Davis, Constitutionalist,* 5:332.

125. Jennings Cropper Wise, *The Long Arm of Lee: The History of the Artillery of the Army of Northern Virginia* (New York: Oxford University Press, 1959), 255.

126. Davis to Lee, August 28, 1862, in Rowland, *Jefferson Davis, Constitutionalist,* 5:332.

127. Davis to Lee, August 30, 1862, Duke University Library.

128. Wise, *The Long Arm of Lee,* 255.

129. Lee to Davis, August 29, 1862, in Freeman and McWhiney, *Lee's Dispatches,* 55.

130. Lee to Davis, August 30, 1862, ibid., 56–59.

131. Lee to Davis, August 30, 1862, *Lee's Dispatches,* 59–60.

132. Davis to Lee, August 30, 1862, Duke University Library.

133. Lee to Davis, September 3, 1862, O.R. 19, pt. 2:590–91.

134. Lee to Davis, September 3, 4, 5, 6, and 7, 1862, ibid., 590–94, 597–98, and in Freeman and McWhiney, eds., *Lee's Dispatches,* 61.

135. Lee to Davis, September 9, 1862, O.R. 19, pt. 2:602–3.

136. Lee to Davis, September 8, 1862, ibid., 600.

137. Lee to Davis, September 8, 1862, ibid., 600–601.

138. Lee to Davis, September 9, 1862, ibid., 602–3; Walter H. Taylor, *Four Years with General Lee* (Bloomington: Indiana University Press, 1962), 66.

139. Taylor to Davis, September 10, 1862, O.R. 51, pt. 2:617.

140. Lee to Davis, September 12, 1862, O.R. 19, pt. 2:604–5.

141. Lee to Davis, September 5, 1862, ibid., 593–94.

142. Lee to Davis, September 9, 1862, ibid., 602–3.

143. Herman Hattaway and Archer Jones contend in *How the North Won: A Military History of the Civil War* (Urbana: University of Illinois Press, 1983) that Lee's 1862 Maryland campaign was a raid (233, 240, 244). Beringer, Hattaway, Jones, and Still assert in *Why the South Lost* (166) that Lee planned to draw only "such key items

as ammunition, salt, and coffee" through the Shenandoah and shortly "having exhausted the resources of the region he would have to return to Virginia." Jones, in *Civil War Command and Strategy* (93–94), makes the same argument: "This would be a raid, a transitory rather than a permanent occupation." He also states that "Lee expected to remain in Maryland unmolested for two or even three months." Finally, he points out, quite correctly, that Lee wanted to get all the supplies he could from Maryland while his army was there and have all possible supplies secured in northern Virginia while the Union army was not there. However, Jones believes this to be the sole purpose for the raid. Further, he asserts that Lee sought battle neither in this nor in any other campaign after the Seven Days, having realized the costly futility of such encounters (71–73, 135, 227–28). Although these closely reasoned conclusions by such able scholars deserve careful consideration, the present writer is convinced that the evidence can better be interpreted in other ways. Whether Lee at any time considered a raid across the Potomac, he had, at least by the time of his September 9 letter to Davis, shifted to a policy of opening a full supply line–ammunition and subsistence–through the Shenandoah, thus making his campaign a sustained offensive rather than a raid. It may be true that he considered his presence there temporary. At worst, he felt he might be forced back across the river (Lee to Davis, September 3, 1862, O.R. 19, pt. 2:590–91), having managed "to annoy and harass the enemy" (Lee to Davis, September 5, 1862, ibid., 593–94). At best, as he revealed in his September 8 letter, he hoped to compel the North to recognize Confederate independence. Thus, as Lee planned it, the move was temporary in the sense that the army would withdraw once a treaty of peace was signed. Although the gathering of supplies was important to Lee, his actions indicate that such activities provided a useful way to improve the time until the Army of the Potomac did attack him and a useful redeeming factor should the campaign fail to produce the results he hoped for. That Lee wished to avoid pitched battle after the Seven Days is plainly and compellingly contradicted by his actions. His maneuvers in the Second Manassas and Maryland campaigns were inherently such as to produce battle, and it is impossible to believe that he thought he could remain for weeks on end north of the Potomac without battle. Had McClellan sought to ignore such an overwhelming political and military reality, he would, as Lee undoubtedly could have guessed, have been relieved forthwith. Although Lee certainly expected McClellan to move more deliberately than he in fact did, Lee must have known that any northern commander would be forced to attack him under any and all circumstances. The clear indication is that Lee was counting on it.

144. Lee to Davis, September 12, 1862, O.R. 19, pt. 2:604–5.

145. Lee to Davis, September 9, 1862, ibid., 602.

146. Lee to Davis, September 12, 1862, ibid., 604–5.

147. Foote, *The Civil War*, 1:671.

148. Lee's report, O.R. 19, pt. 1:151; McClellan's report, ibid., 67.

149. This account is drawn from Edward Porter Alexander, *Fighting for the Confederacy*, ed. Gary W. Gallagher (Chapel Hill: University of North Carolina Press, 1989), 153; Jedediah Hotchkiss, *Confederate Military History*, vol. 3, *Virginia*, ed. Clement A. Evans (Dayton, Ohio: Morningside, 1975), 357; James V. Murfin, *The Gleam of Bayonets: The Battle of Antietam and the Maryland Campaign of 1862* (Baton

Rouge: Louisiana State University Press, 1965), 294–95; Stephen W. Sears, *Landscape Turned Red: The Battle of Antietam* (New York: Warner Books, 1983), 325–26, 328.

150. Lee to Davis, September 20, 1862, National Archives, Records Group 109.

151. Ibid.

152. Lee to Davis, September 25, 1862, O.R. 19, pt. 2:626–27.

153. Ibid.

154. G. W. C. Lee to Davis, September 25, 1862, Autograph File, Dearborn Collection, Houghton Library, Harvard University.

155. Lee to Davis, September 23, 1862, O.R. 19, pt. 2:622–23.

156. Lee to Davis, September 7, 1862, ibid., 597–98.

157. Lee to Davis, September 13, 1862, ibid., 605–6.

158. Piston, *Lee's Tarnished Lieutenant*, 28.

159. Lee to Davis, September 21, 22, 23,and 25, 1862, O.R. 19, pt. 1:142, and pt. 2:617–18, 622–27; Piston, *Lee's Tarnished Lieutenant*, 28.

160. G. W. C. Lee to Davis, September 25, 1862, Autograph File, Dearborn Collection, Houghton Library, Harvard University.

161. Lee to Davis, September 25, 1862, O.R. 19, pt. 2:626–27.

162. Alexander, *Fighting for the Confederacy*, 153.

163. Lee to Davis, September 25, 1862, O.R. 19, pt. 2:626–27.

CHAPTER 6

1. Lee to Davis, September 7 and 13, 1862, O.R. 19, pt. 2:597–98, 605–6.

2. Lee to Davis, September 23, and to Randolph, September 28, 1862, ibid., 622–23, 632.

3. Douglas Southall Freeman, *Lee's Lieutenants: A Study in Command*, 3 vols. (New York: Charles Scribner's Sons, 1944), 2:254.

4. Davis to Lee, September 28, 1862, in Dunbar Rowland, ed., *Jefferson Davis, Constitutionalist: His Letters, Papers, and Speeches*, 10 vols. (Jackson: Mississippi Department of Archives and History, 1923), 5:345–46.

5. Davis endorsement on Lee to Randolph, September 28, 1862, O.R. 19, pt. 2:632.

6. Freeman, *Lee's Lieutenants*, 2:254.

7. Ibid., 255–56.

8. Davis to Lee, September 28, 1862, in Rowland, *Jefferson Davis, Constitutionalist*, 5:345–46.

9. Clement Eaton, *Jefferson Davis* (New York: Free Press, 1977), 249.

10. Ibid.

11. Davis to Lee, Spetember 28, 1862, in Rowland, *Jefferson Davis, Constitutionalist* 5:345–46.

12. Ibid.

13. Lee to Davis, October 2, 1862, O.R. 19, pt. 2:643–44.

14. Davis to Lee, September 28, 1862, in Rowland, *Jefferson Davis, Constitutionalist*, 5:345–46.

15. Lee to Davis, October 2, 1862, O.R. 19, pt. 2:643–44. Some scholars have actually interpreted Lee's praise for Jackson—and silence about Longstreet—as an

indication of his confidence in Longstreet and lingering doubts about Jackson. Frank Vandiver, *Mighty Stonewall* (College Station: Texas A&M University Press, 1957), 408; Freeman, *Lee's Lieutenants*, 2:238–39; Jeffrey D. Wert, *General James Longstreet: The Confederacy's Most Controversial Soldier–A Biography* (New York: Simon and Schuster, 1993), 205.

16. Lee to Davis, October 2, 1862, O.R. 19, pt. 2:643–44.

17. Ibid.

18. Douglas Southall Freeman, *R. E. Lee: A Biography*, 4 vols. (New York: Scribners, 1934), 2:418–19.

19. Freeman, *Lee's Lieutenants*, 2:414; Seddon to Lee, Dec. 4, 1862, O.R. 21:1045.

20. Lee to Randolph, with Davis endorsement, October 25, 1862, O.R. 19, pt. 2:681.

21. Special Orders no. 231, Army of Northern Virginia, October 27, 1862, ibid., 684; Lee to Randolph, October 27, 1862, ibid., 683–84.

22. Lee to Davis, November 6, 1862, ibid., 697–98.

23. Davis to Lee, November 7, 1862, in Rowland, *Jefferson Davis, Constitutionalist*, 5:367.

24. Featherston and officers to Davis, October 25, 1862, with endorsements by Davis and Lee, letters received by the Confederate Adjutant and Inspector General's Office, National Archives, microfilm 474, reel 19, frames 140–44; Davis to Lee, November 7, 1862, in Rowland, *Jefferson Davis, Constitutionalist*, 5:367.

25. Lee to Davis, November 25, 1862, O.R. 21:1029–30.

26. Lee to Secretary of War, November 25, 1862, ibid., 1030.

27. Lee to Davis, October 2, 1862 ibid., 19, pt. 2:643–44.

28. Ibid.; Davis to Lee, September 28, 1862, in Rowland, *Jefferson Davis, Constitutionalist*, 5:345–46.

29. Lee to Davis, October 22, 1862, O.R. 19, pt. 2:675.

30. Freeman, *R. E. Lee*, 2:426–27.

31. Davis to Lee, October 28, 1862, O.R. 51, pt. 2:638; Michael B. Ballard, *Pemberton: A Biography* (Jackson: University Press of Mississippi, 1991), 114, suggests that Davis sent Pemberton to visit Lee so that he could "benefit from Lee's thoughts regarding the Mississippi command" to which Pemberton had just been assigned.

32. Freeman, *R. E. Lee*, 2:427.

33. Lee endorsement, November 4, 1862, letters received by the Confederate Adjutant and Inspector General's Office, National Archives, microfilm 474, reel 19, frames 140–44.

34. Lee to Davis, November 6, 1862, O.R. 19, pt. 2:697–98; Lee to Randolph, November 6, 1862, ibid., 697.

35. Freeman, *R. E. Lee*, 2:428; James Longstreet, *From Manassas to Appomattox*, ed. James J. Robertson, Jr. (Bloomington: Indiana University Press, 1960), 291.

36. Lee to Davis, November 17, 1862, O.R. 21:1014–15; Lee to Secretary of War, November 17, 1862, ibid., 1015.

37. Lee to Davis, November 19, 1862, ibid., 1020–21.

38. Lee to Davis, November 20, 1862, in Douglas Southall Freeman and Grady McWhiney, eds., *Lee's Dispatches: Unpublished Letters of General Robert E. Lee, C.S.A.*

to Jefferson Davis and the War Department of the Confederate States of America, 1862–65 (New York: G. P. Putnam's Sons, 1957), 66.

39. Lee to Davis, November 22, 1862, O.R. 21:1026–27.

40. Lee to Davis, November 25, 1862, ibid., 1028–29; Davis to Lee, November 26, 1862, ibid. 51, pt. 2:651; Davis to Lee, December 8, 1862, in Rowland, *Jefferson Davis, Constitutionalist,* 5:384–86.

41. Davis to Lee, December 8, 1862, in Rowland, *Jefferson Davis, Constitutionalist,* 5:384–86.

42. Lee to Davis, November 25, 1862, O.R. 21:1028–29.

43. Ibid.

44. Ibid.

45. Lee to Davis, December 6, 1862, ibid., 1049–50.

46. Lee to Davis, December 8, 1862, ibid., 1052–54.

47. Davis to Lee, December 8, 1862, in Rowland, *Jefferson Davis, Constitutionalist,* 5:384–86.

48. George C. Rable discusses the political factors that impelled Davis to endeavor to hold territory in *The Confederate Republic: A Revolution Against Politics* (Chapel Hill: University of North Carolina Press, 1994), 127, see also Freeman, *R. E. Lee,* 2:480.

49. Lee to Davis, November 25, 1862, O.R. 21:1028–29.

50. Davis to Lee, December 8, 1862, in Rowland, *Jefferson Davis, Constitutionalist,* 5:384–86.

51. Ibid.

52. Lee to Seddon, December 13, 1862, O.R. 21:546.

53. Davis to Seddon, December 15, 1862, ibid., 1062.

54. Jefferson Davis to Varina Davis, December 15, 1862, in Varina Howell Davis, *Jefferson Davis: Ex-President of the Confederate States of America, A Memoir by His Wife,* 2 vols. (New York: Belford, 1890), 2:366–67.

55. Seddon to Davis, December 15 and 16, 1862, O.R. 21:1062–63, 1065; Lee to Seddon, December 15 and 16, 1862, ibid., 548, 1064.

56. Shelby Foote, *The Civil War: A Narrative,* 3 vols. (New York: Vintage Books, 1986), 2:41–45.

57. Lee to his wife, December 16, 1862, in Clifford Dowdey and Louis H. Manarin, eds., *The Wartime Papers of R. E. Lee* (New York: Bramhall House, 1961), 364–65.

58. Lee to Cooper, April 10, 1863, ibid., 366–74.

59. Lee to Jackson, November 19, 1862, O.R. 21:1021.

60. Lee to Seddon, December 16, 1862, in Dowdey and Manarin, *Wartime Papers,* 363–64.

61. Lee to Davis, January 6, 1863, ibid., 387–88.

62. Lee to Seddon, January 10, 1863, ibid., 388–90.

63. Lee to Smith, January 4, 1863, Lee to Seddon, January 5, 1863, Lee to Davis, January 6, 1863, ibid., 383, 385–88.

64. Davis to Lee, January 12, 1863, in Rowland, *Jefferson Davis, Constitutionalist,* 5:416.

65. Davis to Vance, January 12, 1863, ibid.

66. Lee to Davis, January 13, 1863, O.R. 21:1091–92.

67. Lee to Davis, January 12, 1863, Tulane University Library.

68. Freeman, *R. E. Lee,* 2:479.

69. Lee to Davis, January 19, 1863, O.R. 21:1096–97.

70. Lee to Davis, January 21, 1863, ibid., 1103–4.

71. Davis to Lee, January 22, 1863, in Rowland, *Jefferson Davis, Constitutionalist,* 5:421–22.

72. Lee to Davis, January 23, 1863, O.R. 21:1111.

73. Lee to Seddon, January 29, 1863, in Dowdey and Manarin, *Wartime Papers,* 397.

74. William C. Davis, *Jefferson Davis: The Man and His Hour* (New York: Harper Collins, 1991), 494; Lee to Davis, February 26, 1863, O.R. 25, pt. 1:642–43.

75. John B. Jones, *A Rebel War Clerk's Diary,* ed. Earl Schenck Miers (New York: Sagamore, 1958), 172; Robert Garlick Hill Kean, *Inside the Confederate Government,* ed. Edward Younger (New York: Oxford University Press, 1957), 48.

76. G. W. C. Lee to R. E. Lee, February 4, 1863, in Rowland, *Jefferson Davis, Constitutionalist,* 5:429–30; Lee to Davis, January 16, 1863, O.R. 25, pt. 1:627; Hamilton J. Eckenrode and Bryan Conrad, *James Longstreet: Lee's War Horse* (Chapel Hill: University of North Carolina Press, 1986), 158.

77. Wert, *General James Longstreet,* 206, 228; Eckenrode and Conrad, *James Longstreet,* 159; William Garrett Piston, *Lee's Tarnished Lieutenant: James Longstreet and His Place in Southern History* (Athens: University of Georgia Press, 1987), 26–28.

78. Wert, *General James Longstreet,* 228.

79. Eckenrode and Conrad, *James Longstreet,* 159–60.

80. Lee to Davis, February 18 and 26, 1863, O.R. 25, pt. 1:631–32, 642–43.

81. Davis to Lee, March 10, 1863, in Rowland, *Jefferson Davis, Constitutionalist,* 5:446.

82. Eckenrode and Conrad, *James Longstreet,* 159–63; Freeman, *R. E. Lee,* 2:498–501; Wert, *General James Longstreet,* 231–33.

83. Freeman, *R. E. Lee,* 2:498–99; Lee to Davis, March 19, 1863, O.R. 25, pt. 1:675.

84. Eckenrode and Conrad, *James Longstreet,* 159–63; Lee to Davis, April 2, 1863, O.R. 25, pt. 1:700–701.

85. Lee to Cooper, March 28, 1863, with Davis endorsement, O.R. 25, pt. 1:689.

86. Davis to Lee, April 1, 1863, in Rowland, *Jefferson Davis, Constitutionalist,* 5:463.

87. Lee to Davis, April 2, 1863, O.R. 25, pt. 1:700–701.

88. Lee to Seddon, April 9, Lee to Cooper and Davis, April 16, Cooper to Lee, April 14, 1863, ibid., 713–14, 720, 724–26; J. B. Jones, *Rebel War Clerk's Diary,* 190; James S. Phelan to Davis, April 25, 1863, letters received by the Confederate War Department, National Archives, microfilm 473, reel 106, frames 954–55.

89. Edwin B. Coddington, *The Gettysburg Campaign: A Study in Command* (New York: Charles Scribner's Sons, 1968), 8–9; Russell F. Weigley, *The American Way of War: A History of United States Military Strategy and Policy* (New York: Macmillan, 1973), 113.

90. Lee to Davis, April 16, 1863, O.R. 25, pt. 1:725–26.

91. Lee to Davis, April 20, 1863, ibid., 740–41.

92. Lee to Davis, April 27, 1863, ibid., 752–53.

93. J. B. Jones, *Rebel War Clerk's Diary*, 192.

94. Davis to Seddon, April 29, 1863, O.R. 25, pt. 1:757.

95. Seddon to Cooper (two dispatches), April 29, 1863, Cooper to Lee, May 1, 1863, ibid., 758–59, 763.

96. Davis to Lee, April 29, 1863, in Rowland, *Jefferson Davis, Constitutionalist*, 5:477.

97. Lee to Davis, April 29 and 30, 1863, O.R. 25, pt. 1:756–57, 761; Lee to Davis, April 30, 1863, in Freeman and McWhiney, *Lee's Dispatches*, 86.

98. Lee to Davis, May 2, 1863, O.R. 25, pt. 1:765.

99. Mary Boykin Chesnut, *Mary Chesnut's Civil War*, ed. C. Vann Woodward (New Haven, Conn.: Yale University Press, 1981), 477–78.

100. J. B. Jones, *Rebel War Clerk's Diary*, 198.

101. Chesnut, *Mary Chesnut's Civil War*, 477–78.

102. Ibid.; J. B. Jones, *Rebel War Clerk's Diary*, 200.

103. Lee to Davis, May 3, 1863, O.R. 25, pt. 1:768.

104. Ibid.

105. J. B. Jones, *Rebel War Clerk's Diary*, 202. Eckenrode and Conrad (*James Longstreet*, 166–67) maintain that Longstreet "had no desire to rejoin Lee" and deliberately delayed his return. Wert (*General James Longstreet*, 239) hotly denies this and labels it "ludicrous."

106. Lee to Davis, May 7, 1863, in Freeman and McWhiney, *Lee's Dispatches*, 90.

107. Freeman, *R. E. Lee*, 2:557.

108. Ibid., 3:5–6.

109. V. H. Davis, *Jefferson Davis*, 2:382–83.

110. Freeman, *R. E. Lee*, 2:561–62.

111. Lee to Seddon, May 10, 1863, O.R. 25, pt. 1:791.

112. Davis to Lee, May 11, 1863, ibid.

113. J. B. Jones, *Rebel War Clerk's Diary*, 207.

114. V. H. Davis, *Jefferson Davis*, 382–83.

115. Herman Hattaway and Archer Jones, *How the North Won: A Military History of the Civil War* (Urbana: University of Illinois Press, 1983), 397; Archer Jones, *Civil War Command and Strategy: The Process of Victory and Defeat* (New York: Free Press, 1992), 158–59.

116. Freeman (*R. E. Lee*, 2:477) suggests that by the winter of 1862–1863, the Army of Northern Virginia as a whole was "fearful of economic disaster behind the lines" due to "the inevitable consequences of economic attrition." "Before the winter was to end," Freeman writes, "the danger of starvation and of immobility, resulting from a collapse of transportation, was to be plain to every private in the ranks."

117. Lee's Chancellorsville report, O.R. 25, pt. 1:803.

118. Freeman, *R. E. Lee*, 3:1.

119. Richard E. Beringer, Herman Hattaway, Archer Jones, and William N. Still, Jr., *Why the South Lost the Civil War* (Athens: University of Georgia Press, 1986) take as their central argument the thesis that the Confederate will to resist crumbled when southerners were convinced by battlefield defeats that God was not on their side.

120. J. B. Jones, *Rebel War Clerk's Diary*, 201–2.

121. Ibid., 204.

122. Lee to Davis, May 7, and to Seddon (telegram), May 10, 1863, O.R. 25, pt. 1:782–83, 790. Freeman (*R. E. Lee,* 2:560) tends to think that Lee was in fact suggesting that he might be superseded by Beauregard.

123. Lee to Seddon, May 10, 1863, O.R. 25, pt. 1:790.

124. Davis endorsement on Lee to Seddon telegram, May 10, 1863, ibid.

125. Lee to Davis, May 11, 1863, ibid., 791–92.

126. Lee to Davis, May 7, 1863, ibid., 782–83.

127. R. E. Lee to G. W. C. Lee, May 11, 1863, in Dowdey and Manarin, *Wartime Papers,* 484.

128. J. B. Jones, *Rebel War Clerk's Diary,* 209–10.

129. Ibid., 210.

130. John H. Reagan, *Memoirs,* ed. Walter F. McCaleb (New York: Neale, 1906), 121–22, 150–51. In these memoirs, written many years after the fact, Reagan consistently confuses this meeting with another held ten days later.

131. Ibid., 122.

132. Lee to Davis, May 20, 1863, O.R. 25, pt. 1:810–11.

133. J. B. Jones, *Rebel War Clerk's Diary,* 211.

134. Davis to Lee, May 20, 1863, O.R. 25, pt. 1:810–11.

135. Reagan, *Memoirs,* 121, 151.

136. J. B. Jones, *Rebel War Clerk's Diary,* 214.

137. Reagan, *Memoirs,* 121, 151.

138. Davis to Lee, May 26, 1863, in Rowland, *Jefferson Davis, Constitutionalist,* 5:496–98.

139. Lee to Hood, May 21, 1863, in Dowdey and Manarin, *Wartime Papers,* 490.

140. R. E. Lee to G. W. C. Lee, May 11, 1863, ibid., 484.

141. Lee to Davis, May 20, 1863, O.R. 25, pt. 1:810–11.

142. Davis to Lee, May 31, 1863, ibid., 841–43.

143. Lee to Davis, May 20, 1863, ibid., 810–11.

144. Lee to Davis, May 25 and 28, 1863, in Freeman and McWhiney, *Lee's Dispatches,* 91–92, 96–99.

145. Lee to Davis, May 20, 1863, O.R. 25, pt. 1:810–11; May 20, 25, and 28, 1863, letters received by the Confederate Adjutant and Inspector General's Office, National Archives, microfilm 474, reel 135, frames 302–4 and 308–9; May 25, 26, and 28, 1863, in Freeman and McWhiney, *Lee's Dispatches,* 91–92, 94–95, 96–99; Davis to Lee (two dispatches), May 26, 1863, in Rowland, *Jefferson Davis, Constitutionalist,* 5:496–98.

146. Lee to Seddon, May 20, 1863, O.R. 25, pt. 1:811; Lee to Davis, May 25 and 28, 1863, in Freeman and McWhiney, *Lee's Dispatches,* 91–92, 96–99.

147. Davis to Lee, May 26, 1863, in Rowland, *Jefferson Davis, Constitutionalist,* 5:496–98.

148. Lee to Davis, May 29, 1863, in Freeman and McWhiney, *Lee's Dispatches,* 99–100; Lee to Hill, May 30, 1863, O.R. 25, pt. 1:834.

149. Davis to Lee, May 29, 1863, O.R. 25, pt. 1:831.

150. Davis to Lee, May 30, 1863, in Rowland, *Jefferson Davis, Constitutionalist,* 5:500.

151. Lee to Davis, May 30, 1863, O.R. 25, pt. 1:832–33.

152. Davis to Lee, May 31, 1863, ibid., 841–43.

153. Lee to Seddon and to Davis (separate dispatches), June 2, 1863, ibid., 848–49; Lee to Davis June 7, 1863, in Rowland, *Jefferson Davis, Constitutionalist,* 5:506–7; Lee to Davis, June 8, Lee to Cooper, June 23, Davis to Lee, June 28, Cooper to Lee, June 29, 1863, O.R. 27, pt. 1:75–77 and pt. 3:868–69; Lee to Davis, June 20, 1863, Library of Congress.

154. Lee to Davis, June 23, 1863, O.R. 27, pt. 3:924–25.

155. Ibid.

156. Lee to Cooper, June 23, 1863, ibid., pt. 1:77.

157. Davis to Lee, June 28, and Cooper to Lee, June 29, 1863, ibid., 75–77; J. B. Jones, *Rebel War Clerk's Diary,* 239.

158. Lee to Seddon, May 30, 1863, O.R. 25, pt. 1:834.

159. Seddon to Hill, May 30, 1863, ibid., 833–34.

160. Lee to Davis, June 2, 1863, ibid., 848–49.

161. Elzy to Pettigrew, June 5, 1863, O.R. 27, pt. 3:861; Davis to Lee, June 6, 1863, in Rowland, *Jefferson Davis, Constitutionalist,* 5:505.

162. Seddon to Lee, June 9 and 10, 1863, O.R. 27, pt. 3:874–76, 882.

163. Lee to Seddon, June 13, 1863, ibid., 886.

164. Lee to Davis, June 19, 1863, ibid., 931–33.

165. Davis to Lee, June 28, 1863, ibid., 904.

166. Davis to Lee, June 28, 1863, ibid., pt. 1:76–77.

167. Lee to Davis, July 8, 1863, in Rowland, *Jefferson Davis, Constitutionalist,* 5:537–38; Stanton to John A. Dix and to Lorenzo Thomas, July 4, 1863, O.R. 27, pt. 3:526, 529.

168. Davis to Beauregard, June 25, 1863, in Rowland, *Jefferson Davis, Constitutionalist,* 5:531–32.

169. The issue of the divergence of Lee's and Davis's strategic views has been addressed recently, with similar conclusions, by Emory Thomas, "Ambivalent Visions of Victory," *Freeman Historical Review* (1994):19–27. James Lee McDonough also gives an intelligent and thoughtful discussion of issues of Confederate strategy in *War in Kentucky: From Shiloh to Perryville* (Knoxville: University of Tennessee Press, 1994), 323–25.

170. Lee to Seddon, June 8, 1863, O.R. 27, pt. 3:868–69; Lee to Davis, June 7, 1863, in Rowland, *Jefferson Davis, Constitutionalist,* 5:506–7.

171. Lee to Davis, June 10, 1863, O.R. 27, pt. 1:880–82.

172. Lee to Davis, June 25, 1863, ibid., pt. 3:930–31.

173. Lee to Davis (two letters), June 25, 1863, ibid., 930–33.

174. Ibid.

175. Ibid.

176. Lee to Davis, June 19, 1863, in Rowland, *Jefferson Davis, Constitutionalist,* 5:526.

177. Davis to Lee, June 19, 1863, O.R. 27, pt. 3:904.

178. Lee to Davis, June 25, 1863, ibid., 930–31.

179. William Garrett Piston, "Cross Purposes: Longstreet, Lee, and Confederate Attack Plans for July 3 at Gettysburg," in Gary W. Gallagher, ed., *The Third Day at*

Gettysburg and Beyond (Chapel Hill: University of North Carolina Press, 1994), 31–51. Piston believes Lonstreet's mistake was failing to bring up Pickett's division during the night of July 2 in order to be ready for an early assault on the third. He believes Lee had probably given Longstreet notice of a planned early attack on July 3.

180. Longstreet, *From Manassas to Appomattox,* 358, 361; Wert, *General James Longstreet,* 261–62; Eckenrode and Conrad, *James Longstreet,* 191.

181. Lee to Davis, July 8, 1863, in Rowland, *Jefferson Davis, Constitutionalist,* 5:537–38.

182. Davis to Lee, July 9, 1863, O.R. 27, pt. 3:986. This is revealed by the fact that Davis did not know Lee had abandoned his supply line, something Lee stated in his June 25 letter.

183. J. B. Jones, *Rebel War Clerk's Diary,* 220.

184. Ibid., 234.

185. Seddon to D. H. Hill, July 2, 1863, O.R. 27, pt. 3:956–57.

186. J. B. Jones, *Rebel War Clerk's Diary,* 237.

187. V. H. Davis, *Jefferson Davis,* 2:392.

188. Seddon to Davis, July 8, 1863, Davis Papers, Tulane University; J. B. Jones, *Rebel War Clerk's Diary,* 238.

189. Hill to Seddon, July 8, 1863, O.R. 27, pt. 3:984.

190. Davis to Lee, July 9, 1863, ibid., 986.

191. J. B. Jones, *Rebel War Clerk's Diary,* 239.

192. Hill to Seddon, July 8, 1863, O.R. 27, pt. 3:984.

193. Davis to Lee, July 9, 1863, ibid., 986.

194. W. C. Davis, *Jefferson Davis,* 507.

195. Lee to Davis, July 4, 1863, in Rowland, *Jefferson Davis, Constitutionalist,* 5:535–36.

196. Lee to Davis July 7, 8, 10, 12, 16, and 24, 1863, ibid., 536–39, 543, 567–68, 575–76; Lee to Davis, July 17, 1863, O.R. 27, pt. 3:1016.

197. Lee to Davis, July 27 and 29 and August 1, 1863, O.R. 27, pt. 3:1040–41, 1048–49, 1068–69; Davis to Lee, July 21 and 28 and August 2, 1863, ibid., 1030–31, and in Rowland, *Jefferson Davis, Constitutionalist,* 5:578–80, 583–84.

198. Lee to Davis, July 29, 1863, O.R. 27, pt. 3:1048–49.

199. Davis to Lee, August 2, 1863, in Rowland, *Jefferson Davis, Constitutionalist,* 5:583–84.

200. Davis to Lee, July 21 and 28 and August 2, 1863, O.R. 27, pt. 3:1030–31, and in Rowland, *Jefferson Davis, Constitutionalist,* 5:578–80.

201. Kean, *Inside the Confederate Government,* 84; Piston, *Lee's Tarnished Lieutenant,* 65; V. H. Davis, *Jefferson Davis,* 2:392.

202. Gary W. Gallagher, "Lee's Army Has Not Lost Any of Its Prestige: The Impact of Gettysburg on the Army of North Virginia and the Confederate Home Front," in Gallagher, *The Third Day at Gettysburg and Beyond,* 1–22.

203. J. Davis, *Rise and Fall,* 2:447–49.

204. Davis to Lee, July 28, 1863, in Rowland, *Jefferson Davis, Constitutionalist,* 5:578–80.

205. Gallagher ("Lee's Army Has Not Lost Any of Its Prestige," in *The Third Day at Gettysburg and Beyond,* 21) surmises Lee's post-Gettysburg state of mind thus: "Lee

did not believe he had been defeated in Pennsylvania, [but] he harbored a sense of lost opportunity that left him easily wounded by criticism."

206. Lee to Davis, August 8, 1863, in Rowland, *Jefferson Davis, Constitutionalist*, 5:585–87.

207. Davis to Lee, August 11, 1863, O.R. 29, pt. 2:639–40.

CHAPTER 7

1. Gary W. Gallagher, "Lee's Army Has Not Lost Any of Its Prestige: The Impact of Gettysburg on the Army of North Virginia and the Confederate Home Front," in Gary W. Gallagher, ed., *The Third Day at Gettysburg and Beyond* (Chapel Hill: University of North Carolina Press, 1994), 1–8; Paul D. Escott, *After Secession: Jefferson Davis and the Failure of Confederate Nationalism* (Baton Rouge: Louisiana State University Press, 1978), 189–90, 195.

2. Lee to Davis, July 27 and 29, and to Seddon, July 30, 1863, O.R. 27, pt. 3:1040–41, 1048–49, 1052; Davis to Lee, July 28, 1863, in Dunbar Rowland, ed., *Jefferson Davis, Constitutionalist: His Letters, Papers, and Speeches*, 10 vols. (Jackson: Mississippi Department of Archives and History, 1923), 5:578–80.

3. Davis proclamation, August 1, 1863, O.R. series 4, 2:687–88.

4. Escott, *After Secession*, 189–90, 195.

5. Lee to Davis, August 8, 1863, in Rowland, *Jefferson Davis, Constitutionalist*, 5:585–87.

6. Lee to Davis, August 17, 1863, O.R. 29, pt. 2:649– 50.

7. Lee to Davis, August 22, 1863, ibid., 660–61.

8. Lee to Davis, August 24, 1863, ibid., 664–65.

9. Davis to Lee, August 24, 1863, in Rowland, *Jefferson Davis, Constitutionalist*, 5:598.

10. Douglas Southall Freeman, *R. E. Lee: A Biography*, 4 vols. (New York: Scribners, 1934), 3:163–65.

11. Robert Garlick Hill Kean, *Inside the Confederate Government*, ed. Edward Younger (New York: Oxford University Press, 1957), 403; Lee to Davis, September 14, Davis to Lee, September 16, 1863, O.R. 29, pt. 2:720–21, 725–27.

12. Lee to Davis, September 6, 1863, O.R. 29, pt. 2:700–701.

13. Davis to Lee, September 8, 1863, ibid., 702.

14. Lee to Davis, September 9, 1863, in Douglas Southall Freeman and Grady McWhiney, eds., *Lee's Dispatches: Unpublished Letters of General Robert E. Lee, C.S.A. to Jefferson Davis and the War Department of the Confederate States of America, 1862–65* (New York: G. P. Putnam's Sons, 1957), 126.

15. Lee to Davis, September 11, 1863, O.R. 29, pt. 2:711–12.

16. Lee to Davis, September 11, 14, and 18, 1863, ibid., 711–12, 720–21, 730–31.

17. Ibid; Lee to Davis, September 23 and 27, 1863, ibid., 742–43, 752–53.

18. Davis to Lee, September 16 and 21, 1863, ibid., 725– 27, 738–39.

19. Lee to Davis, September 28, 29, and 30, and October 1 and 3, 1863, ibid., 753–54, 756–58, 766, 769.

20. Freeman, *R. E. Lee*, 3:171.

21. Kean, *Inside the Confederate Government*, 406.

22. Lee to Davis, October 5, 1863, O.R. 29, pt. 2:771–72.

23. Foster to Halleck, October 8, 1863, ibid., 268; Davis to Lee, October 5, 1863, in Rowland, *Jefferson Davis, Constitutionalist,* 6:56–57.

24. Freeman, *R. E. Lee,* 3:171–87; James I. Roberston, Jr., *General A. P. Hill: The Story of A Confederate Warrior* (New York: Random House, 1987), 233–40.

25. Lee to Davis, November 10, 1863, O.R. 29, pt. 1:610–11; Freeman, *R. E. Lee,* 3:188–92.

26. Lee to Seddon, November 10, 1863, O.R. 29, pt. 2:830.

27. Lee to Davis, November 12, 1863, ibid., 832.

28. Lee to Seddon, November 12, 1863, ibid., 832–33.

29. Lee to Davis, November 12, 1863, ibid., 832.

30. Davis to Lee, November 14, 1863, in Rowland, *Jefferson Davis,* 6:80.

31. Seddon to Lee, November 14, 1863, O.R. 29, pt. 2:835.

32. Lee to Seddon, November 19, 1863, ibid., 837–38.

33. Seddon to Lee, November 20, 1863, ibid., 838–39.

34. G. W. C. Lee to Davis, November 18, 1863, Schoff Collection, Clements Library, University of Michigan.

35. That this matter was discussed in these terms is indicated by Davis's December 6 telegram to Lee (Rowland, *Jefferson Davis, Constitutionalist,* 6:93), "Could you *now* consistently go to Dalton *as heretofore explained?*" [emphasis added] and Lee's reply the next day (O.R. 29, pt. 2:861), "Unless it is intended that I should take *permanent* command, I can see no good that will result" [emphasis added]. These dispatches must refer to a discussion that occurred at this time.

36. Freeman, *R. E. Lee,* 3:193–94; J. Robertson, *General A. P. Hill,* 243.

37. Lee to Davis, November 25, 1863, telegrams received by the Confederate Secretary of War, National Archives, microfilm 618, reel 16, frame 447.

38. Davis to Lee, November 25 and 27, 1863, in Rowland, *Jefferson Davis,* 6:90–92.

39. Lee to Davis, November 25, 1863, O.R. 29, pt. 2:846.

40. Lee to Davis, November 27, 1863, ibid. 51, pt. 3:788.

41. Bragg to Davis, November 29, Cooper to Bragg, November 30, 1863, ibid. 31, pt. 2:682.

42. Bragg to Davis and Cooper, December 1, 1863, William P. Palmer Collection of Braxton Bragg Papers, Western Reserve Historical Society, Cleveland; Hardee to Davis, December 2, 1863, O.R. 38, pt. 5:988.

43. Lee to Davis, December 3, 1863, O.R. 29, pt. 3:858–59.

44. Davis to Lee, in Rowland, *Jefferson Davis, Constitutionalist,* 6:93.

45. Lee to Davis, O.R. 29, pt. 2:861.

46. Davis to Lee, in Rowland, *Jefferson Davis, Constitutionalist,* 6:128.

47. Lee to Stuart, O.R. 29, pt. 2:866.

48. Freeman, *R. E. Lee,* 3:214–15.

49. Davis to Northrop, January 4, 1864, William J. Rucker Collection, University of Virginia Library; Davis to Lee, January 4, 1864, O.R. 33:1064; Lee to Northrop, January 5, 1864, ibid.; Lee to Davis, January 11, 1864, ibid., 1076–78.

50. Whiting to Seddon, August 24, 28, 31 and September 2, 8, and 30, 1863, O.R. 29, pt. 2:670–72, 678–79, O.R. 33:1071–72, O.R. 29, pt. 2:695–96, 703–4, 761; to Davis, October 1 and December 21, O.R. 29, pt. 2:766–67, 886–87; to Cooper, October 4, 1863, and January 4, 12, 1864, O.R. 29, pt. 2:770–71, O.R. 33:1064,

1084–85; to Col. Wm. M. Browne, December 20, 1863, February 3, 1864, O.R. 29, pt. 2:881, O.R. 33:1145. See also Seddon to Whiting, September 8, O.R. 29, pt. 2:702–3, and Whiting to Martin, August 26, O.R. 29, pt. 2:675–76.

51. Lee to Seddon, January 11, 1864, O.R. 29 pt. 2:910.

52. Davis to Lee, January 4, 1864, ibid. 33:1064.

53. Lee to Davis, February 3, 1864, ibid., 1144.

54. Ibid.

55. Lee to Davis, February 18, 1864, ibid., 1185.

56. Freeman, *R. E. Lee,* 3:218–19.

57. W. P. Johnston to Cooper, with endorsements by Cooper and Davis, letters received by the Confederate Adjutant and Inspector General's Office, National Archives, microfilm 474, reel 93, frame 658.

58. William C. Davis, *Jefferson Davis: The Man and His Hour* (New York: Harper Collins, 1991), 541.

59. Judith Lee Hallock, *Braxton Bragg and Confederate Defeat,* vol. 2 (Tuscaloosa: University of Alabama Press, 1991), 165, 169, 171.

60. Clement Eaton, *Jefferson Davis* (New York: Free Press, 1977), 243.

61. Freeman, *R. E. Lee,* 3:218–19.

62. Lee to Davis, February 18, 1864, O.R. 33:1185; Freeman, *R. E. Lee,* 3:261; W. C. Davis, *Jefferson Davis,* 530; Hamilton J. Eckenrode and Bryan Conrad, *James Longstreet: Lee's War Horse* (Chapel Hill: University of North Carolina Press, 1986), 291; Jeffrey D. Wert, *General James Longstreet: The Confederacy's Most Controversial Soldier–A Biography* (New York: Simon and Schuster, 1993), 369–70. Wert maintains that Lee approved of Longstreet's plan.

63. Lee to Davis, March 25, 1864, in Freeman and McWhiney, eds., *Lee's Dispatches,* 140–45.

64. Lee to Davis, March 30, 1864, O.R. 33:1244–45.

65. Lee to Davis, April 5 and 8, 1864, ibid., 1260–61, 1267.

66. Lee to Davis, April 9, 12, and 15, 1864, ibid., 1268–69, 1276, 1282–83.

67. Lee to Davis, April 12, 1864, in Rowland, *Jefferson Davis,* 6:224.

68. Lee to Davis, April 15, 1864, O.R. 33:1282–83.

69. Lee to Davis, April 18, 1864, ibid., 1290–91.

70. Bragg to Lee, April 8, 1864, O.R. 51, pt. 2:1076–77; Kean, *Inside the Confederate Government,* 143–44.

71. Bragg to Lee, April 8, 1864, O.R. 51, pt. 2:1076–77.

72. Cooper to Beauregard, April 15, 1863, O.R. 33:1283; T. Harry Williams, *P. G. T. Beauregard: Napoleon in Gray* (Baton Rouge: Louisiana State University Press, 1956), 207; Alfred Roman, *The Military Operations of General Beauregard in the War Between the States, 1861–1865,* 2 vols. (New York: Harper and Brothers, 1884), 2:193.

73. William Glenn Robertson, *Back Door to Richmond: The Bermuda Hundred Campaign, April–June 1864* (Newark: University of Delaware Press, 1987), 47–50, 53; P. G. T. Beauregard, "The Defense of Drewry's Bluff," in Robert U. Johnson and Clarence C. Buel, eds., *Battles and Leaders of the Civil War,* 4 vols. (New York: Thomas Yoseloff, 1956), 4:195; Beauregard to Bragg, April 22 (two dispatches), 25 (three dispatches), and 29 (two dispatches), with endorsements by Bragg, Cooper, Seddon, and Davis, O.R. 51, pt. 2:872, 876, 880, and ibid. 33:1326–28.

74. Lee to Davis, April 25, 1864, in Freeman and McWhiney, *Lee's Dispatches*, 166.

75. Lee to Davis, April 24, 1864, ibid., 165.

76. Varina Howell Davis, *Jefferson Davis: Ex-President of the Confederate States of America, A Memoir by His Wife*, 2 vols. (New York: Belford, 1890), 2:496.

77. Lee to Davis, April 28, 1864, O.R. 33:1320–21.

78. V. H. Davis, *Jefferson Davis*, 2:496.

79. Davis to Lee, May 2, 1864, in Rowland, *Jefferson Davis, Constitutionalist*, 6:239.

80. Ulysses S. Grant, *Personal Memoirs of U. S. Grant*, 2 vols. (New York: Charles L. Webster, 1885), 2:177.

81. Lee to Davis, May 4, 1864, in Freeman and McWhiney, *Lee's Dispatches*, 169–74.

82. Beauregard to Bragg, May 3, 1864, O.R. 51, pt. 2:886.

83. Davis to Beauregard, May 4, 1864, in Rowland, *Jefferson Davis, Constitutionalist*, 6:246–47.

84. Beauregard to Davis, May 4, 1864, O.R. 51, pt. 2:889.

85. Lee to Bragg (two dispatches), May 4, 1864, ibid. 36, pt. 2:950.

86. Davis to Lee (two dispatches), May 4, 1864, ibid. 51, pt. 2:867, and in Rowland, *Jefferson Davis, Constitutionalist*, 6:247.

87. Lee to Davis, May 5, 1864, O.R. 36, pt. 2:951.

88. Lesley J. Gordon-Burr, "Pickett After Gettysburg," in Steven E. Woodworth, ed., *Leadership and Command in the American Civil War* (Campbell, Calif.: Savas Woodbury, 1995), 83; W. G. Robertson, *Back Door*, 66–69.

89. Beauregard, "Defense of Drewry's Bluff," in Johnson and Buel, *Battles and Leaders*, 4:196; Beauregard to Bragg May 5, 1864 (two dispatches), with Davis endorsement, O.R. 51, pt. 2:890.

90. Gordon-Burr, "Pickett After Gettysburg," in Woodworth, *Leadership and Command*, 44.

91. Beauregard to Bragg, May 5, 1864, O.R. 51, pt. 2:891.

92. Freeman, *R. E. Lee*, 3:287–88. Freeman assumes Lee acted entirely in the excitement of the moment.

93. Lee to Seddon, May 6, 1864, O.R. 36, pt. 2:561.

94. Cooper to Beauregard, May 6, 1864, ibid., 964.

95. Beauregard to Cooper, May 6, 1864, ibid.

96. Whiting to Cooper, May 6, 1864, ibid. 51, pt. 2:897.

97. Davis to Beauregard, May 6, 1864, in Rowland, *Jefferson Davis, Constitutionalist*, 6:248.

98. Beauregard to Davis, May 6, 1864, O.R. 51, pt. 2:894.

99. Beauregard to Cooper, Seddon, and Bragg, May 6, 1864, ibid. 36, pt. 2:963–64.

100. Beauregard, "Defense of Drewry's Bluff," in Johnson and Buel, *Battles and Leaders*, 4:196; Gordon-Burr, "Pickett After Gettysburg," in Woodworth, *Leadership and Command*, 45; W. G. Robertson, *Back Door*, 66–67.

101. Lee to Seddon, May 7, 8 (three dispatches), 9, and 10, 1864, O.R. 36, pt. 2:966–74, 982–83, and in Freeman and McWhiney, *Lee's Dispatches*, 174–77.

102. Davis to Lee, May 9, 1864, in Rowland, *Jefferson Davis, Constitutionalist*, 6:249.

103. Gordon-Burr, "Pickett After Gettysburg," in Woodworth, *Leadership and Command*, 45.

104. Davis to Bragg, May 8, 1864, O.R. 51, pt. 2:902.

105. Beauregard to Bragg (four dispatches), May 8, 1864, ibid., 903–4.

106. Ransom to Bragg, May 9, 1864, ibid. 36, pt. 2:977; W. G. Robertson, *Back Door*, 122–23; Douglas Southall Freeman, *Lee's Lieutenants: A Study in Command*, 3 vols. (New York: Charles Scribner's Sons, 1944), 3:471.

107. Davis to G. H. Terret, May 10, 1864, in Rowland, *Jefferson Davis, Constitutionalist*, 6:249; Terret to Davis, May 10, 1864, O.R. 36, pt. 2:986.

108. W. G. Robertson, *Back Door*, 128.

109. Ibid.

110. Beauregard to Bragg, May 10, 1864, O.R. 51, pt. 2:915.

111. Beauregard to Bragg (second dispatch), May 10, 1864, ibid.; W. G. Robertson, *Back Door*, 128.

112. Beauregard to Bragg, May 11, 1864, O.R. 51, pt. 2:920; W. G. Robertson, *Back Door*, 139–40. That the order directed—or at least assumed—that Beauregard would lead the advance himself is demonstrated by Davis's assumption in his 2:15 P.M., May 11 dispatch that Beauregard had already left. Rowland, *Jefferson Davis*, 6:250.

113. Beauregard to Bragg, May 11, 1864, O.R. 51, pt. 2:919.

114. Beauregard to Bragg, May 11, 1864, ibid., 920.

115. Freeman, *Lee's Lieutenants*, 3:474.

116. Beauregard to Seddon, May 11, 1864, O.R. 36, pt. 2:992; to Davis, May 11, 1864, ibid. 51, pt. 2:920.

117. Beauregard to Bragg, May 11, 1864, ibid. 51, pt. 2:921.

118. Beauregard to Bragg, May 11, 1864, ibid., 919.

119. Seddon to Beauregard, May 11, 1864, ibid. 36, pt. 2:991.

120. Beauregard to Seddon, May 11, 1864, ibid., 992.

121. Freeman, *Lee's Lieutenants*, 3:473.

122. Seddon to Beauregard, mistakenly dated May 10, 1864, O.R. 36, pt. 2:986. See W. G. Robertson, *Back Door*, 140–42.

123. Beauregard to Seddon, May 11, 1864, O.R. 36, pt. 2:992.

124. Seddon to Beauregard, May 11, 1864, ibid.

125. V. H. Davis, *Jefferson Davis*, 2:498; Davis to Lee, May 11, 1864, in Rowland, *Jefferson Davis, Constitutionalist*, 6:250; W. C. Davis, *Jefferson Davis*, 556.

126. Davis to Commanding Officer, Petersburg, May 11, 1864, in Rowland, *Jefferson Davis, Constitutionalist*, 6:250.

127. Beauregard to Davis, May 11, 1864, O.R. 51, pt. 2:920.

128. Beauregard to Bragg, May 11, 1864, ibid.

129. W. G. Robertson, *Back Door*, 140–42.

130. Seddon to Bragg, May 11, 1864, O.R. 51, pt. 2:918.

131. John B. Jones, *A Rebel War Clerk's Diary*, ed. Earl Schenck Miers (New York: Sagamore, 1958), 373.

132. W. G. Robertson, *Back Door*, 146; Seddon to Bragg, May 11, 1864, O.R. 51, pt. 2:918.

133. Jefferson Davis, *The Rise and Fall of the Confederate Government*, 2 vols. (New York: Appleton, 1881), 2:510; V. H. Davis, *Jefferson Davis*, 2:500.

134. Beauregard to Bragg, May 12, 1864, O.R. 51, pt. 2:923; Beauregard to Davis, May 13, 1864, ibid., 927.

135. W. G. Robertson, *Back Door,* 146– 47.

136. Ibid. 149; Bragg to Beauregard, May 13, 1864, O.R. 51, pt. 2:927; Freeman, *Lee's Lieutenants,* 3:476.

137. Jones, *Rebel War Clerk's Diary,* 375.

138. Lee to Davis, May 12 and 13, 1864, O.R. 36, pt. 2:993, 998; Davis to Lee, May 13, 1864, in Rowland, *Jefferson Davis, Constitutionalist,* 6:251.

139. Lee to Davis, May 11 and 12, 1864, O.R. 36, pt. 2:988, and ibid. 51, pt. 2:922.

140. Davis to Lee, May 11 and 13, 1864, in Rowland, *Jefferson Davis, Constitutionalist,* 6:250–51.

141. Beauregard to Bragg, May 14, 1864, O.R. 36, pt. 2:1024; Freeman, *Lee's Lieutenants,* 3:478–79.

142. Freeman, *Lee's Lieutenants,* 3:479–81; Beauregard, "Defense of Drewry's Bluff," in Johnson and Buel, *Battles and Leaders,* 4:199.

143. Davis to Beauregard, May 14, 1864, in Rowland, *Jefferson Davis, Constitutionalist,* 6:252; Beauregard to Davis, May 14,1864, O.R. 51, pt. 2:930.

144. Beauregard to Bragg, May 14, 1864, O.R. 36, pt. 2:1024.

145. Beauregard, "Defense of Drewry's Bluff," in Johnson and Buel, *Battles and Leaders,* 4:198–200; Davis to Lee, May 14, 1864, in Rowland, *Jefferson Davis, Constitutionalist,* 6:252; J. Davis, *Rise and Fall,* 2:511–13; W. G. Robertson, *Back Door,* 153.

146. Beauregard to Bragg, May 14, 1864,O.R. 51, pt. 2:934.

147. Beauregard "Defense of Drewry's Bluff," in Johnson and Buel, *Battles and Leaders,* 4:200.

148. Bragg to Beauregard, May 15, 1864, O.R. 51, pt. 2:934.

149. Bragg to Beauregard (second dispatch), May 15, 1864, ibid.

150. Beauregard to Bragg, May 15, 1864, with Bragg and Davis endorsements, ibid. 36, pt. 2:1004.

151. Whiting to Beauregard, May 15, 1864, ibid. 51, pt. 2:935.

152. J. Davis, *Rise and Fall,* 2:512–13.

153. Beauregard to Davis, May 15, 1864, O.R. 51, pt. 2:1077.

154. J. Davis, *Rise and Fall,* 2:512–13.

155. Beauregard, "Defense of Drewry's Bluff," in Johnson and Buel, *Battles and Leaders,* 4:200.

156. Beauregard to Bragg, 5:00 A.M. and 8:30 A.M., May 16, 1864, O.R. 51, pt. 2:938, and ibid. 36, pt. 2:196–97.

157. Beauregard to Bragg, May 16, 1864, ibid. 36, pt. 2:197.

158. Freeman, *Lee's Lieutenants,* 3:488–89; W. G. Robertson, *Back Door,* 194.

159. Beauregard to Bragg, May 16, 1864, O.R. 36, pt. 2:197.

160. J. Davis, *Rise and Fall,* 2:513.

161. Freeman, *Lee's Lieutenants,* 3:488–89; W. G. Robertson, *Back Door,* 205–6; W. C. Davis, *Jefferson Davis,* 557; John H. Reagan, *Memoirs,* ed. Walter F. McCaleb (New York: Neale, 1906), 190–91.

162. W. G. Robertson, *Back Door,* 206, 209, 214–16; Reagan, *Memoirs,* 190–91; Freeman, *Lee's Lieutenants,* 3:492–95; Beauregard to Bragg, 5:45 P.M. and 10:50 P.M.,

May 16, and 11:00 P.M., May 17, 1864, O.R. 36, pt. 2:198; Grant's report, ibid. 36, pt. 1:20–21.

163. J. Davis, *Rise and Fall*, 2:514–15; Davis to Lee, May 18, 1864, in Rowland, *Jefferson Davis, Constitutionalist*, Beauregard memorandum, in V. H. Davis, *Jefferson Davis*, 2:521–23; Bragg to Davis, May 19, 1864, O.R. 36, pt. 2:1024; Davis to Lee, May 20, 1864, in Rowland, *Jefferson Davis, Constitutionalist*, 6:256–58.

164. Beauregard to Bragg, May 19 (three dispatches) and May 20, 1864, Bragg to Beauregard, May 19, 1864, O.R. 51, pt. 2:947–48, 953; W. G. Robertson, *Back Door*, 223; Davis to Lee, in Rowland, *Jefferson Davis, Constitutionalist*, 6:255–56.

165. Davis to Beauregard, May 20, 1864, in Rowland, *Jefferson Davis, Constitutionalist*, 6:258–59.

166. Lee to Davis, May 15, 16, 17, 18, and 19, 1864, in Freeman and McWhiney, *Lee's Dispatches*, 181–86, and O.R. 36, pt. 2:1011, 1015, 1019, 1022.

167. Lee to Davis, May 22, 1864, in Freeman and McWhiney, *Lee's Dispatches*, 190–93.

168. Lee to Davis (two dispatches), May 18, 1864, ibid., 186–88.

169. Davis to Lee, May 20, 1864, in Rowland, *Jefferson Davis, Constitutionalist*, 6:256–58.

170. Davis to Lee, May 15, 1864, ibid., 235.

171. Davis to Lee, May 15, 1864, ibid., 259–60.

172. Freeman, *R. E. Lee*, 3:356.

173. Lee to Davis, May 20 and 23, 1864, in Freeman and McWhiney, *Lee's Dispatches*, 188–89, 194–97.

174. Lee to Davis, May 28, 1864, ibid., 202–3.

175. Freeman, *R. E. Lee*, 3:351–64.

176. Davis to Lee and Beauregard, May 28, 1864, in Rowland, *Jefferson Davis, Constitutionalist*, 6:261–62.

177. Davis to Lee, May 28, 1864, ibid., 262.

178. Lee to Bragg and Davis, May 29, 1864, in Freeman and McWhiney, *Lee's Dispatches*, 204–5.

179. Beauregard to Lee, May 30, 1864, in Roman, *Military Operations*, 2:563.

180. Lee to Davis, May 30, 1864, O.R. 36, pt. 3:850.

181. Davis to Lee, May 30, 1864, in Rowland, *Jefferson Davis, Constitutionalist*, 6:263.

182. Bragg to Beauregard, May 30, 1864, O.R. 36, pt. 3:857.

183. Davis to Lee, May 31, 1864, ibid. 51, pt. 2:973–74.

184. Ibid.

185. Davis to Ransom, June 1, 1864, in Rowland, *Jefferson Davis, Constitutionalist*, 6:265.

186. Lee to Davis, June 3, 1864, in Freeman and McWhiney, *Lee's Dispatches*, 212–14.

187. Lee to Davis, June 5 and 6, 1864, ibid., 215–18; Bragg to Seddon, June 6, 1864, O.R. 37, pt. 1:150; Seddon to Davis, June 6, 1864, ibid. 51, pt. 2:989–90.

188. Bragg to Davis, June 12, 1864, O.R. 37, pt. 1:758.

189. Davis to Lee, June 9, 1864, in Rowland, *Jefferson Davis, Constitutionalist*, 6:269–70.

190. Lee to Davis, June 14, 1864, in Freeman and McWhiney, *Lee's Dispatches,* 226–32.

191. Lee to Davis, 3:45 P.M., June 14, and 12:45, 6:50, and 8:20 P.M., June 15, 1864, Lee to Bragg, 4:00 P.M., June 14, and 12:20 P.M., June 15, 1864, ibid., 232–43.

192. Lee to Davis, June 15, 1864, ibid., 239–40.

193. J. William Jones, *Personal Reminiscences of Gen. Robert E. Lee* (New York: Appleton, 1875), 40.

194. Lee to Davis, June 15, 1864, in Freeman and McWhiney, *Lee's Dispatches,* 242–43.

195. Davis to Lee, June 15, 1864, in Rowland, *Jefferson Davis, Constitutionalist,* 6:273.

196. Beauregard to Lee, June 16 (six dispatches) and June 17, 1864, O.R. 51, pt. 2:1078–79; Lee to Davis, June 16, 1864, in Freeman and McWhiney, *Lee's Dispatches,* 243–45.

197. Lee to Davis, June 18, 1864, in Freeman and McWhiney, *Lee's Dispatches,* 249–50.

CHAPTER 8

1. J. William Jones, *Personal Reminiscences of Gen. Robert E. Lee* (New York: Appleton, 1875), 40.

2. Alan T. Nolan, *Lee Considered: General Robert E. Lee and Civil War History* (Chapel Hill: University of North Carolina Press, 1991), 85.

3. Lee to Davis, June 21, 1864, in Douglas Southall Freeman and Grady McWhiney, eds., *Lee's Dispatches: Unpublished Letters of General Robert E. Lee, C.S.A. to Jefferson Davis and the War Department of the Confederate States of America, 1862–65* (New York: G. P. Putnam's Sons, 1957), 253–57.

4. Lee to Davis, June 26, 1864, O.R. 37, pt. 1:766–68.

5. Lee to Davis, June 29, 1864, ibid., 769–70.

6. Lee to Davis, July 21, 1864, in Freeman and McWhiney, *Lee's Dispatches,* 285–86.

7. Lee to Davis, July 23, 1864, in Dunbar Rowland, ed., *Jefferson Davis, Constitutionalist: His Letters, Papers, and Speeches,* 10 vols. (Jackson: Mississippi Department of Archives and History, 1923), 6:299.

8. Lee to Davis, August 22, 1864, in Freeman and McWhiney, *Lee's Dispatches,* 289–93.

9. Davis to Lee, August 23, 1864, O.R. 42, pt. 2:1197–98.

10. Seddon to Lee, August 23, 1864, ibid., 1199.

11. Lee to Seddon, August 23, 1864, ibid., 1199–1200.

12. Seddon to Lee, August 26, 1864, ibid., 1203–4.

13. Lee to Davis, September 2, 1864, in Rowland, *Jefferson Davis, Constitutionalist,* 6:327–29.

14. Lee to Davis, September 9, 1864, in Freeman and McWhiney, *Lee's Dispatches,* 293–95.

15. Lee to Seddon, September 12, 17, and 20, Seddon to Lee, September 18 and 22, Lee endorsement, October 5, 1864, O.R. 42, pt. 2:1245–46, 1256–57, 1260–61, 1269–70, 1281–82.

16. Lee to Seddon, October 4, 1864, ibid., pt. 3:1134.

17. Seddon to Lee, October 5, 1864, ibid., 1134–35.

18. Lee to Davis, November 2, 1864, in Freeman and McWhiney, *Lee's Dispatches*, 304–6.

19. Lee to Seddon, August 14, Seddon to Lee, August 17, 1864, O.R. 42, pt. 2:1175–76, 1182–83.

20. Davis speech, September 9, 1864, in Rowland, *Jefferson Davis, Constitutionalist*, 6:341–44.

21. Lee to Seddon, October 10, 1863, O.R. 29, pt. 2:806–7; Davis to Lee, January 6, February 23, March 17 and 25, August 31, and September 8 and 13, in Rowland, *Jefferson Davis, Constitutionalist*, 6:143, 188, 208–9, 326, 333–34.

22. Latrobe to Taylor, with endorsements, November 14, 1864, O.R. 42, pt. 3:1213.

23. Lee to Davis, June 21, 1864, in Freeman and McWhiney, *Lee's Dispatches*, 253–57.

24. Lee to Davis, June 29, 1864, O.R. 37, pt. 1:769–70.

25. Lee to Davis, July 3 and 5, 1864, in Freeman and McWhiney, *Lee's Dispatches*, 269–71, 275–76. Lee refers to other letters no longer extant.

26. Davis to Lee, July 8, 1864, in Rowland, *Jefferson Davis, Constitutionalist*, 6:285; Lee to Davis, July 8, 1864, in Freeman and McWhiney, *Lee's Dispatches*, 278.

27. Lee to Davis, July 11, 1864, O.R. 37, pt. 2:594–95.

28. Davis to Lee, July 12 and 13, 1864, in Rowland, *Jefferson Davis, Constitutionalist*, 6:291–92; Lee to Davis, July 12, 1864, in Freeman and McWhiney, *Lee's Dispatches*, 280.

29. Varina Howell Davis, *Jefferson Davis: Ex-President of the Confederate States of America, A Memoir by His Wife*, 2 vols. (New York: Belford, 1890), 2:494–95; Davis to Lee, June 21, 1864, in Rowland, *Jefferson Davis, Constitutionalist*, 6:276.

30. Pemberton to Seddon, August 7, 1864, O.R. 42, pt. 2:1164–65.

31. Lee to Davis, August 4, 1864, ibid., 1161–62.

32. Lee to Davis, July 6 and 23, 1864, in Freeman and McWhiney, *Lee's Dispatches*, 367–68, and O.R. 37, pt. 2:599.

33. John B. Jones, *A Rebel War Clerk's Diary*, ed. Earl Schenck Miers (New York: Sagamore, 1958), 410–11.

34. Davis to Lee, August 23, 1864, O.R. 42, pt. 2:1197–98.

35. Davis speeches, September 29 and October 3, 1864, in Rowland, *Jefferson Davis, Constitutionalist*, 6:341–47.

36. Douglas Southall Freeman, *R. E. Lee: A Biography*, 4 vols. (New York: Scribners, 1934), 3:507–9.

37. Nolan, *Lee Considered*, 115, 117–19; Richard E. Beringer, Herman Hattaway, Archer Jones, and William N. Still, Jr., *Why the South Lost the Civil War* (Athens: University of Georgia Press, 1986), 333–34.

38. Davis to Lee, November 18, 1864, in Rowland, *Jefferson Davis, Constitutionalist*, 6:407.

39. Davis to Lee, November 21, 1864, ibid., 408; Lee to Davis, November 21 and December 5, 6, and 13, 1864, O.R. 42, pt. 3:1222, 1254–56, 1271.

40. Davis to Lee, December 19 and 20, 1864, in Rowland, *Jefferson Davis, Constitutionalist,* 6:423–24, 433; V. H. Davis, *Jefferson Davis,* 2:206.

41. Davis to Lee, December 30, 1864, January 2 and 18 and February 25, 1865, O.R. 51, pt. 2:1055, ibid. 46, pt. 2:1118, and in Rowland, *Jefferson Davis, Constitutionalist,* 6:434, 488; Lee to Davis, December 30, 1864, Davis Papers, Tulane University Library.

42. Freeman, *R. E. Lee,* 3:533–34.

43. Jones, *Rebel War Clerk's Diary,* 469, 471.

44. Robert Garlick Hill Kean, *Inside the Confederate Government,* ed. Edward Younger (New York: Oxford University Press, 1957), 185.

45. James Longstreet, *From Manassas to Appomattox,* ed. James I. Robertson, Jr. (Bloomington: Indiana University Press, 1960), 582–83; Thomas S. Bocock to Davis, January 21, 1865, O.R. 46, pt. 2:1118.

46. Davis to James F. Johnson and Hugh W. Sheffey, January 18, 1865, in Rowland, *Jefferson Davis, Constitutionalist,* 6:454–55.

47. Davis to Seddon, February 1, 1865, ibid., 458–61.

48. Davis to Johnson and Sheffey, January 18, 1865, ibid., 453–54.

49. Davis to Lee, January 18, 1865, in Rowland, *Jefferson Davis, Constitutionalist,* 6:452.

50. Lee to Davis, January 19, 1865, in Freeman and McWhiney, *Lee's Dispatches,* 322–23.

51. Jones, *Rebel War Clerk's Diary,* 490–91.

52. Kean, *Inside the Confederate Government,* 190–91; Davis to Seddon, February 1, 1865, in Rowland, *Jefferson Davis, Constitutionalist,* 6:458–61.

53. J. B. Jones, *Rebel War Clerk's Diary,* 483, 488, 490–91; Frank E. Vandiver, *Their Tattered Flags: The Epic of the Confederacy* (College State: Texas A&M University Press, 1987), 295; Douglas Southall Freeman, *Lee's Lieutenants: A Study in Command,* 3 vols. (New York: Charles Scribner's Sons, 1944), 3:634–35); Longstreet, *From Manassas to Appomattox,* 582–83.

54. Jones, *Rebel War Clerk's Diary,* 490–91.

55. Lee to Davis, February 9, 1865, O.R. 51, pt. 2:1082–83.

56. Longstreet, *From Manassas to Appomattox,* 587–89.

57. Lee to Davis, February 9, 1865, O.R. 51, pt. 2:1082–83.

58. A. P. Hill to W. H. Taylor with Lee endorsement, December 1, 1864, B. R. Johnson to Major Duncan, December 26, 1864, ibid. 42, pt. 3:1249, 1311; Freeman, *Lee's Lieutenants,* 3:623.

59. Lee to Davis, February 9, 1865, O.R. 51, pt. 2:1082–83; Freeman, *Lee's Lieutenants,* 3:623.

60. Davis to Lee, February 10, 1865, in Rowland, *Jefferson Davis, Constitutionalist,* 6:478–79.

61. Davis to Lee, February 10, 1865, ibid., 479.

62. Lee to Seddon with Davis endorsement, February 8, 1865, O.R. 46, pt. 1:381–82.

63. Kean, *Inside the Confederate Government,* 200.

64. Richard D. Goff, *Confederate Supply* (Durham, N.C.: Duke University Press, 1969), 231.

65. Bromfield Ridley to Davis, February 10, 1865, letters received by Confederate Secretary of War, National Archives, microfilm 437, reel 150, frames 644–47.

66. Davis paper, February 18, 1865, in Rowland, *Jefferson Davis, Constitutionalist,* 6:491–503.

67. Davis to James Phelan, March 1, 1865, ibid., 491.

68. Davis to Lee, February 24, 1865, ibid., 484.

69. Davis to James Phelan, March 1, 1865, ibid., 491.

70. Jeffrey D. Wert, *General James Longstreet: The Confederacy's Most Controversial Soldier—A Biography* (New York: Simon and Schuster, 1993), 397.

71. Davis to Lee, February 28, 1865, in Rowland, *Jefferson Davis, Constitutionalist,* 6:489.

72. Lee to Davis, March 2, 1865, in Freeman and McWhiney, *Lee's Dispatches,* 371–72.

73. Wert, *General James Longstreet,* 397.

74. Freeman, *R. E. Lee,* 4:8–9.

75. Ibid., 9–10.

76. Jefferson Davis, *The Rise and Fall of the Confederate Government,* 2 vols. (New York: Appleton, 1881), 2:648–49.

77. Ibid., 649–50; Lee to Davis, March 26, 1865, in Freeman and McWhiney, *Lee's Dispatches,* 341–46.

78. Lee to Davis, March 23, 1865, in Freeman and McWhiney, *Lee's Dispatches,* 339.

79. Lee to Breckinridge, March 25, and to Davis March 26, 1865, ibid., 341–47.

80. V. H. Davis, *Jefferson Davis,* 2:575.

81. Davis to Lee, April 1, 1865, in Rowland, *Jefferson Davis, Constitutionalist,* 6:526–27.

82. Lee to Davis, April 1, 1865, in Freeman and McWhiney, *Lee's Dispatches,* 358–60.

83. Kean, *Inside the Confederate Government,* 205; John H. Reagan, *Memoirs,* ed. Walter F. McCaleb (New York: Neale, 1906), 196; J. Davis, *Rise and Fall,* 2:655–56, 667–68.

84. Davis to Lee, April 2, 1865, O.R. 46, pt. 3:1378.

85. Freeman, *R. E. Lee,* 4:55.

86. Lee to Davis, April 2, 1865, in Freeman and McWhiney, *Lee's Dispatches,* 375.

87. Lee to Davis, April 2, 1865, in J. Davis, *Rise and Fall,* 2:660–61.

88. Ibid., 675–76.

89. Ibid., 667–68.

90. Reagan, *Memoirs,* 198.

91. J. Davis, *Rise and Fall,* 2:676–77.

92. Davis to Beauregard (2 dispatches), April 4, and to Johnston, April 5, 1865, in Rowland, *Jefferson Davis, Constitutionalist,* 6:529, 532.

93. J. Davis to V. H. Davis, April 5 and 6, 1865, ibid., 532–34.

94. Davis proclamation, April 5, 1865, ibid., 529–31.

95. J. Davis, *Rise and Fall,* 2:676–77.

96. Lee to Davis, April 6, 1865, O.R. 46, pt. 3:1386.

97. Davis to Lee, April 9, 1865, in Rowland, *Jefferson Davis, Constitutionalist,* 6:541–42.

98. J. Davis, *Rise and Fall,* 2:677–78; Reagan, *Memoirs,* 199–200; Davis to Johnston, April 10, 1865, in Rowland, *Jefferson Davis, Constitutionalist,* 6:542–43.

99. Davis to Johnston, April 11, 1865, in Rowland, *Jefferson Davis, Constitutionalist,* 543–44.

100. J. Davis, *Rise and Fall,* 2:679–83; Reagan, *Memoirs,* 199–200; Craig L. Symonds, *Joseph E. Johnston: A Civil War Biography* (New York: W. W. Norton, 1992), 354–55; William C. Davis, *Jefferson Davis: The Man and His Hour* (New York: Harper Collins, 1991), 615–17. Some discrepancies exist in the recollections of the various participants as to the exact times, dates, and sequences of these events.

101. J. Davis, *Rise and Fall,* 2:689; W. C. Davis, *Jefferson Davis,* 622–26.

102. W. C. Davis, *Jefferson Davis,* 629–39.

103. This view is best set forth by Nolan, *Lee Considered,* 59–106.

104. Clement Eaton, *Jefferson Davis* (New York: Free Press, 1977), 250.

BIBLIOGRAPHY

PRIMARY SOURCES

Confederate Museum, Richmond, Virginia.
Dearborn Collection, Houghton Library, Harvard University.
Jedediah Hotchkiss Papers, Manuscript Division, Library of Congress.
Jefferson Davis Papers, Rice University.
Jefferson Davis Papers, Tulane University Library.
Leonidas Polk Papers, Southern Historical Collection, Library of the University of North Carolina at Chapel Hill.
Letters received by the Confederate Adjutant and Inspector General's Office, National Archives.
Letters received by the Confederate Secretary of War, National Archives.
Manuscript Department, Perkins Library, Duke University.
Mrs. Mason Barret Collection of Albert Sidney and William Preston Johnston Papers, Tulane University Library.
Records Group 109, National Archives.
Schoff Collection, Clements Library, University of Michigan.
Telegrams received by the Confederate Secretary of War, National Archives.
William P. Palmer Collection of Braxton Bragg Papers, Western Reserve Historical Society.
William J. Rucker Collection, University of Virginia Library.

SECONDARY SOURCES

Albright, Harry. *Gettysburg: Crisis of Command*. New York: Hippocrene Books, 1989.
Alexander, Bevin. *Lost Victories: The Military Genius of Stonewall Jackson*. New York: Henry Holt, 1992.
Alexander, Edward Porter. *Fighting for the Confederacy: The Personal Recollections of General Edward Porter Alexander*. Ed. Gary W. Gallagher. Chapel Hill: University of North Carolina Press, 1989.
——. *Military Memoirs of a Confederate*. New York: Scribners, 1907.

Angle, Paul M., and Earl Schenck Miers. *Tragic Years, 1860–1865*. 2 vols. New York: Simon and Schuster, 1960.

Bailey, Ronald H. *The Bloodiest Day: The Battle of Antietam*. Alexandria, Va.: Time-Life Books, 1984.

——. *Forward to Richmond: McClellan's Peninsular Campaign*. Alexandria, Va.: Time-Life Books, 1983.

Ball, Douglas B. *Financial Failure and Confederate Defeat*. Urbana: University of Illinois Press, 1991.

Ballard, Michael B. *The Long Shadow: Jefferson Davis and the Final Days of the Confederacy*. Jackson: University Press of Mississippi, 1986.

——. *Pemberton: A Biography*. Jackson: University Press of Mississippi, 1991.

Baltz, Louis J., III. *The Last Battle of Cold Harbor: May 27–June 13, 1864*. Lynchburg, Va.: H. E. Howard, 1994.

Bearss, Edwin C., and Chris Calkins. *The Battle of Five Forks*. Lynchburg, Va.: H. E. Howard, 1985.

Beck, Brandon, and Charles Grunder. *The First Battle of Winchester*. Lynchburg, Va.: H. E. Howard, 1992.

Bellah, James Warner. *Soldiers' Battle: Gettysburg*. New York: David McKay, 1962.

Beringer, Richard E., Herman Hattaway, Archer Jones, and William N. Still, Jr. *Why the South Lost the Civil War*. Athens: University of Georgia Press, 1986.

Boritt, Gabor S., ed. *Why the Confederacy Lost*. New York: Oxford University Press, 1992.

Brice, Marshall Moore. *Conquest of a Valley*. Charlottesville: University Press of Virginia, 1965.

Bridges, Hal. *Lee's Maverick General: Daniel Harvey Hill*. Lincoln, University of Nebraska Press, 1991.

Calkins, Chris M. *Battles of Appomattox Station and Appomattox Court House, April 8–9, 1865*. Lynchburg, Va.: H. E. Howard, 1987.

Cannan, John. *The Antietam Campaign, August–September 1862*. Conshohocken, Pa.: Combined Books, 1990.

——. *The Wilderness Campaign, May 1864*. Conshohocken, Pa.: Combined Books, 1993.

Cannan, John, ed. *War in the East: Chancellorsville to Gettysburg, 1863*. New York: Gallery Books, 1990.

Casdorph, Paul D. *Lee and Jackson: Confederate Chieftains*. New York: Paragon House, 1992.

Cate, Wirt Armistead. *Lucius Q. C. Lamar: Secession and Reunion*. New York: Russell and Russell, 1935.

Catton, Bruce. *The Coming Fury*. New York: Doubleday, 1961.

——. *Gettysburg: The Final Fury*. Garden City, N.Y.: Doubleday, 1974.

——. *Glory Road: The Bloody Route from Fredericksburg to Gettysburg*. New York: Doubleday, 1953.

——. *Mr. Lincoln's Army*. New York, Doubleday, 1951.

——. *Never Call Retreat*. New York: Doubleday, 1965.

——. *A Stillness at Appomattox*. New York: Doubleday, 1953.

——. *Terrible Swift Sword*. New York: Doubleday, 1963.

——. *This Hallowed Ground*. New York: Doubleday, 1955.

Cauble, Frank P. *The Surrender Proceedings: April 9, 1865–Appomattox Court House*. Lynchburg, Va.: H. E. Howard.

Chambers, Lenoir. *Stonewall Jackson*. 2 vols. New York: William Morrow, 1959.

Chesnut, Mary Boykin. *Mary Chesnut's Civil War*. Ed. C. Vann Woodward. New Haven, Conn.: Yale University Press, 1981.

Clark, Champ. *Decoying the Yanks: Jackson's Valley Campaign*. Alexandria, Va.: Time-Life Books, 1984.

——. *Gettysburg: The Confederate High Tide*. Alexandria, Va.: Time-Life Books, 1985.

Clark, James C. *Last Train South: The Flight of the Confederate Government from Richmond*. Jefferson, N.C.: McFarland, 1984.

Coddington, Edwin B. *The Gettysburg Campaign: A Study in Command*. New York: Charles Scribner's Sons, 1968.

Collins, Darrell L. *Jackson's Valley Campaign: The Battle of Cross Keys and Port Republic, June 8–9, 1862*. Lynchburg, Va.: H. E. Howard, 1994.

Connelly, Thomas L. *The Marble Man: Robert E. Lee and His Image in American Society*. New York: Alfred A. Knopf, 1977.

Cooling, Benjamin Franklin. *Jubal Early's Raid on Washington, 1864*. Baltimore: Nautical and Aviation Publishing Company of America, 1989.

Cormier, Steven A. *The Siege of Suffolk: The Forgotten Campaign, April 11–May 4, 1863*. Lynchburg, Va.: H. E. Howard, 1989.

Crist, Lynda Lasswell, and Mary Seaton Dix, eds. *The Papers of Jefferson Davis*. 7 vols. to date. Baton Rouge: Louisiana State University Press, 1971– .

Cullen, Joseph P. *The Peninsula Campaign, 1862: McClellan and Lee Struggle for Richmond*. Harrisburg, Pa.: Stackpole, 1973.

Cummings, Charles, M. *Yankee Quaker, Confederate General: The Curious Career of General Bushrod Rust Johnson*. Cranbury, N.J.: Farleigh Dickinson University Press, 1971.

Cutting, Elisabeth. *Jefferson Davis, Political Soldier*. New York: Dodd, Mead, 1930.

Davis, Burke. *Gray Fox: Robert E. Lee and the Civil War*. New York: Rinehart, 1956.

——. *Jeb Stuart: The Last Cavalier*. New York: Rinehart, 1957.

——. *The Long Surrender*. New York: Random House, 1985.

Davis, Jefferson. *The Rise and Fall of the Confederate Government*. 2 vols. New York: Appleton, 1881.

Davis, Varina Howell. *Jefferson Davis: Ex-President of the Confederate States of America, A Memoir by His Wife*. 2 vols. New York: Belford, 1890.

Davis, William C. *Battle at Bull Run: A History of the First Major Campaign of the Civil War*. Garden City, N.Y.: Doubleday, 1977.

——. *The Battle of New Market*. Garden City, N.Y.: Doubleday, 1975.

——. *Breckinridge: Statesman, Soldier, Symbol*. Baton Rouge: Louisiana State University Press, 1974.

——. *Brother Against Brother: The War Begins*. Alexandria, Va.: Time-Life Books, 1983.

——. *Death in the Trenches: Grant at Petersburg*. Alexandria, Va.: Time-Life Books, 1986.

——. *First Blood: Fort Sumter to Bull Run*. Alexandria, Va.: Time-Life Books, 1983.

——. *"A Government of Our Own": The Making of the Confederacy.* New York: Free Press, 1994.

——. *The Imperiled Union.* 2 vols. Garden City, N.Y.: Doubleday, 1982–1983.

——. *Jefferson Davis: The Man and His Hour.* New York: Harper Collins, 1991.

Davis, William C., ed. *The Confederate General.* 6 vols. N.p.: National Historical Society, 1991.

Dodd, William E. *Jefferson Davis.* Philadelphia: George W. Jacobs, 1907.

Donald, David, ed. *Why the North Won the Civil War.* New York: Collier, 1960.

Dowdey, Clifford. *Death of a Nation: The Story of Lee and His Men at Gettysburg.* New York: Alfred A Knopf, 1958.

——. *Lee's Last Campaign: The Story of Lee and His Men Against Grant–1864.* Boston: Little, Brown, 1960.

——. *The Seven Days: The Emergence of Lee.* Boston: Little, Brown, 1964.

Dowdey, Clifford, and Louis H. Manarin, eds. *The Wartime Papers of R. E. Lee.* New York: Bramhall House, 1961.

Early, Jubal A. *Narrative of the War Between the States.* New York: Da Capo, 1989.

Eaton, Clement. *A History of the Southern Confederacy.* New York: Macmillan, 1954.

——. *Jefferson Davis.* New York: Free Press, 1977.

Eckenrode, Hamilton J. *Jefferson Davis: President of the South.* New York: Macmillan, 1930.

Eckenrode, Hamilton J., and Bryan Conrad. *James Longstreet: Lee's War Horse.* Chapel Hill: University of North Carolina Press, 1986.

Eckert, Ralph Lowell. *John Brown Gordon: Soldier, Southerner, American.* Baton Rouge: Louisiana State University Press, 1989.

Epstein, Robert M. "The Creation and Evolution of the Army Corps in the American Civil War." *Journal of Military History* 55 (January 1991): 21–46.

Escott, Paul D. *After Secession: Jefferson Davis and the Failure of Confederate Nationalism.* Baton Rouge: Louisiana State University Press, 1978.

Evans, Eli N. *Judah P. Benjamin: The Jewish Confederate.* New York: Free Press, 1988.

Farwell, Byron. *Stonewall: A Biography of General Thomas J. Jackson.* New York: Norton, 1992.

Feis, William B. "A Union Military Intelligence Failure: Jubal Early's Raid, June 12–July 14, 1864." *Civil War History* 36:3 (1990): 209–22.

——. "Neutralizing the Valley: The Role of Military Intelligence in the Defeat of Jubal Early's Army of the Valley, 1864–1865." *Civil War History* 39:3 (1993): 199–215.

Foote, Shelby. *The Civil War: A Narrative.* 3 vols. New York: Random House, 1958–1974.

Freeman, Douglas Southall. *Lee's Lieutenants: A Study in Command.* 3 vols. New York: Charles Scribner's Sons, 1944.

——. *R. E. Lee: A Biography.* 4 vols. New York: Scribners, 1934.

Freeman, Douglas Southall and Grady McWhiney, eds. *Lee's Dispatches: Unpublished Letters of General Robert E. Lee, C.S.A. to Jefferson Davis and the War Department of the Confederate States of America, 1862–65.* New York: G. P. Putnam's Sons, 1957.

Fremantle, Arthur J. L. *Three Months in the Southern States, April–June 1863.* Ed. Gary W. Gallagher. Lincoln: University of Nebraska Press, 1991.

Furgurson, Ernest B. *Chancellorsville, 1863: The Souls of the Brave*. New York: Alfred A. Knopf, 1992.

Gallagher, Gary W. "The Army of North Virginia in May 1864: A Crisis of High Command." *Civil War History* 36:2 (1990): 101–17.

———. "Scapegoat in Victory: James Longstreet and the Battle of Second Manassas." *Civil War History* 34:4 (1988): 293–307.

———. *Stephen Dodson Ramseur: Lee's Gallant General*. Chapel Hill: University of North Carolina Press, 1985.

Gallagher, Gary W., ed. *Antietam: Essays on the 1862 Maryland Campaign*. Kent, Ohio: Kent State University Press, 1989.

———. *The First Day at Gettysburg: Essays on Confederate and Union Leadership*. Kent, Ohio: Kent State University Press, 1992.

———. *The Second Day at Gettysburg: Essays on Confederate and Union Leadership*. Kent, Ohio: Kent State University Press, 1993.

———. *Struggle of the Shenandoah: Essays on the 1864 Valley Campaign*. Kent, Ohio: Kent State University Press, 1991.

———. *The Third Day at Gettysburg and Beyond*. Chapel Hill: University of North Carolina Press, 1994.

Georg, Kathleen, R., and John W. Busey. *Nothing But Glory: Pickett's Division at Gettysburg*. Hightstown, N.J.: Longstreet House, 1987.

George, Joseph, Jr. " 'Black Flag Warfare': Lincoln and the Raids Against Richmond and Jefferson Davis." *Pennsylvania Magazine of History and Biography* 115:3 (July 1991): 291–318.

Glatthaar, Joseph T. *Partners in Command: The Relationship Between Leaders in the Civil War*. New York: Free Press, 1994.

Goff, Richard D. *Confederate Supply*. Durham, N.C.: Duke University Press, 1969.

Goolrick, William K. *Rebels Resurgent: Fredericksburg to Chancellorsville*. Alexandria, Va.: Time-Life Books, 1985.

Gordon, John B. *Reminiscences of the Civil War*. 1903. Reprint. Baton Rouge: Louisiana State University Press, 1993.

Gordon-Burr, Lesley J. "Pickett After Gettysburg." In Steven E. Woodworth, ed., *Leadership and Command in the American Civil War*, pp. 81–107. Campbell, Calif.: Savas Woodbury, 1995.

Gorgas, Josiah. *The Civil War Diary of General Josiah Gorgas*. Frank E. Vandiver, ed. Tuscaloosa: University of Alabama Press, 1947.

Govan, Gilbert E., and James W. Livingood. *A Different Valor: The Story of General Joseph E. Johnston, C.S.A.* Indianapolis: Bobbs-Merrill, 1956.

Gragg, Rod. *Confederate Goliath: The Battle of Fort Fisher*. New York: Harper Collins, 1991.

Graham, Martin F., and George F. Skoch. *Mine Run: A Campaign of Lost Opportunities*. Lynchburg, Va.: H. E. Howard, 1987.

Grant, Ulysses S. *Personal Memoirs of U. S. Grant*. 2 vols. New York: Charles L. Webster, 1885.

Greene, A. Wilson. " 'Stonewall' Jackson: The Man Behind the Legend." *Journal of Confederate History* 5 (1990): 1–33.

Hagood, Johnson. *Memoirs of the War of Secession*. Columbia, S.C.: State, 1910.

Hallock, Judith Lee. *Braxton Bragg and Confederate Defeat.* Vol. 2. Tuscaloosa: University of Alabama Press, 1991.

Hamlin, Percy Gatlin. *"Old Bald Head": The Portrait of a Soldier.* Strasburg, Va.: Shenandoah, 1940.

Harris, William C. *Leroy Pope Walker: Confederate Secretary of War.* Tuscaloosa, Ala.: Confederate Publishing, 1962.

Haskell, John Cheves. *The Haskell Memoirs.* Ed. Gilbert E. Govan and James W. Livingood. New York: G. P. Putnam's Sons, 1960.

Hassler, Warren W., Jr. *Crisis at the Crossroads: The First Day at Gettysburg.* Tuscaloosa: University of Alabama Press, 1970.

Hassler, William Woods. *A. P. Hill: Lee's Forgotten General.* Richmond, Va.: Garrett and Massie, 1957.

Hattaway, Herman. *General Stephen D. Lee.* Jackson: University Press of Mississippi, 1976.

Hattaway, Herman, and Archer Jones. *How the North Won: A Military History of the Civil War.* Urbana: University of Illinois Press, 1983.

Heleniak, Roman J., and Lawrence L. Hewitt, eds. *The Confederate High Command and Related Topics–The 1988 Deep Delta Civil War Symposium: Themes in Honor of T. Harry Williams.* Shippensburg, Pa.: White Mane, 1990.

——. *Leadership During the Civil War: The 1989 Deep Delta Civil War Symposium.* Shippensburg, Pa.: White Mane, 1992.

Henderson, G. F. R. *Stonewall Jackson and the American Civil War.* 2 vols. New York: Longmans, Green, 1909.

Hendrick, Burton J. *Statesmen of the Lost Cause: Jefferson Davis and His Cabinet.* Boston: Little, Brown, 1939.

Hennessy, John. *Return to Bull Run: The Campaign and Battle of Second Manassas.* New York: Simon and Schuster, 1993.

Heth, Henry. *The Memoirs of Henry Heth.* Ed. James L. Morrison, Jr. Westport, Conn.: Greenwood Press, 1974.

Hoehling, A. A., and Mary Hoehling. *The Last Days of the Confederacy.* New York: Fairfax Press, 1986.

Hood, John B. *Advance and Retreat: Personal Experiences in the United States and Confederate States Armies.* Bloomington: Indiana University Press, 1959.

Hotchkiss, Jedediah. *Confederate Military History.* Vol. 3, *Virginia.* Ed. Clement A. Evans. Dayton, Ohio: Morningside, 1975.

Johnson, Robert U., and Clarence C. Buel, eds. *Battles and Leaders of the Civil War.* 4 vols. New York: Thomas Yoseloff, 1956.

Johnston, Joseph E. *Narrative of Military Operations.* New York: Appleton, 1874.

Jones, Archer. *Civil War Command and Strategy: The Process of Victory and Defeat.* New York: Free Press, 1992.

Jones, J. William. *Personal Reminiscences of Gen. Robert E. Lee.* New York: Appleton, 1875.

Jones, John B. *A Rebel War Clerk's Diary.* Ed. Earl Schenck Miers. New York: Sagamore, 1958.

Kean, Robert Garlick Hill. *Inside the Confederate Government.* Ed. Edward Younger. New York: Oxford University Press, 1957.

King, Alvy L. *Louis T. Wigfall.* Baton Rouge: Louisiana State University Press, 1970.

Klein, Maury. *Edward Porter Alexander.* Athens: University of Georgia Press, 1971.

Krick, Robert K. *Stonewall Jackson at Cedar Mountain.* Chapel Hill: University of North Carolina Press, 1990.

Lash, Jeffrey N. *Destroyer of the Iron Horse: General Joseph E. Johnston and Confederate Rail Transport, 1861–1865.* Kent, Ohio: Kent State University Press, 1991.

Lewis, Thomas A. *The Guns of Cedar Creek.* New York: Harper and Row, 1988.

Loehr, Charles T. "The Battle of Drewry's Bluff." *Southern Historical Society Papers* 19:100–111.

Longstreet, James. *From Manassas to Appomattox.* Ed. James I. Robertson, Jr. Bloomington: Indiana University Press, 1960.

McDonough, James Lee. *War in Kentucky: From Shiloh to Perryville.* Knoxville: University of Tennessee Press, 1994.

McElroy, Robert. *Jefferson Davis, The Unreal and the Real.* New York: Harper and Brothers, 1937.

McMurry, Richard M. *Two Great Rebel Armies: An Essay in Confederate Military History.* Chapel Hill: University of North Carolina Press, 1989.

McPherson, James M. *Battle Cry of Freedom: The Civil War Era.* New York: Oxford University Press, 1988.

McWhiney, Grady. *Braxton Bragg and Confederate Defeat.* Vol. 1. 1969. Reprint. Tuscaloosa: University of Alabama Press, 1991.

McWhiney, Grady, and Perry D. Jamieson. *Attack and Die: Civil War Military Tactics and the Southern Heritage.* Tuscaloosa: University of Alabama Press, 1982.

Mapp, Alf J. *Frock Coats and Epaulets.* New York: Thomas Yoseloff, 1963.

Matter, William D. *If It Takes All Summer: The Battle of Spotsylvania.* Chapel Hill: University of North Carolina Press, 1988.

Maury, Dabney. *Recollections of a Virginian.* New York: Charles Scribner's Sons, 1894.

Miller, William J. *Mapping for Stonewall: The Civil War Service of Jed Hotchkiss.* Washington, D.C.: Elliott and Clark, 1993.

Miller, William J., ed. *The Peninsula Campaign of 1862: Yorktown to the Seven Days.* Vol. 1. Campbell, Calif.: Savas Woodbury, 1993.

Murfin, James V. *The Gleam of Bayonets: The Battle of Antietam and the Maryland Campaign of 1862.* Baton Rouge: Louisiana State University Press, 1965.

Murphy, James B. *L. Q. C. Lamar: Pragmatic Patriot.* Baton Rouge: Louisiana State University Press, 1973.

Neely, Mark E., Jr. *Confederate Bastille: Jefferson Davis and Civil Liberties.* Milwaukee: Marquette University Press, 1993.

Newton, Steven Harvey. *Joseph E. Johnston and the Defense of Richmond.* Ann Arbor: UMI, 1991.

——. *The Battle of Seven Pines.* Lynchburg, Va.: H. E. Howard, 1993.

Nolan, Alan T. *Lee Considered: General Robert E. Lee and Civil War History.* Chapel Hill: University of North Carolina Press, 1991.

——. "The Price of Honor: R. E. Lee and the Question of Confederate Surrender." *Virginia Cavalcade* 41, pt. 1 (Winter 1992): 124–31 and pt. 2 (Spring 1992): 178–91.

Osborne, Charles C. *Jubal: The Life and Times of General Jubal A. Early, C.S.A., Defender of the Lost Cause.* Chapel Hill, N.C.: Algonquin Books, 1992.

Parks, Joseph H. *General Leonidas Polk, C.S.A.: The Fighting Bishop.* Baton Rouge: Louisiana State University Press, 1954.

Parrish, T. Michael. *Richard Taylor: Soldier Prince of Dixie.* Chapel Hill: University of North Carolina Press, 1992.

Patrick, Rembert W. *The Fall of Richmond.* Baton Rouge: Louisiana State University Press, 1960.

——. *Jefferson Davis and His Cabinet.* Baton Rouge: Louisiana State University Press, 1944.

Paxton, John Gallatin, ed. *The Civil War Letters of General Frank "Bull" Paxton, C.S.A.: A Lieutenant of Lee and Jackson.* Hillsboro, Tex.: Hill Junior College Press, 1978.

Pender, William Dorsey. *The General to His Lady: The Civil War Letters of William Dorsey Pender to Fanny Pender.* William W. Hassler, ed. Chapel Hill: University of North Carolina Press, 1965.

Pfanz, Harry. *Gettysburg: Culp's Hill and Cemetery Hill.* Chapel Hill: University of North Carolina Press, 1993.

——. *Gettysburg: The Second Day.* Chapel Hill: University of North Carolina Press, 1987.

Pindell, Richard. "The Vice President Resides in Georgia." *Civil War Times Illustrated* 29 (January/February 1990): 36–43.

Piston, William Garrett. *Lee's Tarnished Lieutenant: James Longstreet and His Place in Southern History.* Athens: University of Georgia Press, 1987.

Procter, Ben H. *Not Without Honor: The Life of John H. Reagan.* Austin: University of Texas Press, 1962.

Rable, George C. *The Confederate Republic: A Revolution Against Politics.* Chapel Hill: University of North Carolina Press, 1994.

Reagan, John H. *Memoirs.* Ed. Walter F. McCaleb. New York: Neale, 1906.

Rhea, Gordon C. *The Battle of the Wilderness, May 5–6, 1864.* Baton Rouge: Louisiana State University Press, 1994.

Robertson, James I., Jr. *General A. P. Hill: The Story of a Confederate Warrior.* New York: Random House, 1987.

Robertson, William Glenn. *Back Door to Richmond: The Bermuda Hundred Campaign, April–June 1864.* Newark: University of Delaware Press, 1987.

Roland, Charles P. *Albert Sidney Johnston: Soldier of Three Republics.* Austin: University of Texas Press, 1964.

——. *An American Iliad: The Story of the Civil War.* Lexington: University Press of Kentucky, 1991.

Roman, Alfred. *The Military Operations of General Beauregard in the War Between the States, 1861–1865.* 2 vols. New York: Harper and Brothers, 1884.

Rowland, Dunbar, ed. *Jefferson Davis, Constitutionalist: His Letters, Papers, and Speeches.* 10 vols. Jackson: Mississippi Department of Archives and History, 1923.

Sanger, Donald B., and Thomas Robson Hay. *James Longstreet: Soldier, Officeholder, and Writer.* Baton Rouge: Louisiana State University Press, 1952.

Savas, Theodore P. "The Life Blood of the Confederate War Machine: George Washington Rains and the Augusta Powder Works." *Journal of Confederate History* 5 (1990): 87–110.

Schiller, Herbert M. *The Bermuda Hundred Campaign: Operations on the South Side of the James River–May 1864.* Dayton, Ohio: Press of Morningside Bookshop, 1988.

Sears, Stephen W. *Landscape Turned Red: The Battle of Antietam.* New York: Warner Books, 1983.

——. *To the Gates of Richmond: The Peninsula Campaign.* New York: Ticknor and Fields, 1992.

Simpson, Craig M. *A Good Southerner: The Life of Henry A. Wise of Virginia.* Chapel Hill: University of North Carolina Press, 1985.

Smith, Gustavus Woodson. *Confederate War Papers.* New York: Atlantic Publishing and Engraving, 1884.

Sorrel, Gilbert Moxley. *Recollections of a Confederate Staff Officer.* Bell I. Wiley, ed. 1905. Reprint. Jackson, Tenn.: McCowat-Mercer, 1958.

Stern, Philip Van Doren. *An End to Valor: The Last Days of the Civil War.* Boston: Houghton Mifflin, 1958.

Strode, Hudson. *Jefferson Davis, American Patriot.* New York: Harcourt Brace, 1955.

——. *Jefferson Davis, Confederate President.* New York: Harcourt Brace, 1959.

——. *Jefferson Davis, Tragic Hero.* New York: Harcourt Brace, 1962.

Strode, Hudson, ed. *Jefferson Davis, Private Letters, 1823–1889.* New York: Harcourt Brace, 1966.

Symonds, Craig L. *Joseph E. Johnston: A Civil War Biography.* New York: W. W. Norton, 1992.

Tanner, Robert G. *Stonewall in the Valley: Thomas J. "Stonewall" Jackson's Shenandoah Valley Campaign, Spring 1862.* Garden City, N.Y.: Doubleday, 1976.

Tate, Allen. *Jefferson Davis: His Rise and Fall.* New York: Minton, Balch, 1929.

Taylor, Richard. *Destruction and Reconstruction: Personal Experiences of the Late War.* Ed. Richard B. Harwell. New York: Longmans, Green, 1955.

Taylor, Walter H. *Four Years with General Lee.* Bloomington: Indiana University Press, 1962.

Thomas, Emory M. "Ambivalent Visions of Victory: Jefferson Davis, Robert E. Lee, and Confederate Grand Strategy." *Freeman Historical Review* (1994): 19–27.

——. *Bold Dragoon: The Life of J. E. B. Stuart.* New York: Harper and Row, 1986.

Thompson, William Y. *Robert Toombs of Georgia.* Baton Rouge: Louisiana State University Press, 1966.

Trudeau, Noah Andre. *Bloody Roads South: The Wilderness to Cold Harbor, May–June 1864.* Boston: Little, Brown, 1989.

Tucker, Glenn. *High Tide at Gettysburg: The Campaign in Pennsylvania.* Indianapolis: Bobbs-Merrill, 1958.

U.S. War Department. *The War of the Rebellion: A Compilation of the Official Records of the Union and Confederate Armies.* 128 vols. Washington, D.C.: Government Printing Office, 1880–1901.

Van Creveld, Martin. *Supplying War: Logistics from Wallenstein to Patton.* Cambridge: Cambridge University Press, 1977.

Vandiver, Frank E. *Basic History of the Confederacy.* Princeton, N.J.: Princeton University Press, 1962.

——. *Mighty Stonewall.* College Station: Texas A&M University Press, 1957.

——. *Ploughshares into Swords: Josiah Gorgas and Confederate Ordnance.* Austin: University of Texas Press, 1952.

——. *Rebel Brass: The Confederate Command System.* Baton Rouge: Louisiana State University Press, 1956.

——. *Their Tattered Flags: The Epic of the Confederacy.* College Station: Texas A&M University Press, 1987.

Warner, Ezra J. *Generals in Gray: Lives of Confederate Commanders.* Baton Rouge: Louisiana State University Press, 1959.

Weigley, Russell F. *The American Way of War: A History of United States Military Strategy and Policy.* New York: Macmillan, 1973.

Wellman, Manly Wade. *Giant in Gray: A Biography of Wade Hampton of South Carolina.* New York: Charles Scribner's Sons, 1949.

Wert, Jeffry D. *From Winchester to Cedar Creek: The Shenandoah Campaign of 1864.* Carlisle, Pa.: South Mountain Press, 1987.

——. *General James Longstreet: The Confederacy's Most Controversial Soldier–A Biography.* New York: Simon and Schuster, 1993.

Wheeler, Richard. *Lee's Terrible Swift Sword: From Antietam to Chancellorsville–An Eyewitness History.* HarperCollins, 1992.

——. *On Fields of Fury: From the Wilderness to the Crater–An Eyewitness History.* New York: Harper and Row, 1991.

——. *A Rising Thunder–From Lincoln's Election to the Battle of Bull Run: An Eyewitness History.* New York: HarperCollins, 1994.

——. *Sword Over Richmond: An Eyewitness History of McClellan's Peninsula Campaign.* New York: Harper and Row, 1986.

——. *Witness to Appomattox.* New York: Harper and Row, 1989.

——. *Witness to Gettysburg.* New York: Harper and Row, 1987.

Williams, T. Harry. *P. G. T. Beauregard: Napoleon in Gray.* Baton Rouge: Louisiana State University Press, 1956.

Wilson, Clyde N. *Carolina Cavalier: The Life and Mind of James Johnston Pettigrew.* Athens: University of Georgia Press, 1990.

Wise, Henry A. "The Career of Wise's Brigade, 1861–1865." *Southern Historical Society Papers* 25:1–13.

Wise, Jennings Cropper. *The Long Arm of Lee: The History of the Artillery of the Army of Northern Virginia.* New York: Oxford University Press, 1959.

Woodworth, Steven E. *Jefferson Davis and His Generals: The Failure of Confederate Command in the West.* Lawrence: University Press of Kansas, 1990.

Woodworth, Steven E., ed. *Leadership and Command in the American Civil War.* Campbell, Calif.: Savas Woodbury, 1995.

INDEX